GRATIS

RADICAL CAMPUS

HUGH JOHNSTON

radical

MAKING
SIMON FRASER
UNIVERSITY

campus

DOUGLAS & McINTYRE
VANCOUVER/TORONTO

Douglas & McIntyre Ltd.
2323 Quebec Street, Suite 201
Vancouver, British Columbia v5t 4s7
www.douglas-mcintyre.com

Library and Archives Canada Cataloguing in Publication
Johnston, Hugh J. M., 1939–
Radical campus : making Simon Fraser University / Hugh Johnston.
Includes bibliographical references and index.

ISBN 13: 978-1-55365-140-6   ISBN 10: 1-55365-140-5

1. Simon Fraser University—History. I. Title.
LE3.S82J63 2005   378.711′33   C2005-903345-2

Jacket design by Peter Cocking
Interior design by Jessica Sullivan
Jacket photograph of Simon Fraser University in 1965 by John Fulker
Printed and bound in Canada by Friesens
Printed on acid-free paper that is forest friendly (100% post-consumer
recycled paper) and has been processed chlorine free.

We gratefully acknowledge the financial support of the Canada Council
for the Arts, the British Columbia Arts Council, and the Government of
Canada through the Book Publishing Industry Development Program
(BPIDP) for our publishing activities.

Contents

Preface
Freedom Square and SFU's History

This book had its start nearly five years ago when Jack Blaney was president and looking for someone to tackle a history of Simon Fraser University. It is not the first attempt to tell this history. In fact, it has been told many times and in many ways, orally and in print—although never before at this length. From the beginning, faculty members, students, journalists and others have written or talked about it and much of what they have related is accessible in the back files of magazines and journals, in a variety of SFU publications and in manuscripts, theses and essays, as well as in taped interviews and even on Web pages on the Internet. And SFU is young enough that its early history lives in the memories of many who were there—sometimes in stories well honed by repetition. But memories are uneven. Interestingly, what people retain most vividly is what happened recently or what happened long ago, with the intervening years falling into much flatter, less distinguishable territory.

But the early SFU story is escaping us as one generation of students replaces another and as professors and staff members retire and are replaced. More than ten years ago an SFU student, Robert Wilkins, wrote a regretful article in *The Peak* shortly before he graduated. He had been asking everyone he could what they knew about Freedom Square and he had been getting blank looks. Today he would get a better response. Freedom Square is the area where SFU students held mass rallies in the 1960s. Its location is more easily identified now that the Freedom Square plaque, missing for more than thirty years, has been restored to its place on the podium where it was first mounted. When Wilkins was asking, however, it took him several days before he found someone who could locate the square and who knew that there had been a plaque. It seemed to Wilkins that an era of SFU history had fallen into wanton ignorance; and from what he knew, that did not seem right.[1]

The plaque had originally been installed on September 11, 1968, and it was stolen the next day by University of British Columbia engineers. The wording—commemorating mass student rallies in defence of academic freedom—had been accepted by a conservative and reluctant board of governors after they had previously rejected an earlier wording put forward by a radical Student Council.[2] When the plaque—which is quite heavy—went missing, nobody noticed right away because the UBC engineers had substituted a replica that spoofed the wording of the original, yet looked the same from a distance. Stealing the plaque was a prank and the engineers would have returned it if they had not lost it. It spent many years in the trunk of someone's car—a weight for winter traction—and then served indoors in a living room as a TV stand long after that. The person who possessed it finally returned it to SFU in 1990, when he became aware that the SFU Alumni Association was looking for it. He returned it only to have it disappear into a cubbyhole in an administration office. Thanks to the efforts of one student the plaque resurfaced in 1999, and with the plaque restored, Freedom Square has found a place in the SFU vocabulary as a bit of reclaimed history.[3]

The student was Amanda Camley, an activist who uncovered some of the university's history when she began investigating SFU spaces and their meanings as an honours anthropology project. Freedom Square was a space she had not been aware of, but it acquired a lot of significance for her when she began digging into the past, interviewing as many people as she could and going through all the pictures and records that she could find. In 1999, when she asked fellow students about Freedom Square, she got much the same response as Robert Wilkins had five years earlier. They did not know about it. But she discovered that when she began to talk about it, they were very interested. For Camley, Freedom Square opened up issues of the 1960s and 1970s: the New Left and student radicalism, controversies over university government and academic freedom, and the women's movement. What she came to understand was that these had all been hot topics at her university, vigorously debated and contested by students and faculty.[4]

The SFU story is also about the creation of a new university in an era of expansion in higher education: about choices made, directions taken, people hired in a period of ferment and flux; and about changing directions in academic disciplines, rival conceptions of a university—conceptions that clashed with new intensity when the future seemed to have so much possibility. Every decade of SFU's history has left its stamp. This book, however, is about the beginnings. As students like Robert Wilkins and Amanda Camley would say, the beginnings are worth our attention. SFU's early years coincided with great change in higher education, and that was especially obvious for people creating a new university. SFU had no tradition when it opened but quickly established one, and if its mission and culture have since taken new forms, the university's present personality is still an outgrowth of the original. To understand why we do what we do, it helps to go back to the beginning.

What people remember has been vitally important in reconstructing SFU's past; and the results would have been much poorer without the interviews of the past five years. But I am indebted to students, professors, staff members and other researchers who conducted interviews in the more distant past and gave copies of their tapes and transcripts to SFU Archives. They include Dennis Roberts, Liisa Fagerlund, Ken Nielsen, Elika Kohler, Terry Spurgeon, Robin Fisher and Peter Stursberg. Some of their interviews are now invaluable because the people they talked with are no longer with us. The core of this book, however, comes from the main archival record: the minutes, memos, correspondence, reports and statements generated daily by SFU's academic and administrative departments and its committees and by the societies and organizations that make the university what it is, as well as the personal papers that have been donated by faculty, staff and alumni over the years.

While working in the SFU Archives I saw a steady stream of students and other researchers using the collections housed there; and from their vantage point and from my own I gained great appreciation for our Archives staff, both for their work in organizing and describing collections and for their effectiveness in directing researchers to what they need. The archivists that I worked with most directly were Frances Fournier, Enid Britt, Paul Hebbard, Richard Dancy and Ian Forsyth. Frances in particular has a lot invested in this book in time and in creative suggestions.

My thanks to John-Henry Harter and Dionysios (Dino) Rossi, my research assistants, and to Ruth Sandwell for her interview of Arthur Erickson. Dino's contribution to SFU's history includes not just an extraordinary effort in collecting material, but a wonderfully researched MA thesis on SFU and the Politics, Sociology & Anthropology strike. I am grateful to Robin Fisher and Stephen Hicks for their generosity in giving me boxes of material on SFU that they collected in the 1980s. My work has been speeded along by the transcripts typed by Joan MacDonald and by my wife, Patricia. I have also appreciated the comments and corrections of those who have read the draft manuscript or parts of it, particularly Frances Fournier, Ian Forsyth, Paul Dutton, Scott McIntyre, Elizabeth Lo, Penny and John Spagnolo and Bill Bruneau. The final text has had the great advantage of Mary Schendlinger's discerning editorial eye. It has been a rare privilege to research and write about a university where I have taught for thirty-six years. I believed from the beginning that I could do it with reasonable detachment because I was not at the centre of the action in any of the events I describe. Readers can make their own judgement. In any case, I appreciate the hands-off encouragement given me initially by President Jack Blaney and Vice-Presidents Jock Munro and David Mitchell, and subsequently by President Michael Stevenson and Vice-President Warren Gill. I have been left free to tell the story as I chose.

Hugh Johnston
Simon Fraser University
January 24, 2005

1

The Instant University

The science centre at Simon Fraser University is named after Gordon Shrum; and there couldn't be a better place on the campus to acknowledge him. After his long career in physics, the science departments were closest to his heart. But the whole campus was his creation. When the university first opened, it was really Gordon Shrum University. The actual name remembered a nineteenth-century adventurer, Simon Fraser, who had never attended a university or thought of endowing one. (Fraser was not the education supporter that his fellow fur trader James McGill had been.)

No one ever considered naming the university after Shrum. The B.C. minister of education had already decided to call it Simon Fraser University before Shrum became involved and, for all manner of reasons, that closed the question. There came a time, however, when students and faculty would have revolted if anyone had put Shrum's name forward. He became immensely unpopular on the campus he had created.

Unpopularity probably cost Gordon Shrum little sleep. He was not remembered for self-doubt. By habit and discipline he kept busy, whether about his house and garden—in the little spare time he had— or as a man of power and influence in the province. He shouldered administrative responsibility well into his mid-eighties, believing that public involvement was the best way to preserve his grey matter. Only when he was eighty-seven did he set time aside to tell his life story. In this, SFU was an important late chapter. He was proud of his achievement with SFU, and if there had been trouble there, which people did ask about, he did not accept blame or see that as the main point.

In the early months of 1983 Shrum recorded his recollections in a series of taped interviews with Peter Stursberg, a well-known broadcaster and oral historian.[1] These interviews became the basis of an edited autobiography and a documentary. Shrum's ability, at an advanced age, to recall the substance and detail of nearly nine eventful decades was remarkable, but not surprising given his active intellect and punctilious nature.

It took five meetings and ten hours of audio tape to cover his first sixty-five years: his origins on a farm in the fruit-growing area of Ontario's Niagara Peninsula; his undergraduate career at the University of Toronto, interrupted by three years' service with a volunteer artillery unit raised on the Toronto campus; the action he saw at Vimy Ridge in 1917; his outstanding post-graduate work at Toronto under John McLennan, the physicist and star of Toronto's science faculty; his long career at the University of British Columbia and the application of his singular energy in an extraordinary variety of offices, mostly held concurrently—head of Physics, director of Extension, dean of Graduate Studies, and colonel in command of the Canadian Officers Training Corps (COTC), which, during the Second World War, provided compulsory training for every male student at UBC; his wartime and post-war membership on the National Research Council when its primary concern was the development of nuclear energy; and then the new career and larger theatre that he stepped into, after he reached the age of sixty-five, as chair of B.C. Hydro, overseeing the Peace River Hydro-Electric Power Development.

In the sixth interview Shrum reached the founding of SFU. Stursberg, the interviewer, suggested that SFU was his greatest work. The answer was not a contradiction, but it had Shrum's characteristic emphasis on action. "Well," said Shrum, "it was certainly the most unique thing I ever did because I am certain that nobody, in any part of the world, ever built a university in two years and six months that accommodated 2,500 students at the opening."[2] Building a university quickly had been a challenge that Shrum had relished, and it was an aspect of the story of SFU that he promoted from the beginning.

His involvement began the moment that the SFU project received legislative authorization and continued through the university's exciting, turbulent and creative first six years. In fact he was named as chancellor before the legislation was passed. His appointment was announced in the B.C. Legislative Assembly during the second reading, several days before the Universities Act became law. It was a safe announcement because the government's action received general congratulations, both for its commitment to the expansion of higher education and for its choice of chancellor for the new university. The minister of education, Leslie Peterson, in making the announcement commented on Shrum's capacity for work. Peterson and Premier W.A.C. Bennett, on past experience, were impressed by Shrum's ability to get things done.[3]

As co-chair of B.C. Hydro, Shrum already had one of the biggest jobs in the province. How he got that job, with a more than twofold jump in salary, on the day of his retirement as a physics professor, is a testament to the years of energetic service that he gave to UBC. Generations of students had encountered him, as dean, department head and COTC colonel. Some of them had moved on to positions of influence and power and kept in touch with their mentor. Shrum was UBC President Norman (Larry) MacKenzie's right-hand man from 1944 to 1961; and he was famous for cutting though or ignoring red tape in commandeering more than three hundred army huts and moving them to the UBC campus at the end of the Second World War.[4] These huts, no longer needed by the army, vanished from camps as distant as the west coast of Vancouver Island and reappeared at UBC to accommodate the flood of army veterans entering university. In accumulating them on the UBC campus, Shrum had moved so fast that, to give one example, while municipal councillors in North Vancouver were vacillating from one meeting to the next whether or not to appropriate huts at a camp on the North

Shore, Shrum simply loaded them onto barges and towed them to the university. Possession, he knew, was nine points of the law.

Robert Bonner was among the thousands of UBC students who encountered Shrum on the parade square as a tall, imposing commanding officer with a rasping parade-ground bark. When Bonner returned from active duty at the end of the war, Shrum recruited him as a COTC training officer. A decade later, Bonner was a cabinet minister in W.A.C. Bennett's Social Credit government. Bonner recommended Shrum to Bennett, who was looking for someone to chair a commission on the financing of the B.C. Power Commission. The press had been demanding an investigation, and a Royal Commission was the answer. Shrum produced a report that delighted the government and Bennett in particular.[5] This led to Shrum's appointment, while still at UBC, as chair of the B.C. Energy Board in 1958 and, on retirement from UBC in 1961, as co-chair of B.C. Hydro when it was created as a publicly owned electric-power monopoly.

Shrum had been in his B.C. Hydro position for less than two years when the premier asked him to take on the extra job of chancellor of a projected new university. The request was unexpected. Shrum was eating lunch in the executive dining room in the B.C. Hydro Building in downtown Vancouver when a temporary secretary timidly interrupted to say there was a call from the premier. Shrum and Bennett were not personal friends or social acquaintances. Their relationship, as Shrum explained it, was based on business. The premier, Shrum observed, always called him Dr. Shrum, although one should not make too much of this because, as the premier's wife once explained to an interviewer, her husband—in the manner of the small-town merchant he had been—was habitually formal. Shrum remembered the phone conversation this way: after explaining that the government was acting on a recommendation to build a new university, Bennett said, "We want you to be chancellor. Select a site, and build it and get it going. I want it open in September 1965."[6]

With his years of university experience, Shrum knew that a chancellor's position was voluntary and essentially honorary, and that the effective executive officer in a North American university was the president. He also understood that Premier Bennett, who had prospered in business and politics with a grade-eight education, had little knowledge of the way universities worked and was under the impression that the chancellor ran the show. Shrum had no desire to correct him. The prospect of a free hand to build a university as he saw fit was too enticing. In his interview with Peter Stursberg, Shrum recalled that Bennett offered to let him think about it before accepting; but Shrum did not want time and accepted on the phone immediately. He was afraid, he explained, that if he delayed, Bennett might change his mind. The opportunity and challenge of getting something built against an extraordinarily tight deadline were what he wanted. The fact that the position paid nothing was immaterial.

Those who knew him have described Shrum as impressive and formidable. He could be brusque and aggressive in meetings and interviews; but he also looked out for his proteges. Grace McCarthy, the Social Credit cabinet minister, asked Shrum when he was eighty-one to supervise the Pier B.C. project, the first stage of the Canada Trade and Convention Centre. She observed that he didn't suffer fools gladly and she said she found this refreshing. Presumably she had never been the target of his impatience. John Ellis, the first director of Educational Foundations at SFU, came to the conclusion, after a couple of early brushes with Shrum, that if you stood up to him you got his respect. But the stories that circulate about Shrum suggest that many people hesitated to challenge him, or challenged from a weak position, and came away bruised.[7]

Shrum himself attributed his daunting work ethic to wartime service. He had survived a battlefield in France where 3,598 Canadians died in a single day; he had been wounded in action seven months later, and he had returned to the front for the final push to the end of the war. When he resumed his university education at twenty-two, it was with a sense that time was not for wasting. His drive overlay a farm boy's practicality, and years of academic life effected no change. He looked for decisiveness. He impressed this on his son Gordon, telling him that deciding was more important than the decision. Sixty per cent of the time, Shrum said, you would be making the best decision; and one hundred per cent of the time you would then be free to act. Perhaps the point was meant for a particular set of facts, but it defined Shrum's character. The example that Shrum set his children for the many years he had them in his sole care was always to be productive. Gordon Jr. remembered that his father, if he ever did watch TV, would be occupied peeling a bucket of apples or with some such task.[8]

For a man of Shrum's makeup, the SFU chancellorship was irresistible. He had the resources of the provincial government behind him and the confidence of the premier, to whom he reported directly. It was W.A.C. Bennett's style, he knew, to give general direction—build a university—but not otherwise to interfere. For his first six months as chancellor, Shrum had no one else to answer to: no board of governors, no community group, no advisory committee and no staff. During this half year, he made a series of absolutely critical decisions that set the direction SFU would take. He had few qualms about the wisdom or difficulty of the deadline of September 1965 or the objective of opening with buildings already erected. Among those who became involved in the project, there was common consent that it would not have happened without Shrum's energy and drive.

AN EXCEPTIONAL CHALLENGE

There was no idle boasting in Shrum's claim to have done something remarkable at SFU. One needs only to look at the origins of other universities, both contemporary and older.

SFU in Vancouver and York University in Toronto took shape at much the same time. York's start, however, was much more measured and deliberate. York had community involvement from its inception: it was not a one-man show. Like SFU, York was built to relieve pressure on an older, established university. Unlike SFU, the genesis of York began with a community group. The York group formed a board, found a president and with support from the University of Toronto secured funding from the provincial government. The first president, Murray Ross, began recruiting faculty in June 1960 and York started the 1960–61 academic year with sixty-seven students and as an affiliate of the University of Toronto. The students took University of Toronto courses and wrote University of Toronto exams. In its first year, York was housed in an old residential building on the Toronto campus. By the second year it had its own building on the 34-hectare Glendon campus. York continued looking for a 200-hectare site for its main campus, and only in its sixth year did it have some buildings up and classes running on that campus. It remained an affiliate of the University of Toronto for its first four years and waited for that affiliation to end before establishing its own curriculum.

SFU compressed all of this development into thirty months. In September 1965, the two universities were roughly the same size and operating on brand-new campuses. But York had been offering classes for five years and SFU was just starting. The comparison underscores the reality that in the 1960s there was no trouble-free way to create a university. Despite its measured development, York still had a crisis in its third year, with a staff revolt, sharp criticism of the president and bad publicity in the press.

In the early 1960s, Britain also expanded its university system, upgrading colleges to university status, enlarging existing universities and building new ones. The "Shakespeare Seven"—Sussex, Essex, York, Lancaster, Kent, Warwick and East Anglia—were SFU's contemporaries. The story of Sussex illustrates the way in which the British went about creating these new universities.

In Britain, a central government agency, the University Grants Commission, determined the national pattern—deciding which school got funded and which did not—but local initiative was part of the story. In Sussex, local authorities began agitating for a university five years before getting a charter. Public meetings and deputations to London generated momentum. The creation of a local committee was an instrumental starting point. That committee determined a potential site, petitioned the University Grants Commission for funding and recruited an external group of academic administrators as a planning committee. It took two years to get a go-ahead from the University Grants Commission and another year to select an architect, who then began to design a campus. All this had happened before a chief executive officer (the vice-chancellor) took up his position. In its second year of operation, beginning October 1962, Sussex had just four hundred students.[9]

This pace of development, with its careful apparatus of consultation and planning, would not have suited Shrum. He had witnessed years of slow development at UBC before the dramatic growth of the post-war era. He knew how long one could wait for all the elements of a complete campus to come together; and he believed that when a government began to loosen its purse strings, it was necessary to act quickly because the moment was not likely to last.

If Shrum had been operating within the development process employed at York or Sussex, he would have had contrary views thrown at him. Some planning committee members would have argued that a university is first of all people and only secondarily buildings and that the people for whom the university was built should have a say in its design. In the vital initial planning of SFU, however, Shrum had to contend with no other opinions.

The freedom that Shrum enjoyed at SFU was without precedent in Canadian higher education. He and his university were independent from the start. He did not begin as an affiliate of an older institution, although that had been the model, not just for York and other contemporary universities but for older universities like UBC. SFU's sister institution, Victoria, which also became a university in 1963, had once been affiliated with McGill; then it became a college affiliated with UBC. When it finally gained university status, it enjoyed strong community involvement and the support of generations of former students.[10]

Victoria's history was typical of the new generation of Canadian universities. Most had community roots and long histories before achieving university status. They had begun as branches or affiliated colleges of existing universities or developed from junior colleges, technical institutes or seminaries. The multi-campus Université du Québec, created three years after SFU, was an exception, a radical new departure in higher education in Quebec. But among the new English-speaking universities of the 1960s, none had such an ambitious start from zero as SFU.[11]

INNOVATION AND HASTE

"Instant university" was a phrase coined for SFU by Donald Stainsby, a Victoria journalist writing for the national magazine *Saturday Night*.[12] His article appeared in March 1964 as tenders were being called for the first phase of construction. Stainsby did his research late in 1963, before SFU's first president took up his post and while the university's only employee was an engineer, hired to oversee construction. At that early moment in the genesis of the new university, Stainsby got wind of nervous and hostile speculation at UBC and elsewhere about what Shrum was doing. Was he creating a degree factory? Was his university siphoning funds away from UBC? And what was the hurry? Why was speed so essential? In answering these questions for Stainsby in December 1963, Shrum had spoken of "instant tradition," to suggest the fully formed character—forward looking, meeting current needs and maintaining high standards—that SFU would have when it opened its doors. SFU was in a hurry because it had to relieve growing enrolment pressure on UBC. He knew that he was working against a seemingly impossible deadline.[13]

Getting buildings up and bringing roads and services to the site on a normal schedule would have taken far more time than the deadline allowed. Those who subsequently worked for Shrum would have agreed. Arthur Erickson, the architect, explained to a researcher years later that on a project of this scale, the drawings alone should have taken two years and construction another two.[14] When Erickson began detailed drawing, however, opening day was only twenty-five months away. Shrum understood that staffing was also a huge challenge, and a much greater challenge in the early 1960s than it would be today. Canada then had a limited pool of university teachers, researchers and administrators to draw on.

In 1963, most of Canada's thirty-two English-speaking universities and colleges were small and intimate, with teaching faculties numbering 150 or fewer. But all were expanding, and new universities like SFU, Brock and Trent were coming on stream. PhD programs, especially in the humanities and social sciences, were embryonic. In the 1950s, Toronto ran the only graduate school in the country that covered all the disciplines. UBC, the second largest university, had produced its first PhD in 1950, and by 1963 had graduated only two PhDs in the humanities.[15] Shrum needed to hire 115 or 120 faculty by September 1965, and that number could not be found in Canadian universities.

The country entered the 1960s producing no more than seventy-five PhDs a year in the humanities and social sciences. Graduates in the pure sciences were more numerous, but demand for them by business and government was also greater. In some disciplines, Canadian graduate schools did scarcely anything. In the social sciences, for example, most graduate students took economics, political science or history, and few studied sociology or anthropology. Experienced librarians and people with an understanding of university administration were hard to locate and harder to recruit. Shrum and the tiny administrative staff he first appointed began searching for Canadians, whether trained at home or abroad, and in assembling an initial nucleus of faculty and administrators they did quite well. Understandably, to make the bulk of their appointments, they had to cast a wider net.

Shrum did not anticipate the exact nature of the "instant tradition" that was born at SFU, but he did get an adventurous and forward-looking university community. There were many factors in this development. The explanation begins with the rapid change in student and faculty attitudes and values on North American campuses during the thirty months that SFU was taking shape. And the speed with which SFU was created, its rootless start and its institutional independence all made it open to change and challenge. York, which was three years older, had its beginnings under the University of Toronto, because its founders assumed that this was necessary to ensure academic standards and reputation. After four years York was able to go its own way. But its initial years were intentionally conservative, and inevitably confining.

Until the late 1950s and early 1960s, in the world of higher education, educators—certainly in Britain and Canada—took it for granted that a new institution needed to start off with ties to an older one. But when emphasis shifted from maintaining traditional standards to encouraging experimentation, educational planners saw new universities in a different light. In Britain, by 1958, the University Grants Commission had begun to focus on the potential that new universities had to innovate. The inertia of an eight-hundred-year-old Oxford or even a sixty-year-old Leeds could be escaped in a new university. This could be expressed another way. As governments invested more money in universities, they became interested in changing them. The University Grants Commission understood this. The result was a policy giving universities like Sussex an unfettered and independent start. If one wanted to reinvent the university, the new ones would make the most headway. The same policy also projected modest enrolments for new universities. Older and more traditional universities like Leeds could absorb most of the predicted student influx, and the new could experiment without being overwhelmed.[16]

SFU AND UBC

SFU was another story. It was to be new and independent, but also capable of absorbing many students. The rush to get it going was a quick-fix solution in the absence of any long-term planning by the provincial government. If relations between the established university—UBC—and the provincial government had been better, SFU might never have been built or, if built, it would not have been the "instant university" that a late start demanded.

It took a change of presidents and a change in thinking at UBC to set SFU in motion. A core group of faculty at UBC had long felt that Vancouver needed a second campus; and a new president, influenced by current ideas, recommended creating a second campus that was autonomous and innovative—free to set its own direction. His recommendation, however, contained none of the caution of the contemporary British approach. He envisaged a new campus in operation in short order with an ambitious enrolment target. When he made his recommendation, half the universities and colleges of Canada enrolled two thousand students or fewer. In the other half, UBC with thirteen thousand students was among the largest. SFU was to start in the middle of the pack with twenty-five hundred.

UBC had enjoyed a monopoly in B.C. and instinctively the president who had taken it through a period of tremendous growth wanted to keep it that way. The UBC charter of 1908, renewed in 1936, made it the only degree-granting institution in the province; and Norman MacKenzie, the president down to 1962, resisted any division or sharing of this role.

In his eighteen years at UBC, MacKenzie presided over a transformation of the UBC campus. New federal funding, increased provincial funding and private and corporate donations all contributed to an energetic building program and expanded operations for a rapidly growing student population. Federal funding was the starting point and MacKenzie, in concert with other university presidents, campaigned first to get that funding and then to increase it.

Over a period of twelve or thirteen years, MacKenzie and his fellow presidents recast their campaign for federal funding several times. Each time they were successful, and each time they asked for more. The first call was for a program of federal assistance for returning World War II veterans. The second was for continued federal funding after the veterans were gone. Universities needed this funding, they argued, to preserve the quality of university education. The third call followed on the heels of the second as UBC and other universities realized that a drop in income from veterans was not their only challenge: they were experiencing, year by year, a progressive increase in students coming directly from high school. A precipitous decline in enrolment at UBC between 1948 and 1952 had reversed itself and by 1957 the university had more students than ever before.[17]

In their first analysis, university presidents believed that they were simply encountering the consequences of general population growth, especially in the population of youth. By the mid-1950s they could see that something else was happening. In the affluent post-war world, many young people from families with no university tradition were now choosing to attend. In September 1951, universities and colleges in Canada were enrolling forty-two of every one thousand young Canadians of university age. The following year it was fifty, and ten years later it was seventy-five.[18] Today the figure is four times greater than that: the product of a long-term trend. By 1956–57, universities had identified the beginnings of this trend and raised an alarm.[19]

In selling universities to a federal government and a Canadian public that in the past had been largely indifferent, university presidents, with striking ease and assurance, adopted the argument of utility. They encouraged parents and young people to see a university education as a route to better-paying jobs and more security. And they promoted the idea of the modern university as an engine of economic growth. This idea materialized from observation of the world's strongest economy. In the United States, the proportion of university-educated people had long been much higher than in Canada; and since 1945 the Americans had been pouring increasing amounts of money into universities. The belief that universities were a key to economic development found early expression in Canada in the 1957 Report of the Royal Commission on Canada's Economic Prospects.[20] This new emphasis on the pragmatic, vocational (rather than educational) value of a university made some university teachers acutely uncomfortable.

In October 1957, the case for universities acquired Cold War justification. Gordon Shrum happened to be passing through London on a European trade junket along with the B.C. minister of trade and industry when Russia launched the first of its Sputnik series of artificial satellites. Years later he remembered the excitement of the news. What he could not know was that within six years he would be building a university with Sputnik as one of the given reasons. The West became obsessed with Russia's apparent technological advantage. Americans immediately began to throw more money at education; and in the National Defense

Education Act of 1958, the American federal government formalized for the first time its role in higher education.[21]

Canadians were comparing their education systems, their universities and their research spending not just with the Soviet Union, but with the U.S., Japan and Europe. The striking economic success stories of Japan and West Germany and the spending of those countries on higher education were the subjects of repeated media reports. In a competitive world, Canadians heard and read that they were losing ground. By the end of the 1950s, as a product of public discussion before and after Sputnik, most Canadians were believers in educational spending. The federal government was onside and provincial governments were moving rapidly in that direction.[22]

By the end of his regime, although he did not appreciate it himself, the UBC community regarded Norman MacKenzie as an obstacle to achieving a comprehensive policy for higher education in the province. His national standing and his connections with the Liberal government in Ottawa—in 1952 St. Laurent offered him a cabinet position—had served the university well. In the early years of his tenure he had enjoyed good relations in Victoria with two Liberal premiers, first John Hart and then Byron Johnson. From 1952 on, however, he had difficulty approaching Social Credit Premier W.A.C. Bennett. That problem along with his insistence on maintaining UBC's control over higher education made some key faculty members look forward to his departure.[23]

INVESTING IN HIGHER EDUCATION

MacKenzie had done a good job of selling higher education to the federal government but a poor one of selling it to the provincial, even though public belief in its value was rising. And he was out of touch with the aspirations of localities across the province that wanted postsecondary institutions close to home.

In 1962, when he was sixty-six, the UBC board sent MacKenzie unwillingly into retirement. (He had an appointment without term so retirement had not come automatically at sixty-five.) If he had gone earlier, the province might have opened its pockets sooner. In that scenario, the imperative to build SFU in thirty months would have been less pressing. MacKenzie's ineffectiveness in dealing with the premier had a personal dimension. But many people at UBC shared a conviction that the premier did not like the university; it wasn't just MacKenzie. A hostile reception that students gave Premier Bennett on a couple of occasions in 1958 when he visited the UBC campus had not helped. Back in 1955, a delegation of faculty who went to see Bennett to press their case for improved salaries got a taste of his attitude. He dismissed them with the comment that they were being paid more than his cabinet ministers.[24]

Bennett, however, had a great sense of public expectations. A review of his twenty years as premier shows a flexible politician who moved with the times. The Social Credit label under which he operated said little about his political philosophy. Social Credit had been a fringe movement based on eccentric ideas on monetary reform. In British Columbia under Bennett it became a conservative–centrist party that adopted much the same menu of initiatives as provincial governments in Ontario, Alberta and elsewhere. In the 1950s, Bennett in B.C., like Leslie Frost in Ontario, had been building infrastructure. His highway budget was huge. His public hydroelectric power projects (with Shrum as a partner) were massive. In the 1960s he turned to social programs, with education and universities at the top of the list.

In investing in universities at this time, Bennett was doing what governments throughout the western world were doing. Before he could begin, however, he needed a blueprint and, as the decade began, that was coming neither from the provincial Department of Education nor from UBC. The department had never attempted to supervise the university. While department and university officials would meet to set matriculation exams and award entrance scholarships, they did so in the spirit of practical co-operation between separate jurisdictions. Neither the minister nor the deputy minister ever bothered to create a division in the department that would be responsible for higher education.

For several years, a variety of voices in the province had been calling for local post-secondary institutions. Bennett was aware of the potential votes that these voices represented. He could not miss the campaign going on in the provincial capital. Influential Victoria citizens like General George Pearkes, now the lieutenant-governor and previously a federal cabinet minister, wanted Victoria College to drop its UBC affiliation and become a university in its own right. In 1961, Pearkes's group secured land at Gordon Head in Victoria for a campus. In Nelson, the Catholic bishop, W.E. Doyle, wanted a university charter for the tiny college he was running in affiliation with St. Francis Xavier in Nova Scotia.

Members of the Evangelical Free Church had plans for a college in Langley; Bishop John Fergus O'Grady had formed an interdenominational board for a college in Prince George. For some time, Kelowna had been promoting the idea of a community college for the Okanagan Valley and there was similar talk in Kamloops and Trail.[25]

Back in 1957, with a number of these projects already in the wind, the *Vancouver Sun* had offered a caution: this was not the time to siphon funds from the provincial university.[26] The *Sun* was endorsing Norman MacKenzie's position. But members of his faculty were worrying about the effects of growth on their campus. The UBC Faculty Association, unsatisfied with the way MacKenzie was handling the issue, began calling for a provincial review of higher education. Their agitation had begun during a recession in 1957, when funding and enrolments appeared to be getting completely out of alignment. The university could not take in all of these students, they argued, and maintain its standards. Ron Baker, then a professor of English at UBC (and later SFU's first academic planner), offered a vision of the future. Let us continue as we are going, he suggested ironically, and witness a campus covered by parking lots and student cars.[27]

One solution—described by faculty at UBC as the University of California model—would be a multi-campus system operating under a single governing board or authority. Following this model, UBC would have branch campuses at Victoria, in the Lower Fraser Valley and in the interior. These campuses would offer a common curricular program and conform to a common procedure for hiring staff. At that time, eight states in the U.S. supported unified multi-campus systems. Strictly speaking, California was not one of them. Its system was more complex. The California public system included the multi-campus University of California with its single governing authority. In addition, there were state colleges under a separate authority and junior colleges under yet another authority. It was the attractive complexity of the California system that caught the eye of John Barfoot Macdonald, who became president of UBC when Norman MacKenzie retired on the first of July 1962.[28]

A PLAN FOR HIGHER EDUCATION IN B.C.

In remarkably short order, the new UBC president gave the provincial government the incentive it needed to build SFU, and to build it quickly. He produced a plan for the expansion of higher education that was also a plan for diversification—and for a tiered system with, not surprisingly, UBC alone at the apex. It took Premier Bennett no time to decide that he liked most of it and to proceed.

Macdonald had been a UBC Faculty Association nominee for president. This was evidence of changing times. For the Faculty Association, getting a chance to make a nomination had been a major gain. The UBC board, acting on its own, had originally offered the presidency to Murray Ross, who was at York in Toronto. Faculty at UBC found out after Ross turned the offer down. This was the way things had always been at UBC. The Faculty Association protested and demanded its own representative on the presidential search committee. The board refused but let the association name a candidate. After interviewing Macdonald, the board decided he was the right person for the job.[29]

Members of the UBC Faculty Association had been impressed by Macdonald in 1955, when he had conducted a survey for UBC on the feasibility of a dental school. He was then director of dental research at Toronto. By 1962 he was director of the Forsyth Dental Infirmary at Harvard and, at forty-four years of age, a generation younger than MacKenzie. According to Macdonald, he was only "dimly aware" of the issues when he took up the presidency, but found himself thrust into the middle of them. He understood that something had to be done and he moved with dispatch.[30] What he could see was that UBC's differences with Victoria College and with community groups across the province had to be sorted out before the Bennett government would substantially increase its spending on higher education. He also got the message from members of the UBC faculty that the Point Grey campus had to have relief from rising enrolments.

Within six months, Macdonald produced his revolutionary new design for higher education in B.C., which had the great merit of making political sense to Premier Bennett. Less than nine months after Macdonald arrived from Harvard, the government had a new Universities Act before the legislature and the premier was on the phone to Gordon Shrum about a new university. After several years in which little seemed to be happening, the difference was dramatic.

Prominent among the recommendations of the Macdonald Report, released in summary form in December 1962, was a call for a second campus in the Vancouver area. Tentatively, Macdonald termed it Burnaby College because the municipality of Burnaby appeared to be the best location for a campus serving the eastern part of the greater metropolitan area. After he first took stock of the situation, in the first few weeks of his presidency, Macdonald got agreement from the Pearkes group at Victoria to hold off on their campaign for university status.[31] He wanted a chance to make a recommendation himself. When he reported, he coupled the idea of a new campus in Burnaby with independent status for Victoria.

Two words defined Macdonald's approach. From the moment he started, he had these in mind and he spelled them out for the UBC board at the end of his first month as president. The province's system of higher education needed to provide for *diversification* while protecting *excellence*. In practical terms that meant that British Columbia needed a variety of independent institutions to fulfill a variety of functions. In Macdonald's thinking, decentralization had become essential. The multi-campus, University of California model was not the one to choose. But California was still an example with its independent tiers and the University of California at the top.

Macdonald had in mind a special place for UBC in a decentralized system. Here would be the place of excellence. Looking across the border, he saw how important graduate studies were in the U.S. UBC's graduate program was still very small and he believed it needed to grow. Macdonald was aware that UBC was in eighth place among leading Canadian universities in the relative size of its graduate program. American universities had long before moved heavily into graduate studies. The University of California, which was determinedly expanding its graduate program, already enrolled half as many graduate students as undergraduates. At Chicago, Columbia, Harvard and Yale, the emphasis on graduate studies was even greater. No Canadian university came close. At Toronto and McGill, about one student in ten was doing graduate work, and at UBC only one in sixteen.[32]

When Macdonald spoke of excellence, he was also thinking of undergraduates. In his report he gave some space to what he called wastage. About 40 per cent of UBC's first-year students were not returning for their second year, and only half of the students admitted to UBC ever graduated. Either the university was not giving them what they wanted, he reasoned, or they did not have enough ability. In either case, admitting them was "a waste of time and money" for them and for the university. Macdonald thought that California had it right with its multi-tier system. In California, state colleges and two-year junior colleges absorbed enrolment pressure that otherwise would be felt by the university.[33]

The University of California protected its standards by admitting only the top 12.5 per cent of high-school graduates. State colleges and junior colleges admitted students with lower grades. If college students did well, some were able to transfer to the university, but transfer was not automatic. The junior colleges offered programs that could not be found at the university; and generally they served a different clientele. The absence of perfect transferability between colleges and the university was, in Macdonald's mind, a necessary and acceptable part of the system. Although he did not say it explicitly, he was describing the virtues of a system that preserved the elite character of the university.

The two-year junior or community college was a California phenomenon that had been replicated across the United States in the decades since the First World War. By 1960 there were nearly seven hundred such colleges in the U.S., and during the following decade another four hundred were created. This American development had been ignored in Canada right up to the writing of Macdonald's report. Lethbridge, in southern Alberta, was the only place in the country with a community college.[34] Macdonald did not mention it; so one can gather that as an experiment, it was not well known.

For British Columbia, Macdonald wanted what he called a two-level system, but might more explicitly have called a three-level system—with overlaps. UBC would be the centrepiece with a large graduate program and a research emphasis. Victoria and Burnaby would have autonomous four-year, degree-granting undergraduate colleges. In his report Macdonald described these three institutions as the first level, but his relegation of Victoria and the new Burnaby college to undergraduate work suggested a clear division within this level. In proposing autonomous college status for Victoria, Macdonald seemed to think he could satisfy Victoria's ambitions. This proved not to be true.

What Macdonald proposed was to establish a hierarchy of institutions of higher education that had no Canadian precedent; although, as the decade progressed, established universities in Ontario and Quebec began to argue in support of the same thing. They put it this way: excellence could best be achieved by concentrating graduate and research funding in a few places. Everyone could not do everything; and a division of function between elite and lesser universities would make the most rational use of public money. That made sense at Toronto or McGill or UBC. But it read differently elsewhere. Smaller universities and colleges would not equate size with merit. Politically, the idea was not attractive.

COMMUNITY COLLEGES

Macdonald's proposed system also included two-year colleges operated by local school boards. When the provincial government acted on his report, these colleges became a vital component of the expansion of higher education in B.C.—in a chronological sense they were sister institutions with SFU. These colleges now have a forty-year history and their students take them for granted, but they did not exist prior to the Macdonald Report. As we have observed, he called them a second level of higher education, but if he had wished to be more explicit, he would have called them a third: first (if he had had his way) would be UBC with the only graduate school and the main research mission; second, the undergraduate colleges at Victoria and Burnaby; third, the two-year community colleges.

The idea of two-year community colleges made political sense to Premier Bennett. It had already been endorsed by the B.C. Association of School Trustees and numerous school boards and municipalities. With the Macdonald Report in hand, the provincial government moved immediately to enable school boards to run post-secondary colleges. The first of these, Vancouver City College, amalgamating a continuing education centre, a vocational institute and an art school, opened in September 1965. During the next five years, seven more opened: Capilano and Douglas in the Greater Vancouver area; Malaspina in Nanaimo, and Selkirk, Okanagan, New Caledonia and Cariboo in the interior.

Community colleges were part of the solution that Macdonald proposed in December 1962 for British Columbia. When the provincial government adopted this part of his report, higher education in B.C. became much more accessible while also taking a very different and more complex shape. One problem for students that immediately manifested itself was the absence of a system of credit transfer from one institution to another. In California, Macdonald had observed the absence of a fluid transfer system. From his perspective as a university president, that absence seemed fine: it served to screen students. In Simon Fraser University's early years, however, the community college transfer issue excited a huge controversy.

In 1963, B.C. adopted a community college model that no other province subsequently chose to follow. This model had been advocated for several years by a member of the UBC Geography Department, Walter Hardwick—later a prominent Vancouver city councillor and subsequently the deputy minister of education. When he arrived at UBC, Macdonald adopted the Hardwick model and incorporated it into his report. Hardwick had taken an interest in the American community college system during a year's study in Wisconsin, and he had been promoting it for B.C. since the enrolment crunch of 1957.[35]

He saw the community college as a low-cost solution with numerous advantages. It could respond to local needs. It could offer vocational and general education programs as well as academic; it could provide students from small cities and outlying areas in the interior and on Vancouver Island with the first two years of a degree program before they made the often difficult adjustment to a big city and a big campus; it could save those students and their families money while they stayed at home for those two years; it could have a regional identity and serve as a general educational and cultural centre for people at a distance from the metropolis. And it could be staffed by "senior and successful" secondary school teachers with MAs who had roots in the community or were familiar with it.

The community college that Hardwick envisaged, that Macdonald recommended and that the provincial government endorsed, overlapped the existing functions of B.C. secondary schools as well as the university. Many B.C. schools were then running grade-thirteen classes, which were accepted as the equivalent to the first year of university. About 60 per cent of UBC's incoming students were arriving straight out of grade twelve, and 30 per cent were entering second year after completing grade thirteen. (Two other provinces, Ontario and New Brunswick, offered grade thirteen; it was something of a Depression-era legacy, placing some of the cost of advanced education with school boards and saving students and parents money.) Macdonald recommended phasing out grade thirteen, and in B.C. it was gone by the early 1970s.[36]

With grade-thirteen classes, school boards were already involved in post-secondary education. Community colleges were a next step. In Vancouver, a grade-thirteen class of 750, at King Edward School, became the first year of Vancouver City College's academic program. By placing community colleges under the jurisdiction of local school boards, as Macdonald and Hardwick recommended, the B.C. government put its faith in decentralization. This made it possible for each college to design itself according to the needs of its regional community.

The Department of Education expected each community college to take its own direction. In contrast to the college systems in other provinces, the management and financing of B.C. community colleges were locally controlled. This meant that curriculum was locally controlled. And, as did not happen in Ontario and most other provinces, in addition to technical, vocational and general education, B.C. community colleges were able to compete with universities in offering the first two years of degree programs. In other provinces, when community colleges came onto the scene, provincial universities fought to control their academic programs or to prevent them from offering credits towards a degree. UBC, under Macdonald, was the exception.[37]

A FOUR-YEAR CAMPUS IN BURNABY

When the provincial government decided to make up for lost time by rapidly expanding and immediately diversifying higher education, it had no plan of its own, but relied on the report that UBC President Macdonald had prepared. This contained specific recommendations about the mission and location of the four-year institution in Burnaby that was to become SFU.

Macdonald's report was an admirably complete, succinct and innovative document of 119 pages. It contained too much to have been researched and written in six months. As the surviving minutes of Macdonald's deliberations show, the main outlines and much of the detail were already at hand on the day he arrived. Faculty at UBC had not waited for Macdonald's arrival before looking for answers to the enrolment pressures they faced. Walter Hardwick's contribution is a case in point. Macdonald found a number of other people at UBC with well-developed ideas on what needed to be done. They included Ron Baker from English, who was later to become SFU's first academic planner.

Macdonald recruited these people as members of a committee that, without delay, gave him the substance of his report. They had settled on the main elements by the end of the summer and needed the fall only for drafting: by September they had agreed on four-year colleges in Burnaby and Victoria and on school board-controlled community colleges. And they had agreed on the principles of decentralization and institutional autonomy. This meant, among other things, that the new college at Burnaby should have its own act and the same independence that UBC enjoyed and that Victoria was to receive.[38]

In the years before Macdonald arrived, Baker and Hardwick, acting independently, had begun to consider the logic of a second campus in the Vancouver area. Baker used student telephone numbers to plot the geographical centre of UBC's student catchment area. The centre had always been in the affluent west side of Vancouver, but Baker observed that it was moving eastward at the rate of a block a year. During the 1961–62 academic year, Hardwick gave his graduate geography students an exercise in the application of location theory by asking them to collect and analyze data on the whereabouts of university-aged individuals throughout the province.[39] Within metropolitan Vancouver he calculated travel times and looked for potential sites. By June 1962, before Macdonald took office, Hardwick set out the results in a document placed on the agenda of the UBC senate. Macdonald subsequently incorporated this material into his report.[40]

When they looked at the growing parking lots on their campus, people at UBC could see that the age of the automobile had come. (The 1961 ratio of one car for every five people in B.C. was 50 per cent higher than it had been ten years earlier; and that meant more young people with wheels. At UBC that translated into eighteen thousand students, staff and faculty arriving each day in eight thousand cars.[41]) For Hardwick, driving time had to be a key determinant in deciding where a new campus should go. He observed that UBC, situated at the western end of a peninsula, was too far away for students to commute by bus or car from the southern and western parts of the metropolis. From most of the North Shore via Lions Gate Bridge, and from the northeastern sections of Vancouver, as well as from New Westminster, it took thirty-five to sixty minutes to drive out to the UBC campus. Students from east of New Westminster did not attempt it, but had to live on or near the campus if they were going to attend university.

In 1961–62, Hardwick was well aware that the geography of the region would soon be substantially reshaped by the Trans-Canada Highway, which was nearing completion. (Premier Bennett formally opened the B.C. portion of the Trans-Canada in a ceremony at Rogers Pass on July 30, 1962.) When it was finished, the Trans-Canada provided a divided highway that swept from the east through the municipalities south of the Fraser, across the Port Mann Bridge to New Westminster and Burnaby and then over Burrard Inlet by the newly completed Second Narrows Bridge to the North Shore. This, Hardwick could see, would become the main east–west thoroughfare in the Lower Mainland from Hope to Horseshoe Bay. If there was to be a new college, he believed that it should be near this highway at a point within a half-hour drive for the maximum number of students coming either from the east or the west. This point, he determined, was the Cariboo/Stormont Interchange on the Trans-Canada at the foot of Burnaby Mountain.

Near the Cariboo/Stormont Interchange, Hardwick and his students saw four possible sites of 250 acres (100 hectares) or more. One was the land south of the highway owned by the federal government, of which only a portion was used by the George Derby veterans hospital; another was the site of a projected vocational school near Burnaby Lake; a third was the Oakalla Prison Farm, and the fourth was an undeveloped cemetery property owned by the City of Vancouver on the lower south slope of Burnaby Mountain. Hardwick saw disadvantages in the George Derby, Burnaby Lake and Oakalla sites. The first had a northern exposure; the second was on low land with soils that could not support multi-storey buildings, and the third was not immediately available. The Burnaby Mountain site was a few minutes from the highway but had the advantages of well-drained land, southern exposure and a view.

By the time Macdonald had finished his report, he and his committee, with Hardwick's help, had narrowed their choice to the Burnaby Mountain and George Derby sites. Hardwick prepared a map dividing the metropolitan region between UBC and the Burnaby college according to thirty-minute driving times. On the North Shore the boundary ran between the municipalities of North and West Vancouver. In the city of Vancouver there was an area of overlap in the region between Main and Nanaimo streets, with the affluent western section easily within thirty minutes of UBC territory. Richmond, to the south, Hardwick calculated as half an hour from UBC. Otherwise, all the municipalities to the east and south as far away as Langley were within driving range of the proposed Burnaby college.

Hardwick's driving times, incidentally, conformed to the socio-economic divisions of the greater Vancouver area. A college in Burnaby would serve students from high schools in the east that until recently had sent few young people to university. UBC would draw from the more privileged west as in the past. In his report Macdonald did not go out of his way to make that obvious. He stressed instead the advantages of a decentralized system that could provide a variety of options for high-school graduates. Competition, he argued, is a great motivator; and the province would get more out of competing institutions than by concentrating all higher education on the UBC and Victoria campuses. He had evidence from California and Michigan to demonstrate that it would not cost much more to build an entirely new and independent campus for 2,500 students than to provide that much additional space at UBC. In fact, he argued that if the cost of constructing additional residences was added to the calculation, it would be more expensive to keep expansion at UBC. His point was that residences would be needed for students whose homes were beyond an acceptable daily commute.[42]

Macdonald was able to draw on UBC facts and figures to estimate the capital costs involved in building a new campus. That is how he calculated the square footage of classroom, office, laboratory, cafeteria, library and administrative space needed per student and how much, in current dollars, each square foot of building cost. He assumed that the new college would open with two thousand students and reach an enrolment of seven thousand within six years. For capital cost up to 1971 he estimated $9 million, "for bare essentials." This was just for Burnaby. Macdonald was also looking for $20 million in operating costs for UBC and Victoria up to 1965 and $85 million for the whole university system up to 1971.

Speaking in Toronto in 1965, Macdonald remembered his surprise at the initial reaction of the business community in B.C. He held up the example of American business, which, he said, understood the economic value of a university. In Vancouver, by contrast, businessmen had told him that his figures were "utterly fantastic."[43] Early in his tenure as chancellor, Shrum received an objection to the money being spent at SFU from H.R. MacMillan, chairman of MacMillan Bloedel, the giant B.C. forest products company. MacMillan grumbled that education did not seem to be teaching people basic economics. "I am wondering where and how welfare, education, public works and other tasty morsels are going to be paid for."[44]

Macdonald and his committee, however, had satisfied the person who counted most, Premier Bennett. The ink was scarcely dry on the first printing of the Macdonald Report when the premier promised action. The occasion was at the beginning of a session of the legislative assembly at the end of January 1963. Bennett declared himself generally in agreement with Macdonald about what was needed for higher education and promised, in the Speech from the Throne, to create a system of community colleges and to grant Victoria university status.[45] His government also began to prepare legislation to create a university in Burnaby.

THE PREMIER'S PRIORITIES

Bennett had taken what he liked from the Macdonald Report while ignoring major points. The report recommended four-year undergraduate colleges for Burnaby and Victoria, but Bennett's government made them universities. For this change, SFU must thank the supporters of Victoria College, because it was the Victoria lobby that insisted on university status and that had the political muscle to get it. The premier and the minister of education professed to see nothing much in it. They had asked various people about the difference between a college and a university and understood that Canadians had no fixed understanding. If the people at Victoria wanted to call their place a university, why not? It cost no more. For the sake of symmetry it made sense to call SFU a university as well. At that point there was no community group, faculty, staff or chancellor to lobby for SFU or to appreciate what had happened.

The change in designation from college to university erased a distinction that Macdonald had wanted between the two new degree-granting institutions and UBC. The change, he thought, encouraged unrealistic ambitions. Neither Victoria nor the fledgling SFU accepted his idea that they should only be teaching undergraduates. When Gordon Shrum eventually called the first meeting of the SFU board of governors—more than six months after he was named chancellor—he announced in his definitive way that SFU was going to have graduate students. His university was going to seek excellence in the same arena as UBC.[46]

Macdonald brought up the subject at a conference in Toronto that he addressed weeks after SFU opened with seventy-four graduate students. He wished that SFU and Victoria had waited before launching graduate studies. He did not accept their argument that first-class faculty would not come to a purely undergraduate institution, and he cited the existence in the U.S. of many excellent undergraduate colleges. It wasn't fair, he thought, to take in graduate students before you could offer them a strong research library and well-established departments. He had to accept the consequences of the autonomy that SFU and Victoria had received. In principle he believed that he was right in recommending autonomy: "... they can make their own choices, and that we intended. Those of us who do not like the decision can only say that we would have done it differently."[47]

Premier Bennett had calculated the political advantage he could get out of an expansion of higher education. That led him to scatter his largesse in a way that left Macdonald, and other members of the public system, a little disappointed. Since forming his first government, Bennett had established a pattern of calling an election every three years. He was therefore conscious of three-year cycles of accomplishment: what could he tell voters that he had done during his last mandate?

Bennett's last election had been in 1960, and at the beginning of 1963 he was aiming for the vote that he would eventually call for September 30. The creation of two new public universities would be a major part of his record. The promise of community colleges for the Vancouver area, Vancouver Island, the Okanagan, the Cariboo and the Selkirks would help in local constituencies. All this the Macdonald Report had justified. But Bennett and his government could not resist the petition that came from the Selkirk region for university status for Notre Dame, the tiny (seventeen students and seven faculty) private Catholic college operating in Nelson. Instead of one public university and two public four-year colleges, as Macdonald had recommended, B.C. was to have three public universities and one private. Macdonald questioned the political mentality that took the decentralization of higher education that far; but there was nothing he could do about it.[48]

The premier and minister of education also overlooked the sequence of steps that the Macdonald Report outlined for the establishment of a new college (or university) in Burnaby. What they did adopt was Macdonald's deadline of September 1965 and his enrolment target of two thousand or more. Getting a university built within two and a half years matched Bennett's three-year election cycle. He could announce the plan for the 1963 election and have the university up and running before the 1966 election. The best way to accomplish that was to hand over the task to a man like Gordon Shrum.

If the premier and minister had followed the Macdonald Report they would immediately have established a level of supervision for higher education that would protect the universities from direct government interference. The model was the University Grants Commission in Britain, which functioned as a planning and funding body for higher education at arm's length from the government. Macdonald recommended two bodies, a provincial granting agency and a provincial accrediting agency or academic board. He thought that these arm's-length agencies should be in place before the province began establishing new degree-granting institutions.

Macdonald's sequence for establishing SFU would have been: first, for the government to create a provincial academic board; second, for the academic board to recommend a board of directors for SFU; third, for the SFU board of directors to find a president, and fourth, for the president, working with the board of directors, to draft a university act for the provincial assembly to pass.[49] Each step would have taken weeks or months, but the process would have allowed the university, through its board and president, to design its own governing legislation. Instead, the premier picked up the phone and called Gordon Shrum.

The actual sequence was the reverse of Macdonald's recommendation. Bennett named Shrum as chancellor days before the legislature passed a new Universities Act (which Shrum had not seen); Shrum chose a president; and, after that decision, the government, acting on Shrum's advice, named a board of governors for what was to be SFU. Only then did the government name its arm's-length provincial academic board.

This sequence was expeditious, and it was probably the best way to ensure that SFU opened by the target date given in the Macdonald Report. It made decision making simple.

To draft new university legislation, the minister of education, Leslie Peterson, turned to George Curtis, dean of Law at UBC. Curtis has claimed credit for naming SFU. He has said that he wrote the name into the legislation knowing that everyone would associate it with Simon Fraser, the North West Company trader who in 1808 travelled the length of the Fraser River by canoe and foot, beginning in the far northeastern interior. But Curtis was slipping in a tribute to a British officer he had met and been impressed by during the Second World War: Simon Fraser, Lord Lovatt, the head of the Fraser clan.

The logic of the Fraser part of the name was seen by all because the university was to serve half a dozen municipalities in the lower Fraser Valley. Sperrin Chant, the dean of Arts at UBC, reputedly was the person who first questioned the name Fraser University. "Do you want a crowd yelling FU at your football team?" Adding "Simon" was the solution. Most people give Leslie Peterson credit for the choice, not Curtis.[50]

Curtis was given the job of drafting a single act for the three public universities. Macdonald had not anticipated this, but had assumed that each institution would have its own act. Curtis did his drafting between January and March 1963. He made his task simpler by taking the 1936 act under which UBC was then operating and adding sections for SFU and Victoria. He did not have the time, and was not encouraged, to reconsider the provisions for university governance that the 1936 act contained. What he was drafting had more consequence for the immediate future of SFU than he or the minister appreciated.

CHANGING TIMES AND CHANGING ATTITUDES

An "instant university" got an instant act. No one involved in drafting and approving the act anticipated how objectionable that act would later seem to the faculty that would teach at the new university on Burnaby Mountain. It was too American, although the faculty who took jobs at SFU generally assumed that they did not like it because it was too British. In any case, it was too authoritarian.

The 1936 UBC Act, like the university legislation in the three other Western provinces, had been modelled on a University of Toronto Act of

1906. By the time that Curtis replicated that model once again, the leading members of the Canadian Association of University Teachers (CAUT) had become very critical of it. The 1906 Toronto act undoubtedly was an advance on the nineteenth-century legislation it replaced because it interposed a board of governors between the provincial government and the provincial university. Until then, the Ontario government had been exercising direct control over its university. The change had been recommended by an Ontario Royal Commission that, significantly, had surveyed American universities—Chicago, Wisconsin, Harvard, Yale and Princeton—but not British or Canadian universities. When Toronto set up a board of governors appointed by the Ontario provincial government, it was following American practice.[51] This is what SFU inherited in the legislation that Curtis drafted.

This meant, among other things, no faculty or student representation on the governing body of the university. In 1963, faculty members at Canadian universities were not concerned about student representation, but they were beginning to object to being excluded themselves. A sign of the times was the recent insistence of the Faculty Association at UBC on having a voice in the selection of a new president. The executive of the national association, the CAUT and other active members had begun to articulate a comparison of the American and British models of university governance; and their comparison was decidedly unfavourable to the American. They considered it unfortunate that Canadian universities had gone the American route.

What fuelled their unease was the transformation of Canadian and American universities during the previous decade. The growth of universities and the expansion of their programs had consequences that dismayed many university teachers, especially those in traditional academic subjects. At UBC, for example, the administration had mushroomed during the Norman MacKenzie years; by the time he left, half of the positions in the university were administrative. Fifteen years earlier, when the university had been much smaller, three-quarters of the people employed there were teaching. An intimate campus had been lost and the importance of the teaching role on campus had become a little less obvious. Growth came with another price as well. For many, universities were becoming too vocational. And the presidents, politicians and board members could be worrisome when they used business analogies to describe the university as a plant with a product, or to suggest that university administration might follow business models.

Stewart Reid, the first full-time executive secretary of the CAUT, after taking office in 1959, made a study of university government and its history. He described the model at most American universities, and generally in Canada, as authoritarian. In this model, legal and formal control over the university rested with outsiders, the non-university people appointed to the board of governors. In most cases, as in British Columbia, a majority of the board were appointed directly by the provincial government. Everywhere in North America, university boards were made up largely of representatives of the business and professional communities. An important role of the board had always been fundraising, and that consideration had repeatedly led governments and university presidents to select members from business. The problem for Reid and his colleagues in the CAUT was that universities were becoming too businesslike.

Reid thought that a much more desirable form of university government could be found in Britain. The Oxford–Cambridge model was the ideal. There, both at the college and federated university levels, academic staff were in control. At the old Scottish universities and the newer British "red-brick" universities, as far as Reid could see, the principle of academic autonomy and self-determination was also alive and well. It was ironic, he thought, that in Canada a professor, who might be called on to advise the federal government or to act as a United Nations consultant, could not have a voice in the government of his own university.[52]

This thinking was shared by an active and distinguished group within the CAUT. The group included F.R. Scott, Frank Underhill, Donald Rowat, W.L. Morton, George Whalley, Bora Laskin and V.C. Fowke, all profoundly influential within their own disciplines—political science, history, literature, law and economics. These individuals were contributors to a book on university government, published in the spring of 1964, but already in the works when George Curtis began drafting legislation for SFU. The editor, George Whalley, summarized the point of the book in his preface. The media and politicians, he observed, were talking of a "crisis in higher education" without adequate definition or analysis. The public discussion was all about finding enough places for students; but the real crisis was one of preserving the university and its reason for existing. The danger was that as governments spent more money on universities, they would want to call the tune, and their tune would be on the theme of investment and return—the business of education. "That is why," Whalley said, "we feel the need for a revised vigorous university government." Academics had to be in a position to protect the academic life.[53]

ACADEMIC FREEDOM AND UNIVERSITY GOVERNMENT

Stewart Reid had been at the centre of a controversy that had riveted the Canadian academic community only five years earlier, in 1958. That controversy had galvanized the CAUT membership and made the CAUT a much more muscular organization than before. Reid had been head of the three-person History Department at United College in Winnipeg when the college board of regents attempted to dismiss a colleague, Harry Crowe, "with cause." The board did not specify the cause in its initial letter of dismissal, and that was a major procedural omission. But its reasons for acting, when they became known across the country, were seen as highly questionable: statements in a private letter from Crowe to a third party, which had been intercepted and turned over to the principal of the college, were construed by the board as disloyal to the college.[54]

In the dismissal of Harry Crowe, the CAUT had its first academic freedom case. The organization was then only eight years old; it had little revenue and no permanent office, and it was concerning itself mainly with the exchange of information about salaries and benefits for the use of local university faculty associations. In the Crowe case, the CAUT appointed an economic historian, V.C. Fowke from Saskatchewan, and a law professor, Bora Laskin from Toronto, as a special commission. (Fifteen years later, Laskin was chief justice of Canada.) Fowke and Laskin conducted four days of hearings at United College, and found in favour of Crowe. The board did not co-operate with the investigation and did not accept the Fowke–Laskin Report, which they saw as prejudiced. In the end, thirteen faculty and three members of the administrative staff left the college in protest. Stewart Reid was one of them; and so was Percy Smith, who, following Reid, was to become the CAUT's permanent secretary.

For Reid, Smith and the CAUT, academic freedom and university government were inextricably linked. The core of the matter, as they viewed it, was academic control of the university. With the Crowe affair, they generated enough national support from university teachers to put the CAUT at the centre of the university debate. Their next step was to approach the National Conference on Canadian Universities and Colleges (NCCUC) with a proposal for a special commission on university government.[55]

The NCCUC, soon to be called the Association of Universities and Colleges of Canada (AUCC), was an organization of university presidents, although it sought to speak for the whole university community. Norman MacKenzie at UBC had reflected an understandable presidential view that faculty ought to see the NCCUC as their organization and let it speak for them. By the early 1960s, however, presidents were accepting the reality that faculty had their own national organization.

In June 1962, in the month before John Barfoot Macdonald began working on the study that would recommend the creation of SFU, the NCCUC agreed to sponsor jointly with the CAUT a commission on university government. Some university presidents were themselves interested in reform. Prominent among them was Claude Bissell, now at Toronto, who was looking for a simpler structure than the University of Toronto Act provided.

It took more than a year to establish terms of reference, to select commissioners James Duff and Robert Berdahl and to organize their tour. In November 1964, as construction proceeded at the top of Burnaby Mountain, these commissioners had a preliminary meeting with CAUT and NCCUC representatives. Between January and April of 1965 they toured the country, visiting thirty-six campuses. In the second week of March they arrived in Vancouver, where they spent two days at UBC. On March 10, Berdahl went over to Victoria while Duff visited the skeleton staff that SFU temporarily housed in the offices of a B.C. Hydro subsidiary in downtown Vancouver.[56] By then SFU had a president, librarian, registrar, bursar, academic planner, engineer, dean of education and three department heads, who attended a one-hour meeting with Duff before he went to lunch with the board of governors. There was not much any of them could yet say about the way the government of SFU worked, so it was not a very instructive exchange.

While Gordon Shrum was building his university, the commissioners were writing their report, and he moved faster than they did. SFU was in its second semester of operations, in the spring of 1966, when their report became public. In the Canadian academic world, the appearance of this report was a major event. On SFU's brand new campus, it became fuel for an increasingly volatile situation.

Commissioners Duff and Berdahl had supported the CAUT call for faculty representation in university government. Their findings should not have been a surprise because the CAUT had done well in the choice of the two commissioners. The senior was Sir James Duff, former vice-chancellor at Durham University; and the junior was Robert O. Berdahl, professor of political science at San Francisco State University. They had the appearance of balance: one British and one American, one older and one younger (the age difference was twenty-eight years). But their selection ensured that British practice would be the main basis of comparison. Duff, a former chair of the BBC, had twenty-three years' experience as a university vice-chancellor, and had served on the governing bodies of four different British universities. Berdahl had studied at the London School of Economics and had recently published a doctoral dissertation on British universities.

Duff and Berdahl gave CAUT activists the ammunition they wanted. Donald Rowat's April 1966 review of the Duff–Berdahl Report makes that clear. But the spirit of reform on Canadian campuses was already outrunning the document that Duff and Berdahl had produced. Many found it tepid. Claude Bissell, who had chaired the joint CAUT–NCCUC steering committee for the Duff–Berdahl Commission, mused that if the commissioners had started their work a year or two later, they would have written ten times as much on students and student demands. As it was, they had only two and a half pages about students in a report that ran to ninety-seven.[57]

SPEED AND CHAOS

In creating SFU as rapidly as they did, the Bennett government and Gordon Shrum moved too fast to assimilate the changing mood of faculty and students in North America. Perhaps the trouble the university faced in its first few years was unavoidable. After all, commissioners Duff and Berdahl were unable to get ahead of the tide, and they had a better opportunity than most to judge its progress.

In the year and a half that Duff and Berdahl worked on their report, expectations changed rapidly on Canadian university campuses and what the commissioners produced looked conservative to many faculty as well as students. Their recommendations were radical, however, compared with the legislation that brought SFU into existence. And the gap was compounded by the inexperience of the SFU board. In North America generally over the preceding forty or fifty years, boards had been learning not to interfere with education policy or academic freedom. They had learned to distinguish between the formal power that they possessed under the law and the actual power that they should use. The board that governed SFU under Gordon Shrum's guidance had no chance to absorb this lesson before they alienated a large section of the university's faculty.

John Hutchinson, who arrived at SFU as an assistant professor of History in 1966, read the Duff–Berdahl Report during his first days on the job. He later remembered the surprise expressed by members of the SFU board of governors at the tone of a CAUT investigating committee that visited SFU in 1968. "They [the board] clearly hadn't realized that they were twenty, thirty years out of date, in the way in which they were proposing to go about running a university."[58]

From a distance it seemed that things had gone badly wrong at SFU. That was Claude Bissell's perspective from Toronto, offered in a book published in 1970. When built, Bissell said, SFU was the wonder of the academic world with its magnificent mountaintop campus. But it had developed tensions that had not, by 1970, been resolved. For Bissell, SFU illustrated the problem of the instant university.[59]

This did not capture what students, faculty and staff at SFU felt about their university. A sense of academic adventure and opportunity brought many of them there and held them once they became involved. Many found a great learning environment in SFU's chaotic start.

2

Choosing a Site, a Design,
a President and a Trimester System

For an "instant" start, Simon Fraser University needed a
man like Gordon Shrum who could get on with the job
without hesitation. In the six weeks after his acceptance
of the chancellorship and before his formal appointment, he selected the site, set up an architectural competition and approached his first choice as president.
While he was still waiting for the results of the competition and looking for a president, he began making
speeches promising that the new university would be an
all-year operation, not the standard seven months with
a five-month summer break. He was charging ahead
without a budget or funds or even a governing structure. Nobody, however, doubted that the university was
going to happen; and the press marvelled at the speed
with which he moved. In the case of SFU, Shrum's willingness to ignore red tape suited the premier and his
government.

Shrum took on SFU on the strength of a phone call
and a public announcement, and without any written

direction from the premier or his government. Years later he recalled a conversation with the minister of education, Leslie Peterson, in the summer of 1963. Peterson asked how he was going to pay for all the things he was doing. "I don't know," said Shrum. "Don't ask me. That's not my problem. I've only been asked to build a university and get it built on time and I've nothing to do with the financing."[1] Premier W.A.C. Bennett subsequently did let him know that he could not expect the government to pay for everything, and that he would have to raise money privately. This Shrum proceeded to do. But the fast start he made depended on the immense trust that he shared with the premier.

SELECTING BURNABY MOUNTAIN

For guidance, Shrum had to turn to the report prepared by the president of the University of British Columbia, John Barfoot Macdonald. Shrum began reading the Macdonald Report after becoming chancellor, although he had a general sense of its content from the press. There he found enrolment targets (two thousand students in 1965 and seven thousand by 1970–71) and a vastly underestimated capital budget ($9 million to 1971). He also understood that SFU was to be a commuter campus and not residential.

Looking twenty-five kilometres east from his downtown office on top of the B.C. Hydro building, Shrum could see the wooded profile of Burnaby Mountain, the 390-metre summit that old-timers still remembered as Snake Hill. Walter Hardwick and John Chapman, the authors of the demographic section of the Macdonald Report, had a glimpse of that view when they made a presentation to Shrum. They recommended Burnaby Mountain, or the grounds of the George Derby veterans hospital, also in Burnaby, or the Green Timbers area to the east in Surrey. During their conversation, Shrum swung round from his B.C. Hydro desk and pointed to Burnaby Mountain: "I could run both places from here."[2]

Shrum's search for a site drew several municipalities into the bidding, all of them sure a university would be a major asset. Burnaby had the inside track. In 1963, however, every suburban municipality in the Lower Mainland contained extensive woodland and farmland that its council planned to develop. The city of Langley, thirty-five kilometres east of the Cariboo/Stormont Interchange, offered Shrum 800 acres (320 hectares), of which 400 would be free and 400 financed. Delta offered

400 acres in the Sunshine Hills area, about twenty kilometres by road south of the critical interchange. Surrey identified 800 acres south and east of the Pattullo Bridge over the Fraser River, an area that has since been preserved as the Green Timbers Forest Reserve. Coquitlam promised 800 acres at Essondale, which survive today in their semi-natural state as Mundy Park.

To view these sites and the road systems that served them, Shrum took a slow-flying B.C. Hydro seaplane, an amphibious Grumman Goose, over the lower Fraser Valley (at Hydro expense). That gave him a bird's-eye view of all the locations, but the Langley, Delta and Surrey sites never were in the running: they were too far east or south. The Coquitlam site was closer in and had potential; but Shrum had his mind set on Burnaby Mountain.³ He explained years later that in choosing to build on Burnaby Mountain he saw an opportunity to do something spectacular; and while he was looking at other possible sites, he could not get out of his mind the setting "of unsurpassed grandeur" that the Burnaby summit would have.

Shrum did recognize a large drawback in Burnaby Mountain. From the west, one could drive three-quarters of the way up via Curtis Street, which turned into Centennial Way, leading farther to Burnaby Mountain Park and a pavilion. From the park, it was an upward hike of about a kilometre through the woods to the summit. But from the Trans-Canada Highway to the south there was no route, and six kilometres of highway (at a 7 per cent grade) would have to be built. Shrum saw that the problem of developing access to Burnaby Mountain would likely delay the opening of the university.

Although he mentioned nothing about this, he was prepared in his own mind to sacrifice the September 1965 deadline for the sake of the spectacular location.⁴ He gave no hint of concern about delay when he recommended the site to Premier Bennett and the government. It was a gamble, but the Social Credit cabinet was a freewheeling bunch, and strongly behind the SFU project, and Shrum subsequently succeeded in getting his highway at no expense to the university and without much effort. As he recalled, he spoke to the minister of highways, Phil Gaglardi, in the spring of 1965, when university construction was well advanced. Gaglardi said, "Did I promise you a road?" and Shrum said yes, although he had nothing in writing. This was small potatoes to

Gaglardi, whose highways department still spent nearly a quarter of the province's budget, and he replied that if he had promised a road, he would build it. The road was completed that fall, three months after the university opened.

Shrum hid his hand, using the Langley, Surrey, Delta and Coquitlam bids to get more land from the Burnaby council. He didn't have much of a struggle. The progressive reeve of Burnaby, Alan Emmott, was a strong supporter of the idea of a university in his municipality; and he and his council made successive increases to an initial offer of 200 acres (80 hectares).[5]

In the end, Burnaby donated 1,000 acres; the provincial government added 150 acres of Crown land, and the developers, Webb and Knapp, added 18 acres, for a total package of 1168 acres (467 hectares). Within the boundaries of this block were seventeen undeveloped lots that had been in private hands for forty or fifty years. (The lack of a municipal water supply had stopped people from building, but not from camping during summer holidays.) Many private owners agreed to donate their land; others were bought out at expropriated prices. The Department of National Defence had nearly 6 acres (2.4 hectares) for a microwave relay station, which the university was able to purchase, paying for the land and for the removal of the equipment. This gave the university the complete summit: everything above the 300-metre level as well as most of the south slope running steeply down to about 150 metres. Shrum made sure that the natural surroundings would be protected. His deal with Burnaby included zoning restrictions on the slopes of the mountain.

Part of the deal with Burnaby was a road allowance from Curtis Street through Burnaby municipal land. That brought traffic from the west. Access from the Trans-Canada Highway to the south, however, required a road through a 260-acre (104-hectare) property owned by the City of Vancouver—a property that Vancouver had purchased for a cemetery and not developed and that the MacDonald Report had mentioned as a possible site for SFU. In 1964 the provincial government appropriated this property to build the necessary road—Gaglardi Way. This was after Vancouver City Council had tried and failed to make some money out of the situation by getting zoning for a residential development in exchange for road access up to SFU.[6]

Once roads were built, the ascent by car from the east or the south took a good ten minutes. By bus the trip was somewhat longer, and for the hardy few who biked it was at least half an hour. All of this was in addition to the thirty minutes or fewer that Hardwick had figured students ought to travel to get to the Cariboo/Stormont Interchange. For those who used the bus, a commute of an hour or more was common. When Shrum wrote to the premier to recommend the Burnaby Mountain site, he observed that students got more out of university if they lived on campus. Unfortunately, he said, "we have to be realistic," and accept sfu's role as commuter campus.[7]

Shrum's comment about residence living speaks of his own undergraduate experience half a century earlier, when he left the family farm to immerse himself in life at the University of Toronto. He could imagine another kind of university on top of Burnaby Mountain: one that was largely removed from the normal world. There was an impractical factor in his choice. He had selected a splendid retreat—but for students who would be there only between 8:30 AM and 4:30 PM on weekdays.

AN ARCHITECTURAL COMPETITION

While choosing a site, Shrum was already thinking of buildings. On a lined sheet of paper he jotted down a series of brief notes to himself, the essence of his ideas about what was needed. The first was "Architecture determines the nature, the inner philosophy of a university." The second was "SFU—convenient and covered walks, an invitation to students to use the library. Parking too." The third was "On the physical side we wish to create surroundings which will make learning possible and attractive—convenient for and conducive to the work of learning." Finally he wrote: "We have a general artistic responsibility to the whole public to create buildings that set a high standard of beauty and efficiency."[8] Shrum was asked more than once if he had his eye on the army huts, still in use at UBC, for his new campus on Burnaby Mountain.[9] For Shrum it was not a joking matter. His university was going to be defined first and foremost by its site and its architecture.

Warnett Kennedy, the British-born architect who helped Shrum frame the conditions for an SFU architectural competition, found it a tension-ridden task. "From the onset," he recalled, "Dr. Shrum and I were 'eyeball to eyeball' in daily conflict."[10] Shrum had a host of notions about running the competition that would have been unacceptable to professional architects. Kennedy remembered going repeatedly to the president of the Architectural Institute of B.C. for backing. All was forgiven once the winner was announced. "The competition was a success. Gordon Shrum became my friend."

Kennedy came to the conclusion that Shrum himself had the capacity to be a great architect. (Others, including the competition's co-winner, Arthur Erickson, were not so sure.) Shrum had acquired a lot of experience with buildings and design, and he had been accumulating ideas. He had been responsible, as dean of Graduate Studies at UBC, for the award-winning Koerner Graduate Centre and Shrum Block completed in 1960–61. During his professional travels, he took note of what was happening on other campuses, and he paid attention to Vancouver's architectural development. He had ideas about architecture, and on Burnaby Mountain he had an opportunity to put them into effect.

During a visit to Harvard, Shrum visited the Graduate Centre, designed in 1949–50 by the renowned German Bauhaus architect Walter Gropius. For Shrum, the application that this design offered was not the way in which Gropius and his collaborators had used stone and other materials to integrate a modernist complex with older buildings, but his use of covered walkways that allowed students to get from residences to dining halls without getting wet. If this was a good idea for Massachusetts, Shrum thought it a better one for rainy B.C. He employed it at the Koerner Graduate Centre at UBC. On Burnaby Mountain, where it is wet half the year, he wanted it for the complete campus.[11]

Shrum wanted an imaginative and striking design. He also wanted to get it cheaply while creating opportunity for young B.C. architects. On the last point he was critical of UBC, where the firm of Thompson, Berwick, Pratt had been university architects for fifty years, after winning a competition in 1912.[12] The UBC School of Architecture was more than a decade old and it was time to give its graduates a chance at a big project. The cost and complexity of the great bundle of drawings required for a major competition could exclude small firms and junior architects. For this he had an answer.

Shrum had chosen his site by early May. He asked the premier to make the announcement on May 8 and to promise an immediate architectural competition open only to B.C. architects. Shrum circulated details at the end of May and gave contestants two months to submit. He now estimated first- and second-stage construction costs at $15 million; and he set the ultimate student population at eighteen thousand.[13]

What made his competition different was his requirement of an overall concept in just three sheets of drawings: on the first, a site plan showing two phases of construction; on the second, an aerial view locating the various buildings, and on the third, profiles and sections. Written explanation was limited to one legal-sized page. Independent architects and junior members of large firms could manage this on their own: they would not need the resources of a large office.

Shrum expected thirty-five applications and got seventy-one. Nearly half of the architects in B.C. prepared submissions, individually, in partnerships or as members of teams. The panel of five judges included two from Canada and three from the U.S. The competition was local but the panel was international. They assembled on the sunny morning of July 31, 1963 at the Vancouver Art Gallery, then located on Georgia Street—where all of the drawings were on display—and they announced their decision late that afternoon at a ceremony attended by the premier at the pavilion in Burnaby Mountain Park.

The five judges were unanimous about the winning entry, although they did not agree so easily on the order of the next nine. The competition offered five prizes of $5,000, with the provision that the prize would be against fees for design: the five prize winners would all be offered work on the project. The judges also awarded five honourable mentions. Of the architects who contributed to the five prize-winning entries, all were under the age of forty-six. Only one well-established firm, Duncan McNab and Associates, finished in the top five—and that was in fifth place. Arthur Erickson and Geoffrey Massey were in attendance among the crowd of five hundred architects, academics, politicians and media; and they were as surprised as anyone when they learned they had won. They were thirty-nine and thirty-eight.

ARTHUR ERICKSON

Arthur Erickson was then an associate professor teaching design at UBC. He had known Geoffrey Massey, the son of the actor Raymond Massey and nephew of former Governor General Vincent Massey, since the early 1950s. The two had shared a house and had collaborated on the design of residences for common friends, the painter and professor of art at UBC Gordon Smith, and Massey's future wife, artist Ruth Killam. For SFU's competition, Erickson and Massey worked out of Massey's downtown office and took on two of Erickson's former students.[14] Erickson and Massey have both said that the ideas and concepts were Erickson's and that Massey's contribution was in organization, administration and detailed design.

Erickson was the partner who was to attract national and international acclaim such as no Canadian architect had ever before enjoyed. His body of work grew impressively in the next ten years, with major commissions for Expo 67 in Montreal, the MacMillan Bloedel building in Vancouver, the Canadian Pavilion at Expo 70 in Osaka, Japan, the University of Lethbridge, the Museum of Anthropology at UBC, the Bank of Canada Extension in Ottawa, and the courthouse and Vancouver Art Gallery complex in Vancouver. A 1979 article in *The New Yorker* quoted the eminent American architect Philip Johnson as saying that Erickson was the greatest architect in Canada and perhaps the greatest on the continent.[15] SFU was the design that first put the spotlight on him.

Erickson approached the design of SFU with a genuine interest in the history, mission and functioning of universities, arising from his experience as a student at UBC and McGill, his teaching at Oregon and UBC, his reading of history and his extensive travels. Before UBC he had taught in an experimental program at the University of Oregon that emphasized interdisciplinary education and the Socratic method—drawing knowledge from students rather than instructing them. This was much better, in his mind, than the kind of factory process he remembered as an undergraduate.

He was by nature comfortable with classical references and contemporary thought. In Architecture at McGill between 1946 and 1949, he had received a strong dose of the modernists—Gropius and the Bauhaus school, Le Corbusier, Mies van der Rohe—the proponents of an international architectural style that developed in the 1920s and 1930s and flowered after the Second World War. He was also attracted to Frank Lloyd Wright, whom his teachers at McGill tended to disparage, but whom he admired for his blending of landscape and architecture. In his education at McGill he absorbed modernist concerns with simplicity, function, structure and beauty, social responsibility, industrial construction and prefabrication, the exploration of new technologies and new applications for materials, particularly concrete and glass. The modernists at McGill had no interest in architectural history, which they thought stood in the way of new solutions to contemporary problems. If his McGill training left a gap, he more than made up for it in his travels.

At the age of twenty, Erickson found himself in India. As an undergraduate in wartime, he had been recruited into an intensive Japanese language course conducted in Vancouver by the Canadian army for the British. In 1944 the army sent him to India as an intelligence officer in a unit of ten Canadians attached to British military intelligence and expected to interrogate Japanese prisoners of war. He had postings in Delhi, Calcutta and Bombay. After the Japanese surrender in 1945, his army service continued in Malaya as program director for radio Kuala Lumpur. He returned to Canada in 1946 and, after three years' study in Montreal, received a one-year travelling scholarship from the McGill School of Architecture, which he managed to extend to a full three years abroad. He travelled though Egypt, Lebanon, Greece, Italy, France, Spain, England and Scandinavia, with his longest stops in Florence and London, always with an architect's eye for historical detail. For the next eight years he was on the west coast of North America, in Oregon and British Columbia, but by 1961 he had accumulated enough teaching credit at UBC for a sabbatical year, which he spent in Japan, Cambodia and Indonesia.

The Asian experience was fresh in his mind in 1963 when he entered the SFU competition. He was too much of a modernist, however, to consciously borrow styles. As he explained in an interview in 2001, he had studied the history of universities and he had seen where they had begun: Al-Azhar University in Cairo, Bologna, the University of Paris, Oxford and Cambridge. He was aware of the great prototypes and how their architecture reflected attitudes, teaching methods "and everything else." Moreover, he had views about North American universities and how they might develop in the future. He says that at one point he asked Massey if they wanted to win or to show what they believed in, and that they elected the latter.[16] If this was the case, he was fortunate to have a partner who was willing to go along with him.

THE ERICKSON DESIGN

Shrum had prepared a sketchy statement of conditions for the SFU architectural competition, but it was enough to stimulate Erickson's creative juices. About teaching, Gordon Shrum had one conviction that would influence the design: he thought teaching was best done with a combination of large lecture halls and small classes.[17] Aside from this, Shrum had had no teaching program, policy or philosophy to show to the architects who submitted plans and drawings for the SFU competition. He began with a mountaintop, rather than a nucleus of faculty and staff, or an advisory group, or a governing body, and he found himself encouraging architects to provide a vision. He saw no problem with that approach.[18]

Most of the contestants did not take up the challenge, but two did, Erickson and Massey and one other entry; and the judges placed them first and second. The merits of these two entries went beyond their ideas on teaching, but the educational rationales they developed along with their designs gave their submissions coherence and purpose that the others lacked.

The second-place entry belonged to William R. Rhone and W. Randle Iredale. They sought to combine the intimacy of a small college with the advantages of a large campus. They had Oxford and Cambridge in mind as well as what they knew of the recent development of small campuses in California (Rhone had attended the University of California at Berkeley). In their design for SFU they included nine autonomous colleges, each providing the basic subjects along with specializations such as performing arts or physics. Students would register in a home college and take most of their courses there, but could cross the campus for specializations offered elsewhere. Rhone and Ireland arranged the colleges around the perimeter of the site, giving each cluster of college buildings its own distinctive outward view of the mountains or valley, and leaving the highest ground at the centre as green or wooded campus.

Erickson had a more radical concept, a rethinking of the university as it had evolved in North America. In the statement that accompanied their sketches, he and Massey portrayed contrasting models: Oxford and Cambridge, possessing a cohesive philosophy of education, and American universities, where administration and curriculum had become departmentalized. At North American universities, departmentalization determined the layout, with independent buildings for separate disciplines or disciplinary groupings. Erickson and Massey proposed a more efficient layout to encourage interdisciplinary co-operation and to break down departmental barriers. They organized space functionally rather than by academic department.

Organization by function led them to put faculty offices and seminar rooms in one building (the Academic Quadrangle) and lecture theatres and labs on the adjacent, terraced slopes. Service, recreational and library spaces were grouped along a mall; residences went to one end of the campus and the president's residence, faculty club, faculty housing and administration to the other. This concept was largely, although not completely, realized in the final structure.

In their report, the jurors acknowledged the revisionist implications of the Erickson–Massey design. But they had more to say about Erickson and Massey's use of the site, the flexibility of the design and potential to support a variety of educational directions. They were also impressed by the provision that it made for growth. In an article in *Canadian Architect* in 1968, Erickson described the usual solution to growth at American universities as scattering buildings around the campus and then filling in between. That is what had happened at UBC. What he proposed, along with Massey, was to start at the centre and allow growth to proceed outwards. This development plan meant designing a compact structure.

All of the contestants were working with 600 acres (240 hectares) at the top of the mountain; beyond this area, the slopes were too precipitous to support buildings. Arthur Erickson and Geoffrey Massey and the other contestants had hiked up to the summit on a spring day to look it over before developing their ideas. They found a rough clearing at the top that helped them understand the rise and fall of the two-kilometre-long ridge that defined the summit. One can appreciate the originality and attractiveness of their solution by looking again at what their competitors proposed.

Rhone and Iredale would have built around the skirts of the ridge. One of Shrum's requirements was that the design should provide for expansion, but that the campus should look finished from the start. (Shrum had lived too long through the Depression and war years with the unfinished plan for UBC.) Rhone and Iredale answered this with their college concept: the university would open with three complete colleges, and one college would be added for each additional two thousand students. The disadvantage was that the development of colleges involved duplication of facilities.

When they stood in the clearing at the top of the mountain, Erickson and Massey could see the saddle shape of the ridge: highest in the east and lowest in the middle. Three of the other prize winners paid attention to that conformation, but none of them in the way that Erickson and Massey chose.

Zoltan Kiss, the Hungarian-born third-prize winner, saw the dip in the ridge as the natural focal point for the campus, and he projected expansion from there in both directions along the ridge. Robert Harrison, the fourth-prize winner, would also have placed the core facilities at the low point on the ridge and provided for expansion on lines radiating out. Duncan McNab and Associates, the fifth-prize winners, reversed the concept, starting with the two peaks and designing two rings of buildings that overlapped at the low point. This design emphasized the contours of the mountain; however, it would have taken years to complete the rings and the point of the design would not be seen right away.

The genius of the winning Erickson–Massey design was their placement of the university along the ridge and their provision for expansion down the slopes. In this way they perfectly met Shrum's expectation that the university should look finished from the day it opened and that further expansion, from two thousand to seven thousand to eighteen thousand students, should not detract from the original architectural conception. Their design was linear: an arrangement along the ridge of administrative, teaching, service/recreation (library, bookstore, theatre, student centre and gym) and residential buildings. For the core or spine of the campus, Erickson and Massey claimed the ridge, which offered vistas to the north and south, and they took advantage of the east–west axis to put their structures in line with a Vancouver landmark, the First Narrows (Lions Gate) Bridge, visible in the distance at the entrance to Burrard Inlet.

The way in which Erickson and Massey dealt with the saddleback nature of the ridge was key to their design. They saw the dip in the ridge as the hub of the campus, the transportation centre where students debussed and stores were received. This is where they placed a pedestrian mall intended to be the length of two football fields and six metres above grade, bridging the low part of the saddle. This hub remains the central architectural feature of the university today, although the open mall area is half the length specified in the prize-winning design. Underneath the mall is the parkade, which serves to keep some of the parking out of sight. Alongside are the library, theatre and gym, which are original structures, to which the student centre and multi-purpose Maggie Benston Centre have been added. The main road to the campus passes under the mall and that is where a majority of those who arrive by bus still dismount, although a second terminus now exists at the east end of the campus. Students living in residence still walk the length of the mall to reach their classes. In the area between the library and the theatre, the covered section of the mall remains the most dramatic and dynamic open-air space on campus, as the architects planned.

Erickson intended the sequence for the pedestrian walking through the mall and the Academic Quadrangle to be uplifting: moving from an area of activity to one of quiet, and offering the possibilities of walking meditations, as in Buddhist temples or Christian cloisters, or perambulating philosophical discussion, as in the marketplaces of the Greeks or the quadrangle of an Oxford college.[19] In an essay in 1988, Erickson explained the design as a succession of open-air spaces.[20] First, occupying the highest ground, is the three-acre (1.2-hectare) volume enclosed by the Academic Quadrangle. This is a space intended to induce quiet and contemplation through its symmetry and scale. (How many students or faculty, hurrying from car to class, have ever understood this is a good question.)

Erickson has described the Plaza Major, in the historic Spanish city Salamanca, as an influence for the Academic Quadrangle. When, in his travels, he first entered this eighteenth-century arcaded public square (designed for occasional use as a bullring), Erickson said he experienced the shock of its perfect squareness and he attributed the awe that he felt to its visual stillness: nothing directed the eye; there was no hierarchy of attention. In an article in the *Architectural Review* in 1968, Erickson's friend and neighbour, Abraham Rogatnick, observed that Plaza Major was, in fact, not a perfect square or without focal points.[21] That is a caution not to take the reference too literally, but to understand it as a remembered experience that Erickson sought to recapture at SFU with a quadrangle whose features were sufficiently repetitive to serve as a quiet frame for the sky, the garden and the distant view through the pillars supporting the elevated top two floors.

The second major space, Erickson explained, was the mall, especially the covered portion outside the library. In a comment written when SFU was newly opened, Lionel Tiger (then an assistant professor at UBC) described the mall as the triumph of the entire design, the place where the university came together. In a series of lectures given at Harvard in 1962, Clark Kerr, president of the University of California, had coined the phrase "multiversity" to describe what the modern American university had become: complex, balkanized and multi-purpose, with little common interest to integrate all those who came under its umbrella. For Tiger, the SFU mall expressed the unity of the university, the place where people mingled on their way from residences, parking or buses to offices, classrooms and labs, or where they gathered before entering the library or theatre.

Others spoke in Erickson's terms of the mall as the intellectual agora or marketplace.[22] Donlyn Lyndon, then chair of the University of Oregon's innovative Department of Architecture, on first viewing SFU saw the covered mall as the centrepiece: "a great space-framed outdoor room" that—with its three-storey-high glass roof and sense of enclosure, the library on one side and theatre on the other, and its vistas of nature and building—possessed "a visual surround of great intensity."[23] In an interview more than a decade later, Philip Johnson, who had been at the forefront of the evolving international architectural style since the early 1930s, described the "vastness of the covered mall" at SFU as "the best central device for a campus that I know of anyplace."[24] It worked for Ada Louise Huxtable, architectural critic for *The New York Times*, who pictured a noontime concert in the SFU mall as "an exercise in togetherness."[25]

The third and fourth open-air spaces of which Erickson was conscious were the recreational areas around the gym (now represented principally by the playing field and track) and the domestic space around the residences (which has not developed as originally planned). There was a fifth and larger space in the Erickson–Massey conception: the surrounding mountaintop that provided the setting for the built structure.

Erickson has said that he was more landscape designer than architect.[26] In *The Architecture of Arthur Erickson,* he speaks about "the dialogue between a building and its setting," and the low profile and strong horizontal lines of the buildings at SFU were his response to the mountaintop site. The transition from the wooded slopes to the structure at the top was an important aspect of Erickson's vision. His fellow Vancouver architect, Ron Thom, understood this when he described the approach by road, emerging from a cleft in the trees to see the edges of the playing field and then sweeping around to catch a first glimpse of the buildings "appearing as a delicate crown inseparable from the top of the mountain."[27] When Thom wrote this in 1966, a large clearing remained. Here Erickson and Massey wished to develop a mountain meadow with natural grasses and trees; and it is a disappointment to Erickson that alder trees have been allowed to grow back, taking away from a sense of the mountaintop.[28]

The Erickson–Massey design can be seen as a single structure, although it comprises many buildings. The competition called for a design for a complete university with library, administration, classroom and chemistry buildings, office space, physics and biological sciences laboratories, an auditorium/theatre, a gymnasium, a bookstore, a cafeteria, three student dormitories, faculty housing, a house for the president, a student union building, a faculty club and research institutes. In addition, the conditions specified wind-sheltered architectural spaces between buildings, covered walkways, landscaping and outdoor sculpture. By providing nearly all of these elements in one megastructure, Erickson and Massey broke with long-established conventions for the appearance of a college or university campus. In the designs of their rivals, buildings were interspersed with grassy areas, groves of trees and gardens, as at UBC, Edmonton, Toronto or almost every other campus in the country. Many designs combined high-rises with slab structures arranged around a patchwork of open areas. All provided covered walkways to link buildings, but the Erickson–Massey design integrated this feature with the greatest ease.

Lionel Tiger applauded SFU's monumental structure on Burnaby Mountain as neither urban nor rural, but a bold new university environment. The architect Richard Archambault, in submitting plans for a faculty club a few years later, characterized the Erickson–Massey master plan as an urban campus in a rural setting. He meant that it belonged downtown, where a self-contained environment of hard surfaces and formal spaces would make more sense. For Erickson, it was undoubtedly an urban complex—intended eventually to accommodate eighteen thousand students—but an urban complex with a relationship to a magnificent natural setting.

Erickson has spoken of several spectacular hilltop cities as references for SFU: particularly the partially excavated (when he saw it) twenty-eight-century-old Zapotec centre of Monte Albán near Oaxaca in southern Mexico, the ruins of the acropolis of the Greek city of Pergamum in Turkey and the abandoned Mughal city of Fatehpur Sikri near Agra in India. What these places have in common is their command of a height of land, their plazas with distant prospects, as well as an organic fit of structure and site. Erickson has also mentioned at various times the terraced hills of Java, the Acropolis at Athens, the hill towns of Italy, the Inca ruins at Machu Picchu, Peru, and the Chinese imperial Temple of Heaven in Beijing, as well as Plaza Major in Salamanca. Others have suggested—without Erickson's endorsement—that SFU has echoes of the ancient Egyptian complex of Deir el-Behari, or the Roman Forum and the Baths of Caracalla in Rome. None of this should be taken too specifically. As Erickson observed decades later, he was not conscious of influences at the time and only realized later "as people started to visit, and came from all over the place" what all the sources of his inspiration were.[29]

The materials of Monte Albán, Pergamum and Fatehpur Sikri were limestone and basalt, limestone and marble, and red sandstone. Concrete was the material of choice for Erickson and Massey, a structural and finishing material that, when sandblasted, chipped or bush hammered, produced a surface that for Erickson was "as noble as limestone."[30] Erickson had the modernist preference for unpainted stone and concrete and shared a popular appreciation of ancient Greek or Meso-American structures in their weathered state, long stripped of the brilliant colours that had originally decorated them. "As in all serious architecture," Erickson wrote about SFU in 1966, "the structural material is consistent, pervasive and unadorned." He reserved colour for the interior and exposed the concrete of the exterior so that there would be no distraction from the form, proportion and scale that gave the buildings their beauty.

Those who have lived with the concrete and the form and proportion it expresses have had varying reactions, frequently depending on the day and the weather. As the History Department's Tudor and Stuart specialist, Charles Hamilton, put it a few years after he arrived at SFU, on a sunny summer day the university was breathtaking, but on a foggy winter day the unpainted concrete in addition to the isolation could make it feel like a prison. Concrete, however, was such a popular architectural material in the 1960s that there was little chance that sFU would be built or finished with anything else. It was, above all, economical to maintain. Developments in precast and prestressed concrete over the previous twenty-five years had dramatically expanded the possibilities of the material, making it attractive to adventurous architects. All five of the prize-winning entries in the sFU architectural competition specified concrete construction; and in the 1960s, concrete buildings were rising on campuses around the world, from Imperial College, London, to Jawaharlal Nehru University in Delhi.

In their use of concrete, in their organization of the university by function, in their low and compact structure, and in their placement of the spine of the university along the ridge, Erickson and Massey had a design that was not only magnificent and evocative, but also efficient and economical to build. Warnett Kennedy, speaking of the day on which the design was chosen, said that the entire jury realized that it was the one that could be adopted and built without delay.[31] Shrum, who did not have a vote on the jury panel—but did have the ultimate say on what got built—had not picked this design. He conceded later that he did not have an architect's eye to see the potential of the drawings. But when one of the judges took him aside to explain the merits of the design, with its strong axis along the summit and potential for expansion, he had quickly accepted what he was told.[32]

DIVIDING THE WORK

Shrum had warned contestants that he might not use the design that won. He wanted the advice of the jury, but did not want to be hamstrung by their choice. If he did not like the winning design, he would employ the winning architects to develop another design that he liked better. As it happened, the competition produced a design that was practical, aesthetically exciting, and that could be built quickly; and once he saw that, he had no hesitation in moving forward with it. He was also committed to employing the five prize-winning firms.

Shrum pushed the architects to finish their work in a fraction of the time they would normally have taken. When he met the five prize winners in his B.C. Hydro office on the morning after the awards ceremony, he told them he would replace any of them right away if they had hesitations. Nobody withdrew. Erickson and Massey would oversee the project, but Shrum left it to the five firms to decide together how they would share the work. This proved to be difficult and it took two months to sort it out. In the meantime, Erickson and Massey pressed on with a sixty-six-page development plan and drawings, revising and detailing their competition drawings. In this two-month period they did enough to establish their overall conception of the buildings, inside and out.

The problem in deciding how to share the work began with a difference between Erickson and Massey and the others. The others thought that all five should pool the work and commissions. Erickson and Massey insisted on splitting it up while they kept responsibility for the overall design. Shrum supported Erickson and Massey, because Erickson and Massey had the winning design and because dividing the work up among architectural firms, each with its own contractor, would create a competitive situation that would give the university leverage in pushing them to meet targets.

Erickson and Massey wanted four months to complete all of the preliminary design work, including elevations and sections for all the buildings. They were halfway done when Shrum refused to give them more time and told them to involve the other firms immediately. In late September the five firms agreed on a division of work and signed contracts. As a consequence, the Erickson–Massey conception was largely realized, but the other firms were brought in soon enough to initiate some departures.

For the first stage of construction, Erickson and Massey had proposed building part of the student residences, the central section of the gym, the main section of the library, part of the theatre/auditorium complex, the classroom complex, the science centre and the administration building. In their plan, the Academic Quadrangle would wait for stage two. Shrum, in September 1963, decided on another order of priority. There would be no student residences in phase one, no administration building and no classroom complex. Instead he would go ahead with the Academic Quadrangle and the mall—the centrepieces of the Erickson–Massey design—and he would build major sections of the gym, the library and the science centre. He insisted that the heart of the university should be built first, so that it looked finished when it opened, and he put the gym and theatre ahead of classrooms and residences because it would be easier to raise money for the latter later on. The administration offices, he decided, could go into the library in the beginning, when that building would have excess capacity.

The initial budget for six buildings, to be completed for the opening of the university, was $9.56 million. Engineering, site development and miscellaneous costs took the total to $15.06 million. The architects' commission was a standard 6 per cent of the cost of construction less a quarter of a per cent to Erickson and Massey as the coordinating firm. (Erickson and Massey also received $11,690 for their preliminary work.) The five firms divided the project according to their placement in the competition. Erickson and Massey, with the first pick, considered the Academic Quadrangle, but took the mall because it was the central building that integrated all of the others and that they believed really defined SFU. Rhone and Iredale, with second pick, had their eyes on the Academic Quadrangle, but were persuaded by Zoltan Kiss that the science centre would be better because it would expand in subsequent phases of construction, while the quadrangle, once built, was finished.

Zoltan Kiss took the Academic Quadrangle, which he had wanted all along. With a choice of theatre and gym or library, Robert Harrison chose the library. Duncan McNab and Associates were left with the theatre and gym/pool complex, a result that pleased McNab, who had been a diver on the McGill swim team. In dollar terms the science centre was the largest project, followed by the Academic Quadrangle, the mall and the library. With the gym and theatre, McNab and Associates had about an eighth of the work.[33]

With five firms involved, but all working from the same master plan, the question of credit requires some sorting out. How much belongs to Erickson and Massey? In the 1990s, an architectural historian from South Carolina, Gene Waddell, made an admirably thorough study of the design and construction of SFU. His interest developed during three years spent as head of collections in the library of the Canadian Centre for Architecture in Montreal. In 1997 Waddell interviewed a number of SFU's original architects, including Iredale, Kiss, Harrison, McNab, Erickson and Massey.[34] One of his questions was whether Erickson and Massey provided the others with preliminary drawings. Erickson and Massey said that they had completed detailed plans and elevations for every building. The memories of the others were not so clear. Waddell's conclusion, after looking at all the drawings and other evidence, was that Erickson and Massey were right. They remembered the work they had done. The others did not.

The strongest differences that surfaced after the other four firms began working involved Zoltan Kiss and the Academic Quadrangle. He wanted to vary the windows on the principle that a building should reflect its usage: office windows should not look like classroom windows. Such a change would have destroyed the regularity that was so important to Erickson in re-creating the impact of Plaza Major. Shrum took Erickson's side. The other major issue was the colour of the concrete fins hanging between the windows. These fins are a feature of most of the buildings in the sfu complex. They appear to be a Le Corbusier influence: they give the Academic Quadrangle a strong resemblance to Le Corbusier's Monastery of La Tourette, in Eveux, France, completed only a few years earlier. Kiss wanted the fins of the Academic Quadrangle to be white. Erickson objected to this departure from the monochromatic exterior he had envisaged. This time Shrum agreed with Kiss, and the fins are white.

Otherwise one has to move inside to see the design choices of the other firms. Erickson would have kept the interiors of the buildings muted and monastic. The student centre, which his firm did as part of the mall complex, had interior walls of finished concrete. The other firms were responsible for the introduction of a greater variety in materials and colour. Zoltan Kiss, for example, warmed up the rooms and third-floor corridors of the Academic Quadrangle with extensive use of wood panelling.

CONSTRUCTION

The architects signed their contracts on September 27, 1963. Shrum wanted to tender for construction in three months' time, an impossible target that the five firms, working overtime seven days a week, could not meet. In fact, Shrum had to wait five months before advertising for tenders. Even that was a great achievement. Over this period, the approval process for the designs grew progressively more complicated. Shrum ceased to be a committee of one and acquired a board and president, an academic planner, a librarian and the first of his department heads. He remained a singular force, but was obliged to involve a growing number of people in decisions. In the overall Erickson design, however, he had an architectural statement that promised to put SFU on the map.

One cannot leave the architecture of SFU without mentioning leakage, a problem for which Erickson buildings are famous. SFU was a two-hundred-bucket university: that was the number of leaks, large and small, that needed attention during an overhaul in 1969. The worst were in the mall area and the library. The explanation given at the time by SFU's director of physical plant, Bill DeVries, was hasty construction, not bad design.[35] Earlier that same year, Danger signs were up and the mall area was roped off after the glass panels in the roof began breaking under the weight of a freakishly heavy snowfall. Again, haste was the culprit along with cost shaving. During construction, the board under Shrum's leadership had been slow to make a decision on the roof, and then had tried to save money by employing an experimental engineering solution. If there had been any saving, it was lost after the 1968–69 snowfall in the cost of doubling the vertical strips (mullions) supporting the glass panes. To Erickson's regret, that repair slightly darkened the mall. He was conscious of the difference, but thousands who have since walked through probably have not thought about it.[36]

A METEOROLOGIST AS PRESIDENT

Shrum wasted no time in seeking a president. He aimed high and he consulted leading academic administrators in eastern Canada. In Ottawa, during a trip east shortly after becoming chancellor, Shrum pulled a sheet of Château Laurier letterhead from a desk drawer and jotted down eleven names, two of which he pursued. Patrick McTaggart-Cowan, SFU's first president, was not on that list.[37]

Shrum first approached Gordon Robertson, a native of Saskatchewan who had enjoyed a meteoric rise within the federal civil service. Shrum spoke to him in May 1963, when Robertson was about to get the most influential position a Canadian civil servant could achieve, clerk of the privy council and cabinet secretary. Still, he thanked Shrum and said he would give SFU serious consideration. By the end of the month he had written Shrum to decline.

Shrum's second choice was a graduate of UBC, Robert T. McKenzie, who had been on the staff of the London School of Economics since

1949 and who had acquired celebrity in Britain as a radio and TV broadcaster. McKenzie briefly entertained the idea of returning to Vancouver, but by June 6 had decided that he could not give up London or his teaching, writing and broadcast journalism.

Shrum next turned to Howard Petch, a solid state physicist who in 1952 had been one of UBC's earliest PhDs. Petch was still in his thirties, and already had been chair of metallurgical engineering and then director of research at McMaster University. Shrum brought Petch out to Vancouver and introduced him to the premier. But on August 14, Shrum had Petch's letter declining the job. (Petch later served as president pro-tem at Waterloo and after that was president of Victoria for fifteen years.[38])

In his first three approaches Shrum had looked inside academia twice and outside once. His next step was to go outside again, to call on another former student. This was Patrick McTaggart-Cowan, who by 1963 was the director of Canada's meteorological service. Shrum and McTaggart-Cowan had a long and familiar relationship. Their partnership at SFU was a vital part of the SFU story; and to understand it, one needs to know more about McTaggart-Cowan and his previous experience.

McTaggart-Cowan had spent thirty-six years in the meteorological service. He had grown with it as it expanded to support the development of commercial aviation in the post-war era. At SFU he was dismissed by many as an Ottawa bureaucrat, overlooking the fact that the meteorology service was based in Toronto. And the characterization did not do justice to McTaggart-Cowan's career or his past responsibilities. By 1963 he was in charge of a service with professional, technical, administrative and clerical staff numbering well over a thousand and spread across the country and into the high Arctic. This was a research and training service as well as a long-range and spot-weather forecaster; and it had continually accumulated responsibilities, becoming the locus for research on climatology, atmospheric pollution and oceanography. Meteorology itself was an advancing science: the flow of air masses, for example, came to be much better understood in the new aviation age in which McTaggart-Cowan worked.

In 1943 McTaggart-Cowan had received an MBE (Member of the Order of the British Empire) for his wartime service. As a twenty-five-year-old, fresh out of Oxford and with only a few months' meteorological training at Croydon in London, he had been posted to the remote station of Botwood in Newfoundland. He went there for joint British, Canadian and American experimental flights designed to test the viability of regular transatlantic passenger services. The program died after two summers when war broke out in 1939, but was quickly resurrected as a Royal Air Force operation out of Gander, Newfoundland.

To save space on the transport ships being convoyed from Canadian to British ports, the British war ministry decided that the Hudson, Liberator and Ventura bombers that they were getting from the Americans should fly the Atlantic under their own power. This RAF operation was known as Ferry Command. Gander was the main base for departure and the young meteorologist McTaggart-Cowan was in a critically important position. The RAF were pushing the capability of the aircraft and the science of meteorology to the limit. McTaggart-Cowan had to be able to predict not only safe takeoffs but safe landings on the other side of the ocean; and he had sole authority to say when pilots could fly. It was then that he acquired the affectionate nickname McFog. Impetuous air force pilots, impatient with direction from a civilian, learned to accept the fact that when McFog said you couldn't fly, you could not fly. The same nickname, when it followed him to SFU, assumed an entirely different connotation.

Although the meteorological service had installations across the country, most of its work was done in Toronto. The main headquarters were on Bloor Street, just off the University of Toronto campus, although the whole Toronto operation had become geographically dispersed, and it used to be a full-day enterprise for McTaggart-Cowan to drive across the city to visit the ten different locations where he had staff employed.

At the time he accepted the SFU presidency, McTaggart-Cowan was negotiating for a new building on the Toronto campus next to Aeronautical Studies and the University of Toronto Press. He felt himself a part of the university community. For years, the University of Toronto and the meteorological service had jointly offered courses in meteorology, taught by members of the service for recruits entering it. As director, McTaggart-Cowan had secured the introduction of graduate work in meteorology at the PhD level at Toronto, to train his staff and to increase the university's research competence in meteorology. He felt that he had known his way around a university long before he came to SFU, something that his detractors at SFU would not acknowledge.

When Shrum invited him to be president of SFU, the call came out of the blue. He had no expectation of a university position, but he was intrigued and flew to Vancouver to talk it over. He had known Shrum since his first undergraduate year at UBC, when Shrum was a junior member of the Physics Department. Shrum had been a most helpful mentor. When McTaggart-Cowan graduated in 1933 with first-class honours in math and physics and a reputation as a badminton player and oarsman, Shrum had encouraged him to apply for a Rhodes scholarship. When he didn't win it the first time around, Shrum found him a scholarship and an instructorship at UBC so he could enter the graduate program there. The following year McTaggart-Cowan won the Rhodes and left for Oxford.

In 1936, having earned an Oxford BA in addition to his BA from UBC, McTaggart-Cowan wrote Shrum for assistance in finding a job. Shrum produced two possibilities: a position with the Dominion Astrophysical Observatory in Victoria and one with the Meteorological Services of Canada. McTaggart-Cowan chose the latter and left Oxford for his course at Croydon. In 1961, when McTaggart-Cowan received an honorary doctorate from UBC, Shrum had a chance to see his protege at the height of his career accepting recognition from the university where he started. Two years later, after being turned down three times in his search for a president, Shrum decided that he had just the man he needed in his old student.

SHRUM, MCTAGGART-COWAN AND THE BOARD OF GOVERNORS

Shrum and McTaggart-Cowan regarded each other as friends; "good friends," said Shrum when interviewed years later. But given Shrum's personality and their mentor–protege relationship, they inevitably set themselves on a course that would turn bitter. McTaggart-Cowan took little time to decide that he wanted the job and Shrum sent him off to see the premier. In setting up this meeting and suggesting that the premier's approval was necessary for the appointment, Shrum showed no concern for the principle that university appointments should be free from government interference. In the first week of September, McTaggart-Cowan flew straight from Toronto to Victoria and returned home without publicity. At his secret meeting with the premier and the minister of education, Leslie Peterson, they asked whether he could work with Shrum. McTaggart-Cowan reported this question to Shrum himself, saying, with boyish enthusiasm, that he knew he had passed this one "with flying colours."

Eighteen years after he left SFU, and a year after Gordon Shrum passed away, McTaggart-Cowan gave an interview to Robin Fisher, who was then a member of SFU's History Department.[33] The interview took place in the farmhouse on the 80-hectare wooded lot on the Muskoka River, in cottage country north of Toronto, where McTaggart-Cowan enjoyed his retirement. McTaggart-Cowan told Fisher that out of respect for Shrum he had kept his silence since leaving SFU. Now that Shrum was dead, he felt free to speak. He attributed the lion's share of his grief as president to Shrum's heavy hand as chancellor. McTaggart-Cowan said that he had known from the beginning that Shrum would never be able to take a back seat; he raised the issue with him before agreeing to be president; and he thought he had Shrum's promise to step down as chancellor at the end of his first three-year term, which would be soon after the university opened. When Shrum elected to stay on for a second term, McTaggart-Cowan said nothing, but in retrospect he regretted never getting their agreement in writing.

In the tape of the Fisher interview, one can hear McTaggart-Cowan unconsciously mirroring the descent of his relationship with Shrum. Early in the interview, discussing their friendship and the beginnings of their collaboration at SFU, McTaggart-Cowan spoke familiarly of "Gordon." Later, describing the last year of his presidency, he referred formally to "Gordon Shrum" and at some points, icily, to "Shrum."

McTaggart-Cowan's dismissal by the SFU board in May 1968—with Shrum's concurrence—brought a painful end to a job that he had assumed with enthusiasm and energy. Ron Baker, SFU's academic planner, who started on the day that McTaggart-Cowan formally became president, was a McTaggart-Cowan loyalist right up to the end. In 1970, Baker found time to dictate more than forty pages of random recollections about early SFU. From a distance of a few years he remained impressed by McTaggart-Cowan's extraordinary capacity for work, his ability to learn, his willingness to take advice and criticism, his remarkable equanimity and his exceptional effectiveness in representing SFU to the public. (By his own count, McTaggart-Cowan gave 420 public addresses in 365 days leading up to the opening of the university.[40]) Baker did have reservations, partly because he saw McTaggart-Cowan as a bit of a Boy Scout: earnest, keen and willing, and comfortable voicing the platitudes his audiences expected. But this judgement Baker tempered with the possibility that behind the appearance of a Boy Scout was a highly sophisticated man who knew what he was doing.[41]

One of McTaggart-Cowan's great handicaps was his relationship with the SFU board of governors. He had an inauspicious start at the first meeting and never commanded their full respect. As Duff and Berdahl, the authors of the 1966 report on university government, observed, Canadian university presidents of that era were hugely important figures because they were the sole link between the board and the university community. Almost inevitably they exerted great influence through their power to set the board's agenda and to generate the information it got. This was an influence that McTaggart-Cowan never fully achieved. Baker was struck by the fact that at board meetings McTaggart would not sit up at the table, but placed his chair slightly back and, like a secretary, passed material forward to Shrum.[42] He assumed the role of a civil servant, a deputy minister unobtrusively supporting the political chief of his department, and his opinion never carried the weight with the board that it should have.

The pattern was set from the beginning. In early September 1963, when McTaggart-Cowan had his secret meeting with the premier and the minister, SFU had no board. As far as McTaggart-Cowan could see, that was a problem: he had read the Universities Act and it gave the power of appointment to the board, not the chancellor. When he raised this as a question, neither the premier nor the minister expressed concern; they thought Shrum could make the appointment and get it ratified later on. On reflection after the meeting, they decided that the time had come to appoint a board. What was uppermost in their minds when they saw McTaggart-Cowan was an imminent provincial election. They told him they did not want his appointment made until afterwards. If the opposition won, Bennett explained, the new premier should have his say.[43] Bennett took it for granted that as premier, he should be consulted.

Bennett's election victory on September 30 cleared the way for the immediate creation of a board. The government announced the board membership on October 3 and Shrum called the first meeting a week later. According to Shrum, he had suggested most of the board members to the premier: they included the mayor of New Westminster (the only woman), the president of the B.C. School Trustees Association, who was also a lawyer, a retired superintendent of schools, a banker, another lawyer and several business executives and independent businessmen. Five of the nine members had attended university and four had not. None, as Richard Lester, the young Haney lawyer and school trustees president, later conceded, had any experience developing, running or even working in a university.[44] As with board members at established universities, they had been chosen for their broad experience and business and community connections. The difference in their case was that they were all starting with a new university and a commanding Gordon Shrum in the chair.

Their first meeting in the offices of B.C. Hydro took a scheduled two and a half hours. Shrum had a packed agenda of eighteen items, large and small. At the top of his list was the appointment of a president; and regarding it as automatic, he had scheduled a press conference to follow. McTaggart-Cowan had flown in from Toronto and was sitting in the waiting room. Shrum outlined his qualifications and, after a brief discussion, got the board to approve the appointment. "I don't think we really expected him to be there," Lester recalled. "Then he came in and we all met him and we had a president."[45] It was Shrum's own recollection that the flight-weary McTaggart-Cowan, who had only started to think about being a president a few weeks earlier, did not make a good impression. The novice board took the only candidate Shrum offered; but because they had had no involvement in the search, they never felt ownership of the decision.[46]

McTaggart-Cowan came to SFU without a formal contract, just the resolution passed by the board, appointing him effective January 1, 1964, and specifying his salary and benefits (a house, a car and out-of-pocket moving expenses). By the time he left SFU, he had begun to regard this as an anomaly, although he conceded that when he took up the position, formal contracts were not customary for university presidents. When the board sent its delegates to him in the summer of 1968, insisting on a written resignation, his first response was that he had nothing in writing about his appointment and did not see why he should give anything in writing now.[47]

McTaggart-Cowan understood that he served at the pleasure of the board until retirement; and he readily accepted the reality that when he no longer had the board's pleasure, his appointment was over. But he had noticed that university presidents were beginning to get written contracts and that this was becoming the norm. If he had been given a choice, he might not have considered this a better arrangement. Contracts for university presidents had come to mean fixed terms, typically five years, rather than life appointments or appointments to retirement. When McTaggart-Cowan started at SFU he believed he would be guiding the university until he was sixty-five, which would be for a dozen years beyond opening day.

The immediate challenges for McTaggart-Cowan, when he began his presidency, were the recruitment of staff (beginning with an academic planner, a registrar and a librarian), the supervision of construction and the development of an academic program. He had asked for three months to hand over his responsibilities with Meteorological Services, but visited Vancouver for the November and December meetings of the board. In this interval he was developing his ideas of the shape the university should take, while under Shrum's unmistakable tutelage. He put it differently: he said that Shrum's vision happened to accord with his own on nearly every point.[48]

At the same time, the board were commencing their own sharp learning curve. In November, at their second meeting, the board struck three committees: buildings & site, finance, and staff & organization. In the absence of faculty or staff to take on tasks, board members became concerned with the smallest of details and found themselves volunteering far more time than they had expected. They were also caught up in the excitement. As Lester recalled, no board member in those early days ever indicated anything but "complete willingness and enthusiasm" to do what had to be done.[49] This level of involvement proved to be a difficult thing to turn off later on.

Shrum had selected a president with a great many admirable qualities and with broad experience, even if it was all within one government service. Much of McTaggart-Cowan's work within the service had an international dimension, coordinating operations particularly with the Americans and with NATO countries. He had also received recognition for his contribution to the science of meteorology; and in a number of

ways, as a member of the Rhodes scholarship committee, as a participant in scientific conferences, as a recruiter of university graduates for
the service; and through the program in meteorology offered at
Toronto, he brushed shoulders with members of the university academy.
But when he started at SFU he knew less about universities than he realized, or than he ever later conceded. When the members of SFU's fledgling board initially looked around the table, they saw leadership with
Shrum and not McTaggart-Cowan.

OPERATING A YEAR-ROUND CAMPUS

When McTaggart-Cowan first presented himself to the premier and the
minister of education, they had three questions for him—beyond the
initial one of his ability to work with Shrum. Did he understand the urgency with which the university was being built? Was he flexible in his
approach to teaching and willing to try new ideas such as large classes,
automated teaching and making "full use of facilities"? And did he recognize the value of money?[50]

The premier was going to give higher education an infusion of public money, but he still thought that universities should make their
money go further than they did. For his part, Shrum believed that there
were efficiencies to be found, although he never contemplated creating
anything but a first-rate institution. What he advocated was "full use of
facilities" or, in his own words, "year-round classes." He explained to the
journalist Donald Stainsby in December 1963 that this would have a
double advantage: it would make full use of building and plant, and
allow students to get through their education and into their careers as
quickly as possible.[51]

The idea of the year-round-university had surfaced in Canada in the
mid-1950s. Taxpayers and politicians were asking how universities could
expect more money and still take long April-to-September holidays; and
university presidents were trying to explain that professors were not on
holiday when they were away from their classes but doing research and
trying to stay current in their fields.[52]

When Shrum spoke of a year-round operation, he had two models
in mind, although there were at least three possibilities.[53] An American
survey in the spring of 1963 identified sixty-nine colleges and universities in the U.S. already operating year-round or about to do so. Twenty-

seven had chosen the quarter system (four terms a year), twenty-five the trimester (three terms) and nineteen were running two regular terms plus two short summer sessions. Stanford in California had been on the quarter system since 1918; Golden Gate College in San Francisco had been on the trimester system since 1946, and the University of Alabama had split the summer into two sessions since 1942. At these institutions the year-round system was long established, but at most of the others it was new or just planned. As anyone familiar with American higher education would know, sixty-nine colleges and universities was not many. About 96 per cent of American junior and senior colleges and universities were still on the traditional twenty-eight- to thirty-two-week academic year with a long summer break.

In 1963 no one in Canada (or the U.S.) seemed to have a sure grasp of the costs and advantages of the year-round system. It was not a simple matter to compare the different models employed at different kinds of institutions (state colleges, teachers' colleges, colleges with large part-time enrolments, universities with large graduate programs), especially because few institutions had been doing it for long. Shrum saw the choice as either the quarter system or the trimester system; and from the moment that McTaggart-Cowan agreed to be president, he understood that sorting this out was a priority. A couple of weeks later, in Boston, at an executive meeting of the American Meteorological Society, he had a chance to talk to a vice-president from the University of Florida, which had just gone on the trimester system after the Florida state legislature had made year-round operations mandatory. The frank advice that he got was to do something else: the split summer was the least disruptive of the year-round systems.[54]

McTaggart-Cowan handled the question by delegating it to Ron Baker, his academic planner. Baker was SFU's first faculty appointment. He had known Shrum but not well when they met at a UBC symposium at a YMCA camp during the summer of 1963. Shrum had been invited to speak about SFU, but he took note of Baker when he remembered that he was one of the authors of the Macdonald Report. Baker was then forty-one and had been teaching English at UBC since 1951, first as a teaching assistant and then as a regular faculty member. He had come to Canada during the war as an RAF navigator when Canada's open spaces were vital in the training of British pilots and navigators. A couple of years after the war ended, he returned as a twenty-three-year-old immigrant to enrol at UBC, where he completed an honours BA and then an MA in English. His UBC education made him strongly Canadian in outlook, and he was also familiar with the British university system, especially after starting a PhD in linguistics (which he did not finish) at the School of Oriental and African Studies in London.

As a junior faculty member at UBC he was mentored by Roy Daniells, the head of English, for whom he acted as an assistant, and by Geoffrey Andrew, the assistant to the president. He undertook various tasks for the president's office, including the preparation of the president's annual report, and assumed an interest in the broad direction of the university. He was also active in the Faculty Association, and when President Macdonald arrived on the scene, he was an obvious recruit for Macdonald's Committee on Higher Education. Because Baker knew as much as anyone about the recommendation to create SFU, Shrum thought he would be a good person to have around. He discussed this with McTaggart-Cowan on the October weekend when McTaggart-Cowan was appointed president; and they presented Baker's name to the board at the November meeting. In that period of time they had defined his role as academic planner. Shrum had proposed the title of executive assistant, which Baker refused. Baker's appointment was effective January 1, 1964, but he did not have the luxury of waiting until then to get started.[55]

In December, McTaggart-Cowan outlined a list of projects for Baker to research, with year-round operations first. Nearly forty years after he did this research, Baker admitted that he never liked teaching in the trimester system, and he thought the quarter system would have been even worse. He was one of those who preferred the rhythm of the old academic year, with courses running from September to May and with exams at Christmas that gave students an idea of how well they were doing halfway through.[56]

Baker's examination of alternatives had to be a rush job, because the public announcement that SFU was adopting the trimester system came only weeks after he started as academic planner. He sought information from other universities, including the University of California and the University of Manitoba, but had little time to look at what came back. He had written to the University of California because the board of regents there had recently sanctioned the quarter system; but the reply that he got, days before SFU's announcement, was that California was deferring action.[57] Manitoba had been discussing a year-round system for several years and just completed a report rejecting the idea.

Baker did not have a chance to read the Manitoba report before making his recommendation. However, reviewing it now helps to explain how Canadian academics responded to the issue then, and to understand why Canadian universities almost unanimously said no to year-round operations. The authors of the Manitoba report saw the question in terms of a drift away from the British model towards the American. They realized that Canadian universities in 1963 no longer gave the same emphasis as the British to the BA as the culmination of a student's formal education. But Canadians had yet to go as far as Americans in treating the BA as simply preliminary to graduate work.

As the authors of the Manitoba report saw it, the downgrading of the undergraduate degree in the U.S. was allowing it to become merely a matter of accumulating course credits. They offered a dismissive illustration, saying that if you asked British students what they were doing, they would reply, "reading economics" or "reading chemistry," whereas American students would report how many credit hours they had. They believed that American universities were throwing out quality and replacing it with quantity. A quarter system or a trimester system, requiring many short courses, would take universities further down the road of quantification, and it was for this reason, principally, that Manitoba decided that it was the wrong way to go. The American evidence they had also suggested that a year-round system would be more expensive than the traditional seven-month academic year: a small saving in capital costs would be more than counterbalanced by a large increase in operating costs.[58]

Baker had a number of other documents at hand about American year-round systems, and he had a report by a privately funded Montreal-based education researcher who was promoting the idea in Canada.[59] This report had appeared at the end of 1963 just as Baker began to look into the subject and it was creating a stir in academic circles. The UBC faculty association began to look at it in December 1963, and because Baker was still a UBC faculty member, he was invited to serve on the special committee they struck. (Baker had agreed to teach one course at UBC to the end of the academic year, so he was splitting his time between universities.) Before SFU made its announcement about going on the trimester system, Baker had a chance to attend a couple of meetings of this committee and to take part in its discussions. A number of other universities—McGill, Sir George Williams, Bishop's, Carleton, Queen's, York and Western Ontario, as well as Manitoba—were formally examining the subject, but Baker did not have time to exchange information with them.

THE TRIMESTER SYSTEM

Baker picked the trimester system for SFU with the knowledge that his UBC colleagues thought it better than the quarter system but liked the split summer best. In their opinion the quarter system sped things up too much, with shorter courses, greater scheduling problems and more frequent transitions from term to term. He knew that they were concerned about faculty workloads and saw the prospect of stipends for additional teaching as potentially dismal, tempting faculty to give up time they needed for research and scholarship and undercutting the quality of the education they offered. He had also witnessed some willingness among members of the special UBC Faculty Association Committee to accept a year-round system as long as faculty research time was protected.[60]

When he recommended the trimester system, Baker used the financial argument, but he soon afterwards concluded that it was wrong. He originally cited a couple of American studies, published in 1958 and 1961, to argue that although costs for faculty and staff would increase absolutely, there would be proportionate saving because a year-round operation would handle more students. Shrum took this to be definitive and was slow to revise his position.[61] After the university had been running for a few years, he could see that the savings he expected were not there. In hindsight, he came to believe that the quarter system would have been cheaper and therefore better. (Universities on the quarter system expected their faculty to teach three quarters out of four; with the trimester system it was two semesters out of three.[62])

More important to Baker were the advantages of the trimester system to faculty and students. One can see, with experience, that he was wrong in his expectation of advantages to students. He thought that getting through quickly would be a major attraction and he calculated a decided financial gain for students heading into professional careers if they decided to forgo summer jobs so they could start their careers a year earlier. What he did not see was the difficulty that most of the students who came to SFU would have in financing their education without taking jobs along the way. About the advantages to faculty, however, Baker was right. He quickly saw that the trimester system had the flexibility to permit faculty to accumulate credit for teaching that they could use, every so often, to take eight consecutive months for research. He saw this as a recruiting point, and it became central in the pitch that he and McTaggart-Cowan made in their search for department heads and faculty.

As a linguist, Baker knew better than anyone that *trimester* was a misnomer, but he decided to use it anyway. The word was already in the vocabulary of American colleges and universities, and it seemed to convey to the public what it should: a division of the year into three equal parts. Only a purist (or perhaps a doctor speaking of the three trimesters of a pregnancy) would object that *mester* in Latin meant month, that a semester should be six months long and a trimester three months. Rather than invent another word, Baker realistically accepted *trimester* to describe a system of four-month terms.

The *Globe & Mail*'s education columnist, John Bascom St. John, was an immediate critic of the SFU decision, saying that it would be difficult to staff and to schedule a trimester system and correctly predicting that other Canadian universities would be slow to do the same.[63] He made his comment knowing that universities were under government pressure to abandon the traditional academic calendar.[64] That was why a number of universities had the year-round system under review.

Caution was the strong recommendation of a Canadian Association of University Teachers (CAUT) committee that reported in September 1964, seven months after SFU's announcement. The committee had visited nine American universities that operated year-round and had consulted more broadly among Canadian and American faculty and administrators. They did not find much to praise in the publicly funded universities they went to see in Michigan, Pennsylvania, North Carolina, Georgia, Florida and Tennessee. They had the impression that at these institutions, they were witnessing the acceleration of a North American trend towards the mass production of students while the basic requirements of the academic community were "in danger of being forgotten."[65]

In the United States the movement towards year-round operations gained ground throughout the 1960s, with the quarter system a much more common choice than the trimester. By the fall of 1971, about a quarter of all American colleges and universities had adopted one or the other. This did not happen in Canada, although the idea of the year-round university continued to be promoted in the occasional editorial and in speeches by business leaders and politicians. Only three university-level institutions in Canada adopted year-round programming: Simon Fraser, the University of Guelph and Ryerson Polytechnical. Guelph did it in 1964, a year before SFU opened, and Ryerson followed in 1966.[66]

Ryerson kept the trimester system for five years and then abandoned it because summer enrolments were low. By then it was evident at Guelph and SFU that the trimester system was not economical and that it would take careful management to keep its costs down. In 1972 a management consultant firm calculated that the trimester system was costing SFU an extra 19 per cent per full-time student. Low summer enrolments were a major factor. From the beginning most students chose either to take the summer off for work and recreation or to reduce their summer course load. Planning was a challenge because students could start in any semester and could choose to take a semester off in the fall, spring or summer. Departments were quick to learn that most of the enrolments were in the fall and spring, and they distributed faculty teaching time accordingly. But the system was plagued with inefficiencies, the duplication of offerings from one semester to the next and the too frequent underenrolment of courses.[67]

The answer given to SFU by management consultants in 1972 was to be vigilant in the administration of the system. It was apparent that SFU would have to work hard to bring its costs back in line with those of other Canadian universities and obvious that it had not found a cheaper way of operating. The SFU and Guelph examples, as they became known and understood by the early 1970s, eventually silenced those who had thought universities could economize by running continuously. Pierre Trudeau, during a December 1971 radio interview in Vancouver, suggested year-round education as an answer to youth unemployment. But W.A.C. Bennett's provincial government was no longer buying the idea; and the minister of education, Donald Brothers, had his own statement for the press three days later about the difficulties and complications of operating year-round.

By 1971 the trimester system had become such a part of SFU that it was difficult to scrap. Even if summer enrolments were low, the system had a flexibility that attracted students and faculty. One major reason for keeping it was an expectation that SFU would lose students without it. The CAUT committee that reported on year-round operations in 1964 had calculated—incorrectly—that the trimester system would save money. Their opposition had nothing to do with funding. But, as they learned at the American universities they visited, what they saw as problems and dangers could also be described as advantages and opportunities.

Did the trimester system mean the fragmentation of course offerings or the creation of rich and varied choice? Was the intensity generated by short courses and frequent exams something to avoid because it was stressful or something to accept because it encouraged good work habits? Was the loss of identification with a student cohort who started and finished together more than answered by the freedom each student had to follow an individual program? These questions suggest some of the trade-offs that the CAUT committee identified. The committee also expressed concern that faculty would be saddled with increased teaching loads and would have less time for research. Baker was conscious of these issues and protected faculty research time in his design of the trimester system at SFU. As the years have shown, it has contributed to the strong research performance of SFU's faculty without undermining their commitment to teaching.

CONTRADICTIONS

In moving quickly to get SFU started, Shrum had no time to reflect. He chose a mountaintop retreat for students who would rush away at the end of each day of classes. He insisted on a year-round academic calendar requiring short courses that would lead to narrower teaching specializations. Yet he had selected an architectural design that was supposed to bring academic disciplines together. For a university promising to be innovative he chose a president who was nearly thirty years removed from his time at university. Looking back, it is difficult to find a coherent vision in Shrum's choices. What he did bring to his task was publicity, energy and expectation, and that was the chief inheritance of the students, staff and faculty who were subsequently drawn to SFU.

3

Academic Planning

Simon Fraser University's first employee was an engineer. His name was Arthur Orr and Shrum found him at B.C. Hydro. Orr began working for SFU on September 1, 1963, three months ahead of the president and the academic planner. That was because Shrum put construction ahead of academic planning. The second employee was a secretary, Joan Hewitt, appointed in early November. Initially Orr and Hewitt worked in the B.C. Hydro building on Burrard Street. In the New Year they moved, along with the academic planner, Ron Baker, to a suite of eight offices in a building owned by a B.C. Hydro engineering subsidiary at 570 Dunsmuir Street, six blocks from B.C. Hydro. The largest office in the suite became Patrick McTaggart-Cowan's when he finally arrived from Ontario by train in mid-January.

In that office, Baker and McTaggart-Cowan began sorting out what academic departments SFU would have. Baker was also preparing a paper on the trimester system, and he was wrestling with a document defining terms of appointment for academic staff. Other big decisions—admissions policies, instructional methods and curriculum, the approach to teacher education, the place within the university of fine and performing arts and of athletics, and the scope of the graduate program—also needed to be tackled. Shrum had strong views on most of these subjects, and they set the framework for Baker and McTaggart-Cowan.

From Dunsmuir Street, McTaggart-Cowan made frequent trips to Burnaby Mountain, occasionally packing skis so he could traverse the site after a heavy winter snow. He was a university president with a hard hat instead of a mortar board, chasing after architects and contractors.[1] By the time he arrived, bulldozers were ready to grade the site. Fifty acres (twenty hectares) had been cleared: fifty acres of volunteer alder, hemlock and spruce that had grown on the mountain since it had been logged a half century earlier. From the time he started, McTaggart-Cowan oversaw construction with an eye on the urgent September 1965 deadline. Shrum held the big stick with the contractors, who were well aware of the construction money he controlled as co-chair of B.C. Hydro. McTaggart-Cowan fell naturally into the role of troubleshooter, especially in dealing with the unions and union grievances. One such grievance that he remembered many years later was the problem that workers had in getting to "johns" after an exceptional snowfall and his own prompt action in getting snowplows and more portable "johns" on the site.

SHRUM ON TENURE

Gordon Shrum liked to stir the pot, and the trick was to know when to take him seriously. McTaggart-Cowan and Baker frequently found themselves repairing damage after one of his public utterances.[2] Shrum made some early comments on tenure that got more circulation than he had probably counted on. In early November 1963, he gave a talk about SFU to the University of B.C. Faculty Association; and when he took questions, members of the audience challenged him about tenure. He said that if he had his way, there would be no tenure at SFU because academic freedom could be protected without it. His implication was that if you were really good at what you did, you did not worry about job security: that was for the second-rate.[3]

These remarks caused a fuss among faculty at UBC and with the Canadian Association of University Teachers.[4] In Ottawa, Stewart Reid, the executive secretary of the CAUT, immediately got reports of Shrum's remarks. From this moment, Shrum and SFU were in the bad books of the CAUT—not that Shrum felt the least repentant. Reid wrote from Ottawa asking for a statement of SFU's policy on tenure; and Shrum gave an impatient and frosty reply.[5] All this happened before SFU had a single faculty member or even a president established in his office or a secretary who had been more than two weeks on the job.

Ron Baker, working intensely alongside Shrum and McTaggart-Cowan, learned to take the rough with the smooth. He observed that while Shrum liked to provoke an audience, his most outrageous statements were generally qualified. In Baker's paraphrase, Shrum had said something like this: "If I had my way, there would be no tenure, but I won't because there will be a senate, faculties and so on." The qualification did not allay alarm; it was the part of his statement that most people missed.[6]

With tenure, Shrum managed to create controversy on a subject that had no clear and consistent meaning, at least in Canada. It was frustrating for Baker, when he was drafting a policy for SFU on terms of employment, not to be able to find an obvious model to work from. The CAUT, a dozen years after it came into existence, had no comprehensive statement on tenure to explain how it should be awarded and protected and how it could be lost.[7] Baker wrote to the CAUT and to various Canadian universities to find out what current practice was, but he found no simple answer.

In the fall of 1964, Baker had an unsatisfactory discussion in Ottawa with J. Percy Smith, who had become executive secretary of the CAUT a few months after Stewart Reid's premature death. It was a conversation in a public area while the annual meeting of the CAUT was in session, and they were subject to repeated interruptions. It might not have gone well in any case. Their misunderstanding demonstrated some of the vagueness that surrounded the subject. Was tenure justified because university professors were so specialized and had invested so many years in their training that they needed job security? Or was it justified because they needed to be free to follow their research and to speak their minds without fear of repercussion? Baker had tried to say that the second reason was the only valid one. In this opinion he had a lot of company within the CAUT. And if Smith had been less suspicious of SFU, he would likely have accepted the point in better spirit.

Ironically, Baker had already persuaded the SFU board—despite Shrum's pronouncements—to adopt a policy on tenure. His reasoning was pragmatic. As he saw it, the legal basis for tenure was weak. (A report prepared for the CAUT by a Queen's University law professor, Daniel Soberman, and published eleven months later, said the same thing, but with ideas on how that might be changed.[8]) Baker had concluded that tenure had moral force rather than legal. But he told the SFU board that many faculty placed a high value on it.[9] If it had not already become an issue, he thought a decision could wait until the university had faculty and a faculty association to negotiate a policy. Many Canadian universities then had no written statements on tenure policy, so a little delay on SFU's part would not in fact have made it anomalous.

Having made this point, Baker warned that the negative symbolism would do the university no good. Too many academics would conclude that academic freedom was not protected at SFU and would class it with "bush league colleges." Baker thought that the hunt for faculty was going to be arduous enough and this would make it worse. In his recommendation to the board, Baker underscored the problem that had developed with the CAUT. "We appear to be in some danger of being informally blacklisted if we do not make a clear statement,"[10] he wrote in early March 1964, anticipating much of what was to follow.

Curiously, when asked nearly twenty years later whether SFU had had tenure while he was chancellor, Shrum was not sure.[11] His memory was sharp on so many items that this gap is striking, especially because the issue was the cause of so much controversy. The SFU board did adopt a tenure policy in 1964, on Baker's advice, and had it in place by the time the university began recruiting. It was posted in the March 1965 issue of the CAUT *Bulletin*. If Shrum forgot that, it was probably because the policy was under continuous criticism by the CAUT. What Shrum remembered was that whatever SFU had, the CAUT did not like it.

THE NOVELTY OF A FORMAL TENURE POLICY

SFU came into existence on the crest of change in many areas of academic life and tenure was one of them. Baker modelled his recommendations on the Canadian examples he was able to get in 1964. These were examples of an informal system, based on custom and usage rather than written definition. Moreover, the written statements that did exist fell short of the standards that were coming over the horizon. What Canadian universities and faculty members had long assumed, likely without giving the question much thought, was an atmosphere of trust and goodwill. Most Canadian university charters—like American charters—said that appointments were "during the pleasure" of the board. But that language did not come into play when there were no problems and when tenured faculty served their years without threat of being fired.

Tenure had not, until recently, been a great issue in Canada. Bora Laskin, then a law professor at Toronto and president of the CAUT, made a list of seven Canadian dismissal cases involving tenure. It is true that he could have made his list longer if he had not been looking for full documentation for each one. Nonetheless, the shortness of his list demonstrates how infrequently Canadian universities found themselves in any kind of a crisis over tenure and dismissal. The first of Laskin's cases was in 1861, the second in 1864, the third in 1884, the fourth in 1920 and the fifth and sixth in 1922. He had to reach a long way back to make any kind of list at all.[12] The seventh case, the Crowe case at United College in Winnipeg in 1958, was the one that still reverberated in Canadian academic circles. Laskin knew a lot about that one. Along with V.C. Fowke of Saskatchewan, he had investigated it on behalf of the CAUT. And Stewart Reid, the executive secretary of the CAUT, had been a professor at United College and had resigned over the Crowe dismissal. This was the case that gave the CAUT executive a heightened sense of purpose from 1958 onward.[13]

The Crowe case led the CAUT along a path already well beaten by the American Association of University Professors (AAUP). The American association had investigated or mediated hundreds of dismissal cases since its formation in 1915. In 1930 it had begun blacklisting universities and colleges that did not guarantee tenure; and by 1940 it had secured agreement with the American Association of Colleges on a joint statement on academic freedom.[14] By the end of 1963, twenty-three associations—the American Library Association, the Association of American Law Schools, the American Political Science Association and so on—had adopted this statement; and the list was growing. The statement had been published most recently in the summer 1963 issue of the *AAUP Bulletin*.

The AAUP had been defending academic freedom for half a century because in the U.S. it had frequently been under attack—most recently and most seriously during the McCarthy anti-communist witch hunt of the early 1950s. In Britain, where faculty were not subject to the control of lay boards as in North America, and where they appeared to enjoy complete security in their positions, academic freedom and tenure was not an issue; tenure was scarcely mentioned; there was no literature on it, and there were no dismissal cases before the courts. By contrast, as Daniel Soberman reported to the CAUT, the body of case law on tenure in the U.S. was immense.[15]

There had been an excusable Canadian inclination to see formal statements on academic freedom and tenure as an American response to an American problem. During the McCarthy era, Canadian universities had been havens for American academics targeted for their leftist views. This witch hunt had not come to Canada. One reason was that Canadian universities, most of which were still run by the churches, were not subject to the same political pressures as American state colleges and universities. Still, as Michiel Horn in his study of academic freedom in Canada has pointed out, there was a Cold War chill in Canadian academia in the 1950s, and professors tended to silence themselves, even if there was no campaign from outside to police them.[16]

SFU'S INITIAL TENURE POLICY

Baker sold tenure to the SFU board by saying that in North America, one had to have it to be taken seriously as an academic institution. Shrum, who could back down when he heard a good argument, offered no opposition. In the original policy on terms of employment, presented to the board in March 1964 and approved in April, Baker included the AAUP statement on academic freedom—in the absence of any CAUT statement.[17] Sensibly, SFU policy left the matter of rank and tenure open to negotiation at the time of appointment (which meant that someone who was already a full professor with tenure at another university might keep that status if he or she came to SFU). Otherwise, assistant professors would be eligible for tenure after seven years, associates after four and full professors after three, with the proviso that tenure was not automatic and would be granted only after the board reviewed a scholar's teaching and research record. Baker had used UBC policy as his main model, although he made the probationary period longer at SFU.

This early SFU policy on tenure did not have the procedural detail of later policy. It assumed no problems and took it for granted that trust and goodwill were what one really needed, not procedures. This was in an era in which tenure decisions were not as fraught as they later became. Getting tenure was very much a matter of time serving. It was still not standard at Canadian universities to make tenure an absolute condition for continuing beyond a probationary period. One consequence of raising the profile of tenure, as the CAUT did in the 1960s, was to invite a public backlash: why did university professors deserve this kind of security? Part of the answer was to conduct a more elaborate review of a scholar's work before granting tenure. With that came an elaboration of procedures. In 1964, however, Baker had little indication that this is what the immediate future held.

The policy of the future would formalize the granting of tenure: requiring faculty to apply for it, creating procedures to review applications and making the tenure decision a final yes or no, stay or go, without the option of renewing probationary contracts. It would also spell out grounds for dismissal as well as more elaborate dismissal procedures. None of this was in the document that the SFU board approved in 1964. Tenured faculty at Canadian universities could be dismissed for cause; and due process at a university like UBC meant that an individual had to have advance notice of the charges and a chance at a hearing to offer a defence. But this was a bare bones apparatus compared to the procedures that members of the CAUT executive were beginning to think were required.

A critical assessment of the tenure situation in Canada appeared in the March 1965 issue of the CAUT *Bulletin*. In this report, by Daniel Soberman of Queen's, SFU's tenure policy received caustic treatment for what it did not say: for the absence of description and procedural rights. The consequence, said Soberman, was that the policy offered faculty no legal protection. He did not mention SFU by name, but quoted directly from its policy, which happened to be printed on the next page, so the connection was not difficult for readers to make. To illustrate his general point, he had reviewed the policies of nine Canadian universities and found them confused, vague, incomplete, ambiguous, procedurally faulty and, in one case, of no value whatsoever in protecting tenure. If sfu's policy was bad, it had plenty of company.[18]

Shrum's original remarks reverberated for a long time and, as the countdown to opening day proceeded, the noise continued. Bora Laskin, as CAUT president, delivered a blast while in Vancouver in June 1965 for CAUT meetings held at UBC. As he read the SFU policy, there was no guarantee that anyone at SFU would get tenure. He delivered this opinion in an interview with a reporter for the *Vancouver Sun,* whose headline read: "No Job Security Simon Fraser Told."[19]

GOVERNMENT BY DEPARTMENT HEADS

Much early decision making at SFU boiled down to choosing either to accept or reject the UBC example. UBC was the primary model. This was certainly the case with the administrative structure that SFU chose. The board, under Shrum's influence, elected to launch the university without permanent deans of Arts or Science. The board did make an exception for Education, which was to have a permanent dean from the beginning, presumably because Shrum, McTaggart-Cowan and Baker believed that they would need strong leadership in Education if they were to achieve a fresh and creative approach. (They knew that they did not want to replicate UBC in this area.) In the arts and sciences, on the other hand, Shrum strongly believed that the leadership should come from the heads of departments, and that all would work best if the deanship simply rotated among the heads.

Baker has explained that Shrum really looked at the university from the perspective of a department head.[20] That is what he had been for twenty-four years at UBC. Deans were people who got in your way, and he had rankled particularly at the enlargement of the dean's role after the Second World War. In the university that Shrum had known in the 1920s and 1930s, a major portion of the administration fell to regular faculty members, and to department heads like himself who took on added jobs without extra pay while continuing to teach. The move towards full-time administrators had been recent, a trend of the 1950s. In this aspect of university development, Shrum wanted to put the clock back.

In addition to full-time deans, Canadian universities, following the American example, had begun to acquire vice-presidents. In the early 1970s, Toronto expanded its tier of vice-presidents to five, something that Toronto's President Sidney Smith could see coming when he appointed the first one in the 1950s. Smith understood that with all the various duties descending on a university president in record keeping, accounting, purchasing, building and maintenance, the days of the teacher–administrator were fading fast.[21] Moreover, in the U.S., the office of vice-president academic was being introduced to relieve presidents of the weight of academic matters so they could concentrate on external relations, fundraising and building.[22] UBC had not yet taken that step, but it was among the many Canadian universities that had a group of senior permanent and professional administrators on whom the president relied increasingly for advice and information.

Shrum wanted power back in the trenches, and the system that he blessed at SFU had department heads reporting directly to the president. These were department heads like those at UBC with permanent positions held at the pleasure of the board. As soon as a few had been appointed, a Committee of Heads and senior administrators (the academic planner, dean of Education, librarian, registrar, bursar and engineer) began to function as the president's main consultative body. This system saw the university through the fifteen-month countdown to opening day and into the third year of operations, but it collapsed in the turmoil and excitement of 1968.

THE ORIGINAL DEPARTMENTS

As Baker has conceded, the list of departments with which SFU began was quite traditional. This was an almost inescapable consequence of the decision to make department heads the senior administrators under the president. It also happened because the rush to get SFU going and the expectation that it would start with a large enrolment left little opportunity for experiment. Everyone involved in the early planning had to feel a little apprehensive that perhaps students would not enrol. A lot of work went into avoiding that failure. A radically different program would have been risky, given the conservatism of most incoming students. SFU's British contemporary, the University of Sussex, by contrast, began with an emphasis on interdisciplinary studies organized within schools of humanities, life sciences, science and technology and social and cultural studies; but it did not have the same hurried planning or enrolment expectations.

SFU was very successful in recruiting people with fresh and experimental ideas, and many of their ideas did find expression in a variety of interdisciplinary programs, which, for most of the 1970s, were nurtured within a venturesome faculty of interdisciplinary studies. These programs, however, developed after people came to the university. When faculty first arrived, particularly in the arts and sciences, they found an academic program based on a familiar selection of academic disciplines. The barons of the university were the department heads, each with an academic domain to develop and protect. That had made the definition of these domains a critical and virtually irreversible early decision.

Baker made his comment about SFU's traditional lineup of departments with an understanding of the broad background of evolution and change in academia. By "traditional" he did not mean timeless. McTaggart-Cowan, on the other hand, had been out of university for thirty years and had little sense of the developments overtaking a number of disciplines. He had a lot of catching up to do. This is evident in the hasty jottings in the pocket-sized notebook that he kept in the fall of 1963. These jottings include a couple of tentative lists of the departments he imagined the university should have. By December he was thinking of four science departments: Physics, Chemistry, Biological Sciences and Environmental Sciences; and six arts departments: History, English, Economics & Political Science (together), Philosophy & Psychology (together), Modern Languages, and Commerce & Business Administration (together).

The most dated choices on his list—the ones that made it look like a university of his undergraduate days—were the combinations of Economics with Political Science and of Philosophy with Psychology. His omission of Math was curious but probably explained by his graduation from a program in which Math and Physics went together. With Biological Sciences he agreed with Shrum that the broad discipline should be kept together and not allowed to fragment into separate departments of Plant Sciences and Zoology. The department closest to his interests was Environmental Sciences, which he also identified as Geography. This is where Meteorology would have been located if his tentative early planning had borne fruit. Geography was missing from his Arts departments: in his mind it was a science. Commerce had become a separate department at UBC in the 1930s and Business had been linked with it; so in contemplating a Commerce & Business Administration department, McTaggart-Cowan was thinking of something that had been new a generation earlier.

In 1960, one needed to go back no more than seventy or eighty years to explain the history of the modern Canadian university curriculum. That does not look like a long time now that SFU is forty years old. In the late nineteenth century, at a university such as Toronto, a student's choices were wonderfully simple. would it be Science (either natural or practical), Philosophy, Classics, Modern Languages or English? In natural science one studied Physics, Chemistry, Biology and Mathematics. Philosophy included Economics, Political Science and Psychology. Classics incorporated Ancient History and Geography. A single subject encompassed a great range of knowledge.

The curriculum that McTaggart-Cowan knew when he was an undergraduate in the early 1930s had become much more segmented. At the larger Canadian universities, Physics, Biology, History and Economics & Political Science were independent departments. Economics & Political Science went together in the political economy tradition of the nineteenth century that treated the two as a single subject. Disciplines like Sociology and Anthropology were still marginal and generally subsumed under Economics & Political Science. Psychology still had not broken free of Philosophy.

As an outsider up to 1964, it was easy for McTaggart-Cowan to miss evidence of the continuing multiplication of disciplines. In any case, as he indicated with Biological Sciences, he felt that specialization could go too far. Most Canadian universities still combined Economics and Political Science (UBC was one of the exceptions). Only three universities in the country had Sociology departments, and Toronto was the only one with an Anthropology department. Psychology, however, had become independent nearly everywhere; and by 1964 the Canadian Psychology Association had been around for twenty-five years. Economics, Political Science, Sociology and Anthropology were all on divergent paths. Two years after SFU opened for classes, the Canadian economists and political scientists split their association into two, each with its own journal. Geography, scarcely represented in Canada as a discipline in the 1930s, had made rapid progress in the 1950s—promoted by a post-war consensus that geographical knowledge was vital. By the 1960s it was being taught at all Canadian universities.

One thing that McTaggart-Cowan had not missed was the long de-cline of Classics. It would have been difficult to do. Right up to the end of the nineteenth century, the classic Latin and Greek languages and their literatures had been at the centre of the university curriculum; but from 1900 on, their undergraduate enrolments had fallen. Graduate studies had helped to sustain them down to the 1960s, and when SFU was conceived, one could still find more classics professors around than psychologists.[23] At Canadian universities, despite the charge of irrele-vance coming from many quarters, classicists were holding on to about 10 per cent of faculty positions in the humanities—which also included English, History, Philosophy and Modern Languages. McTaggart-Cowan, however, left Classics off his list, and he wouldn't find anyone else in the early planning stages at SFU who disagreed. In the beginning Shrum had talked of including Latin, thinking of it as a foundation for the study of French, Spanish and English, and for nomenclature in the sciences; but he did not insist on it.[24]

By early February 1963, Baker, Shrum and McTaggart-Cowan had settled on twelve departments in Science and Arts, as well as a Faculty of Education.[25] In this trio, Baker proposed, Shrum disputed and McTag-gart-Cowan went along with the outcome. For the most part, Baker says, the three of them reached agreement fairly easily. Their objective was to have fewer and larger departments, reversing the trend towards subdivi-sion. Baker looked at enrolments at other universities, with UBC the main example, and that was a major criterion in their selection of de-partments. He found that Shrum was most skeptical about the social sciences, but when he was shown that students would enroll in psychol-ogy, for example, he let it in. If a proposal had Shrum's backing, Baker observed, the board generally supported it.[26]

In early March, McTaggart-Cowan announced SFU's arts and science departments: Economics & Commerce; English; Geography; History; Modern Languages (including French, German, Russian and Spanish); Philosophy; Politics, Sociology & Anthropology (PSA); Psychology; Bio-logical Sciences; Chemistry; Mathematics, and Physics. Baker, Shrum and McTaggart-Cowan considered making two departments out of the disciplines that went into PSA, with Political Science & International studies in one and Sociology & Anthropology in the other. They had also thought of Economics as a department on its own; and Commerce had been added at the insistence of a board member, with Shrum's last-minute backing. (Baker had assumed that Education would be SFU's only professional program; and that Commerce and the rest would be left to UBC.[27]) In each case, they chose to create a bigger unit. PSA came to be viewed at SFU as an experimental department, a new (and failed) adventure in interdisciplinary studies. In reality, it brought together three disciplines that traditionally had been associated in Canada under the umbrella of Economics & Political Science.

A LIBRARIAN

Shrum made the search for a librarian a priority, a fact that belies his anti-library reputation. He got bad publicity when provoked by a presumptuous letter from the Canadian Library Association. He had dismissively and irresponsibly replied that SFU could manage without a library: there was the UBC library, the Vancouver Public Library and lots of books around. But what he said in pique did not represent his thinking.[28] He had already acted on the advice of the chief librarian at the University of Toronto, Robert Blackburn, who told him that it took longer to develop a book collection than to put up a building and that he needed a top-notch librarian and a budget for books without delay.

The search began in the fall of 1963, while McTaggart-Cowan was still in Toronto. Shrum had McTaggart-Cowan seeking suggestions from Blackburn, and over Christmas they had several candidates to think about. One was Don Baird, who was then chief cataloguer at the University of Alberta. McTaggart-Cowan arranged to meet Baird (who had to drive down from Edmonton) on a Calgary railway platform at 12:55 on a wintry Friday afternoon during a half-hour stop of the CPR transcontinental on its way to Vancouver. He was impressed by Baird's energy and experience. Baird was from B.C.; he had a second degree from Columbia, and he had worked in the Vancouver and Victoria public libraries before going to Alberta. At Alberta he had introduced open stacks, a novel and exciting reform for generations of Canadian students who had been kept out of the stacks and who had ordered their books one or two at a time by handing slips to a librarian.[29] In February McTaggart-Cowan recommended Baird to the board, and on April 1 he started. Open stacks would be the rule in his SFU library.

With Shrum as chancellor, the sciences at SFU were in no danger of neglect. Shrum was also an advocate for the fine arts, humanities and athletics, as his early decisions demonstrate. But it was the science world that he knew inside out, and he did not wait for McTaggart-Cowan to start beating the bushes for science heads. His opening shots in December 1963 were to write to the British-born A.E. (Ted) Litherland, one of the key young nuclear physicists at Atomic Energy of Canada's laboratories at Chalk River, and to UBC graduate Bertram Brockhouse at McMaster, who thirty years later (in 1994) received a Nobel prize in physics for research that he had started at Chalk River in the 1950s.[30] McTaggart-Cowan did not get either man, but in January 1964, he was in Ottawa talking to people at the National Research Council (NRC). This visit gave him a dozen names, including two people whom SFU ultimately hired: Rudi Haering in physics and Donald Nelson in biological sciences.[31]

The NRC at that time had a dual function: it ran its own research laboratories and it distributed research money as grants and fellowships to universities. It had been the main engine of scientific research in Canada from the time it was created during the First World War, and Atomic Energy of Canada, the Defence Research Board and the Medical Research Council had all been spinoffs. In the post-war era, in Canada as in the United States, the federal government had started shifting research spending from government laboratories to universities (transforming the universities in the process). By the mid-1960s, the NRC was keeping about half of its funding for its own research and distributing half to the universities. Its in-house scientists adjudicated applications for university grants. In 1964 this was the one-stop place to go to find out who the up-and-coming scientists in Canada were.[32] (Fifteen years later that was no longer so: with the creation of the National Sciences and Engineering Research Council, adjudication committees were filled by university scientists drawn from across the country.)

It was not Shrum's idea to hand-pick department heads—or to appear to do so. He wanted good people, but he also wanted appointments to have credibility, and he knew that would come if the appointing committees had strong academic credentials. The obvious problem at the beginning was that SFU had no faculty. In order to assemble an SFU committee, Shrum and McTaggart-Cowan involved members of the board. The Staff and Organization Committee of the board became the academic hiring committee, interviewing those candidates who came to town (not all of them did) and making recommendations to the board. This committee had two lay members, retired Burnaby school superintendent C.J. Frederickson, and Dick Lester, the Haney lawyer who was president of the B.C. School Trustees Association. McTaggart-Cowan, Shrum and Baker were the other three members.

Fredrickson and Lester worked hard on this committee, expanding the decision-making circle beyond the tight trio of Baker, Shrum and McTaggart-Cowan. But Shrum sought to bolster the search process with advisory committees. He did this better in the sciences than the arts, and imperfectly overall. In Physics, he involved George Volkoff from UBC, Gerhart Hertzberg, director of Physics at the NRC, and the nuclear physicist Martin Johns at McMaster. They recommended six possibilities, with Rudi Haering ranked high.[33] In Biological Sciences, the advisory committee was Ian McTaggart-Cowan from UBC (Patrick's brother), Kenneth Clarke Fisher, head of Zoology at Toronto, and W.H. (Bill) Cook, director of Applied Biology at the NRC. They produced three names, including Don Nelson. Chemistry proved more difficult. Shrum was not happy with the suggestions he got from Charles McDowell, head of Chemistry at UBC, and he suspected McDowell of pushing second-rate people at him.[34] Without someone at UBC to anchor an advisory committee, he let the idea of such a committee ride, although he continued to get suggestions from McDowell and followed up on some.

With the appointments of Swiss-born Rudi Haering in Physics and Ontario native Don Nelson in Biological Sciences, Shrum showed that SFU could go out and get first-rate people. Haering was an outstanding UBC graduate who had done a PhD at McGill and post-doctoral work at Birmingham. At the age of thirty-one, he was a professor of Physics at Waterloo and a member of the research staff at the IBM Research Laboratory at Yorkton Heights, New York, where he was working on semiconductors and superconductivity, a rapidly developing field since the late 1940s. Nelson, who was just a few years older, was an associate professor with a PhD from Pennsylvania and four years' experience at the National Research Council prior to his arrival at Queen's University in Kingston. Nelson had a reputation as an excellent lecturer and educator and also as good a person for getting things done, as he had shown with the School of Plant Physiology and as co-chair of Biology at Queen's.[35] As a plant physiologist he was already widely known in Canada and internationally.

With Mathematics and Geography, Shrum and McTaggart-Cowan may have taken advice from the UBC heads, Ralph James and John Chapman, although years later Chapman could not remember being involved. In the search for a dean of Education they shrewdly recruited the help of John F.K. English, deputy minister of education at Victoria, as well as Dean Walter Gage of UBC. That made five searches in which they formally used external advisors. In one way or another they sought guidance from all the relevant Arts and Science heads at UBC; and McTaggart-Cowan liked to mention this in public talks as an example of co-operation between the two universities.[36] But the consultation was more substantial in some cases than in others. Time, politics and gaps in their knowledge of some disciplines did not allow them to approach all the searches in the same way. McTaggart-Cowan, through meteorology, could connect more readily with geographers than historians or sociologists. Baker, with his footing in the arts, made up for much of the deficit. But it was only in Physics and in Biological Sciences, where Shrum got off to a fast start, that they were able to put together a full two-tier search-committee structure.

Geoffrey Bursill-Hall in Modern Languages was the first head appointed and the second faculty member after Baker; and he was recruited from across town without a formal search. He had been teaching French at UBC since 1949 with two years out to earn a PhD in medieval linguistics (completed in 1959) at London. Like Baker, he was a post-war British immigrant to Canada, with the difference that all of his formal education had been in Britain. With Baker, he shared an interest in linguistics; and his appointment at SFU grew out of their conversations during the fall of 1963, after Baker agreed to come to SFU. What Bursill-Hall promised was an emphasis on spoken language, something that literature-oriented Canadian modern language programs did not provide.[37] His appointment gave SFU an early example of how it was going to be new and different. It made a good press release.[38] The appointment, made in February 1964, was effective from July 1; but the board granted Bursill-Hall a year's unpaid leave of absence to take a visiting professorship at Cornell, where he could see first-hand a leading university language program (based on the Intensive Language Program of the U.S. Army) that gave priority to oral communication.

English was to be one of the biggest departments in the university; and this everyone recognized as a vital appointment. In the end, the board gave it to Baker on McTaggart-Cowan's recommendation, but only after a long and strenuous effort to find someone else. The choice of Baker was somewhat expected from the beginning; but in Baker's own mind it was a second option, not a first.

The first prospect was Roy Daniells, the long-time head of English at UBC, who was in his early sixties. In October 1963, Daniells made a lunchtime appointment with Shrum. He said he wanted to come to SFU because he was no longer happy with the administration at UBC. This was months before the first advertisements for headships were posted. Shrum was excited. He thought Daniells would "transfer tremendous prestige from UBC to SFU."[39] Daniells was evidently still keenly interested in early December. One of his expectations was that he could go to Europe for research for the coming academic year, with SFU paying 60 per cent of his salary.[40] That did not seem to be a problem for Shrum or McTaggart-Cowan.

In late December, Daniells withdrew. The University of Western Ontario had made him an unexpected offer and UBC had made a counteroffer, reducing his teaching, promising a research leave and keeping open the possibility of post-retirement reappointment. This left Daniells content to stay in Vancouver and at UBC.[41] That may have been all there was to it, but Ron Baker has a more entertaining explanation. Daniells did not drive, and his wife did not want him to go to SFU. She chose the worst possible day in December to drive him to Burnaby Mountain by the most circuitous route she could. He did not want to make that trip across town on a regular basis.

George Whalley was the senior academic from eastern Canada whom SFU could have had and did not take. He was a Coleridge scholar, a classicist, a poet, an occasional CBC broadcaster and head of the English Department at Queen's University in Kingston. He is remembered today at Queen's as one of the most distinguished former members of a department that is now over a century old. At the age of forty-nine in 1964, he was in the prime of his career. Whalley was also a supporter of the main thrust of CAUT activity. He had been asked to edit *A Place of*

Liberty, the collection of essays on university government to which all the CAUT heavyweights—Bora Laskin, Stewart Reid, Percy Smith, Frank Underhill and V.C. Fowke—contributed. It had appeared in the spring of 1964, when Whalley was contemplating coming to SFU; and its publication had been timed to make the case for reform in anticipation of a formal review of university government in Canada by the Duff–Berdahl Commission.

Bringing Whalley to SFU would have been a triumph for McTaggart-Cowan and it might have helped smooth over SFU's differences with the CAUT. McTaggart-Cowan knew Whalley from the Rhodes Scholarship Committee, on which both served. (Whalley had been a Rhodes scholar after graduating from Bishop's University in Lennoxville, Quebec.) After an interview in Vancouver in May, Whalley followed up by letter with queries about teaching, research and administrative support for a head of a department, as well as salary, pension, moving expenses and schools for his two youngest children. He did not raise the tenure issue or comment about the way SFU was run. McTaggart-Cowan asked him about the potentially contentious subject of *A Place of Liberty* and its ideas on university government, because they implied a strong criticism of the governing structure at SFU. But Whalley answered that this book had not disturbed the administration at Queen's and should not worry SFU. He said he knew that the justness of a system was determined by the people in it and not the system alone, and he liked and trusted McTaggart-Cowan.[42]

In late July, Whalley made his decision: yes, he would come to SFU. At this point Shrum turned thumbs down. His objection began with *A Place of Liberty,* but Shrum also convinced himself that Whalley's letters showed an unbalanced mind. (Whalley had jokingly said that it would be either a monastery or an institution for him if he did not have enough secretarial support as a department head.) McTaggart-Cowan accepted Shrum's veto in silence and the full episode never became general knowledge. He told the board and staff that Whalley had declined the job. He might have asserted himself—he was the president—but he did not.[43]

The English headship should have been the easiest to fill, outside the sciences. On every campus in the country, English was the largest discipline, employing the most faculty. The advantage one had in looking for scientists was that they could be found in government or industry. But within the Canadian university system, English was decidedly the largest discipline, followed by Modern Languages and then by the sciences, Biology, Math, Physics and Chemistry.

Numbers alone do not describe the problem that SFU faced in finding senior Canadians in smaller disciplines like Political Science, Psychology and Geography—where growth had been recent and faculty were comparatively young and therefore junior. In 1964, nearly two hun dred political scientists were teaching at Canadian universities; but a dozen years earlier there had been only thirty.[44] The ranks of the Sociologists and Anthropologists were so thin that the chances of finding a senior person were slight. Economics, History and Philosophy should have been easier: they were medium-sized and established disciplines. In these cases, the scarcity of qualified Canadian candidates suggests that Shrum's comments on tenure scared people away.

While Baker, McTaggart-Cowan and Shrum were proactive from the onset, seeking suggestions and inviting applications, they found themselves increasingly dependent on what arrived in the mail. Their advertisements in the vacancies listing of the Canadian Universities Foundation (the predecessor to the newsletter of the Association of Universities and Colleges of Canada) and in *Crusade for Education* (published by the Advancement and Placement Institute in New York) brought in the usual pile of underqualified and unlikely applications, but also a few of the eventual heads. What the advertisements failed to attract, however, were applications from senior faculty from Canada's older, established universities.

SFU was fortunate to get an inquiry about the Economics headship from Parzival Copes, who was teaching at Memorial University in Newfoundland. Copes was another B.C. expatriate, but with an exceptional history. His family had left Vancouver at the beginning of the Depression and returned to the Netherlands; and when the Germans invaded in 1940, they narrowly missed getting out. Copes completed his secondary schooling under Nazi occupation; and in the desperate winter of 1944–45, when the Allied advance stalled, he attempted to cross the country in search of work and food and ended up in a German concentration camp. His freedom came with the arrival of the First Canadian Army, and he became an instant recruit when the troops he met discovered they had liberated a Dutch-speaking Canadian. After the war, he returned to Vancouver to complete a BA and MA at UBC. He finished a PhD at the London School of Economics and from there went to Memorial, where, over seven years, he built up an Economics program with five faculty.

Copes had seen the SFU advertisement in the vacancies listed by the Canadian Universities Foundation. He wrote at the end of March and McTaggart-Cowan answered immediately. Two months passed before the last of his reference letters reached the Dunsmuir Street office in Vancouver; so it was June 23 when McTaggart-Cowan phoned Copes, catching him on the way out the door to board an aircraft for Europe on a sabbatical leave. Copes responded by letter from the Netherlands; and his appointment went to the board at its July 9 meeting. This chronology, with its delays, illustrates how difficult it was to meet the deadlines that the SFU timetable required. McTaggart-Cowan was trying to hire twelve heads and a dean by July 1, with his first advertisement appearing in March. It could not be done; and attempting to do it meant taking some risks.

Brian Pate, the first head of Chemistry, was another who wrote to SFU soon after the first advertisement appeared. He was a British-born scholar with a McGill PhD who was teaching chemistry at Washington University in St. Louis, Missouri. He gave two references from Washington University and one from Columbia, but it was the endorsement of his former supervisor at McGill that made the difference. Shrum and McTaggart-Cowan looked at a couple of other prospects before taking Pate's name to the board in July. Pate was nine years beyond his PhD and an associate professor at Washington University.[45]

In the late spring of 1964, Lorne Kendall applied to SFU from Princeton, New Jersey, where he was working for an education testing service as a section head in the statistical analysis division. He was a thirty-one-year-old Canadian from the town of Tofield, Alberta, with a PhD from Cornell completed in 1963. As the summer passed without bringing more senior prospects, McTaggart-Cowan and his Staff and Organization Committee began looking closely at Kendall's file. The board approved his appointment as head of Psychology at its September meeting.[46]

Early in their search for heads, Baker, McTaggart-Cowan and Shrum began to focus on Britain. On April 15, SFU ran the first of three advertisements in the *Times* of London; and acting on various leads, McTaggart-

Cowan and Baker directly contacted several British scholars. Shrum did a number of interviews when he passed through London in April and again in May of 1964, on his way to and from meetings in Stockholm and Moscow. Each time he booked into the convenient Park Lane Hotel in Mayfair and made B.C. House on Lower Regent Street his secondary headquarters. He interviewed in his hotel room, sitting on his bed with the files beside him and offering the chair to his guest.

While in London, Shrum saw candidates for English, Geography, Chemistry and Mathematics, but the two consequential interviews were for PSA and History. The candidate for History was Allan Cunningham; and on Shrum's recommendation, Cunningham got the job. For PSA, the field had narrowed to T.B. Bottomore, then a reader in sociology at the London School of Economics, and one other British scholar. Shrum saw them both in London and approved Bottomore.[47]

Bottomore was a big catch. For a decade he had edited *Current Sociology,* the widely cited journal of the International Sociological Association, and he had recently published an edition and translation of Karl Marx's early writings. At UBC, the Department of Sociology and Anthropology had adopted his text, *Sociology: A Guide to Problems and Literature,* for its introductory course after it appeared in 1962, so he was known there; and the head of the department, Harry Hawthorn, endorsed him as one of Britain's leading sociologists. The coup of getting Bottomore was so obvious, and time so pressing, McTaggart-Cowan did not wait to write to Britain for references, but got them from Hawthorn and Dean Kaspar Naegle at UBC, who knew him by reputation, if not in person. Allan Cunningham was not well known, but looked like an interesting Renaissance prospect: a former Royal Air Force pilot, a painter, sportsman, mountaineer and historian who had taught for five years at the University College of the West Indies and then at the University of London, and who recently had held a two-year senior research fellowship at Oxford. Shrum pronounced him a good man; and McTaggart-Cowan instantly liked him when they first met in London in September. About Bottomore he was not so sure.[48]

Archie MacPherson's name came up for Geography early in the hunt, through Lewis Robinson at UBC, who mentioned him to McTaggart-Cowan.[49] (Robinson happened to live half a block from McTaggart-Cowan's brother Ian.) MacPherson was another RAF veteran who had received wartime training in Canada, in both Alberta and Quebec City. Robinson got to know him during a spring in Edinburgh and later brought him to UBC as a visiting professor. MacPherson was one of those British scholars who had begun lecturing almost immediately on completion of a first-class undergraduate degree and who had done no graduate work. His degree was from Edinburgh and that is where he had taught since 1951, with the exception of two years at Aberdeen and his year at UBC. MacPherson sent in his vita in May, before Shrum left London; and McTaggart-Cowan held the file until he reached a dead end in his search for a Canadian. That took him to September, when he took MacPherson's file to the board and got him appointed.

In September, two headships were still unfilled: Philosophy and Mathematics. In November the Staff and Organization Committee stopped looking for a Philosophy head, and began the department with two assistant professors who were finishing their PhDs. The grand plan had been to appoint heads in time to give them a year to find faculty. In Philosophy, with no senior candidates and opening day fast approaching, that was not going to work. For Mathematics, the committee had looked at couple of impressive Canadian candidates during the summer but in the fall were still searching.[50] By November they had two well-qualified British candidates, D.H. Parsons of Reading and Ronald Harrop, who was then a senior lecturer at Newcastle. When the former withdrew, the job went to Harrop in December.[51]

THE BRITISH FACTOR

Once the heads had been found, Shrum stepped back and adopted a more chancellor-like role with regular faculty appointments. These he defined as McTaggart-Cowan's responsibility; and in any case he would not have had the time to involve himself. The roster of heads that he along with McTaggart-Cowan and Baker assembled were the foundation for the whole academic program. It was their vision that defined the academic objectives of their departments; and they made the initial faculty selections that were crucial in setting the tone of the university. Significantly, the haste with which they made appointments, and perhaps their own inclinations, stopped them from replicating themselves. The result was a sharp contrast in the composition of the group of heads and the main body of faculty who filled out their departments. This contrast was most apparent in the Faculty of Arts.

By the end of 1969, all of the original heads, except Parzi Copes, had been replaced. Lorne Kendall, with heart problems at an early age, gave up his headship in 1967, and Don Nelson, sadly, stepped down in March 1968, terminally ill with leukemia, a victim of the work he had done ten years earlier as research assistant with Atomic Energy at Chalk River. The rest had resigned, accepting the demands of their colleagues for a system of elected chairs. Some of the resignations came in the midst of the SFU revolution of 1968 and some in the following year, all in the aftermath of McTaggart-Cowan's forced departure. A factor in that crisis of the summer of 1968 was the composition of the original group of heads.

Seven of the eleven originals were British. The first time that the president of SFU met with a group of his heads was in London, at the London School of Economics, in September 1964, an unusual beginning for a new Canadian university.[52] As a legacy of a colonial past, most Canadian universities still had a core of British faculty; but by 1964–65, it was a small core. (Twenty years earlier, UBC's faculty had been more than 80 per cent Canadian, and if that proportion was dropping, it was with the addition of Americans as well as British.[53]) The SFU heads were a diverse group in style, character and experience, but their Britishness struck many of the faculty that they hired, especially the Americans—in spite of the considerable North American experience that three of them had.

Bottomore, Cunningham, Harrop and MacPherson came directly to SFU from Britain. But Pate had studied in Canada and the U.S. and had taught in the U.S. Baker had taken most of his post-secondary education in Canada and had taught at UBC for over a decade. Bursill-Hall had been teaching at UBC since 1949. Like nearly every faculty member that they recruited, the original heads were attracted by the possibility of doing things differently at a new university; and collectively they were open to experiment and change. Heads like Allan Cunningham explored the city and the province with great zest in the months before their faculty arrived, and became their guides to the city when they first settled in. From the outside, however, the heads could look like a closed club. McTaggart-Cowan, with his Oxford degree and Scottish family background, tended to blend in. Little things reinforced the impression: for example, McTaggart-Cowan drew Klaus Reickhoff aside, during Reickhoff's time as acting dean of Science, to let him know that a sweater was not appropriate dress for a meeting of the Committee of Heads.[54]

Terms of appointment for heads at sFU—at the pleasure of the board with no fixed term—were standard in Canada at the time. (UBC did not begin electing chairs until well into the 1970s.[55]) And that did not seem remarkable to British academics used to permanent chairs or heads of departments at British universities. Americans were more familiar with elected chairs who served limited terms, although the practice was neither as universal nor as established as some of them thought. The American Association of University Professors had surveyed 177 American colleges and universities back in 1940. The findings showed that presidents and boards at 80 per cent of these places did not consult faculty before appointing department heads. The Columbia University historian Richard Hofstadter, when he surveyed the scene in the early 1950s, had the impression that nothing much had changed. But by the mid-1960s, a predominantly American faculty at sFU saw the system of permanent heads as British; and they saw the heads themselves as people who did not know how a North American university should operate. What no one quite comprehended was how quickly things were changing and how little anyone knew what the standard practice was.[56]

THE CULTURE OF THE PhD

The British heads were concentrated in the Faculty of Arts; and this was the faculty that absorbed the largest number and the greatest percentage of Americans. Everyone at sFU got a hasty education in differences in the British, American and Canadian academic traditions. The PhD was one illustration. At American universities, the PhD or the "ABD" (all but dissertation) was the assumed entry-level qualification for university teaching, and this had increasingly become the case in Canada since the 1940s. Among British academics lingered a dismissive attitude towards the PhD: that it was a specialized degree for the earnest and possibly second-rate academic—something that Americans and Canadians wanted and that British universities provided for foreigners, more than for their own students. If you were really talented, you did not need it. Tom Bottomore was an outstanding scholar in the British tradition without a PhD. Archie MacPherson had been teaching with an MA that at Edinburgh was an honorary degree granted automatically after an earned BA. And Ron Baker's success at UBC with an MA and an abandoned PhD was evidence that the British attitude persisted in Canada.[57]

With the culture of the PhD came an expectation of scholarly production. American universities had travelled down this road much earlier and further than Canadian. In the U.S., the dividing line between the top forty or fifty universities and the rest was measured in graduate teaching and research programs.[58] Where undergraduate teaching was the main focus, research and publication got less emphasis. Canadian universities, like the British, put undergraduate education front and centre and expected less in scholarly publication. But a post war emphasis on research was having a profound effect. Even in the pure sciences, Canadian universities had done little research before the war; but this had changed, especially with the increase in research funding directed to the universities.

Shrum had looked for department heads with research reputations, and he made sure he got them in the sciences, particularly Physics and Biological Sciences. But he had no question in his mind about SFU's primary mission—undergraduate teaching. He knew that was what the provincial government was paying for; and he was clear in his own mind that research institutes devoted to research alone, which one could find in abundance at major American universities, had no place at SFU. Shrum was one of those who did not like the increased emphasis on research at North American universities; and he was happy to offer his views in a national magazine. "I sometimes feel," he wrote in *Saturday Night* shortly after SFU opened, "that there should be some penalty imposed upon those who clutter up the literature of their subject with mediocre publications produced either by contract research or under the pressure of a misguided university policy of 'publish or perish.'" It was important to Shrum that a faculty member should be a researcher because it made him or her a better teacher. But teaching was the mission.[59]

In the publicity they generated about SFU, Shrum, Baker and McTaggart-Cowan got across the message that this would be a university where teaching came first. This looked refreshing to many Americans coming onto the job market, with newly earned PhDs or with ABDS, having heard enough or read enough about the "publish or perish" regime that was said to dominate the first-rank American universities. Shrum's notion of the relationship between teaching and research was probably shared by most of the early faculty at SFU. That did not mean that the "publish or perish" yardsticks had been thrown away. Instead, one had some junior faculty looking critically at the publication records of their heads and finding them wanting.

TEACHER TRAINING AT SFU

Shrum, along with Baker and McTaggart-Cowan, wanted an Education program at SFU that broke with the UBC model. Education, or teacher training, was one of the many subjects on which Shrum had a strong opinion; and he did not like what he knew of it at UBC. There were people in Education there whom he did respect, but the emphasis, he believed, was wrong: too much time on teaching methods and educational psychology and not enough on academic subjects.[60] This was the former head of Physics who believed that to teach a subject you needed to have a specialized knowledge of it.

Shrum had been watching the evolution of teacher training in Canada for a long time. When he had finished secondary school in Hamilton, Ontario, on the eve of the First World War, teacher training had been offered at the University of Toronto for only a few years, and only for secondary school teachers. Nearly everywhere else in the country, teacher training was the function of one- or two-year normal schools, the traditional name for a teachers' college. Primary-school teachers attended normal school after high school and high-school teachers went to normal school after university. For many of Shrum's high-school classmates in 1913–14, further education meant either university or normal school, and for those without the money or without the grades, it was the latter.[61]

British Columbia, following Alberta's example, closed its two normal schools (in Vancouver and Victoria) in the mid-1950s and moved the teacher training programs to the university, to UBC and its affiliated college at Victoria. This became a nation-wide pattern; and it supported two developments already well advanced in the U.S. One was the upgrading of teachers' credentials, and the other was the growth of the science of pedagogy. In the normal schools, teacher training had little theory behind it. Students learned something of child development and child psychology, but spent much of their time going over the subject matter they were going to teach, reviewing grade-four arithmetic or grade-five social studies, and learning how to do lesson plans and keep a daybook. In 1962, when B.C. and Alberta already had the highest standards in the country for elementary teachers, B.C. raised the bar again—requiring three years of degree work before an elementary teacher could get a permanent certificate to teach. At that point, only one elementary teacher in four had a degree, but many of the others were taking summer and extension courses.[62] No one was arguing against teachers staying longer at university, but Shrum was not alone in questioning the substitution of pedagogy for arts and science courses in the BEd degree that UBC introduced in 1956.

Teacher training in the new Education programs at UBC and Victoria came under sharp criticism from a Royal Commission on Education chaired by UBC's dean of Arts and Science, Sperrin Chant. The report was three years old when planning began for SFU, but it was not forgotten. Chant and his fellow commissioners found student teachers disturbingly unenthusiastic about their Education courses—complaining that they were dull and repetitive—while these same students were excited about the opportunity they got (limited as it was) to go into schools for practice teaching. One solution, the Chant Commission offered, would be to insert a one-year teaching internship between the first and second year of the Education program.[63]

The shaping of SFU's approach to this involved Ron Baker, the academic planner, Archie MacKinnon, the first dean of Education, and John Ellis, who became the first director of SFU's Education Development Program. Ellis remembers many Sunday afternoons in conversation with MacKinnon over coffee and cigarettes at a café across the street from the SFU offices at 970 Dunsmuir Street. This was in the months before Ellis had agreed to come to SFU from UBC.[64] From these conversations, the SFU approach materialized: student teachers would go into the schools for four months at a time, and would have more than a semester of practice under their belts before spending a full semester on theory. This was a refinement of the one-year internship idea in the Chant Commission report. The essential idea was that theory made more sense when it followed experience.

ARCHIE MACKINNON AND EDUCATION

Shrum saw the dean of Education as one of the most important early appointments that SFU would make. He began asking about prospects when he was still searching for a president, and long before he looked for candidates for the Physics, Biological Sciences and Chemistry headships.[65] He knew that preparing teachers for elementary and secondary schools was going to be one of SFU's central missions. In the early 1960s, about 30 per cent of UBC's students planned to go into teaching: two-thirds of them were in Education and one-third in Arts and Science.[66] At SFU, the proportion would be higher because SFU would not be offering Law, Medicine, Nursing, Pharmacy, Dentistry, Forestry or Engineering. Given the existing criticism of the UBC Education program, SFU had an opportunity to make a reputation for itself, and Shrum was aware of it. The formal involvement of John F.K. English, the deputy minister of education, on the interview committee tells us how important this decision was seen to be. If SFU was going to bring in a dean to shake up teacher education in B.C., it was going to be with the concurrence of the person at the top of the provincial education system.

SFU found Archie MacKinnon thanks to the first head of Biological Sciences, Don Nelson. The two of them had known each other while attending normal school in the small Ontario city of Stratford. (MacKinnon was from a farming community near Lake Huron, and Nelson was from Stratford.) Both had taught elementary school and then gone to Queen's University in Kingston. MacKinnon later completed a PhD in Education at Edinburgh. In 1964 he was director of research for the Toronto Board of Education and on leave for twelve months as a visiting professor at Harvard. Nelson mentioned him during his own interview for the Biological Sciences headship, and Baker and McTaggart-Cowan immediately phoned him. SFU had other candidates under consideration, but MacKinnon made such a positive impression during his interview that the others paled by comparison. MacKinnon, however, was more of a gamble than the interview committee appreciated. Most of his teaching, aside from his year at Harvard, had been at a normal school in North Bay, Ontario, and that stifling environment was the main incubator of his breakout ideas on education.[67]

John Ellis, who saw a lot of MacKinnon when they put the teacher training program together, described him as a very interesting guy, but admitted that people found him hard to follow. "He could make the simple obscure, but at times he made the obscure simple." In the judgement of Ken Strand, who had to deal with a radical revision of MacKinnon's education curriculum when he was president, MacKinnon could not explain clearly to the university community what his Education curriculum actually was. The problem was a speaking style that seldom gave a succinct answer.[68]

MacKinnon arrived at SFU quoting Alfred North Whitehead on the aims of education and "the seamless coat of learning."[69] At a practical level, that meant integrating elementary- and secondary-school programs and treating elementary teaching as a specialization rather than a second-class vocation (as normal school training had implied). But MacKinnon's thinking was larger than this; and here people had difficulty grasping what he was talking about. He was reaching beyond the compartments of elementary, secondary, university and adult education; and this led him to assemble a mini-university within the Education faculty and to put a lot of emphasis on informal teaching.

MacKinnon built his faculty around five programs: one practical (Professional Development or teacher training); and four that defied categorization but were described as Behavioural Science, Social and Philosophical Studies, Physical Development, and Communication and the Arts. He had the grand idea that the permanent faculty in the other four programs would function as a resource for the teacher training program. They could offer special lectures, give workshops and give guidance to individual students to supplement required courses. It didn't work; and one explanation was that the faculty, as a group, had trouble figuring out what they could do for student teachers. Under MacKinnon's system, the people most directly involved in teacher training were the faculty associates who were teachers on loan from the schools.

The Faculty of Education did offer many non-credit activities and elective courses for the whole university student population. The Physical Development Centre, for example, ran the university's intercollegiate and intramural sports programs, and recreational activities like swimming, dance and weightlifting, as well as recreation clubs, while offering physical development studies—which had courses on human anatomy and health as well as human motor behaviour. But the Faculty of Education had only a couple of required courses of its own and its students did most of their undergraduate work in the Arts and Science faculties. Without many scheduled classes of their own, MacKinnon's Education professors did not do much teaching, or not much that could be measured.

Yet Education was a happening place. Under MacKinnon, the Faculty of Education brought some of the most stimulating and memorable contributors to the SFU scene. These included Murray Schafer and Jack Behrens in music, Iain Baxter in visual arts and John Juliani and Michael Bawtree in theatre—all resident artists located in the Faculty of Education. Schafer introduced the world to the notion of the "soundscape" and "acoustic ecology" during his ten years at SFU. Baxter's influence as a conceptual artist, particularly through the NE Thing C., dates from his time at SFU. John Juliani launched his experimental Savage God Theatre Company while he was at SFU.

The outline of MacKinnon's grand design survived for a half dozen years before pressure from inside and outside the Faculty of Education forced a complete overhaul. Concerns about costs and about faculty who did little teaching, objections to duplication and a general failure to see why all these programs were in Education were factors in this overhaul. Several units were eliminated and some of their people moved out of Education and into new departments in a new Faculty of Interdisciplinary Studies.

One major objection to MacKinnon's programs was the cost of their non-credit activities. In terms of students graduated, the Faculty of Education appeared extravagant. The answer that the university eventually found was to create conventional departments or schools that offered courses for credit. That was a practical step, but it was also a step away from the idea that a university education involved more than courses taken for credit.

The great and lasting success was the year-long Professional Development Program, headed by John Ellis, which got students into schools within six weeks and allocated half their total time for practice teaching. The essential idea was that pedagogical theory had more meaning for students once they had teaching experience. By the time they started their last semester they had spent a semester and a half in the schools. Similar thinking lay behind the co-op program in Engineering at Waterloo, which had been operating since 1957, although there was no direct influence. MacKinnon brought some ideas from the Harvard–Newton Summer Institute with which he was familiar from his year at Harvard. The SFU program, however, was a joint creation by MacKinnon and Ellis.

Ellis was one of the very few early faculty members at SFU who had been born in Vancouver. This made him "an oddity," he recalled. He had gone to normal school and taught at a rural elementary school before earning a BA at UBC and becoming one of the youngest school principals in the Vancouver area. In 1956, when the two normal schools in B.C. closed and UBC took over elementary- as well as secondary-school teacher training, he became an instructor in the UBC Faculty of Education. Subsequently he finished an MEd at UBC and a PhD at Berkeley. He was an associate professor of Education at UBC when he began the conversations with MacKinnon that led to his appointment at SFU. He had two main criticisms of the Faculty of Education at UBC. One was that students needed to get into classrooms sooner and for longer. The second was that the faculty, like Ellis himself, were former teachers who year by year became more removed from their classroom experience. The solution that Ellis and MacKinnon produced was to borrow teachers from the schools for a year or two only. These are the faculty associates whose service to teacher training at SFU has been vital from the beginning.

DOING THINGS DIFFERENTLY AT SFU

An interview with Ron Baker in the spring of 1965 became the text for a small promotional pamphlet used to recruit SFU's first students.[70] The interviewer was the *Vancouver Sun*'s education writer, John Arnett. SFU was going to be different, Baker told Arnett, first of all because it was not going to insist on the standard core of compulsory subjects. Students would not be required to take English or a foreign language or a science. If they took any of these subjects it would be by choice. Second, SFU was going to achieve both quality and efficiency by combining large lectures with small tutorials and seminars (an idea that Shrum had had from the beginning). Third, SFU would take the emphasis off exams: some courses might have final exams but in others the grades would be based on term work. Fourth, SFU would admit students who did not meet the normal requirements: bright students who had not yet finished high school and mature students who did not have the standard entrance qualifications, but who could be judged good prospects by other measures. Finally, SFU was going to have a radically new system of teacher training.

In the planning of the SFU curriculum, Baker had been opposed to English, foreign language and science requirements. Here he differed with Shrum, and their argument had lasted for weeks before Baker prevailed. Shrum said he had been embarrassed when accompanied on foreign trade missions by Canadians who could not speak a foreign language; and he was appalled by the written English of university graduates. (Shrum was a grammarian who would compulsively circle errors in incoming letters, including those from his president, McTaggart-Cowan.) Baker's telling reply was that these problems existed despite the compulsory English and foreign language that all Canadian university students took. There had to be a better way. Making students take subjects in which they were not interested dragged everyone down.

Baker was speaking from experience because he had taught the required English courses for engineers, architects and forestry students at UBC. He also proceeded from an assumption common among English professors at Canadian universities: they taught literature and composition as a single subject, rather than separately as had become the practice at many American universities. In their classes, students improved their writing while reading and writing about English literature. English was a large department everywhere because it was a required subject in many professional programs as well as in the arts and sciences. And it was required because people saw it as utilitarian: engineers, foresters and accountants all needed to be able to write. Generally, English professors did not enjoy freshman grammar and composition classes; and Baker reasoned that English ought not carry the sole responsibility for teaching writing. It belonged to History and Philosophy and every subject in which students wrote essays.

Shrum was the person who pushed the use of large lectures and small tutorials and seminars; but Baker knew what it was about because that was how engineers had been taught English at UBC. It was in fact a standard way of teaching at some Canadian universities, particularly Toronto, although Baker and Shrum seem not to have been aware of it. Shrum's ideal would have been to have lectures given by the university's star faculty for five hundred to a thousand students. The tutorials and seminars, he imagined, could be handled by undergraduate and graduate students and by qualified part-timers: housewives trapped at home with first-rate degrees. He thought it would be a good idea to give second- and third-year students the opportunity to tutor freshmen; and he believed that by the time students were in their fourth year, they could tutor those in the second and third. Fourth-year classes could be taken by graduate students. The system would be economical because it would require fewer faculty. It would expose students to the best: lecturers who, as he put it, could light a fire and not just fill a vacuum. And he believed that the chance to teach would be good for undergraduates. "I know from personal experience that one never understands a subject completely until one has taught it."[71]

Perhaps we should discount some of what Shrum said because he liked to be contentious and he knew that the large lecture system had many opponents. The largest lecture hall that he built at SFU would seat 504, so there would be no lectures for a thousand students. Baker, who was more directly involved with scheduling and class planning, assumed that tutorials and seminars would be covered by graduate students and part-timers. Although undergraduates have been used occasionally, SFU has never set about systematically to employ them as tutors.

When SFU opened, tutorials and seminars were limited to fifteen students each (Allan Cunningham, who was more familiar with the lecture/tutorial system than most of the other founding heads, had suggested a maximum of ten to twelve). Over the last forty years, faculties and departments have raised that limit considerably, progressively converting a tutorial system into one of the larger and less intimate classes. This has been an almost inevitable outcome of course proliferation and a decline in the average size of lecture classes.

In the first year the system operated more or less as Baker had conceived it. Very quickly, however, as departments divided their students among more and more courses, the large lecture idea went out the window, except at the introductory level. Even there it was quickly compromised. At the third- and fourth-year level, some departments abandoned lectures altogether, allowing their faculty to offer a variety of specialized seminars. Because seminars were limited in size, professors never saw more than fifteen fourth-year students at a time. This was not what Shrum had been talking about.

Although it was not his intention, Baker's de-emphasis on final exams undermined the lecture system, especially in the senior courses. At Canadian universities, final exams (taken during the last two or three weeks of the academic year) had long been the measure of student performance. Term work based on essays, or lab reports and mid-year tests, counted for only a small portion of the final grade. Baker, with the backing of the Committee of Heads, opened up the possibility of no exams at all and grades based just on term work. That tended to shift weight from the lectures, which were no longer so vital for marks, to the tutorials and seminars, where most of the marks were earned. Not everyone wished to get rid of exams and one of Baker's objections to them—that they took too much time out of the academic calendar—proved irrelevant because SFU ended up scheduling as many weeks for this purpose as any other university.

Tutorials and seminars with an emphasis on term work became the SFU way. The contrast with a large American university was exciting for a graduate student like Steve Duguid, who arrived at SFU in 1967. He had a BA in history from Illinois, where he could not remember a class with fewer than one hundred students in it and where, in four and a half years, he actually got to know one faculty member.[72] The SFU system was also far removed from undergraduate education in Britain. McTaggart-Cowan's experience at Oxford in the 1930s still described what one could expect in the 1960s. At Oxford, where a student's standing depended on a set of exams taken after three years, there was lots of time for extracurricular activity. Things got serious as final exams approached, but until then there was room for diversions. McTaggart-Cowan was conscious of three parts to his Oxford life: his personal contact with the scholars there, particularly his tutor; his formal study in preparation for the exams, and his involvement in student associations and sports. Most of his studying he did between terms, when he stayed south of London, in Surrey, with an aunt and uncle in a large house with servants.[73] When he was at Oxford, studying was at the bottom of his list. This was a gentleman's education, which SFU never attempted to provide. In this education, university was a total experience granted to young people in the expectation that if they had three years to mingle with scholars and other students, as well as to study, they would emerge as more thoughtful and mature human beings.

Canadian universities were then offering a modification of the Oxford experience. They gave final exams every year rather than at the end of three; but students had lots of opportunity to avoid study until the last panicked weeks of the spring. The examination results ruled, and students either went on to the next year or were held back. Students who entered in 1962 could be expected to graduate in 1966 or, if they missed a year, in 1967, and they moved through their program as a group. SFU struck out in a new direction, not just with its emphasis on term work but also with the introduction of credit hours and grade-point averages. These innovations made it easier to track the records of students who followed individualized programs and completed their degrees at varying speeds. They were necessary tools for a university on a trimester system, although they moved SFU away from a traditional notion of what a university education involved. A degree became 120 credit hours rather than three or four years of study.

Since the 1960s, Canadian universities have adopted various credit-hour and grade-point-average systems. In 1965 they were widely used in the U.S., but not in Canada; and SFU was in the forefront in writing them into its calendar. One might wonder how life went on without them. The answer is that it was simple when there were few or no part-time students, when nearly every student took a full set of courses and when students either passed a year and advanced, or failed and repeated. Baker, when he first broached the notion of credit hours at SFU, explained it as a system of course accounting that should be treated as a guide to the amount of work courses entailed and not an exact record of hours spent in class. It took scarcely a decade, however, for that understanding to disappear and for faculty committees to begin to insist that credit hours should equate with hours in class.

Saskatchewan and Memorial were the first Canadian universities with highly developed grade-point-average systems. In 1964, Alberta, Toronto, Western, Queen's and Acadia had rudimentary systems and McGill, Manitoba and New Brunswick had none at all.[74] Where there was no grade point average, students could graduate by simply passing all of their courses. It is probably no coincidence that as enrolments began to skyrocket, universities began to question a practice that allowed graduates to leave the university with a bare pass in every subject. The answer was to require an average grade well above a pass, and that was the genesis of the grade-point system. The same system proved a useful standard to use with part-time students—who did not have the challenge of completing a full slate of subjects at the same time, but who could be required to do better than a minimal pass in each course they took.

The SFU program worked well for mature students, and one factor was its accommodation of part-time attendance. Shrum had promised a flexible admissions policy that Baker and the Committee of Heads readily supported. Baker himself had been a mature student at UBC who got in as a veteran after being out of school from the age of fifteen. He knew that UBC and other universities did on occasion make allowances for older students. SFU was different mainly because it made this possibility better known. Baker himself had been surprised by the reaction he got to an interview he did with Adrienne Clarkson, then the host of the CBC daytime television program *Take Thirty.* He mentioned mature admissions, and the CBC as well as SFU received a flood of phone calls and letters from across the country from people who had not imagined that this was possible.[75]

SFU's distinctiveness was also evident in its handling of an honours program modelled on what was done at UBC. The early calendars gave it a prominent display, which it has long since lost, although it remains an option for students to the present. The honours program at Canadian universities offered a more specialized and intensive degree than the general or pass or majors program. Many bright students went through the general program and many not so bright went through honours. The difference was that honours gave a more thorough and extensive grounding in a single discipline. At most Canadian universities it took an extra year, although at UBC and McGill it was not longer than the general degree but required more work.

The honours degree was the standard Canadian requirement for entry into graduate school; and honours classes were the ones faculty preferred to teach. They provided the opportunity that at most American schools existed only at the graduate level, and that was to go further into a subject with students who were seriously specializing in it. If one had asked Canadian professors then how they ranked the honours degree, the chances are that they would—accurately or not—have put it at the level of the American MA. When George Whalley was considering the move from Queen's to SFU, one of his insistent points was that SFU should have an honours program: he did not want to give up his honours students.

Most of the Canadians that SFU hired in the early years had come through honours. But for their colleagues from the U.S., the specialized honours degree was a novelty. (A few American universities had introduced honours with tutorials to cater to their better students, but they were exceptional.) And although British universities distinguished between honours and pass students, and invested more time and effort with the former than the latter, their programs were even more specialized than Canadian. All of this meant that the honours program was not well understood by most faculty at SFU. And the name and idea were also out of tune with the times. No Canadian university had made more of the honours program than Toronto, and faculty there were proud of it to the end. But Toronto threw it out in 1967 after a student–faculty committee found fault with it, not because it was a poor program—they recognized its merits—but because the distinction between honours and general made the general students feel bad.[76] At Toronto a century-old tradition died in the ferment of the 1960s. The fact that the honours program survived at SFU tells us that it never had a high enough profile to become objectionable.

FUNDRAISING

SFU opened as the favoured child of the conservative Social Credit government of W.A.C. Bennett. In the spring of 1964, Bennett was pumping money into SFU to get its construction underway, while UBC waited for funding for the expansion that the Macdonald Report had said it needed. Understandably, faculty and administration at UBC began to comment on the absence of any system or order in the allocation of capital funds. They thought a university grants commission was needed to distribute funds in a rational way. Why was there such a rush to get SFU going if the government was not going to take care of UBC as well?

Fortunately, the premier and the minister of education did have a sense of the larger picture and UBC did get its funding. This, however, meant working with SFU and the University of Victoria. In June 1964 all three B.C. universities joined forces in a common fundraising campaign. While speaking in Toronto, UBC's President Macdonald described this campaign as an exceptional example of co-operation among universities. What he did not mention was the leading role that SFU played as a consequence of its favoured status with the government.

Shrum's opening position and that of the SFU board was that Victoria and UBC should delay their campaigns so that the public would not have three universities knocking on doors at the same time.[77] UBC came back with the statesmanlike suggestion that they work together. Although UBC, with graduates distributed throughout the B.C. corporate sector and the moneyed elements of B.C. society, had every advantage in going after private funds, it did not have the easiest path to Premier Bennett's office. When the three presidents met—and working out a deal took several meetings—they gathered at McTaggart-Cowan's suite at 570 Dunsmuir. McTaggart-Cowan chaired the meetings and negotiated with the government on behalf of them all. The two people who agreed to spearhead the campaign, Cyrus McLean, chair of B.C. Telephone, and Allan McGavin, a prominent local businessman and amateur athletics supporter, were recruited by SFU; and the national canvassing company employed by the combined campaign was chosen by SFU, although the choice was the same company that had handled UBC's last capital fund drive back in 1958.[78]

What Premier Bennett finally approved, in June 1964, was a government commitment to the three universities of $40,700,000 in capital funds over five years, while they jointly raised $28 million in the private sector. Victoria would get 16 per cent and SFU and UBC would split the balance, 42 per cent each. The agreement met the projected needs of all three universities.

The agreement also allowed SFU to draw the first $4 million. The SFU timetable gave the fundraisers less time for preparation than they normally took. It was a success nonetheless; with individuals, foundations and B.C. corporations (and their head offices in Toronto and Montreal) responding generously to the call. The funding and construction timetables came together to produce a university that on opening day still looked like a construction site on the outside, but that was nearly finished on the inside. The president, registrar, bursar and English, Geography and History department heads had been able to move into their offices a month earlier, although when they did, McTaggart-Cowan still had an electrician crawling on the floor behind his desk.

The road from the south side, from the Lougheed Highway and the Cariboo/Stormont Interchange, was not finished and would not be for another three months; in the meantime everyone made their way around to Curtis Street to arrive from the east. The sound of jackhammers and bulldozers still reverberated. Some offices and classrooms were unfurnished; and the bookstore had no shelves. On opening day, registration was a shambles; but when it was completed, 2,578 students were enrolled—above all expectations.

The head of the Fraser clan, Lord Lovatt, was a featured guest at the opening-day ceremony in the mall. He had flown in from Scotland at the university's expense to be presented with one of its first two honorary degrees. (The other went to Premier Bennett.) Lovatt was a war hero who had been portrayed by Peter Lawford in the 1962 film about the D-Day landing, *The Longest Day.* Like all first sons in his lineage, he was named Simon (Simon Christopher Joseph Fraser), so he had the same first name as the explorer who canoed down the Fraser River. McTaggart-Cowan had first contacted Lovatt in 1964 to get his permission to use the Fraser coat of arms and the Fraser motto for SFU— permission that Lovatt had willingly given.

At SFU, Lovatt was a great hit, brandishing a three-hundred-year-old claymore, which he gave to the university along with a powder horn, and beginning his remarks by quoting Marc Antony entering Cleopatra's tent: "I didn't come here to talk." By all accounts he stole the show, and a mistake about his relationship to the explorer seems to have made little difference. In its pre-ceremony publicity, SFU had described Lord Lovatt as a descendant, which he was not. His lineage and the explorer's had diverged about three centuries earlier. Lovatt straightened it out when interviewed by the *Vancouver Sun* education reporter, John Arnett. "But of course," he said, "we are all related by blood lines."[79]

During the ceremony, Arnett found another Fraser sitting unnoticed in the audience. His name was Donald Fraser and he was a postmaster from Fargo, North Dakota, who had come with his wife at his own expense. He was a great-great-grandson of the explorer, and that morning he had quietly given the university some Simon Fraser memorabilia— letters, an inventory, a picture and some embroidery done by Simon Fraser's widow. Donald Fraser had been corresponding with the university about this donation before making the trip; but he neither expected nor got any fuss or special attention.[80] The objective on opening day was to have a show, and that was a war hero wielding a claymore, not a postmaster with old letters. An honorary degree for a coat of arms was a fair exchange. Still, looking back, and knowing the kind of university SFU became, the lionizing of Lord Lovatt seems incongruous, and very much a McTaggart-Cowan kind of idea.

4

Berkeley North

CHAOS AT REGISTRATION TIME

In the rush and confusion before opening day in 1965, the Simon Fraser University registrar lost complete control of the registration process. Nobody knew how many students were enrolled or what classes they were in. The registrar was locked in his office and refusing to answer the phone. Shrum had picked him because he had been effective running the physics lab at University of B.C., but he had little experience in a registrar's office. During the first week of classes, the newspapers carried brief reports that he had resigned for health reasons caused by stress. By then a group of department heads had gone into his office to try to straighten it out. They had found empty files, boxes of applications waiting for attention, and bundles of uncashed cheques as much as a month old.[1]

The person McTaggart-Cowan called on to take over was Lolita (Letty) Wilson, the dean of women. On the third day of classes, she arrived on campus to teach her course in Psychology (she was also an associate professor), and she left that day as acting registrar. This position she filled for four months until SFU brought D.P. (Pat) Robertson from the University of Waterloo. Letty Wilson had been hired as dean of women on the recommendation of Don Baird, the librarian. They had first met at UBC, when she went back to study as an army veteran. Subsequently they had known each other at the University of Alberta, where he worked in the library and she was deputy director of counselling services. When Baker and McTaggart-Cowan recruited her, she was dubious about the dean of women position because she thought it antiquated. But a job on the west coast was enticing and she accepted. After a couple of years she convinced the president and the board to make her dean of student affairs and the dean of women position lapsed.

When Letty Wilson took over the registrar's office, she had no satisfactory record of the students registered or of the classes they were in. She chose not to advertise this, but to quietly rectify the problem. What she did, a few weeks into the semester, was to ask students to fill out forms for the final exams. In actuality, she was re-registering them, finding out how many there were and what courses they were in and entering the data on the computer for the first time. On opening day, Gordon Shrum had announced an enrolment of 2,207.[2] Letty Wilson's re-registration established the count at 2,528.

THE STUDENTS WHO CHOSE SFU

Thanks to Letty Wilson it is possible, forty years later, to construct a statistical profile of SFU's early student population. When she re-registered students in October of 1965, she gave them a demographic form to complete; and as dean she administered the same form in subsequent semesters. It asked about age, sex, place of high school, year of last high-school attendance, citizenship, religion and parents' occupations. In the early years of SFU, she also conducted employment, housing and transportation surveys as well as a study of student withdrawals. Her primary objective was to assess students' needs and requirements, but her work is helpful now in indicating who the students were who chose SFU.

The campus had been built for the eastern part of metropolitan Vancouver and located according to a calculation of driving distances. When President John Barfoot Macdonald of UBC wrote his report recommending the creation of SFU, he was thinking of a convenient central point for commuting students. However, Letty Wilson's surveys suggest that proximity was not a consideration for a great many. One learns this by talking to former students.

Stan Wong, who is now a Vancouver lawyer specializing in competition law and commercial litigation, was one of SFU's most prominent and active citizens during its first four years: at various times he was a student ombudsman, student president, contributor to the student newspaper and student senator; and on graduation he was a Woodrow Wilson fellowship winner. In the fall of 1965 he, along with his older brothers Ed and Fred, chose SFU because what he read in the press—particularly the appointments of Rudi Haering in Physics, Don Nelson in Biological Sciences, Geoffrey Bursill-Hall in Modern Languages and Tom Bottomore in Politics, Sociology & Anthropology (PSA)—made SFU seem like a centre of learning that was going places. In Wong's case, Shrum's penchant for publicity worked. Wong had also checked SFU out. Before enrolling, he had visited the auditorium of North Burnaby Secondary, where SFU's heads and deans had temporarily set up shop, each with a desk, two chairs and a filing cabinet, waiting for the move to the Burnaby Mountain campus. There he had seen the head of Economics, Parzival Copes, and had found him most persuasive.

Wong, when he left Vancouver Technical Secondary, was not a typical Vancouver secondary-school graduate. His father was a University of Toronto graduate and an industrial development consultant who had worked abroad for the Columbo Plan, the International Labour Organization (ILO), the UN Food and Agriculture Organization and other international aid agencies. Stan Wong had spent his grade-ten year in Malaysia and his grade-eleven year in Singapore. By the time he was eighteen he had lived seven years of his life overseas, in Hong Kong, Burma, India and Pakistan as well as Malaysia and Singapore. When he started university, his father took a posting with the ILO and his parents moved to Geneva. For their university years, Stan and his brothers maintained the family home in east Vancouver, cooking and eating together. In Letty Wilson's survey, they would have fallen under the category of "living at home," but it was living at home without parents.[3]

SFU attracted students who were not inclined to follow a crowd. Jane Martin and Norma Marier were among them. Both were charter students. After graduation, Martin spent a dozen years in a management position off campus but came back to complete an MBA and then found an administrative job at SFU. Marier has worked for years in the SFU library. Martin and Marier remember that they did not want to be among the "snobby kids" from West Vancouver going to UBC and were attracted by the adventure of attending a brand-new university. The others in their car pool thought the same way. At SFU, Martin learned to suppress the fact that she was from West Vancouver with its upper-middle-class connotations.[4] Working-class origins were a badge of honour at SFU, although claiming them was a stretch for more than half of the students who turned up there.

When SFU opened, British Columbia, as a comparatively wealthy and heavily urbanized province, had the highest university participation rate in Canada. (It cannot make that claim today.) But this participation rate was still only one student-aged person in eight.[5] The rate for females was even lower. At SFU in its first year, 62 per cent of those attending were male and 38 per cent were female. Students like Martin and Marier were enjoying an opportunity that was available to very few contemporary young women. When SFU students gave their fathers' occupations, 35.8 per cent said self-employed businessman, 16.4 per cent said doctor, lawyer, engineer or other professional, and 28.2 per cent said electrician, plumber or other skilled tradesman. Only 11.5 per cent said unskilled. Significantly, at a time when most married women stayed home, 10 per cent of SFU's first generation of students reported professional occupations for their mothers and 13 per cent reported self-employed businesswoman.

In most cases, these students were able to complete their degrees as full-time students with their parents paying their way or with scholarships, bursaries, loans and semesters off for employment. Just over a third had part-time jobs while they were students. In many instances it was a matter of pocket money rather than survival. The job prospects for student-aged women were especially limited and low paying, although they took part-time work in the same proportion as the men. What they earned in a few hours a week as cashiers and retail clerks gave them cash for clothing and entertainment but not much else. More than 60 per cent of the student population attended without taking outside employment, at least during their semesters on campus. For a few, studying every semester without a break was a financial possibility, even if it took a mental toll.

About half of the students at SFU in the 1960s were living with their parents. This is a low figure for what was intended as a commuter campus. (In contrast, 80 to 90 per cent of the students at Vancouver's new community colleges lived at home.[6]) When it opened, SFU had accommodation for only 65 women at Madge Hogarth House. Shell House, completed in 1967, took another 159 men and women; and Louis Riel House, finished in September 1969, offered 209 apartments for married students.[7]

Inevitably, at the beginning of each semester, hundreds of students scrambled for off-campus places—rooms, apartments and shared houses or co-ops—and found it difficult to get anything within close commuting distance. Well into September each year, many were still in motels and hotels. When it opened, the university had no housing service (no one had thought of it), and students fended for themselves. Five months later, Dean Wilson suggested putting up a bulletin board for housing; and by the end of the second semester the university had a housing service. There one could survey a list of rooms for rent: $75–$90 a month for room, board and laundry (with no ironing) and perhaps a packed lunch thrown in; $30 or $40 for a sleeping room; $40 each for a group of ten male students renting a house together, and another $35 for food. We should remember that coffee then cost 10 cents a cup and bus fare was 35 cents. Burnaby had few apartments in the 1960s, and those that existed were generally in four- or five-storey walk-up buildings. Nonetheless, more students elected to share rent for apartments or houses than took rooms in private homes.[8]

Rooms and apartments were in demand because so many SFU students came from out of town. SFU did well recruiting in the region it was supposed to serve—east Vancouver and the municipalities of North Vancouver, Burnaby, New Westminster, Coquitlam, Maple Ridge, Delta and Surrey. In Burnaby's three high schools, about two-thirds of those going on to university chose SFU over UBC. But SFU's appeal reached far. In fact, only 36 per cent of the students who chose this new university came from within its intended territory. As one would expect, on Vancouver's affluent west side and in West Vancouver, UBC was the first choice of the majority, but it wasn't the only choice, and for every three students who headed for the older, established university, there was a fourth, like Jane Martin or Norma Marier, who preferred the new. The fall 1965 sfu student directory contained a surprising number of addresses within twenty city blocks of the green belt that borders ubc.

Among sfu's charter students were more than seven hundred British Columbians from outside the Vancouver metropolitan area. They came from at least two-thirds of the school districts of the province; and a great many were from the distant reaches of the province. For example, eight were from Fernie near the Alberta border in the south, eleven from Kitimat on the north coast, and four from the Peace River country. In its first year, sfu attracted at least half as many students as ubc from the interior, the north coast and Vancouver Island.[9] That was an achievement given the advantage of size, history and familiarity that ubc had; and it speaks of the instant recognition that sfu achieved.

sfu also attracted a good number of students from outside B.C., particularly from Ontario and Alberta. Out-of-province Canadians made up 15 per cent of the charter student population—a percentage that exceeded many times what was found in typical freshman classes at ubc or Victoria. Norma Marier found a circle of friends from Ontario and, by chance, Kimberley, B.C. In the 1960s, however, sfu students were, culturally and socially, remarkably homogeneous despite geographical differences. Most belonged to mainstream churches: United, Anglican, Roman Catholic, Presbyterian, Lutheran and Baptist. Of those who had no church, or who described themselves as agnostic or atheist (about a quarter), nearly all came from a Christian cultural background.[10] Less than 1 per cent were Jewish. A Sikh, Hindu or Muslim student would have been hard to find, especially among the undergraduates. The last names of sfu's charter students were British or northern European, or in a few cases eastern or southern European. The Asian minority was minuscule, although it included a number of the very best students. In general, sfu students came from an economic middle class, from families that were neither exceptionally wealthy nor poor. In fact, these students conformed well to a mid-section profile of English-speaking Canada at the time. What made them exceptional was their choice of an experimental new university.

This was Letty Wilson's analysis based on her statistical evidence and the campus environment that she was observing. "When you planned the university," she wrote to McTaggart-Cowan in a memo accompanying her charts and graphs, "you built a magnet whose strength you may have underestimated."[11] She had in mind what she had assimilated from research reports on student activism as it had emerged in North America in the mid-1960s. SFU was born with an image that was bound to attract students who were likely to become activists. This image included its promise of innovation, academic excellence and openness. Shrum boasted that SFU, in the twenty-nine months before it opened, got more national publicity than all five of the new Ontario universities combined.[12] The architecture, the trimester system, the emphasis on teaching, the openness to mature students, the lecture–tutorial system and the faculty appointments that SFU announced all supported an exciting image and drew students, especially in the humanities and social sciences, who were looking for the kind of academic engagement that SFU seemed to offer.

MATURE STUDENTS

SFU's older students also made it a different campus. Colin Yerbury, now SFU's dean of Continuing Studies, started at SFU after working for a few years in the Creston, B.C., area where he grew up. He tried one semester at the University of Alberta in Calgary but left after a brief illness. When he arrived at SFU, looking for more academic excitement than he had discovered at Calgary, he was twenty-two, but he found that in any student crowd, there were generally people older than himself. Nine per cent of the students admitted in the first year had not completed high school and had entered as mature students over the age of twenty-five. And there were older students who for one reason or another had not gone to university after high school graduation and now chose to do so. Twenty per cent of the students that SFU took in its first academic year were twenty-two and over; and they brought with them a lot of experience. Like the veterans who came back to university in 1945, these students did not take everything they were told for granted; and because they had the confidence of a few more years, and had done more, a number of them stepped forward as student leaders.

The point can be illustrated with two of SFU's first three student senators. In 1967 SFU was the first Canadian university to elect students to its senate; and the three elected were Stan Wong, Sharon Yandle and Simon Foulds. Wong was nineteen; but Yandle at twenty-five and

Foulds at twenty-nine were older than most undergraduates. Yandle was among the many young women of her generation who had not gone to university after high school because her family could not afford it. She had worked on several weekly newspapers and then hitchhiked in Europe before going to Australia, where she studied for a year. She went on to New Zealand and had travelled in twenty-two countries by the time she was twenty-four. While abroad she had been active with the World Union of Students. When she started at sfu she was married with two children; and after her marriage broke up she was a single mother coping at a campus without daycare facilities. After her first semester she plunged fully into campus life as a student politician, contributor to the student newspaper, research assistant, and organizer and participant in a great many special events and activities. Few people on campus at the time had a higher profile. In the fall of 1967, when university government was the subject of a national conference at the University of Toronto, she was the novelty, a student senator who stood up to say that anything less than real participation and some real control for students would not do.[13]

Simon Foulds had attended the London Academy of Music and Dramatic Art and had worked in a variety of jobs in journalism, advertising and public relations in Britain and Canada before enrolling in arts at sfu. He was landed immigrant no. 3/SA9249, as he informed his readers in one of his columns in the student newspaper, *The Peak*.[14] In the spring semester of 1967, when he edited *The Peak,* he turned it into a quality production, expanding it to twenty pages, with a magazine section featuring extended reviews of theatre, music and the arts, as well as articles on topics such as the New Left and Canadian economic nationalism. He was an advocate, along with Wong and Yandle, of more student representation, and of more open processes. But he was a moderate activist, willing to proceed step by step.[15]

The first editor of *The Peak,* Sam Steenhuus, was married and in his thirties when he started in arts at sfu.[16] The first president of the Student Society was Tony Buzan, a graduate student in psychology who had completed a double honours at ubc. (Buzan, in his post-sfu career, is best known for the concept of mind mapping.) The ultimate student ombudsman was Ace Hollibaugh, an avowed radical nearing fifty years of age and, in his words, a "shit-kicker." He was re-elected by acclamation three times and stayed in the position for seven semesters. Hollibaugh had been an insurance agent in California. In opposition to the Vietnam War he had given up his job, sold his property and with his wife migrated north to Vancouver in 1968 to live in a trailer in Port Moody while attending PSA classes at SFU.[17]

Hollibaugh was a mentor for Bill Birge, who, in 1969 at the age of thirty-six, decided to attend SFU to become a teacher. Birge had lost his job with the service station department of an oil company; his wife had gone back to work and he had three children, so SFU's fast-track trimester system seemed to be the answer. Birge turned up with his executive crewcut and a three-piece suit for a Senate Appeals Board hearing after being told that his Ontario high-school results were not good enough for admission. He immediately felt out of place when he ran into Ombudsman Hollibaugh, who was wearing a jean jacket and cut-offs, and whose hair was down over his ears. But with Hollibaugh representing him, Birge did get admitted as a mature student. In short order, Birge became a long-haired student himself, experimenting with pot and playing an active role in student politics. After the passage of the B.C. Universities Act of 1974, which allowed student membership on the board of governors, Birge became one of SFU's first two student governors.[18] After graduating from SFU, he went to Athabasca College in Alberta, to become director of facilities and then vice-president.

In 1984 a McMaster University sociologist, Cyril Levitt, published the classic study of Canadian student activism in the 1960s. Levitt also looked at student activism in the U.S. and West Germany; and his title, *Children of Privilege,* neatly expresses his characterization of the 1960s student generation. Levitt identified the vanguard of the baby boom as the activists. These were the children born between 1945 and 1950 who entered university at age eighteen between 1963 and 1968. He characterized them as the offspring of cautious and conformist parents who were shaped by the Depression and war years; and, as such, they had grown up pampered and protected in the new suburbs of the post-war era. Their assertiveness, activism and nonconformity were a consequence and a reaction.

Like most generalizations, this one was not meant to cover every particular. At SFU, older students were a vital part of the mix; and if SFU was a radical campus, they were part of it. And they did not fall neatly into Levitt's time frame.

When one looks at photographs of students in early issues of *The Peak,* or in SFU brochures, or the Vancouver daily press, they have a neat and tidy appearance. Males have clean-shaven faces and hair cut short on back and sides—in the style of their fathers and grandfathers, not their bearded and mustachioed great-grandfathers and great-great-grandfathers. White shirts, ties and sports jackets, although the choice of a minority, appear frequently, and not just on picture taking occasions but in crowd scenes. For females, the Jackie Kennedy bouffant hair style is giving way to the Sassoon bob or the longer sleek pageboy. The mod look is in with Carnaby Street styles, geometric patterns in skirts and dresses, hems rising above the knees, and Mary Quant makeup. A letter to *The Peak* from a male student complains about the fashionable purple stockings.[19]

Year by year one sees more hair, first with the men and then the women. One can chart the evolution with Allen Garr, who started SFU in 1965 at the age of twenty-four—one of the older students. Garr was on *The Peak* staff continuously during his undergraduate career, as the editor for one semester, as the business manager and as a long-time contributor of an irreverent humour column. His picture appears frequently. The beard comes and goes, but in 1968 his hair begins to creep over his ears. A large crowd scene in the mall in the summer of 1968 might have been taken two years earlier, so many students have trim hair, but a picture of the staff of *The Peak,* taken at the same time, shows a predominantly hairy group with beards or sideburns extending down the cheeks and hair over the ears.

The hair bothered members of the general public. During the summer of 1968, Martin Loney, SFU's best-known student radical, appeared on the same TV program as Prime Minister Pierre Trudeau, and hotly castigated him for Canada's complicity in the Vietnam War. His effort earned him a letter from the angry parent of an SFU student from Salmon Arm, who was upset by Loney's manners and argument, and by his appearance. "Why couldn't you have worn a shirt and tie and cut your hair?"[20] This parent may not have realized it, but longer hair was progressing through the age groups. It had appeared on a few Beatles-inspired students in some high schools in the year SFU opened. Then it moved to university and college campuses. By 1970, Trudeau had long sideburns and locks reminiscent of Canada's first prime minister, John A. Macdonald.

The new look perplexed an older generation conditioned to judge people by dress and deportment. Murray Ross, the first president of York University, had a student come to see him in the fall of 1965 wearing dirty jeans, sneakers and a sweatshirt. Ross says he was shocked. It was the first time in all his years as a professor and university administrator that a male student had appeared in his office without a jacket and tie. When he took time to talk to this student, it was a revelation to find him "intelligent, alert, and able."[21]

Students were adopting a bohemian style that had not been seen on campuses before. The beatniks of the 1950s were not a campus phenomenon, but the hippies of the 1960s, or their imitators, were. The bundle of values that they espoused and that found expression on university campuses were summed up in 1972 by the American pollster Daniel Yankelovich under the heading "The New Naturalism."[22] Co-operation was better than competition; living in communes was real and families were artificial; the community should come ahead of the individual; official forms of authority were out; objectivity was impossible; being in the moment was the thing rather than planning and preparing; non-verbal expression was in; sensory perception was the way to the truth; and the natural look was what one wanted, not three-piece suits or crew-cuts or bouffant hairstyles or bras. Drugs, in this ideology, were okay—marijuana more than LSD—and those who experimented with them believed that public acceptance was really a matter of public education.

The hippie scene had coalesced in the low-rent Haight Ashbury district of San Francisco about the time SFU opened. Ken Kesey, the proto-hippie and transitional link from the beatniks to the hippies, had taken his famous acid-popping trip from San Francisco to New York and back in 1964, in an old, wildly painted, rock-blaring school bus. Tom Wolfe wrote about the trip in the subjective style of the new journalism that he was pioneering. This became his second book, *The Electric Kool-Aid Acid Test,* published in 1968 and quickly adopted as supplementary reading for introductory sociology courses. His subject, Kesey, was a defining figure for the hippie movement and its social philosophy; and Kesey's experimentation with drugs happened to parallel that of Timothy Leary, the acknowledged guru of the psychedelic drug culture. Leary was fired from Harvard in 1963, a year after he began his self-experimentation with LSD. That placed him in the public eye, and by 1968 he was estimating that there were 100,000 LSD users in North America.

Reading about Kesey or Leary or listening to Leary lecture, however, did not have the powerful effect of the music that supported their message. All over North America, youth were tuning in to the San Francisco acid rock band the Jefferson Airplane, which produced its first huge hit in 1966. On their second album in 1967, the Jefferson Airplane slipped in the words of the Grace Slick song "White Rabbit" that gave Alice's pill-popping adventure in Wonderland—pills to make her larger or smaller—an entirely new connotation. But of course it was not the words, but the experience of the music that drew audiences. In 1968 the Jefferson Airplane were on the cover of *Life* magazine, exemplifying the psychedelic sound that was grabbing youthful audiences, not just their sound but that of bands like the Grateful Dead, Jimi Hendrix, the new electronic Bob Dylan and the post-1966 Beatles. If hippie culture needed any more promotion, the film industry also got into the act with two movies that would be long forgotten except for their easy acceptance of the hippie lifestyle, including drugs. These were *Alice's Restaurant* with Arlo Guthrie in 1967 and *Alice B. Toklas* with Peter Sellers in 1968.

The hippie message was something that SFU students were figuring out along with the general public, although usually with much more sympathy. What were the hippies all about? That was something for students to explain for themselves as well as their parents. By the summer of 1967, Vancouver's own hippies were picketing liquor stores with the message that alcohol was worse than marijuana. Weekend hippies and social dropouts mixed together. As the weather turned warmer, Ken Kesey-inspired youth, hitchhiking the thousands of miles of the Trans-Canada Highway, headed west for Vancouver; and they came in numbers that made them a political issue. Should they be eligible for welfare? Yes, said the social democrat opposition. No, said the Bennett government. The public tended to see hippies and SFU students as one and the same. How did students see it? Mike Campbell, a *Peak* staffer from the beginning, acting editor for three issues and later the editor, wrote an editorial about the hippies in the summer of 1967. The editorial had an "us" and "them" structure. It suggested that hippies might have a point, but they were not us. We attack hippies, he wrote, but they may have something to tell us about our inconsistencies.[23]

Drugs were present on the SFU campus as on others—and also in the high schools.[24] How many students and faculty were experimenting we don't know. No one took a count. But drugs weren't for everyone. Diane Laloge remembered her student days in an essay written twenty years later for *The Peak*'s student handbook.[25] She had started at SFU in its second year when she was twenty-two and already a mother. In those days, she wrote, campus revolutionaries could not think of going to protests or sit-ins and occupations unless absolutely stoned. She was exaggerating for effect, although with a foundation in fact. She herself found a pot-induced hallucination too unpleasant and frightening to repeat a second time. And for the prudent or timid, there was the knowledge that possession even of soft drugs was a serious offence in Canada at the time, and carried a heavy sentence. Smoking pot or taking LSD involved a furtiveness that, for some, was at least part of the kick. The name and the tall, imposing figure of Abe Snedenko, the head of the Vancouver Police Drug Squad in the 1960s, were legendary among pot-smoking students, even if these students were fortunate enough never to encounter him. Students were not sure about Fred Hope, SFU's chief of security, and the Student Council sought clarification about his role after the police arrested a couple of individuals on campus and laid charges for possession in March 1968. The answer they got from McTaggart-Cowan was that Hope was not a law-enforcement officer, and that he called in police only for traffic accidents or threats to university security.[26]

The registrar got an occasional letter like the one from a grade-twelve student who withdrew his application for admission in the spring of 1967 because he had the impression that SFU was a haven for "kooks, marijuana smokers, LSD users, and other nondescripts of questionable character."[27] This notion appeared to be widespread and was promoted by the negative press and radio coverage that SFU began to get after its first two semesters. Jack Webster, the open-line radio show host, was no friend of the university; and Sharon Yandle complained in *The Peak* about the way the local newspapers laid out their pages, grouping a routine story from SFU with stories dealing with marijuana and LSD that had nothing to do with the university. Newspapers, given the way they are assembled, often contain odd juxtapositions, but in the 1960s with stories about SFU, these juxtapositions happened too often to be amusing. Yandle objected to the equation of potheads with student radicals and to the creation of a stereotype of sFU students that most of them did not fit.[28]

THE RISE OF STUDENT RADICALISM

To the public's confusion, potheads and student radicals appeared on the scene simultaneously, first in California and then across the continent. In the autumn of 1965, when sFU offered its first classes, students on many American campuses were carrying signs reading "I am a human being. Do not fold, bend, or mutilate."[29] They were emulating protestors at Berkeley who had begun pinning IBM cards on their chests to symbolize the impersonal and factory character of their university education. (These cards were the eighty-column hole-punch cards for machine sorting that had been in use for nearly forty years, and that would not function if damaged.) A few weeks after classes began at sFU, John Bartoot Macdonald, president of uBC, was speaking in Toronto about the changed atmosphere on university campuses, which he characterized as "a growing tendency towards irresponsibility and a growing incidence of lawlessness among students." It was everywhere, he said, at all universities. The problem was less serious at uBC, but it was there.[30]

Students seemed to have changed overnight. That is evident in a selection of addresses that university president Claude Bissell published from his years at Toronto. His standard message to students altered dramatically in the mid-1960s. He had been telling them to be skeptical rather than passive and tractable, to be adventurous and not obsessed with security, to show that they were not apathetic, to forget protocol and challenge the status quo and, finally, not to make an early entry into middle age. By the spring of 1965 he had a new text. Now he spoke of the aggressiveness of youth, which, having at last encountered it, he found to be a negative as well as a positive thing. When he addressed freshmen in September 1966, he spoke of "The New Radicalism."[31] He was willing to describe the presence of an activist minority as refreshing. Now that students would speak up for themselves, a dialogue was at last possible. But he also felt obliged to comment on the new arrogance and surliness of student leaders.

Students were no longer easy to deal with; and Bissell and Macdonald were looking for explanations. That led them to the writings of educators like the Canadian-born Harold Taylor, former president of Sarah

Lawrence College, who from the early 1960s had been saying that students wanted a new freedom to determine their own education, and a new equality with faculty. It also led Bissell to quote Clark Kerr, the president of the University of California, where the problems had begun. Kerr attributed the activism of the current crop of students to the permissiveness of their parents. His point: Dr. Benjamin Spock, the author of the 25-cent pocketbook on child care first published in 1946, had had too much influence.[32]

What brought student issues resoundingly to public attention in Canada and the United States were the disturbances in the fall of 1964 on the campus of the University of California at Berkeley. North American students did not connect with contemporary stories about the harsh repression of student demonstrators in Turkey or South Korea or Latin America, or to the successes of student demonstrators in Japan or the Philippines. Very few would have known or guessed that in India, with its expanded but underfunded university system, there were 700 student demonstrations in 1964 alone, and that 113 of them became violent.[33] But when massive student demonstrations erupted at Berkeley, with a series of sit-ins, the occupation of Sproul Hall (the central administration building), a strike and the intervention of hundreds of police twice within a three-month period, all of North America took note.[34]

At Berkeley, students were employing tactics long used by African-American civil-rights activists: tactics that finally had gained national attention and generated national action when adopted by African-American students and their supporters in the anti-segregation campaigns of the early 1960s. The central figures in the Berkeley student revolt, Mario Savio and Jack Weinberg, were products of these campaigns. In the summer of 1964, Savio had joined in the Student Nonviolent Coordinating Committee's efforts to register African-American voters in Mississippi. Weinberg was a member of the Congress for Racial Equality at Berkeley, organizing demonstrations against racially discriminatory hiring practices by employers in the San Francisco Bay area. The Berkeley troubles began with the administration's attempt to shut down the public presence of civil-rights and other left-leaning political groups on campus. The jumble of tables, chairs, lecterns, posters and picket signs employed by activist organizers and open-air orators at the entrance to the university (situated at a major Berkeley intersection) were too visible to passersby, and especially to the state's conservative politicians. When the university tried to close down this speakers' corner, it provoked a protest that began with the Free Speech Movement and quickly expanded as it captured issues that reflected general student discontent.[35]

As some protestors later admitted, their motivation could be quite superficial. Going to demonstrations was more fun than going to class. But what happened at Berkeley resonated on other campuses. John Seeley's response to the Berkeley student revolt is interesting for anyone reviewing SFU's chaotic summer and fall of 1968. Seeley was the candidate for president that SFU students unsuccessfully put forward after McTaggart-Cowan resigned and when Archie MacPherson was temporary acting president. The British-born Seeley was then sixty-five and living in California, but he had been the first chair of sociology at York and was internationally known for his 1956 book *Crestwood Heights*, which had examined tensions and anxieties among the children of an upper-middle-class neighbourhood in Toronto. It was not for *Crestwood Heights*, however, that SFU students knew him. He had gone into print in 1965 expressing sympathy for Berkeley's students. They were questioning legitimacy, he said; and the answers they were getting were not good enough: "in every confrontation, over panty raids, marijuana, dormitory hours, dress regulations, or food they were asking 'who says and by what right?'" They were not satisfied to be told that the university administration or board had the power under the law, or that attending university was a privilege, not a right. Berkeley's students, said Seeley, were asking the question that free people had always asked of arbitrary authority.[36]

There were no Berkeley imitators at SFU during the first eight months of classes, although it did not take long after that for the university to gain its reputation as Canada's Berkeley North. When, mid-way through the first semester, two or three thousand UBC students marched on the Bayshore Inn (where Canadian university administrators were meeting) to protest tuition fees, SFU's new Student Council declined to join in. The action was too radical, they said, and the objective too unrealistic.[37]

A number of semesters later, Parzival Copes, the head of Economics, told the *Vancouver Province*'s education reporter that in the beginning he worried about a lack of concern among SFU students about social issues and the great debates of the day.[38] That lack of concern disappeared during the second academic year, and didn't return for the balance of the 1960s.

SFU's first student protest, in the summer and fall of 1966, was over the construction of a service station. The second, in the spring of 1967, was a reaction to the firing of five teaching assistants for their part in an off-campus demonstration (the Templeton Secondary affair). Then followed a prolonged agitation over student and faculty representation in university government. In the fall of 1968, the student issue was transfer credit; and in the fall of 1969, student radicals were supporting striking faculty in the PSA Department. The issues were all local, with the exception of student representation, which had become a demand on campuses across the U.S. and Canada.

In the U.S., student protests in the 1964–65 academic year (the year of Berkeley) were about civil rights, food services, dormitory rules, the Vietnam War and dress codes, in that order. Anti-war protests on American campuses escalated after U.S. President Lyndon Johnson doubled the military draft in August 1965; and the anti-war movement played a large role in the unrest that disrupted nearly two hundred American campuses during the 1967–68 school year and five hundred campuses in 1968–69. But the other issues remained. A 1969 survey showed that American students demonstrated most frequently about African-American rights, secondly for the advancement of student power (student representation in university government), thirdly for campus reforms like revision of the curriculum and the grading system, and fourthly about the war. The war, of course, was something that sharply divided American students, because it had its student supporters as well as opponents.[39]

Most SFU students, like most Canadians, opposed the war. SFU students took a vote in the summer semester of 1967 and registered 69.4 per cent against American involvement in Vietnam and 63 per cent against Canada selling arms to the U.S.[40] But the war did not touch them as it did draft-age students in the U.S. About two hundred students and faculty showed up on campus on a Saturday morning in October 1967 for a pre-demonstration rally prior to a main demonstration downtown. That was a respectable turnout during a national day of anti-war rallies, when three hundred people had marched in Halifax and four thousand in Toronto, and when, in Vancouver, a crowd of fifteen hundred (described in the papers as "hippies, students, and others") had gathered at city hall for the city's main rally.[41] But it was a one-time event, aside from the occasional symposium in the mall, and Vietnam rested mainly as a background issue about which SFU students, and Canadians generally, had strong opinions, but little incentive or opportunity for action. By the fall of 1966, a few American draft dodgers had enrolled at SFU; and two newly arrived SFU faculty members, Mordecai Briemberg in PSA and Paul Ivory in Economics, were active with the Vancouver Committee to Aid War Objectors, which was receiving draft dodgers and providing them with initial shelter as well as helping them to apply for landed immigrant status. (Briemberg was later a central figure in the PSA strike of 1969.[42])

A controversy that fall offers a snapshot of student opinion at SFU. President Macdonald of UBC had questioned what people like Briemberg and Ivory were doing. American citizens, he argued, had a legal responsibility to serve their country and Canadians should not be working to subvert it. One of SFU's recently arrived draft dodgers, Anthony Westman (now a Vancouver-based cinematographer), answered in the student newspaper that there were times when individuals had to act according to their own moral values because their country could be wrong. How were these positions understood at SFU? An assistant professor in economics tried to find out by sending members of his class into the cafeteria and library to do a rough sampling of opinions. The result he got was that more than half of those questioned thought that draft dodgers should stay home.[43]

It was a hit-and-miss survey but it reminds us of the complexity of the Canadian response to the war. You could not be sure that someone who opposed American involvement in Vietnam would welcome American draft dodgers. It is also another reminder that SFU earned a reputation that never did fit its whole student population. Steve Duguid, who has enjoyed a long career at SFU in a variety of capacities, including chair of Humanities, was a 1960s draft dodger. He had worked for a year in Washington, D.C., after graduating from Illinois and had begun graduate studies at Chicago when he lost his draft deferment. Canada was his solution. During the summer of 1968, he drove up to the border between International Falls, Minnesota, and Fort Francis, Ontario, travelling by car with his wife and two dogs and pulling a crammed U-Haul trailer.

He was admittedly long-haired and scruffy-looking but was carrying a student visa. Of the moment of paranoia he experienced before being allowed into Canada, what registered most unforgettably was the immigration officer's reaction to his letter of admission to SFU. "You know they teach revolution out there."[44]

A Harris poll done in the spring of 1968 reported that one American college student in five had participated in protests, and that between 1 and 2 per cent of students in the U.S. were radicals.[45] At that time, the primary radical organization among youth in the U.S. was the Students for a Democratic Society (SDS) which had six thousand card-carrying members—those who had paid a $5.00 fee—and a membership list of thirty thousand. As an organization, the SDS did not extend into Canada, although its organizers appeared on some Canadian campuses. The Canadian counterpart, the Students for a Democratic University (SDU) emerged first in Ontario and Quebec and most visibly at Sir George Williams and McGill in Montreal. In January 1968, when radicals at SFU organized an SDU chapter, they drew two hundred people for their first meeting, less than 5 per cent of the student body. But they had a leadership of determined activists who became an unavoidable force on campus over the next twelve months.[46]

Their aims mirrored those of the SDS as it had evolved since the escalation of the Vietnam War in 1965. At their first meeting, Simon Fraser's SDU organizers explained themselves as a radical group that wanted an alternative system of education and a democratized university that would play an activist role in society.[47] A PSA student had already explained these goals in the pages of The Peak many months earlier. In his article, this student expressed the frustration felt within the SDS and the SDU and the broad coalition of organizations that made up what was known as the New Left. Where were the results of their efforts? The war went on; governments remained in place; society didn't change. "In the one segment of society in which the New Left has very real, albeit potential power, it makes the least use of it. If the guts and determination that went into the civil rights movement were applied now on campus the New Left could secure a base from which to spring into society."[48] These were the words of charter student John Olsen, written halfway through his second academic year, and they reflected an argument being made within the SDS and the New Left.

Students like Olsen were reading C. Wright Mills, the Columbia University sociologist who had died in 1962 at the age of forty-six, leaving an influential legacy of academic scholarship and scholarly journalism produced over twenty-three years. Out of his whole corpus on union leadership, the labour movement, the new middle class, power elites and social structure, the publication that students were most likely to come across was the much reprinted "Letter to the New Left," which appeared in the fall of 1960 in the first edition of the *New Left Review*. (The *New Left Review* appealed to campus radicals who rejected Russian Communism but were attracted to Marxism, anarchism and anti-authoritarian thought.) By 1960, Mills had been long disillusioned with the labour movement's potential to promote radical social change. His prediction in "Letter to the New Left" was that it would be intellectuals, not workers, who would be the agents of revolution. This was a much-cited source of the New Left's belief that the university was the place to start because the university could command society's attention.[49]

Students were also reading the anti-establishment, German-American philosopher Herbert Marcuse—particularly his *One-Dimensional Man*, which appeared in 1964. In the 1960s Marcuse was a frequent speaker at student protests; and in March 1969, when the PSA Department brought him to SFU from San Diego, where he was teaching in retirement, an estimated thirteen hundred students and faculty turned out for his midday lecture, too many to be contained within a single lecture hall.[50] Mills and Marcuse helped to turn students on to Marxism; and two other popular books of the era, by the psychoanalyst Erich Fromm—*Marx's Concept of Man*, published in 1961, and *Beyond the Chains of Illusion*, published in 1962—did so as well. This interest in Marx was a departure in Canada and the U.S. from the earlier years of the Cold War, when the campus Marxist was an exceedingly rare individual.

Cyril Levitt, and others who conducted an autopsy of the student movement after it was over, have linked its increasingly ideological bent, and its internal ideological quarrels, with its ultimate collapse. A movement created around civil rights objectives and opposition to the Vietnam War transformed itself after 1965 into a movement to effect fundamental social change. A quick summary of this analysis would be that discouragement with progress towards immediate goals led to an increasingly ideological and visionary posture. Levitt also joined in the general view that the economic downturn at the end of the decade contributed to the demise of student radicalism. Jobs were no longer assured after graduation, and that put a new perspective on everything.[51]

At the height of student agitation it looked like the movement had more lasting potential. What happened in New York at Columbia University in April 1968 was a great incentive to the radical wing of the student movement; and it ushered in twelve months of repeated confrontation between students and university and civil authorities, not just in Canada and the United States, but in western Europe and Britain. At Columbia, the university administration called in police to clear five buildings that had been occupied for a week by up to a thousand students, faculty and residents of Harlem. (One of the objectives of the occupation was to stop the construction of a gymnasium that would have taken a portion of a park used by the adjoining Harlem neighbourhood.) In the riot that ensued, the police made 712 arrests and 148 people were injured; and the Columbia University administration suffered a huge public-relations defeat. Columbia seemed to show that confrontation worked. There was strong support for the occupation, not just among students and junior faculty but among some senior faculty as well; and after the riot and an inquiry, the university gave way to the demands of the occupiers.[52]

A year later, the SDS led an occupation of the administration building at Harvard, which the police and state troopers broke up in the early hours of the morning, again with arrests and injuries. At Harvard, as well, the administration found itself out of step with its constituency, which was generally sympathetic to the protestors, and under this pressure made major concessions. Between the Columbia occupation in 1968 and the one at Harvard in 1969, hundreds of North American campuses experienced student-led disruptions, which in about two dozen cases reached serious proportions. In Canada, during this period, the three most restive campuses were SFU, Regina and Sir George Williams, but every Canadian campus was affected to some degree.

It was in the second week of May 1968 that newspapers and TV carried dramatic reports and images of twenty to thirty thousand French students behind barricades in the streets of Paris, heaving paving stones at helmeted and shield-bearing riot police. The trouble had begun at the new and still unfinished campus in the industrial suburb of Nanterre, where the administration had cracked down on student protests, closing the campus and disciplining six student leaders. The Nanterre students had been agitating about dormitory rules, overcrowded classrooms, poor instructors, compulsory exams and, as the situation escalated, about expulsions and free speech. What started at Nanterre had moved to the centre of Paris, bringing out students from the Sorbonne, and then it involved university and lycée students across France. It became a national crisis when the entire union movement supported the students in a general strike; and the government of Charles de Gaulle, for a moment, looked vulnerable. Within two months, the student-led revolt in France had run out of steam and de Gaulle had secured a conservative majority in assembly elections.[53] But these developments were not immediately disheartening to members of the SDS or SDU or other radical student organizations in North America. For those who believed that the university could be the starting place for revolution, French students seemed to have shown how it could happen.

SFU held its second convocation on May 15, 1968, a date that followed two weeks of headlines about the French student revolt. A last-minute choice as convocation speaker, after the intended speaker fell ill, was Leslie Peterson, the provincial minister of education who had been instrumental in the original decision to build SFU. Unwittingly, Peterson presented himself as a target for anti-government and anti-business protest. When he took his place on the platform in the mall, forty student demonstrators, members of the SDU, were standing along the elevated walkways and sitting on the steps leading up to the Academic Quadrangle. As he spoke, some of them were writing signs like "Shrum Sells Degrees." Long afterwards, he remembered the situation and his decision in the face of adversity to cut his address short. Facing him was a large banner that read "Internationale for Student Power." He had chosen to talk about student protest. When he spoke critically of what students were doing at Columbia and in France, he earned hisses from the gallery.[54]

THE VALUES AND PRIORITIES OF 1960s STUDENTS

The assertiveness of youth in the 1960s was open to various explanations. Late in 1968, SFU Student Society President Rob Walsh wrote a long response to an exasperated member of the general public who asked, "What do students want?" Walsh was a self-described moderate whose slate of candidates had swept Student Society elections the previous September. His answer tried to explain why students at SFU demanded a voice in running the university. Young people, he said, are "socially, politically and educationally more advanced for their age than previous generations."[55] The general public was rapidly reaching a similar conclusion, because only two years later, in 1970, the B.C. legislature reduced the age of majority from twenty-one to nineteen, and the Parliament of Canada gave the right to vote to citizens over eighteen.

These legislative changes put to rest any question of the university's parental responsibilities. The idea that universities were *in loco parentis* went with the notion that a student's time at university was a halfway house between childhood and adulthood. And it had some real meaning for students in dormitories, especially women, whose hours, visitors and behaviour were monitored and regulated. It had less application at SFU, where only a few students lived on campus and where so many students were older; and it was being challenged. When a majority of university students ceased, in a legal sense, to be children, it became obvious to everyone that *in loco parentis* no longer made much sense.

SFU did open with sixty-five young women at Madge Hogarth House living under residence rules with an older woman as full-time supervisor. (The Madge Hogarth residence was named for a local benefactor, the widow of an iron-mining magnate from northwestern Ontario, who put up the money to build it.) The original residents all came from out of town, and one was from Venezuela. Because the building was not quite finished in September, the university put half of them temporarily into hotel rooms over a beer parlour; and when they finally moved into Madge Hogarth House, they needed to make a special purchase of safety pins to hang up bed sheets over bare windows.[56] The rules of residence they agreed on themselves and then got approval from a house committee under Letty Wilson's jurisdiction. The rules were modelled on other university residences, and the rule-making process—formal supervision by the university but effective determination by the resident students—was the liberal way that *in loco parentis* tended to work on other Canadian campuses at the time.

On the four nights a month when the residents of Madge Hogarth allowed themselves to stay out past 2:30 AM, they had to report to the transportation centre and wait for a security guard to go with them to the west end of an empty campus to open the front door. They were not given keys, although for a while they did have a patrolman with a key posted outside the residence. It was a sign of the changing times that after a couple of years, a delegation from Madge Hogarth House went to the dean of students, Letty Wilson, suggesting that it become coeducational. By then, this was not a shocking proposal, although Wilson thought these young women expected more reaction from her than they got. The only reason something was not done was that the university did not have the funding at hand for a conversion. However, Shell House and later McTaggart-Cowan Hall were built as coeducational residences.[57]

Just after midnight on a Thursday in July 1966, eleven male students with nothing better to do approached Madge Hogarth House from the woods on the south side, away from the main road. Six climbed onto the second-floor balcony, entered through unlocked doors, scuffled with the young women blocking their way, broke into a number of rooms, threw some water balloons, broke a clock and ransacked bureaus looking for underwear. One of the six was a camera-carrying reporter for *The Peak*, who followed along in the mistaken belief that his press credentials could take him anywhere. The perpetrators were apologetic when called before Faculty Council that Saturday morning. By then they realized that the general population at SFU saw nothing amusing in their actions and that the residents of Madge Hogarth did not like it and, understandably, might have been badly frightened.[58]

These young men had discovered that the panty raid was an anachronism at SFU. They found out that other SFU students generally saw it as an act of immaturity, not an amusing prank. Panty raids had been a North American campus sport of the 1950s and early 1960s, with raids at times involving hundreds of male students, and with some women joining in by organizing retaliatory raids or opening doors and windows to let raiders in. University administrators tended to discipline participants in this mass behaviour leniently, recognizing it as a release of energy at exam time, or something students did in the fall before becoming serious about classes. Panty raids died out in the 1960s; and common explanations are the politicization of students, along with the sexual revolution. SFU was both the wrong time and the wrong place to carry one out.

SFU in the 1960s was also the wrong time and place for fraternities and sororities. In a previous age, university presidents in Canada had actively encouraged Greek letter social fraternities—with their long tradition in the U.S.—as a contributing element to campus life. But the 1960s brought a different perception. In Toronto, where fraternities and sororities had been part of the campus scene for more than seventy years, they came under fire in 1960 after publicity about a sorority's refusal to admit a student of African descent. Beginning in the 1965–66 academic year, Toronto insisted that fraternities and sororities neither claim nor suggest any association with the university. (This remains Toronto's position today, although its fraternities and sororities still exist.) Fraternities had been rejected at Carleton; and universities like Manitoba tolerated their activities as long as they did not have the appearance of university sponsorship. At UBC, however, fraternities were well entrenched (as they still are) and had a presence in student government.

Several fraternities, including Alpha Delta Phi, Delta Kappa Epsilon and Phi Kappa Sigma, were interested in colonizing SFU. Representatives of the American national offices of Delta Epsilon and Delta Sigma Phi contacted Patrick McTaggart-Cowan, and the Delta Sigma Phi international field representative visited SFU shortly before opening day.[59]

In October 1965, a couple of SFU students started organizing a fraternity group with the backing of the Delta Epsilon chapter at UBC. They signed up forty members, of which ten would be resident, and with the financial help of a few of their parents, rented Ceperley Mansion, the grand old house on six acres (2.4 hectares) of land that is now the Burnaby Art Gallery. The board had no objections to fraternities, but waited to hear from the student body, which aired the question at a mass meeting in early November, and then voted emphatically against fraternities in the following March. The university's position was formalized by a vote of the senate in April. The "no fraternities" decision was final, although Delta Sigma Phi tried to reopen the issue later in 1966 and again in 1967.[60]

SFU students soon consigned several other traditional student institutions to the trash bin. The Student Society held a president's ball on campus in the fall of 1965, with formal wear specified—tuxedos or dark-coloured suits for the men and long or short gowns for the women. They repeated it the next year in the ballroom of the Hotel Vancouver;

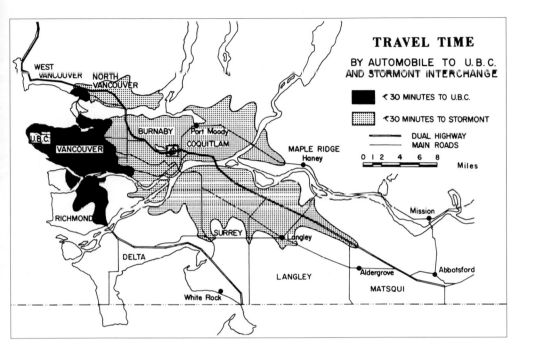

A map of travel times published in December 1962 in *Report on Higher Education in B.C.* by University of British Columbia President John Barfoot Macdonald. The work on the map had been done by Walter Hardwick in the UBC Geography Department before Macdonald arrived at UBC. MACDONALD REPORT, UBC

ABOVE: The Simon Fraser University board of governors at their third meeting in December 1963. *Seated from left to right:* President Patrick D. McTaggart-Cowan, Chancellor Gordon M. Shrum, Mrs. Beth Wood. *Standing:* F.M. Dietrich, A.F.C. Hean, G.D. Wong, C. Bloch Bauer, A.M. Eyre, R.C. Shaffer, C.J. Frederickson, R.E. Lester. HERBERT MCDONALD PHOTO, SFU ARCHIVES

TOP RIGHT: Arthur Erickson and Geoffrey Massey's drawing showing an aerial view of their design for SFU, one of three drawings in their first-prize entry in the SFU architectural competition adjudicated in July 1963. SFU ARCHIVES

BOTTOM RIGHT: William R. Rhone and W. Randle Iredale's aerial view in their second-prize entry. SFU ARCHIVES

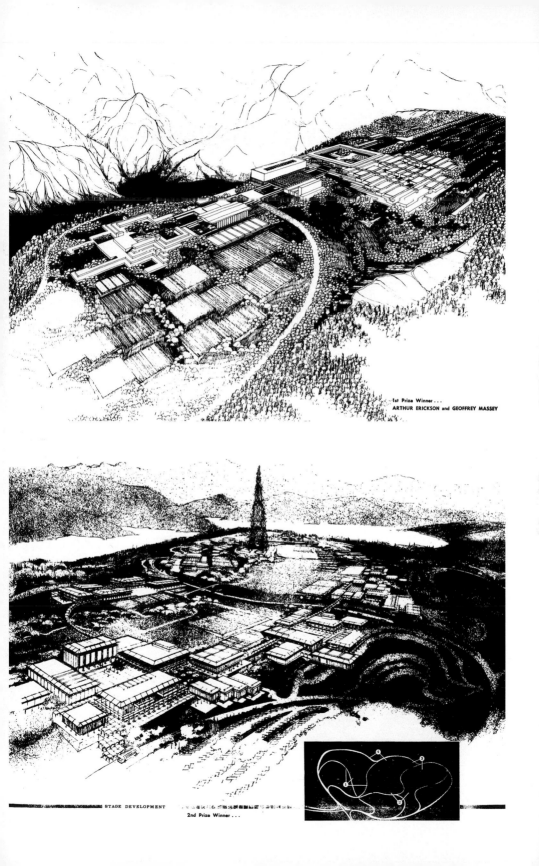

1st Prize Winner . . .
ARTHUR ERICKSON and GEOFFREY MASSEY

STAGE DEVELOPMENT

2nd Prize Winner . . .

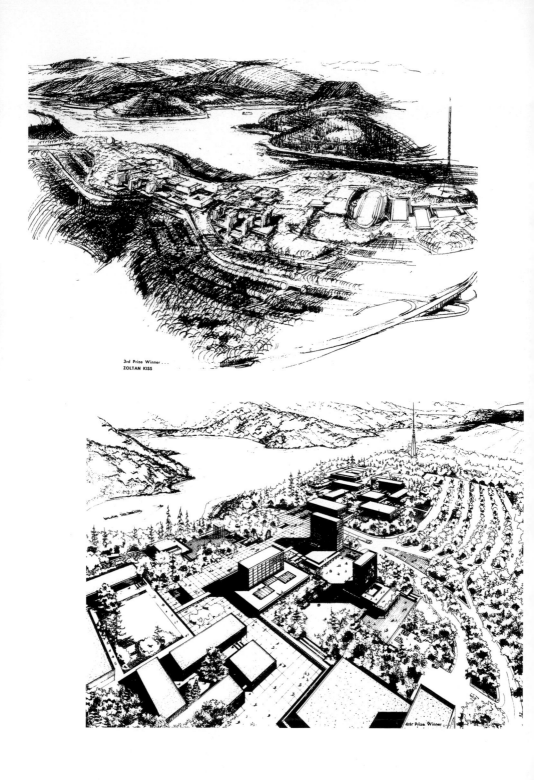

3rd Prize Winner . . .
ZOLTAN KISS

4th Prize Winner . . .

TOP LEFT: Zoltan Kiss's aerial view in his third-prize entry. SFU ARCHIVES

BOTTOM LEFT: Fourth-prize winner Robert Harrison's aerial view.
SFU ARCHIVES

ABOVE: Fifth-prize winner Duncan McNab and Associates' aerial view.
SFU ARCHIVES

TOP LEFT: Aerial photograph of Burnaby Mountain, November 20, 1963, showing the site before construction began. GEORGE ALLEN PHOTO, DEPARTMENT OF GEOGRAPHY, UBC

BOTTOM LEFT: Aerial photograph of Burnaby Mountain, April 1, 1964, showing the site after clearing and construction of access roads. GEORGE ALLEN PHOTO, DEPARTMENT OF GEOGRAPHY, UBC

ABOVE: Geoffrey Massey, Arthur Erickson and Gordon Shrum with the winning design for SFU at the ceremony in Burnaby Mountain Park at which the results of the architectural competition were announced, July 31, 1963. SFU ARCHIVES

SIMON FRASER UNIVERSITY
BURNABY, B.C.
CENTRAL MALL

ERICKSON — MASSEY
ARCHITECTS

JOHN LAING & SON (CANADA) LTD.
GENERAL CONTRACTORS

TOP LEFT: Madge Hogarth, a benefactor who provided funds for a women's residence at SFU. Had such support not been available, Shrum would have left construction of all residences to the second phase of construction. TONY ARCHER PHOTO, SFU ARCHIVES

BOTTOM LEFT: The construction site on May 28, 1964, when the foundations of the mall were being poured. OTTO LANDAUER PHOTO, JEWISH HISTORICAL SOCIETY OF BC

ABOVE: Opening ceremony platform party, September 1965. Gordon Shrum is at centre with mace, with Lord Lovatt and Geoffrey Massey at left, and McTaggart-Cowan and B.C. Premier W.A.C. Bennett at right. SFU ARCHIVES

TOP LEFT: Opening ceremonies, September 1965. The roof over the mall was yet to be completed. SFU ARCHIVES

BOTTOM LEFT: Quebec Premier Jean Lesage greeting Margaret Sinclair (later Margaret Trudeau) during an informal visit to SFU in September 1965. He would have known her through her father, a former Liberal cabinet minister in Ottawa. PEAK PUBLICATION SOCIETY

TOP RIGHT: Aerial view of the campus, April 4, 1966. Work was proceeding on the east side of the Academic Quadrangle and on the science centre. Shrum had left these for the second phase of construction. GEORGE ALLEN PHOTO, DEPARTMENT OF GEOGRAPHY, UBC

ABOVE: President McTaggart-Cowan inspecting the Centrex equipment, the newly installed central electronic switchboard, an advance on the mechanical switchboards that were standard up to the time that SFU opened. SFU ARCHIVES

TOP RIGHT: An aerial photograph taken on May 4, 1966, one of a series of pictures taken monthly throughout construction, both from the air and on the ground. It shows construction slightly advanced from April 4. GEORGE ALLEN PHOTO, DEPARTMENT OF GEOGRAPHY, UBC

BOTTOM RIGHT: A message to Shell Oil from SFU students, written on a gas tank about to be buried for the Shell station under construction, spring 1966. PEAK PUBLICATION SOCIETY

ABOVE: Students in the park across the road from Templeton Secondary School in east Vancouver, at a free speech rally organized by SFU teaching assistants in March 1967. PEAK PUBLICATION SOCIETY

OPPOSITE, CLOCKWISE FROM LEFT: Stan Wong, charter student, economics major and student senator; Sharon Yandle, charter student, Politics, Sociology & Anthropology (PSA) major and student senator; Martin Loney being arrested at Templeton Secondary, after he returned despite a magistrate's order to stay away. PEAK PUBLICATION SOCIETY

Jim Harding, PSA doctoral candidate and Students for a Democratic University leader, addressing a student crowd in the mall. PEAK PUBLICATION SOCIETY

and did it a third time at the end of November 1967, also in a hotel. This time the intermission featured Scottish dancers and pipers, and McTaggart-Cowan enjoyed it so much he told the student president, Arthur Weeks, that it was the best one yet. It was also the last one. A year later McTaggart-Cowan was gone as president, and after an intense, tumultuous, triumphant and bitter year of campus unrest, a president's ball was not in the cards.[61]

In the spring of the first academic year, McTaggart-Cowan was the judge in a student-organized Miss SFU contest, with the standard format except for the bathing suit section. The winner, after each contestant had modelled a tennis outfit, an after-five dress and an evening gown, and after each had delivered a prepared speech, was Rosalind Sinclair, the sister of Prime Minister Pierre Trudeau's future wife. (Rosalind and Margaret Sinclair were charter SFU students.) A year later, when a second-year arts student, Lori Pershick, won, the audience gave most of its attention to a spoof contestant, Michelle Russell, whose brawny male legs were well displayed beneath a short dress made of newsprint. The event was never repeated, although the sports crowd elected a second Miss Clansman later that year. After that, SFU left it to others to carry on with beauty contests, which did continue at twenty or thirty universities in Canada throughout the 1960s. For several years the SFU Student Council ignored invitations to send someone to the Miss Canadian University beauty pageant at the University of Waterloo. Finally, in 1970, the SFU Women's Caucus entered an anti-candidate, Janiel Jolley, who used her two minutes' speaking time to criticize the event, and who did a speaking tour of Ontario campuses while she was out there.[62]

A school yearbook seemed like a good idea in the beginning. The results were two attractive, high-quality coffee-table publications, one for 1965–66 and one for 1966–67, with feature articles and photo essays on the major events of the year. The Wong brothers, Ed, Fred and Stan, were all contributors. The third yearbook was axed by the Student Council during the spring semester of 1968, and there never was another. Cost was the council's stated reason for backing out: the second yearbook had gone heavily into the red. But yearbooks seemed to be something that 1960s students no longer wanted. UBC students got rid of theirs in 1966; so did Sir George Williams and Toronto about the same time. At UBC and Toronto the student populations were becoming too big to include everyone's graduating picture. (With no graduating classes for the first two years, the SFU yearbooks were able to leave that feature out.) But for politicized students of the 1960s, the yearbook was irrelevant, a "Joe College" memento that they did not need.[63]

FURNITURE AND PAPER CUPS

Morris Achtemichuk had an unusual perspective on the new university on Burnaby Mountain. In the fall of 1965, straight out of high school, he took a temporary job in SFU's Stores Department. That led to a career in purchasing, first at SFU, then in the private sector and eventually with the Surrey, B.C., school district. In 1965 his first task was to move furniture into the Academic Quadrangle. His boss was the storekeeper, Matsu Kinoshita, who taught him how to use his 68-kilogram body with the greatest efficiency to manoeuvre heavy furniture into elevators, up stairwells and along corridors. The two of them moved all of the furniture into the three finished sides of the Academic Quadrangle—every desk, filing cabinet, chair and wastepaper basket. The two of them also moved the quality fabric-upholstered oak furniture that went into the wood-panelled faculty lounge and dining room. And a few years later they carried the same furniture out—after it had been trashed by students—and brought in standard metal-frame chairs and sofas that could take abuse. They did the same in the student lounge, and in the rotunda where the student newspaper and Student Society offices were located, eventually carrying out damaged, finer furniture and bringing back sturdier, industrial pieces. Achtemichuk's job left him a dismayed witness to the failure of a genteel vision of what these spaces at a university should look like.[64]

A local area resident took his Swedish guests around the SFU campus on a Sunday in the late spring of 1966. His guests were impressed by the architecture, but as host he was embarrassed by the paper and litter lying in the corridors and lecture halls, and especially in the Student Council area in the rotunda.[65] His was not an isolated reaction. In the files of the dean of student affairs survives a letter from a Canadian-born visitor from California, who was upset during a weekend tour of the campus in the fall of 1966 by the mess of lunch bags, paper cups and candy wrappers in the rotunda area. It had been a continuing problem. President Patrick McTaggart-Cowan saw it as a Student Society responsibility and charged the society president with doing something about it. But if the president of the university could not solve it, the president of the Student Council was unlikely to do much, either. An education campaign did make a difference in the middle of SFU's second year; but in reality, it was a difficult thing to keep a tidy campus without the underpaid help that had picked up after privileged students at older universities in the past.

CHALLENGING FACULTY PRIVILEGE

Separate lounges for faculty and students lasted for three years at SFU and ended during the tumult of 1968. Some faculty wanted no students in their lounge area. Some wanted to bring students in as guests by invitation; and a small minority would have opened up the lounge to everyone. Some students became comfortable enough going in with their professors that they continued to enter freely on their own; and some professors encouraged this. The elevator in the Academic Quadrangle to the lounge was controlled by a key so that students could not use it; but copies circulated with the connivance of a few professors, and at some point someone poured liquid solder into the lock. (When the university opened, all of the elevators had been reserved for faculty, but that privilege had a short life and the elevator to the faculty lounge was the last of its kind.)

In the late spring of 1968, in a spontaneous lunch-time action led by a pregnant young woman looking for a place to sit, a group of students barged into the faculty lounge and briefly liberated it. A partition put up by the administration to restrict access did not last long; students knocked it down during a visit to SFU by the black civil rights leader Stokely Carmichael, and they renamed the area the workers' canteen. Faculty did not get their lounge back, although a vote organized in 1970 showed that many still wanted it.[66]

Jerry Rubin, the co-founder of the Youth International Party, the Yippies, arrived in Vancouver in October 1968, about eight weeks after he had been at the centre of a riot in the streets of Chicago during the Democratic Party national convention. At UBC he led an invasion of the Faculty Club—which did about $3,000 in damage—after asking a crowd of three thousand students what they had to liberate. He had been at SFU on the previous day and *The Peak* ran a picture of him looking like a campus Che Guevara with head scarf, double bandana, wild hair, beard and moustache, and flower-pattern camouflage shirt. He had also asked the SFU crowd what they had to liberate; but they had nothing. They had already done the job.[67]

Democracy also came to the library. SFU had opened in 1965 with a policy of no library fines. Returning books on time was on the honour system. Failure to do so incurred no penalties. The library had a practical reason for this: fines cost more to collect than they brought in revenue. But students objected when books they wanted did not come back within the loan period; and the library began imposing fines in March 1966.

Students had another library issue. Why did faculty have long-term loans when they had to bring books back in two weeks? Why were faculty treated differently? By this time three students were on the senate and in 1969, after these student senators agitated vigorously, faculty found themselves subject to the same rules as students and paying heavy fines when they absent-mindedly brought bags of books in late. Those fines brought strong protest from faculty, loudest from those stuck with the largest bills. Only a small minority found the two-week period too short. And 90 per cent of students surveyed thought it was reasonable. But the objections of the few were strong enough to make change. Parity was now an entrenched principle; so special treatment of faculty was out of the question. The solution was to keep the fines but to extend the loan period to a full semester. This worked for the library because it saved money: with books circulating less frequently, the cost of handling fell. It worked for faculty, who no longer had to keep returning or renewing highly specialized books that they knew were in low demand. And it worked for those students who thought ahead and, early in the semester, picked up every text they would need over the next twelve weeks. It did not work so well for those last-minute operators who would dash into the library to meet an essay deadline only to find the shelves cleared.

Perhaps the most profound instrument of the revolution in relations between faculty and students in the 1960s was the anti-calendar. In 1964–65, in the wake of the Berkeley disturbances, student committees on American campuses began conducting and publishing course evaluations, sometimes with the assistance and co-operation of faculty and administration, and sometimes without. Up to that point, in the centuries-long tradition of university education, professors had enjoyed freedom from formal evaluation of their teaching. They handed out grades, but were never subjected to grading themselves. The anti-calendar changed that.

The appearance of anti-calendars on American campuses provoked a debate about who was qualified to judge teaching. From the faculty side came the stout insistence that students were not competent and that giving weight to student opinion simply turned teaching into a popularity contest. The student answer was that nobody knew better than they who was a good teacher and who was not.[68]

SFU's first two anti-calendars, published by the Student Society in 1968 and 1969, were a direct outcome of the restless activism of that two-year period. Several years passed before another group of students found the time and enthusiasm to attempt a third one, but SFU faculty began conducting student evaluations themselves, partly in self-defence and partly because they were, sometimes reluctantly, persuaded that they had a value. Throughout the 1970s, SFU's academic departments groped their way towards policies that made student evaluation mandatory for all teaching faculty and that required everyone to use the same prescribed form. The Department of Economics was ahead of most departments and by 1975 could print out a table of means and averages that showed the precise ranking of each economics professor according to student responses.[69]

Remarkably, in the 1970s, the grades that students began to get from their professors entered a rapidly inflationary trend that looked like it might never stop. A special Arts Faculty committee on grading found a number of reasons for the trend, including the elimination of final exams in many courses and the more personal nature of SFU's tutorials and seminars. But regular student evaluation deserved some credit. Professors had difficulty sticking to an old grading standard when they were being graded themselves. In 1966, less than 10 per cent of the grades given out in first- and second-year courses were As. In 1980 it was nearly 20 per cent, and in the intervening years it had gone higher.[70] By 1980 the inflation had been reined in, partly as deans and department chairs cracked down, but also with the achievement of a new equilibrium once student evaluation had become familiar and nearly universal.

By its fourth year, SFU also had to rethink the way it handled student discipline. When the university opened, it had a body concerned with student discipline called the Faculty Council—a traditional institution set out in the Universities Act. The membership included the president, registrar, librarian and six elected faculty members, and no students. From the beginning, the members of the Faculty Council had a sense that they were an anachronism and they declared themselves that the university had no parental responsibility for students: it was not *in loco parentis.* American universities were struggling with the concept because students challenged it, while American courts supported it, and the public frequently expected universities to use it.

For three years the Faculty Council did function at SFU: reviewing disciplinary cases involving campus security, traffic and library fines, infractions of rules of residence, damage to university property, pornography in a science student newsletter, cheating and plagiarism. It vetted the Student Society constitution, recommended rejection of fraternities (after the negative student vote) and supported the cancellation of a potentially libellous article in the student newspaper. It also got involved when SFU teaching assistants took part in a demonstration at Templeton Secondary School. But it ceased to meet in 1968. Students insisted that it had no moral authority; and in the revised Universities Act of 1974 it was eliminated.[71] It had no place in a university where the faculty lounge had become the workers' canteen.

5

Student Journalists, Politicians, Athletes and Teachers

The bound and now brittle pages of the Simon Fraser University campus paper, *The Peak,* offer a fascinating introduction to the 1960s. The story is not simply in the content; it is there in the changing voice of the paper. It was an independent paper, like most student papers at Canadian universities and at the more prestigious American ones. But this was not something to take for granted. About a decade and a half earlier at the University of Washington, the editor of the student paper had been dismissed because the paper's faculty advisor objected to a series of articles on a politically contentious subject. Most universities did think at one time that a student paper needed a faculty advisor, but that was never the case at SFU.[1]

How does a student newspaper get off the ground without faculty direction on a campus without tradition where the students initially do not know each other? At SFU it happened through the journalistic aspirations of a few students, and the competitiveness of others. The first issue of *The Peak* appeared five weeks after the start of classes in the fall of 1965, in the tabloid format that it still uses; but it had two short-lived predecessors—rival publications that contained some good reporting, although they were amateurishly produced on mimeograph machines with hand-lettered headlines.

The first was *The Tartan,* whose staff of seventeen got out five hasty issues in a two-week period shortly after the semester began. The second was the *SF View,* which promised a quick conversion to tabloid format in the expectation that it would be the one to get Student Society funding. The editor of *The Tartan,* Lorne Mallin, had been a reporter for the University of B.C. paper, and had transferred to SFU planning to get in first with a student paper. These were the moves of a student with the journalism bug. He had worked the previous summer for a local newspaper and was already doing a shift a week at the *Vancouver Sun.* By contrast, Rick McGrath, the editor of *SF View* (the name mimicking UBC's *Ubyssey*) had no background in journalism, but was the elected choice of a group quickly assembled to challenge Mallin.

By the end of the first week of October 1965, the two groups had joined forces rather than compete for advertisers, and also so they could make a united bid for funding from the Student Society. Part of the argument against Mallin by the *SF View* group was that the editor of the student paper should be chosen by a democratic process and not just be the first on the scene. This required a fresh start rather than simple amalgamation, but it was a fresh start that accommodated members of both groups. At a joint meeting, Mallin, McGrath and their assembled supporters elected a student board of governors that called for applications and appointed staff. Mallin became campus editor and McGrath sports editor, but the board chose an older student with administrative experience as general editor. He was Sam Steenhuus, who had no background on either the editorial or the technical side of producing a paper, but who could run an office. The first issue, produced with Student Society funding, was headed "Name Your Student Newspaper." The names *The Tartan* and *SF View* fell by the wayside. With *The Tartan,* some students had objected to yet another Scottish theme at SFU; and from the second issue the newspaper was *The Peak.*

The original staff of *The Peak* wanted a paper that the university could be proud of. Starting a paper with a staff of novice journalists required some quick and ready research. Looking back, Rick McGrath remembered picking up a phone and getting the tired voice of a night-desk editor at the *New Westminster Columbian.* "Use lots of pictures," is what he was told. Early on, the staff sought membership for *The Peak* in Canadian University Press (CUP), which served most of the English-language university student newspapers in the country. The staff were looking for the respect and stature of membership, the imprimatur of CUP standards, as well as the news services CUP provided. CUP, which professes to be the oldest student news service in the world, was formed in 1938 by a gathering in Winnipeg of Canadian student newspaper editors. It was (and is) protective of the independence of student papers—not just from administration or faculty control but also from control by student societies. The staff of *The Peak* had a chance to see that right away.[2]

The Peak became a full member at CUP's twenty-eighth annual conference held in Calgary over the 1965–66 Christmas holidays. At that conference, CUP suspended the membership of the student paper at Ryerson because it was faculty controlled; and it censured the student council at Saskatchewan for interfering with the student paper there. Later in the same year, CUP went to bat for the editor of the *McGill Daily,* who had been fired by the student council for an article about a McGill professor's Pentagon-funded research. This article was the product of a new, hard-hitting student journalism that emerged in the mid-1960s, a journalism that had an increasingly leftist slant. At its inception, *The Peak* caught a changing tide, but that was not what its staff were seeking, at least in the beginning. They wanted respect for their newspaper; and membership in CUP gave them a line of defence against interference, with the argument that they were meeting national standards for student journalism.[3]

THE PEAK AND EDITORIAL INDEPENDENCE

One thing an editor of *The Peak* could scarcely expect, even before the campus became politicized, was a letter of appreciation from the Student Society president. The responsibilities of the two positions inevitably clashed, when the name of the game for the student newspaper was to preserve its independence while fulfilling its role as a public watchdog. There was a continuing crossover in personnel between the Student Society and *The Peak* because the university's most active students tended to get involved with one and then the other. A byline in

The Peak helped with name recognition at election time. But when a *Peak* staffer became a student politician, he could not count on a cheering section from the newsroom. In April 1967, Stan Wong, as student president, did congratulate Simon Foulds for an excellent job after the latter finished a semester as editor; but this was an isolated moment in a the characteristically abrasive relationship between campus press and campus politicians.[4]

Financial control was an early issue for *The Peak*. The Student Society wanted financial control and the board and staff of *The Peak* resisted because they saw this as a short step from editorial control.[5] To protect the paper, they incorporated as a non-profit society in December 1966, a year before the Student Society got around to doing the same thing.[6] This insulated the Student Society from debts incurred by the paper and it weakened the argument that the Student Society needed to exercise financial supervision. But money spoke, and the paper always had to go to the Student Society for that.

Advertising covered about 65 per cent of *The Peak*'s operating costs; and most of it came from off-campus business looking for student customers—movie theatres, taxi companies, bistros, pizza parlours, bookstores and auto-repair shops. However, this income depended on an advertising monopoly. *The Peak* had a contract with the Student Society that gave it an exclusive right to sell advertising at SFU. (This made such things as the free distribution of handbills or desk blotters by outside advertisers a matter of objectionable competition.) In addition, about one-third of *The Peak*'s income came as a direct grant from the Student Society. Potentially, the Student Society had a whip hand that it could exercise by withholding either the grant or the advertising monopoly or both. These possibilities threatened in the fall of 1966, after several months of fractious relations, when the Student Society executive prepared to cut the paper's grant by more than 40 per cent or even to dissolve it and start a new one.[7] Of course, this did not happen. A change of editors helped; but the administrative structure of *The Peak* as well as its membership in CUP were important elements of the situation.

The Peak was censured once, in the summer of 1966, when Allen Garr was editor. The student chair of *The Peak*'s board cancelled an issue that had already gone to press, because he did not like Garr's reply to a female reader who had criticized an article on birth control. The

Student Society executive said that the issue could go ahead. Then the Faculty Council, on behalf of the administration, cancelled it. The next day Garr produced a renegade tabloid with the name *The Free Peak.*

A couple of principles got trampled in this episode: the independence of the student paper from the Student Society, and its independence from the university administration. But it did not happen again; and the incident did show everyone that there was a functional difference between the governing board and the editorial staff of *The Peak.* This helped in the fall of 1966, when the Student Council threatened to eliminate *The Peak* altogether. At that point, the members of *The Peak*'s board proved to be stout defenders of their newspaper; and they could argue with more detachment than *The Peak* staff possessed.[8]

Over the next six semesters, *The Peak* remained reasonably true to its original vision. Journalistic standards everywhere, however, were shifting. As one would expect, *The Peak* had a core of staff members who stayed with the paper for many semesters, and who could cultivate a shared sense of what the paper should be. Allen Garr, Sharon Yandle and Rick McGrath all wrote for *The Peak* throughout their undergraduate careers. Mike Campbell, Alan Bell, Jaan Pill, Stewart Gold and Gordon Hardy were all editors who came up through the ranks of *The Peak* during its first four years. The pages of the paper they created constitute a remarkably fine record of the issues, events and debates of SFU's early years. If there was a changing of the guard it came in 1969, in the fifth year of the university and of its student newspaper. It coincided with the emergence of a far more abrasive and partisan style.

For someone who wishes to do a quick study of *The Peak* to see how it transformed itself in temper and tone from 1965 to 1969, the cartoons are worth a look. President Patrick McTaggart-Cowan never suffered the savage treatment from early student cartoonists that President Ken Strand later got from Sandy Wilson. (Wilson subsequently made her mark as a film writer and director, most famously with her feature film and box-office success *My American Cousin,* released in 1986.) The ultimate Wilson cartoon—which drew an outraged protest from Dean Dale Sullivan—had another caption but might have been called "The Rape of the PSA Department."[9]

There was no mistaking what side Wilson was on in the Politics, Sociology & Anthropology (PSA) dispute of 1969; and the same statement could be made of the general reporting and editorial comment of *The Peak* at that time. One dismayed economics professor wrote to the editor, complaining that *The Peak* never got things right; it could only have merit as a publication, he said, if you could convince yourself that it was all a put-on, something that "looked, felt and tasted like a newspaper," but was "in reality a serialized shaggy dog story."[10]

This was harsh criticism but the view was widely shared. If there is any doubt about how widely, one has only to look at the frank assessments of two *Peak* editors, George Keter, who ran the paper in the summer of 1970, and Phil Dubois, who did so in the autumn of 1969. Both saw themselves engaged in a salvage effort, trying to recapture lost readership. Keter did not think the paper had been that bad. "But that is the way students were feeling," he said in an interview in November 1970.

Dubois made his assessment in an editorial he wrote in November 1969. He was a history student who placed himself well to the left of the political spectrum. The problem he recognized was that *The Peak* had such a credibility gap no one was reading it any more, or very few were. Dubois expanded the coverage and content so that there was more in the paper for more readers.[11] Keter was doing something similar a few months later, soliciting articles from as many contributors as he could and opening the letters-to-the-editor page to diverse opinions. Their regimes began a shift towards more even-handed reporting, although they did not turn *The Peak* back into the discreet publication it had been in the beginning. In his regular column, John Sawatsky, for example, was honing the journalistic skills that reached maturity with his exposé of the RCMP security service, his first book, published in 1980.

Dubois justified his policy with *The Peak* in tactical terms. He was a socialist and he thought it quite proper to use the pages of a student-subsidized paper to promote socialist ideals. He said quite candidly that the paper had to win readers so it could proceed to educate them. In 1969 the university community was more open to his idea of honest partisanship than it would have been earlier. The viability of objective journalism was now disputed, and not just at SFU.

At its national conference in December 1968, CUP had adopted a statement declaring objectivity a fiction. By that time, as a consequence of the increasingly radical politics of student journalists generally, CUP had been captured by the radicals of the Students for a Democractic

University (SDU).[12] They argued that the pretense of balanced reporting was just a cover for keeping the status quo. But the attack on objectivity came from many quarters. The imitators of the new American journalism of Tom Wolfe and Truman Capote (whose non-fiction novel *In Cold Blood* appeared in late 1965) were dismissing the value of detachment and advocating the open employment of subjective observation. In the spring of 1970, *The Peak* reprinted an article that first appeared in the venerable American weekly *The Nation*. The title said it all: "Objectivity: The Myth that is Destroying Journalism."[13]

For a short time at SFU, these influences expressed themselves in a highly partisan and wildly unpopular student paper; but credibility came back as the staff of *The Peak* began to tell themselves that if they could not be objective, at least they could be fair.[14]

STUDENT GOVERNMENT

In its maturity, SFU's Student Society has faced a nearly impossible task in getting a quorum for its annual general meeting. The standard set when the student population was much smaller now appears to be too high. A strong reaction to the discovery of pornography on some computers in the Student Society offices brought 800 people out for a meeting in freezing weather in the fall of 1996. But that was a rare event. Repeatedly the annual general meeting has fallen far short of its required quorum for a constitutional amendment. In 2002, about 30 showed up when 500 were needed for the meeting to proceed. The student executive prepared a motion to lower the quorum to 200, which they had ready for the annual meeting in October 2003. To ensure a large turnout, they offered a free buffet of hot food, vegetarian and chicken, at a cost to the Student Society of $15,000; and they succeeded in feeding well over 500. Some ate and ran. By the time the meeting came to order, the assembly was down to 430. Opponents of the motion were quick to call for a quorum, and the meeting ended before it began. In 2004, without the hot dinner, the annual meeting drew fewer than 80.[15]

It is true that in the 1960s, student leaders complained often about campus apathy. And similar moments were faced by student president John Mynott in the fall of 1966, when only one hundred people turned out for a special general meeting.[16] Roger Welch was well known on campus as a three-time student councillor and also remembered for eating his way to a weight of 135 kilograms and then, on a diet designed by SFU health services, trimming down to 81 kilos. In the pages of *The Peak,* Welch offered a timeless description of the political divisions of a university campus.[17]

Welch's theme was "SFU, the radical campus." Sure, he said, there were sharp divisions between campus radicals and moderates, but collectively these people did not make up much of the student body. There were three larger and, he judged, more powerful groups—the bridge players, the poker players and the beer drinkers, or, in his actual terminology, the "four clubs, four spades" group, the "raise you 25 cents" group, and the "see you at the Cariboo" group. (The Cariboo, at the foot of Burnaby Mountain just off the Lougheed Highway, was then the favoured campus drinking place.) Welch figured that the "see you at the Cariboo" group alone vastly outnumbered the political students of the right, left and centre. Add in the card players, and the politically active were a tiny minority.[18]

Yet there were highly charged moments in the 1960s when student power showed its face on the Erickson mall or at indoor meetings in the gym, with two-thirds of the student body assembled and intensely debating the future of the university. Even before the radical rhetoric began, a keen core of student leaders emerged from the crowd of strangers on SFU's first registration day. With no guidance other than an item on student government in the material they received at registration, a few took the initiative in calling a general meeting for the day after the opening ceremonies.[19] At the forefront was Lorne Mallin, who was ambitious to start a student paper, and who had posters up to recruit staff for *The Tartan*. What he knew was that $5.00 of the fees that the university collected from every student every semester went to the Student Society. It came to a tidy sum. He was motivated to get the Student Society going so it could direct some of that money to a campus paper. At the third general meeting in a seven-day period, with a large assembly trying to thrash out the outlines of a student government, someone suggested that they draw names from a hat. About 250 students were present; thirty names went into a hat and then were transferred into a paper bag. Ten were drawn, and these ten people—two females and eight males—became a steering committee charged with drawing up a draft constitution.[20] This was how student government began at SFU. It was briefly a perfect democracy.

SFU's first student president, Tony Buzan, was in the group whose names came out of the paper bag. His steering committee—after meeting daily for three weeks, reviewing what was done elsewhere, particularly at Victoria, looking at some American literature and consulting a lawyer—produced a constitution that was approved at a stormy general meeting by a vote of 137 to 98. In the first elections for Student Council, 45 per cent of the student population voted, an exceptional response for a student election. Tony Buzan became president of a council that had six other members. He began his presidency with three general meetings in the mall, all within the space of two weeks. These meetings had their contentious moments but exuded the enthusiasm of a first semester at a new university.[21]

The office of ombudsman was the most original innovation of the newly crafted constitution. It was an idea that had received recent publicity. New Zealand and Norway had created ombuds offices in 1962 and Denmark had done so in 1955. Previously the office had existed only in Finland and Sweden. No Canadian government had yet adopted the idea; and no Canadian university student society had tried it.[22] Over the next fifteen or twenty years, most Canadian provinces and many campuses created ombuds offices; but SFU's charter students were out ahead of the pack.

In the beginning, the ombudsman was a non-voting member of the Student Council who was also seen as a student president in waiting.[23] A constitutional change in 1967 took the ombudsman off the Student Council to eliminate a potential conflict of interest. But the kind of complaint that the ombudsman dealt with rarely had anything to do with the Student Council or student government. Most complaints were directed against faculty and the administration and involved matters like library fines and rejected bursary and scholarship applications or (as in Bill Birge's case) admission applications, as well as issues that students had with their treatment in courses and classes. The office proved its worth and became a permanent institution at SFU because the early ombudsmen were remarkably successful in getting the access, information and co-operation they needed from faculty and administrators.

The effectiveness of the student ombudsman was a boost to those who got involved with the Student Council. In the 1960s, students could be harshly dismissive of student government. "Sandbox government" was what radicals at Berkeley and elsewhere called it—play-acting of no importance. It didn't seem that way at SFU, which ran through twelve student presidents in the first five years. A student president at SFU had a tough job under an intense lens. The trimester system was a factor: a year-round circus that allowed no summer respite. The increasingly fractious nature of the campus was also a major factor. The frustration that Arthur Weeks vented when he resigned in February 1968 showed how difficult a president's role could be. His resignation followed a Student Council vote to censure President McTaggart-Cowan. As Weeks saw it, he had an activist council to his left and an SDU group of confrontational radicals agitating in the wings, while no one spoke for the 75 per cent of the student body who chose not to get involved.[24] Even without politics, a student president had a big task, especially in the early years, when the apparatus of student government was being established.

Money is one measure of the job. A university student council, then as now, had a lot of money in its hands. A $5.00 activity fee per student per semester, in 1968–69, translated into a total Student Society income for the year of $66,670, enough to maintain an academic department with five faculty members—larger than Archaeology and half the size of Philosophy.[25]

Running an office with a bookkeeper, secretary, part-time business manager and various part-time help took 30 per cent of the budget. *The Peak* got about 15 per cent. So did special activities such as concerts, films and visiting speakers. Then there were twenty-one student clubs that altogether received 10 per cent. Elections run by secret ballot, for which the student electoral officer and student electoral clerks received stipends or hourly wages, and membership in the Canadian Union of Students (CUS) and the B.C. Assembly of Students (BCAS) as well as expenses for council meetings took most of the rest. A student president oversaw a large operation, none of which had existed in September 1965, and all of which had to be created during the first few years.

TUITION FEES

The regular business of the Student Society was contentious enough; but major campus issues, like the censure of McTaggart-Cowan, were the ones on which a student president stood or fell. The first big issue was tuition fees, and that was on the table from the day the Student Council was constituted. Student leaders across Canada were pushing for the reduction and elimination of fees. The national student organization, CUS, led this fight and the newly formed provincial one, BCAS, got involved as well. Free university tuition, if it had come, would have been the logical culmination of a century-long progress towards free and universal education. The provincial opposition parties supported it. And in March 1966, the federal Health and Welfare minister, Allan MacEachern, circulated an address in which he advocated it.[26]

That might have been taken as a signal of the direction in which the federal government was moving. But it did not happen. The federal government had introduced a student loan program in 1964, and it was through loans rather than free tuition that the federal and provincial governments chose to extend help to needy students. Additional government support to students through scholarships and bursaries was minimal and in this respect B.C. was well below the national average.[27] Student leaders argued that the large debts that students had to assume through loans should be seen as a national crisis.

In B.C., only half the high-school graduates who had grades high enough to go to university were doing so. CUS did the research to show that a quarter of all students came from the most affluent 6 per cent of the population. And CUS and the BCAS insisted that the lifetime costs for those who did take student loans were too high. Only two years into the student loan program, student leaders were projecting crushing financial burdens for many students when they graduated.[28]

At that time a student could borrow $1,000 a year to a maximum of $5,000, which he or she had to start repaying at 5.75 per cent interest, six months after graduating. At SFU more than 40 per cent of this amount went to pay tuition. (In equivalent dollars, tuition is considerably higher now, but with most of the increase very recent.) Over the years, the loan maximum has increased somewhat: $5,000 then is equivalent to about $27,000 today, or about three-quarters of what a single student can now borrow. Student leaders in the 1960s, who saw these debt loads as unacceptable, found governments unwilling to do things differently; and the student loan program has continued throughout SFU's forty-year history. Generations of SFU students from lower-income families have accepted heavy personal debt as a necessity to get a degree.

The tuition issue engaged SFU's student leaders in a national and provincial crusade. SFU's early student councils joined with their counterparts at the University of Victoria and at UBC in an unsuccessful fight to get the provincial government to change its policy. This was on their agenda in 1965–66, and it was a major incentive in the formation of the BCAS as a provincial organization to augment the national efforts of CUS. With the spectre of tuition-fee increases on the horizon, B.C.'s student societies renewed their campaign in 1966–67.[29] Fees were among the issues that motivated 2,500 university students, mostly from Victoria, to march on the provincial legislature on a soggy Friday in Victoria in January 1967. About fifty SFU students took part in the march. At the steps to the legislature, the minister of education, Leslie Peterson, emerged to tell them that he did not support this kind of demonstration and that they could not expect the millions they wanted for university funding and for free tuition. (The chorus of boos and catcalls that cut him off set the tone for his next encounter with SFU students, when he agreed to be the convocation speaker a year later.[30])

STUDENT REPRESENTATION

A second demand by B.C. students when they marched on the B.C. legislature in January 1967 was for a student role in university government. They carried a twenty-page brief that argued that students should have a say on matters like timetables, entrance requirements, library operations and, most importantly, the curriculum. And they thought students should be involved on committees that governed ancillary services like parking, residences, the bookstore and food services. They wanted student representation on senate and on the board of governors. The issue of student representation had arrived in the wake of the Berkeley disturbances in 1964. The report on university government that Professors Duff and Berdahl produced for the Canadian Association of University Teachers (CAUT) and the Association of Universities and Colleges of Canada (AUCC) in the spring of 1966 recommended increased student involvement—not because Duff and Berdahl thought that was an ideal way to run a university, but because they believed it necessary to avoid Berkeley-like disturbances.[31] Discussion of this report on campuses across the country put the issue clearly on the table. The consequences could be seen at SFU, where the question of student participation had not been visible early in the spring of 1966, but was clearly there in the fall.

Coordinating, encouraging and even driving the student activism that manifested itself from coast to coast in 1966 was the national student organization CUS. SFU's Student Council joined CUS in the fall of 1966, left it a couple of months later and rejoined in the spring of 1967. When SFU came along, CUS was already forty years old. For most of its life, its objectives had been unremarkable, promoting student identity and Canadian (as opposed to regional) consciousness. But what was most apparent when SFU first became a member was CUS's new stridently radical orientation.

CUS had permanent headquarters in Ottawa from the early 1950s, but only in 1965 did it appoint a full-time president. This was the move of an activist leadership that, as a Canadian University Press staff writer observed, saw themselves as participants in a political movement rather than as servants of an organization.[32] Universal access to higher education was a primary goal for them, as well as gaining student and faculty control over university government. They advocated student-centred education and promoted anti-calendars. And they saw CUS as an agency for social change and insisted on taking positions on human rights issues and international affairs—particularly the Vietnam War. Dave Yorke, a history major, was an active CUS supporter and he represented a broad spectrum of opinion among politically involved students. In an article in *The Peak* headed "Activism or Irrelevance," Yorke credited the national organization with the growth of student power at SFU and other Canadian campuses.[33]

The leadership of CUS shifted further to the radical left when SFU's most famous (or notorious) student leader, Martin Loney, became its president. Loney was a graduate student who had come to SFU in 1966 from the University of Durham. His home was Bradford in Yorkshire, not so far from Durham; he had attended Bradford grammar school and one could hear Yorkshire in his accent. Between grammar school and university he had spent what he called "two boring years" as an executive trainee in a textile mill. His parents he described as liberals; his father was a dentist. As with many student radicals of the 1960s, his "libertarian socialism" had little to do with his family or social background.

In 1995, the *Vancouver Sun* columnist Trevor Lautens interviewed Loney in his home in Manotick, a suburb of Ottawa. Loney, who completed a PhD after leaving SFU and taught for twelve years at the Open

University in Britain, could not get a university position in Canada on his return and had made a career for himself as a consultant and researcher. In letters to the papers in 1995, he had railed against the "totalitarianism" of political correctness. In 1998 Loney produced a book—one of many he has published—in which he took aim at equity policies and preferential hiring. Such a book invited the question, "What happened to the student radical?" When Lautens asked him that question, Loney didn't think he had changed much. He said he had always risen to defend free speech.[34]

Loney achieved national attention in 1968. In January he was a principal organizer of the radical SDU group formed at SFU. In February the Student Council president, Arthur Weeks, resigned, complaining of the bullying tactics of the SDU at council meetings. In March the rest of the Student Council resigned after being impeached at a general student meeting for sanctioning a sit-in at a board of governors meeting. In elections held early in the summer, Loney and his group won handsomely—aided by lower summer enrolments. Three months later, at the end of his brief stint as SFU student president, Loney attended the CUS meetings and was elected national president for 1969–70.[35]

By then the SDU had awakened the masses—the politically apathetic—but not as the SDU might have hoped. In August, Loney was predicting a blow-up at SFU in the coming fall semester—a student strike or an occupation of the administration building. An occupation did happen, although without the mass support of the student body. In the council elections in late September, more than 2,700 students turned out in one of the heaviest votes of SFU history; and with two slates to choose from, moderates and radicals, they voted 68 per cent for the moderates. Many students bestirred themselves to vote because they had had enough of campus disruption. And what happened at SFU was happening on other campuses.[36]

University student societies had been dropping out of the radicalized national organization since 1966. The University of Alberta was one of the first, along with the Quebec universities. These losses had been partially offset by new university memberships; but when Loney became president he was faced with an exodus that spelled *finis*. Conservatives and moderates were turned off; and on many campuses their answer was to take their universities out. With this agenda, SFU's moderate council held a student referendum on CUS membership in the fall of 1969. Loney had been CUS president for three months; and he campaigned on his home campus before the vote. He had success to this extent: when the vote was taken, a majority of student voters at SFU favoured staying in. But later that fall, the University of Toronto pulled out, and CUS lost the annual $20,000 that Toronto contributed. That was the end.[37] The national student organization had become a casualty of student radicalism—with an SFU student presiding at the final call.

ATHLETICS AND ATHLETIC SCHOLARSHIPS

The public associated SFU with radicalism and riots, and also with athletes. It seemed at times that these were all the university was known for—negatively for radicalism and positively for sports. George Suart, SFU's vice-president for administration from May 1968, knew that the perception of SFU was not always that stark. But mentioning the public's perception served his argument in 1970, when the intercollegiate athletics program was under attack. The dean of arts, Dale Sullivan, and the chairs of the arts departments wanted to eliminate athletics and redirect its budget to the library. Suart had recently taken athletics under his administrative arm and his opening (and continuing) position was to defend it. Why get rid of something that brought positive publicity? Why target athletics and not other services like the Centre for Communication and the Arts, or the Reading and Study Centre, or psychological counselling? He did not propose to eliminate any of them; but he wasn't volunteering to abandon intercollegiate athletics.[38]

The athletics program, with its athletic scholarships, had Gordon Shrum—a sports fan—written all over it. And like almost everything associated with Shrum, it was controversial. Shrum was often ahead of his time, although in athletics this was only partially true. He wanted an athletics program that would put SFU on the map; and he was solely responsible for the completion of a gymnasium and indoor pool in the first phase of construction. Athletics had been one of Shrum's fiefdoms at UBC. He knew first-hand about the under-the-table funding of a few exceptional athletes at UBC: he had helped to raise it. He also knew that this was not enough to stop the best from going to American universities. (Each year, about forty B.C. high-school graduates were accepting athletic scholarships in the U.S.) He was tired, he said, according to a

Canadian Press quote in January 1966, of seeing UBC teams "go south to get beaten by B.C. boys attending U.S. universities." At SFU, he decreed, athletes would receive scholarships and it would all be in the open.[39]

On the question of women's athletics, Shrum was stuck in the past. Several years after he stepped down as chancellor, an athletics review committee at SFU interviewed him over lunch about the original conception of the program. Shrum said he believed in the educational as well as recreational value of athletics and in competition at the highest possible level. But during this conversation his focus seemed to be on football. And at the age of seventy-five, which is how old he was when this interview took place, he did not see any point in an intercollegiate athletics program for women. Very few women, he thought, would be interested.[40]

SFU began its intercollegiate athletics program with men's basketball, men's swimming and football (also for men). Men's track and field came soon after. Only from SFU's fourth year was there a women's varsity program, beginning with field hockey, track, swimming and basketball. All this happened under the supervision of Lorne Davies, who had been hired as director of athletics in the summer of 1965. Before coming to SFU, Davies had been at UBC as an assistant professor of physical education and an assistant football coach. For the previous few years he had also been a special coaching assistant for the B.C. Lions, then in their fifteenth year in the Canadian Football League. The choice of Davies—which was consistent with Shrum's way of thinking—meant that an intercollegiate program in football would get priority. It also determined the leadership of SFU's exceptionally successful athletics program for the next thirty years until Davies retired.[41]

SFU launched its intercollegiate athletics program in 1965 with fifty scholarships of $219—enough to pay two semesters' tuition for twenty-five athletes. These scholarships were supplemented by a few others that were given by groups or individuals from off-campus. A couple of the latter were enough to pay a year's tuition and leave $250 or $400 for living expenses; the others were enough for tuition only.[42] And SFU limited the total that an athlete could receive to three times the cost of tuition, counting both scholarship money and earnings while enrolled for classes. It was a modest program, attractive to students scrambling to pay their fees, but not the Cadillac treatment that many outsiders assumed it was. To keep their scholarships, athletes had to maintain their grades; and under Lorne Davies, this was an inflexible condition. The Athletics Department had the statistics to show that the average grades of varsity athletes were slightly higher than those of the whole student population.[43]

Ironically, SFU began fielding teams in an era of increased air travel, when national competition became possible. The national university hockey championship dates from 1963 and the football championship from 1967. Basketball, swimming, soccer and volleyball all followed along shortly. It is ironic because SFU, with its athletic scholarships, was ineligible from the start. The national organization, the Canadian Interuniversity Athletic Union (CIAU), prohibited financial aid to student athletes—at least if it came from their universities. The intention was to preserve pure amateurism in intercollegiate sports—to ensure that varsity sports were an outlet for academic students and not monopolized by pre-professional players. CIAU members saw this as preserving the Canadian way, as opposed to the American. They were also afraid of escalating costs if they allowed athletic scholarships.

The CIAU's great inconsistency—as Shrum and others at SFU were quick to say—was the blind eye it turned towards off-campus groups that supported individual athletes. Unfortunately for SFU, people in the CIAU had exaggerated ideas about how much SFU was spending. The president of the CIAU in 1971 seemed to think that an athletics scholarship program would involve annual expenditures of $100,000 or $200,000. In fact, SFU's athletic scholarship budget then was only $25,000—one-quarter or one-eighth of his estimate.[44]

Shrum, for one, was not much bothered about the CIAU. He was looking south. In one of his more famous moments, he promised that within a decade SFU would play in the Rose Bowl, America's most prestigious college football classic. This was bigger talk than SFU football ever had the budget to back up. And there was another fundamental problem: only American teams were eligible to compete in the National College Athletic Association (NCAA). When Peter Stursberg interviewed Shrum in 1983, Shrum admitted he had gone a bit overboard with the Rose Bowl promise.[45]

The choice that SFU actually made, after two years on its own playing exhibition games, was to enter an association of smaller American degree-granting colleges and universities, the National Association of Intercollegiate Athletics (NAIA). This offered competition that SFU could afford and suited its academic emphasis. From its inception in the 1940s, the NAIA philosophy had been the integration of sports and academics; there would be no bogus students on its teams; and it had strict rules about how much financial aid a student athlete could have—no more than needed for tuition, room and board, books and incidentals.[46] Canadians who made derogatory (or envious) remarks about big-money sports at American colleges were thinking of the major schools of the National College Athletic Association (NCAA), not the smaller ones of the NAIA.

When SFU joined the 515-member (and growing) NAIA in 1968, it was the second Canadian university to do so after Lakehead. For SFU, belonging to an American association meant games and meets in the Pacific Northwest and California against institutions that Canadians generally knew little about, like California State University at Chico, California (with an enrolment of about 1,300), or the University of Puget Sound at Tacoma (with an enrolment of around 3,000), or with larger but low-profile schools like Portland State and Central Washington State. But membership in the NAIA also meant a chance for national competition in the U.S.; and in its first three years, SFU sent its swim team and its track team to three American national championships. In those early years the basketball team played in a district championship; and in 1970 the football team achieved a sixth-place national ranking within the NAIA. This was after an undefeated season against opponents on the West Coast. (The NAIA national ranking was based on a complex calculation of the comparative achievements of winning teams from regional conferences that did not play against each other.)

Very quickly, SFU produced a remarkable number of nationally known athletes—as it has continued to do. SFU's media and public relations director, Dennis Roberts, tallied them up when the university was in its twelfth year.[47] By then, 10 per cent of the players in the Canadian Football League were from SFU, more than from any of Canada's other fifty universities. Among them was Dave Cutler, a football Clansman from 1966 to 1969, whose sixteen seasons with Edmonton were to establish him as one of the great place-kickers in CFL history. (Lui Passaglia, who played for twenty-five years for the B.C. Lions beginning in 1976, and who holds the CFL's points record, was the second great kicker to come from SFU.)

Swimming, track and field, soccer, wrestling and basketball were also developing national and international calibre athletes. Roberts counted thirty-eight SFU students in these sports who had represented Canada in international competition by the end of 1976. That included eleven SFU students on the national team at the Montreal summer Olympics that year. At Montreal, Canada won just eleven medals, five silver and six bronze, and one of the silvers belonged to a swimmer from SFU, Gary MacDonald. An SFU diver, Teri York, who had won a bronze at the Commonwealth Games two years earlier, came close to winning a medal at Montreal. At that point, the SFU swim team was in the fifth year of a run of nine consecutive NAIA championships.[48]

Where did SFU find its athletes? Gordon Shrum, when talking to Peter Stursberg in 1983, said he doubted that either Dave Cutler or Lui Passaglia was from B.C.[49] He assumed that assembling a winning football team took aggressive national recruiting, using SFU's lure of athletic scholarships. The best athletes must be from elsewhere. That was a widely shared notion on and off the SFU campus. In 1978, when UBC and SFU resumed their annual football match, the Shrum Bowl, after a hiatus of six years, the UBC coach jokingly told the press that the SFU Clansmen ought to be representing Ontario, it had so many players from Toronto and Hamilton.[50] The team list for that year shows twelve Ontario players out of fifty-five.

Lorne Davies did write to high-school football coaches across the country looking for prospects. But the great majority of his athletes were B.C. boys from Burnaby, North Vancouver, Vancouver and the Lower Mainland, as well as the Okanagan Valley and occasionally elsewhere in the interior. Dave Cutler, although born in Saskatchewan, went to high school in Victoria. He was one of the few SFU football players from Vancouver Island. And Lui Passaglia was from east Vancouver. The Clansmen were not, as Shrum seemed to think, a cast of average local players led by stars recruited from outside. One can see this in the frequency with which local players were named as first or second all-stars in their NAIA conference, or in the number who went on to become professional players. In the first three years of eligibility, from 1969 to 1971, 80 per cent of the SFU football players drafted into the CFL, including Terry Bailey and

John Beaton (who, along with Cutler, survived in the professional game longer than any of the others), were from B.C., most of them from the Vancouver area.[51]

Dave Cutler's story shows a side of athletics at SFU that Shrum did not suspect. Cutler had to ask for a tryout at SFU; he wasn't recruited. He made the SFU team, despite his lack of size and his initially unimpressive play, by proving himself to be too tough to ignore; and he became the team's kicker only after the regular kicker was injured and he asked for a chance to show what he could do. The work he did in the weight room, building himself up from 79 to 95 kilograms between his freshman and senior years, was all part of his development as a football player during his years at SFU. Obviously there was more to SFU's athletic success than simply recruiting outstanding high-school athletes; and Cutler was a prime example.[52]

When the dean and chairs of the Faculty of Arts took aim at the Athletics Department in 1970, they prompted a review of its program. During this review, interesting answers came back from the athletes about why they had chosen SFU. For some, the trimester system was an attraction. A skier, for example, could take the spring off for national and international competition. With the athletic scholarships, which only a minority got, the money was not always as important as the prestige of saying you had one. And the quality of the program, the professional coaching and the good competition were the reasons that many athletes chose SFU. A number had turned down better offers at other Canadian universities, where they could have received free tuition, free books, room and board and other benefits—evidence of the inconsistency of CIAU policy. And American universities, including NAIA members, promised more than SFU. But these students chose SFU because it was strong in the sports they wished to pursue.[53]

Under Lorne Davies, the SFU Athletics Department invested in first-rate coaching for a select few men's varsity sports, employing up to eight full-time coaches year-round and spending substantially on temporary and part-time staff such as assistant coaches, trainers and equipment managers. With this kind of support for varsity teams, SFU was spending at least as much as UBC, a much larger university, and far more than the University of Victoria. Football, with the lion's share of resources, had two or three full-time coaches in addition to Davies. John Kootnekoff with the men's basketball team, Paul Savage with the swimmers and divers, and Donald Steen with track were all full-time coaches in the 1960s. Wrestling got its full-time coach after 1970. Men's soccer, which was to have such success under coach John Buchanan, began as a club sport in 1966.[54]

The soccer story at SFU was one of triumph over neglect. It was also an accidental consequence of the initial placement of athletics in the Faculty of Education. If Dean Archie MacKinnon had still been at SFU when soccer's star shone, he might justly have taken credit for creating an environment in which accidental synchronicities took place. Soccer at SFU began with an effort by Glenn Kirchner, a charter member of the Education Faculty, to create instructional films on sports activities for use in schools. He was instrumental in hiring John Buchanan, a ship's carpenter, as the SFU pool manager, not because Buchanan knew anything about pools—he didn't—but because he knew soccer. Kirchner saw soccer as an especially suitable demonstration sport for instructional films: it could be organized quickly because all you needed was a ball. In Buchanan he had a twenty-six-year-old who had played soccer at an elite junior level in Glasgow and who was on the coaching staff of the B.C. soccer team. By taking Buchanan away from the pool for a few hours at a time, Kirchner had someone to organize twenty-eight kids in soccer drills for filming.[55]

Buchanan's presence on campus led to the formation of a club team composed of students and a few faculty, which he coached. They played in a local league with teams like Croatia and Hungary, made up of immigrant and semi-professional players who produced high-quality soccer. SFU's club team, honed in this league, was too much for the succession of American college and university teams that it met in exhibition matches. Yet it was only in 1975 that soccer became a varsity sport at SFU. (The difference between varsity and club sports was one of funding and competition: a varsity sport needed to have intercollegiate competition, and the Athletics Department had to be able to provide the coaching and facilities.) Somewhat jealously, soccer players attributed their long wait for recognition to the priority given to the prestigious American college sports, football and basketball. By 1975 Buchanan was assistant director of recreation. As a varsity coach he got time off each day for soccer but no additional remuneration; and in this sense, soccer was still a poor cousin to football, basketball, swimming and track. In November 1976, a year after soccer became a varsity sport, Buchanan's team won the NAIA national championship at the Rose Bowl in Pasadena, California. A few months later in Dallas, Texas, his team became the overall American collegiate soccer champions by winning a tournament of the best teams of the NCAA and the NAIA. Here was the champion that Shrum promised, except in low-budget soccer, not big-money football.

THE GOOD AND BAD OF ATHLETICS AT SFU

Although women had four varsity sports by 1968, they were getting crumbs from the Athletics Department budget. Women's basketball started in 1965 as a club sport, played in a local city league and coached voluntarily by a faculty member in the Kinesiology Department, Margaret Savage, who happened to be Paul Savage's wife, and who also coached swimming. Women's field hockey, track and swimming also started on a shoestring. From 1972 the Athletics Department employed a women's athletic coordinator who doubled as the basketball coach. By then the university was awarding athletic scholarships to six or seven women, divided between basketball and field hockey, and to sixty men in football, basketball and swimming. (There were more than five hundred varsity athletes by then, so most did not get scholarships.[56]) Women's soccer first appeared at SFU as a club sport in the late 1970s—early in the development of women's soccer in North America.

When Arts departments wanted to get rid of the athletics program, George Suart asked his assistant, Jake Wyman, to review the program. Wyman interviewed the staff of the Athletics Department and the athletes, administrators and students across the campus. His impression was that SFU students were not very pleased to have an intercollegiate sports program. They had exaggerated notions about how much money athletes got and what special concessions they received. And among students shaped by the 1960s, he encountered objections to competitive sport, or to body-contact sport, or to the Americanization of the sports program.[57]

Aside from the pool and gym, SFU's sports facilities were not very good. The football team had no stadium of its own; there was no ice surface; for soccer and field hockey there were no game-quality fields; and there were no fields on campus with bleachers that could accommodate a crowd. The university had to rent practice fields, rinks, gyms and sports venues off-campus in Burnaby, New Westminster, Coquitlam and Vancouver. Sports at all levels had no visibility: one did not chance upon a soccer game or rugby practice while walking across the campus. And varsity competition with places like Chico State or Yakima Valley College didn't resonate with SFU students. All of this contributed to the anomaly of varsity sports at SFU: outstanding teams were sadly ignored. It was a campus with remarkable athletes and few fans. *The Peak* reflected the attitude of the student body by consigning sports to its back pages and by running critical stories about the Athletics Department.[58]

One game that could generate excitement was the annual Shrum Bowl, when SFU and UBC met in football, playing Canadian rules one year and American the next. The first Shrum Bowl was in October 1967, when a fifteen-minute ruckus involving engineers from UBC and SFU students got overblown treatment in the Vancouver papers—disturbances again, and this time at a sporting event. In fact the Shrum Bowl was a great success. A crowd of fourteen thousand turned out at the (now demolished) Empire Stadium, which was then the home of the B.C. Lions. The press were out in force, and the TV cameras; there was a big half-time show with an American high-school marching band from Bellingham, Washington; and as the teams were getting ready for the opening kickoff, the UBC engineers brought out their naked Lady Godiva mounted on a white horse. Before the game, two thousand students had turned out for a pep rally and dance in the mall. As Lorne Davies remembered, all of the fun things associated with varsity football throughout North America were going on. In other words, it was an exceptional event for SFU.[59]

The Shrum Bowl was a tradition that had to die to be reborn. SFU won the first game and three of the next four. The one it did not win, it tied; and the last two wins were runaways—61 to 6 and 42 to 0. UBC withdrew in embarrassment from the 1971 game with just sixteen days' notice, and refused to play from 1971 until 1978. In 1971, SFU was looking for more Canadian competition, not less, and applied to the western regional association of the CIAU for membership. But SFU's scholarships were still an issue as well as its recruiting. At the insistence of UBC and other western universities, SFU stayed out for another thirty years.

SFU's athletes disagreed amongst themselves about the importance of playing in Canada. For them it was a question not of nationalism, but of sport. Some SFU athletes thought the CIAU would be a step down in competition. Others saw it as a step up. It depended on the sport. In the 1970s, football players, track athletes and wrestlers wanted to continue to go south of the border. The hockey, water polo and rugby players were more interested in the opposition in Canada. Soccer players were also keener to have matches in California than to cross the Rockies to play Calgary or Alberta. The general student body might have preferred to see teams from other Canadian universities, but that was not what a majority of the athletes wanted.[60]

Shrum's legacy was an outstanding program in football and other high-profile men's varsity sports. That was where most of the athletics and recreation budget went in the 1960s. And while SFU was only imitating what was done elsewhere, particularly across the border, expectations were changing, and within short order the Athletics Department was under pressure to make changes.

WOMEN AND ATHLETICS

Women in North America typically received little encouragement in sports when SFU opened; and they had received little in the past. Of course, there were exceptions. Intramural and club sports for women, particularly basketball, had been around since the 1920s. In eastern Canada, where travel distances were shorter, women had been active in basketball, track, indoor tennis, badminton, archery and soccer from the 1920s and 1930s. But SFU had adopted an American model and the sports opportunities for women at American universities and colleges had been even more limited than in Canada.

The NAIA and the NCAA were just for men, and there was no comparable women's association in the U.S. until the formation of the AIAW (Association of Intercollegiate Athletics for Women) in 1972. In Canada, the CWIAU (Canadian Women's Intercollegiate Athletic Union) was only two years older, dating from 1970. Up to that point, athletics specialists generally assumed that women were not built for strenuous sport. In the 1968 summer Olympics, women competed only in track, swimming, gymnastics and volleyball, compared with seventeen sports for men; and in track the longest distance that women ran was eight hundred metres.

In the 1960s a few voices at SFU complained about the neglect of women's sports; and the mumblings increased in the 1970s. By chance, SFU had enrolled a few outstanding women athletes, among them Carol Martin, bronze medal winner in discus at the 1970 Commonwealth Games, and Karen Magnussen, the Canadian figure-skating champion who won a silver medal at the 1972 winter Olympics. However, basketball, field hockey and swimming were the main women's varsity sports. As its field hockey coach, SFU had a national player, Moira Colbourne, who was with the SFU team from the beginning and who became an institution in the twenty-nine years she stayed. But given the status of women's sports, Colbourne was not a full-time coach, nor was Barbara Robertson, who doubled as women's athletic coordinator and basketball coach from 1972. Swimming was taken care of by Paul Savage, assisted by Margaret.

The Athletics Department had appointed Margaret Savage as unpaid women's sports coordinator in 1966, then hired Colbourne as part-time coach and, much later, as the university entered its eighth year, created a paid position for Robertson. (That brought the athletics staff budget on the women's side to one-sixth of the men's.) These hirings measured progress from a zero start. So did the distribution of athletic scholarships. In 1975, men got 83 per cent of the money and women 17 per cent. Ten years earlier, men had got it all. In recreational sports, women were turning up at the gym in greater numbers than the original plan anticipated. By the early 1970s, about one-twelfth of the women on campus were taking part in Athletics Department programs, compared to one-fifth of the men. And reflecting a national trend, the proportion of women on campus was rising, reaching 42 per cent in 1975 (up 5 per cent since 1971). The women who used the old gym facilities, before an addition in 1976, struggled with inadequate washroom, changing and locker space. And they did not like the gauntlet they had to run past the men in the weight-training room to get to the sauna.[61]

Volleyball was the only women's club sport in the early 1970s, and just one of many club sports complaining about meagre funding: the men had about fifteen clubs, including hockey, rugby, soccer, cricket and curling. The women's sports were all looking at the resources given to the men's varsity teams and objecting. The Athletics Department had a mandate to promote sports for everyone and not just elite athletes; and club sports were a major part of its answer. As the department explained, it combined North American and European concepts—sports for excellence and sports for recreation.[62] What made this difficult to sell was a budget that gave more than five times as much to varsity football as to all the clubs together. The imbalance had been greater in 1967, when the cricket and rugby clubs made a major fuss about poor equipment, services and facilities after a cricket player was injured on a badly prepared rented field. Things had improved after that.[63]

In intramural sports, SFU had started traditionally with separate men's and women's programs; then it went coeducational, a 1960s solution that theoretically accommodated everyone. By the mid-1970s, basketball was the only intramural sport with a women's league. Otherwise, intramural volleyball, basketball, soccer, softball, badminton and cross-country running were either coeducational or for men only. This arrangement had its critics, who argued that more women would sign up if they could play in women's leagues. Their point was that women had always been discouraged in sports, that this had been a high-school reality for most of them, and that many needed an alternative to leagues dominated by men. For the students who turned out to participate, however, the coeducational leagues worked, and despite the critique, the day of women-only intramural sports at SFU was over.

In the American model that SFU had adopted, varsity sports like football and basketball were supposed to be money earners that subsidized the rest of the athletics and recreation program. But that was not the way it worked at SFU, where a majority of students showed a tepid interest in their football team, and where there were no alumni to fill the stands. Instead, in the 1960s and 1970s, funding for varsity sports came mostly from the university budget. That is what made the football team a target for complaint, both from the academic side and from competing sports interests, like female athletes and cricket, rugby and soccer players. But SFU's varsity teams were wonderfully successful in giving the university visibility; and they were helpful when the university was looking for support from the public and the business community. From a public relations point of view, varsity football was good for SFU.[64]

STUDENT TEACHERS

Gordon Shrum told the board at its very first meeting that SFU would have graduate students: it wouldn't be the four-year undergraduate college that President John Macdonald of UBC envisaged. In its first year,

SFU enrolled eighty-three graduate students, including thirty-three PhD candidates. About a fifth were from UBC and a quarter were from other Canadian universities, but a majority were foreign, including a contingent from the U.K. and a smaller number of Americans and then a diverse group, making up 20 per cent of the total, from Singapore, Japan, Hong Kong, India, the West Indies, Spain, Germany, South Africa and Australia. The mix in SFU's graduate population was far more international than at other Canadian universities or than at SFU today. The newness of the university, the publicity it had received and the international background of its faculty were all factors.

Eighty-three graduate students spread among fourteen departments were easily lost on a campus with more then 2,500 students; but it was a situation that many of them relished. Graduate studies at SFU began with great informality and flexibility. It was all individual study, and typically faculty were willing to tailor their subjects to the interests of the students. The model was American: a formal structure of coursework or fieldwork prior to a thesis. But individual study blended well with the British model, the research degree that left nearly everything to student initiative. Faculty doors were open and the students and faculty who were there then recall a wonderfully collegial environment. But it was an environment in flux, shaping itself from the moment the university opened, especially in departments whose heads arrived late in the day. There had not been much chance for planning. Physics was an exception. Rudi Haering and his physics faculty saw a strong graduate program as essential for research, which they intended to emphasize They started off with thirteen PhDs, and Haering had drafted an outline of the physics graduate program more than a year in advance.

In the haste to get SFU up and running, no one had looked at a strategy for financing graduate students. Someone might have asked if the university should limit enrolments until it could offer fellowships, but that discussion never took place. In 1965 the university took in graduate students without a plan; and it has lived with the consequences ever since. The situation was compounded by the absence of any province-wide scheme. Ontario offered an example of how things might have been done. In 1964 Ontario introduced a fellowship program covering nearly every student entering graduate school. This supplemented the federal funding available to some PhD students through the Canada Council and the National Research Council. UBC had its own fellowships and awards, but the province of B.C. had nothing, and at SFU the omission fell most heavily on MA students.[65]

Those graduate students who did come to SFU in 1965 were not complaining because department heads had hit on an alternative—teaching assistantships. Shrum, in his enthusiasm for large lectures and tutorials, had imagined using both undergraduates and graduates as tutorial leaders, or TAS as they quickly became known (giving licence to the verb "to TA," which is what people at SFU say they do, rather than "tutor" or "teach"). But Shrum had no notion that graduate students would be the mainstay of the tutorial system. He had spoken of "dentists' wives," the pool of well-qualified housewives that he was sure existed in all subjects. He coined the term and everyone in the university used it in the early years to describe a category of teachers employed by semester who were neither full-time nor students. The teaching assistantship was designed for them as well as for students, both graduate and undergraduate.

"Dentists' wives" were not as easy to locate as Shrum expected, although it depended on the discipline and its needs. In the first year, there were enough qualified people from off-campus looking for part-time teaching to cover more than half of the available positions; and there might have been more if the science departments had wanted them. Instead, the sciences were choosing to support graduate students. Physics, with the largest group of graduate students in the university, gave all of its teaching assistantships to them. It was different in the arts, where temporary instructors from off-campus were initially the main answer. Some arts departments started with no graduate students, or only a couple. Modern Languages, with its emphasis on oral skills, needed tutors who spoke French, Spanish, German and Russian as a mother tongue, and found most of these people off-campus. In English, the composition course was a specialty that faculty did not want to teach and for which graduate students were not fully prepared. Non-student instructors were the answer.[66]

As SFU moved into its second and third years, departments found it easier to expand their pool of graduate students than to find additional qualified non-student instructors. By the beginning of the third year, 250 people were needed as TAS. So the graduate student population grew along with the undergraduate. When Steve Duguid enrolled as a graduate student in History at the beginning of the fall semester of 1968, he was shocked to be offered a TA-ship—and in a field he did not know, African history. He had not expected it although he readily accepted it. What he had run into was the university's shortage of qualified tutorial leaders. Like all things this did not last, but in the first few years the demand for TAs threatened to outrun the supply.

Many Arts departments had turned to graduate students only after looking for non-students. This is what Charles Hamilton found midway through the first academic year. Hamilton had just come from Kenyon College in Ohio, where he had been teaching History, to handle a variety of special assignments in the president's office. One of his first tasks was a report on the use of graduate students and "dentists' wives." Here he recorded a strong reservation expressed by most department heads: the graduate students they hired were putting too much work into their teaching, more than they were being paid for, and it was affecting their progress as students. Tom Bottomore in PSA had been among the first to raise this concern. In the second academic year, McTaggart-Cowan—adopting one of Bottomore's suggestions—offered some TAs funding for one semester free of teaching after teaching two. But he did not promise it for all.[67]

The department heads and faculty who created the teaching system at SFU had no common model to follow. Canadian universities had only recently begun to expand their graduate programs and had not previously relied much on graduate students as teachers. A university like UBC, which did not have the tutorial system, used graduate students as markers and in laboratories, but seldom as classroom teachers. Where the tutorial system did exist (as at Toronto), it had been managed with modest use of graduate students. In the U.S. one could find everything from the Berkeley example, where graduate students seemed to be doing most of the teaching, to Yale, where—in the humanities and social sciences—teaching assistantships were awarded sparingly and mainly to give graduate students some teaching experience before going on the job market. In the British Oxford and Cambridge system, tutorials meant something else again—regular meetings between a single student and a tutor.[68]

In the SFU system, as it developed, TAs took 80 per cent of the first- and second-year tutorials and laboratories. With four to six tutorials, depending on the department, a TA could be handling 60 to 90 students. In the beginning, to cover these positions, departments offered double loads to some non-student instructors and to some graduate students. That could mean 120 students or more. The granting of double TA-ships did not last long, because by the fifth year there were more graduate students applying than TA-ships available.

ORGANIZING GRADUATE STUDENTS

When Steve Duguid walked into a TA job in the fall of 1968, he found himself sharing AQ 5048—now a classroom—with eight or nine other history TAs. The design of the university had made no specific provision for teaching assistants, and their spaces had to be improvised. In the early years they felt the threat of eviction several times as rising enrolments sent deans and vice-presidents searching for places to put people. On those occasions they made themselves heard, petitioning the president, issuing press releases and calling for action by student representatives on senate. At times they found themselves crowded five together in a 13.5 square metre office intended for a single faculty member, or they felt they had no option but to go into the cafeteria or sit in a lounge or find a couple of chairs in a hallway to meet students from their tutorials who wanted guidance about essays or readings. The eventual solution, when the university was more than a decade old, was the construction of what became known as the elevator offices—tiny offices on the sixth floor of the Academic Quadrangle that blocked off all of the windows in the elevator and stairwell areas. It was an architect's nightmare. Only in the 1990s were half of these offices taken out, restoring the views of the mountains and the Fraser River delta.[69]

The other TAs with desks in AQ 5048, besides Duguid, were British or American, with the exception of a couple of Canadians. Most of the Americans were draft dodgers like himself; and, as he remembered it, the TA room was a hotbed of radical ideas. There were some more conservative voices in History among the British, but although they were conservative, they were not quiescent. The History TA room had been the headquarters of a campaign to establish a Graduate Students Association as the negotiating body for TAs. The motivation was that of a group of professionals in training who felt imposed upon, and who were not necessarily imbued with radical ideology.

The president was Ian Spencer, a British student who had come to SFU for a PhD in African history. Spencer's campaign highlighted the anomalous situation of TAS—neither fish nor fowl. They had issues: space (seeking at least a desk, chair, filing cabinet, bookshelves and an enclosed area in which to meet students), salary (objecting to being the only group without an increase since the university opened) and security (wanting some assurance of employment for more than one semester and not wanting to be told at the last minute whether they had jobs). But who were they, students or teachers?

Another group had also been organizing, calling themselves the Non-Faculty Teacher's Union. A married graduate student and TA in biological sciences, Sally Angelo, was a moving force, and her pitch was for a clearly defined employees' group to defend the interests of TAS, whether graduate students or not. (She wasn't using the term "dentists' wives.") She wanted issues related to employment taken out of the basket of graduate student concerns and dealt with separately. And she deliberately called her group a union, anticipating eventual certification under the provincial Labour Relations Act. (Nothing like this had yet been done by TAS anywhere in Canada or the U.S.) If there had been a possibility of co-operation between Spencer's group and Angelo's, it foundered on the word *union*.[70]

Spencer also wanted to pull graduate students out of the Student Society and to have the fees they paid directed to their own association. "Empire building" his critics called it; and members of the Student Society executive opposed it.[71] All this was happening during the 1967–68 academic year, and the three-way tug-of-war among Spencer's association, Angelo's union and the Student Society got lost amidst the larger issues disrupting the campus. The graduate student in the limelight, beginning with the Templeton Secondary affair and continuing through his election as president of CUS, was Martin Loney, not Spencer or Angelo.

In SFU's first eight years, graduate enrolments climbed tenfold while undergraduate increased by a factor of only two and a half. And SFU came to the end of its first cycle of growth and faced retrenchment. One consequence was the disappearance of the non-student TA. The term "dentists' wives," incorrect as it was, passed out of the vocabulary at SFU because departments no longer hired TAS from outside the university. By 1972 the university was able to offer TA-ships to only half of its active graduate students. No longer was it likely that a graduate student would be shocked like Steve Duguid to get a TA-ship he or she had not asked for. Beyond the TA-ship, the university still had little to offer.[72]

The existence of an excess pool of TAs left graduate students in a weak bargaining position. The university had developed a Berkeley view of TA-ships as teaching positions, rather than a Yale view of them as training or practicum opportunities. As the graduate population at SFU increased, the Berkeley attitude hardened. This did not happen as policy: there were no policy statements; but it happened as departments and senior administrators developed an informal rationale for what they were doing. Jean-Pierre Daem, a Belgian-born PhD student in Biological Sciences, ran into this in 1972. He was an environmentalist and activist, already involved on a long list of boards and institutes, when he became chair of a new graduate student organization, the Graduate Student Union (GSU). This group functioned under the umbrella of the Student Society; and it sought recognition from the university administration.[73]

Daem and his group thought the university could do three things for its graduate students: guarantee a minimum level of financial support to all active graduate students; raise TA salaries and link TA and faculty pay scales (giving a TA perhaps 40 per cent of an assistant professor's pay), and abolish graduate tuition fees. From the beginning President Ken Strand gave them no encouragement, although he met with them, listened and promised to consider. After a couple of months his answer was no to all three proposals. He could see no way of doing things differently within SFU's existing budget.

Strand's reasoning drew on assumptions that had been around since 1965. The university's tight finances in the early 1970s explain his unwillingness or inability to increase expenditures. But he was also unwilling to concede to graduate students any preferential claim to TA-ships. These were teaching positions, he told Daem, and the first consideration in filling them should be the welfare of the undergraduate program. The field was open to qualified undergraduates, post-doctoral fellows and faculty as well as to graduate students. (He, like everyone else, was now thinking only of people from within the university.) He had to specify faculty because graduate students were objecting to the assignment of tutorials to faculty to make up their teaching loads whenever enrolments slumped. Graduate students saw this as an encroachment on their own territory. Strand, from a faculty member's perspective, saw it otherwise.[74]

The membership of its executive changed as individuals like Jean-Pierre Daem moved on, but the GSU sustained a remarkable level of activity from 1971 to 1974. The newsletters, briefs and reports now surviving in archival files show it. For a period the GSU had a paid-up membership of over two hundred. Its executive lobbied both within and beyond the university. They met with Eileen Dailly, the minister of education in the new New Democratic Party government, newly elected in September 1972; they addressed the special commissioner on education appointed by Dailly, and they made representations to the governing NDP's standing committee on education—pleading their case for guaranteed graduate student funding. And they energetically petitioned the university administration at all levels on a spectrum of graduate student issues. A number of students worked hard over a three-year period; but in the end they had little to show for it. Halfway through the academic year, the 1973–74 executive began to see unionization under the Labour Relations Act as the only answer. To test the waters, they brought a sign-up sheet to the concourse in the Academic Quadrangle, where graduate students were registering for the spring semester of 1974.[75]

Unionization finally arrived in 1978 with the Teaching Support Staff Union (TSSU), which is still going strong twenty-seven years later. It is not the union of graduate students that the GSU executive wanted in 1974. Instead, the TSSU is a union of temporary or casual teaching staff, even though about 85 per cent of its members *are* graduate students. By contrast, the UBC union—which, incidentally, is not quite as old— defines its members as students (graduate and undergraduate) who are employed either for research or teaching. UBC did not follow the SFU model, and that illustrates a point. Although the TSSU at SFU was among the earliest TA unions in North America, its structure and independent philosophy have not been imitated elsewhere.

One has to look at the University of Wisconsin at Madison, the University of Michigan or the University of Toronto to find TA unions that are older; and they are not older by much. The Madison union was formed in 1969 and Michigan's in 1975; the Toronto union had been formed by 1976. The students who organized the TSSU at SFU were aware of the Toronto union, but knew little about the American precedents. This is an area in which American and Canadian patterns have not been quite the same. Once it started, the impetus towards unioniza-tion was stronger in Canada. Today more than twenty Canadian cam-puses have TA unions, compared with just three times that number in the U.S. (One might expect the U.S. figure to be ten or fifteen times higher given the greater number of universities and colleges there.) The notable Canadian exceptions are the Alberta universities and the fran-cophone universities of Quebec, where TAS are still not unionized. In the U.S., TA unions have mostly affiliated with the powerful American Fed-eration of Teachers. In Canada, nearly all have affiliated with the Cana-dian Union of Public Employees (CUPE). That was a possibility that TAS at SFU looked at but rejected.

Certification of the TSSU at SFU came ten years after Sally Angelo's effort to launch the Non-Faculty Teacher's Union and four years after the executive of the GSU brought a sign-up sheet to the course registra-tion area at the beginning of a spring semester. It was obviously not easy to organize either graduate students or TAS. They presented the problem of all temporary populations; and many of them really did not see the whole campus as their community: they were isolated by disci-pline. Any kind of organized activity, whatever the goal or purpose, went by fits and starts. One had to stick around to see a project like unionization through to the end; but leadership came and went. Those in the greatest hurry to complete their degrees were usually the least likely to get involved. However, the absence of policy at SFU helped the unionization cause in one vital way. There were no university-wide rules on how many TA-ships a student could have. Some depart-ments set the limit at four; others made it eight. In the latter case, graduate students could be around as TAS for four years or more, long enough for it to seem like a semi-permanent career; and these students took more than a passing interest in the conditions under which they were being employed.

At the core of the unionization drive were members of a small net-work of people—faculty, support staff and students—drawn together informally by shared interests, concerns and political perspectives, with a focus on the new left feminism inspired by Betty Friedan's *The Femi-nine Mystique*, published in 1963. A majority of graduate students at SFU in the early 1970s were men, and in every department the number of men employed as TAS far outnumbered the women. But women—and men sympathetic to feminist thinking—were at the heart of the effort to create the TSSU.[76]

The documentation that supported the TSSU's application for recognition includes the minutes of an initial organizational meeting in September 1976. Only thirteen people were present—eight men and five women—representing three departments, Economics, English and Sociology/Anthropology. These were the people who took on the ambitious task of signing up members, dividing up the seventeen departments and programs in the university amongst themselves. This was slow work, for which they were prepared. They expected resistance in the argument that a TA-ship really wasn't a job, that it was preparation for a career or a form of financial assistance. And they expected the consistent winners in the TA lottery, those who regularly got appointments, to be less enthusiastic about change than those who didn't. They also saw jeopardy in what they were trying to do and wondered if they should really delegate the organizing to people who had already had their quota of TA-ships.[77]

After two weeks they had just twenty-nine signatures out of a population of about three hundred TAs currently or recently employed—the group that would constitute their bargaining unit. Getting all of the signatures they would need took over two years; and to keep the list current, they had to go out and ask for the same signatures every semester. Finding time to do the work was a problem. It would have been easiest during an off-semester—when not taking courses—except that for nearly everyone this was the summer. And the rules of the game changed: after they had taken a year to sign up 35 per cent of their bargaining unit, the Social Credit government (back in power from 1975) raised the bar to 45 per cent. After 50 per cent had been signed up, a dispute with the administration about including language assistants delayed the certification vote until November 1978. The union was certified in early December with the language assistants in. The achievement had required a sustained effort over a twenty-eight-month period.[78]

Tom McGauley was a graduate student in English in the 1970s, engaged in research on Samuel Coleridge—which, with all the distractions that SFU offered, he never finished. He now lives in Burnaby and has long been active as a volunteer on various Burnaby boards and commissions—library, parks and recreation and cultural services. He is also a former postal worker. Postal work is what he did during the several years he took away from SFU between his BA and graduate school. McGauley was one of the handful of graduate students at SFU who made the TSSU a reality. Several others were from Economics, notably Michele Pujol, Sid Shniad and Anne-Marie Drosso. After the first meeting Jose Leme from Linguistics was also drawn into the effort. There were others, but these were the key contributors.[79]

The organization of the TSSU was an intersection point for a group of people on a set of remarkably varied paths. Leme went on to the University of Ottawa and then returned home to teach in Mexico City. Shniad became research director for a telecommunications workers' union based in B.C. Pujol and Drosso both completed PhDs at SFU, and Pujol taught at the University of Manitoba and then at Victoria before her death at the age of forty-six in 1997. In Winnipeg she was involved in organizing that city's first gay/lesbian parade and its first women's music festival. Drosso also taught at the University of Victoria and then went to law school at UBC before establishing a second career as a lawyer with the B.C. Workers' Compensation Board. That career has been superseded by marriage and life in Bloomsbury, London, where she began writing short stories, drawing on the insights she acquired growing up in Cairo speaking five languages.

They were an international group and as such characteristic of the graduate student crowd at SFU. McGauley was from the Kootenay region of B.C. and had attended Selkirk College before coming to SFU. But Shniad was an American from California; Pujol was French, born in Niger and educated in Paris; Drosso was Egyptian, and Leme was Mexican of recent Spanish ancestry: his family had left Spain when it fell under the Franco dictatorship. Like all groups, they needed leadership, and the driving force, as McGauley recalls, was Michele Pujol, who had the tenacity, focus and determination that kept the effort on track.

Their immediate motivation sprang from a strike called on September 8, 1976, by seventy-one physical plant employees at SFU who put up picket lines at the traffic lights at the intersection of Gaglardi Way and the route from Curtis Street. This was during the term of SFU's fifth president, Pauline Jewett. Pujol and the others reacted to a direction from Jewett's office to meet classes despite the pickets. They saw it as a challenge and a threat and held their first organizational meeting that day. At that meeting they found the will to persist until they had a union for TAS.

The union that they created became Local 6 of the Association of University and College Employees (AUCE). This was a small and experimental association of autonomous locals that subscribed to feminist and socialist principles and that addressed women's issues. By 1976 it represented clerical and secretarial staff at three universities (UBC, SFU and the tiny and now defunct Notre Dame in Nelson) and at two community colleges. The local at UBC had been the first and the one at SFU the second. The link between them had been the Vancouver Women's Caucus, a group that originated at SFU in 1968 and that had been the catalyst for a feminist union at UBC. One inspiration for AUCE had been the concern expressed within the Vancouver Women's Caucus that traditional unions did not work for women because they were male dominated and male oriented. The TSSU was the last local ever to join AUCE and the only one that represented teaching staff. But it was a natural outcome of the shared perspectives of members of the Women's Caucus, AUCE and the graduate students at SFU who committed themselves to organizing TAS.[80]

Ironically, the only AUCE local still in existence today is the TSSU. The others have all affiliated with the national union, CUPE, which is what most TA unions in Canada have done. The TSSU has chosen to keep its independence, and it continues as a functioning artifact from the past.

When the TSSU was formed, the unionization movement at Canadian universities seemed to have momentum. AUCE was part of this momentum. Faculty at Manitoba and at St. Mary's in Halifax had already unionized; and in 1974 at UBC, faculty got close enough to certification to vote on it, although the vote failed. The founding members of the TSSU were moving with the times. Shortly after they had won their first contract, they were in correspondence with TAS at Toronto, York, Ryerson, McMaster, Lakehead, Carleton, Regina and UBC, all of whom had unionized. Since then the movement has continued at other Canadian universities, but not as rapidly as one might then have expected.

Tom McGauley thinks that unionization at SFU might not have happened without the right combination of personalities and circumstances. When it did happen, however, it helped to confirm the university's radical reputation.

DROPPING OUT AND STAYING ON

Student journalists, student politicians, student athletes and student teachers all contributed to the yeasty atmosphere of the new SFU. Thirty or forty years after the fact, they are the easier students to track down. But one wonders about the rest and what they made of the university. Particularly one wonders about those who dropped out. In the 1960s the attrition rate at SFU was 40 per cent. High as it was, it was lower than the attrition rate that UBC experienced before SFU was built. President John Macdonald of UBC had called it wastage, a waste of time and resources for the university and for the students who came without motivation or ability. He saw it as an entry problem: the university was admitting people who did not belong. SFU's dean of students, Letty Wilson, looked at it differently and set about to ask students why they were leaving. Over the course of about three semesters, she interviewed every student who withdrew. The comment of one young man stuck in her mind. He was surprised to be interviewed and said, "I didn't think anybody around here cared." Wilson sent a questionnaire to every student who had dropped out during the first five years, and got a 29 per cent response.[81]

More than a third left for academic reasons and another third for personal or emotional reasons. Less than 10 per cent left because they could not manage financially. Whatever the primary reason, many expressed disenchantment with life, the world, society and the institution they had attended. A significant proportion cited student unrest as a factor in their decision to withdraw.[82]

That is one side of the story. Ian Andrew, now the director of International Teacher Education at SFU, was a student of the 1960s who fell within nearly every category: the dropout, athlete, activist and eventually graduate student and PhD. He had done poorly at UBC and had been required to withdraw. After working in the Yukon and then taking grade thirteen at King Edward High School—a year before it became Vancouver City College—he had gained probationary admission to SFU. He played on John Buchanan's soccer team and became heavily involved in sports and recreation. He joined the student protest over sFu's policy on transfer credits—having received no recognition for his year at King Edward—but stopped short of joining in the student occupation of the administration building. And he found himself a full participant on a campus that he remembers as academically progressive, although challenged at every level of its administrative structure; but above all a campus of gatherings and occasions and casual meetings where you got to know everyone. "It was an event to come to campus." For him, sFu offered a challenging five years of immense importance. It was his place of connection. His nostalgic memory of the university at that time: "It was easy to think outside the box because there wasn't a box."[83]

6

Young, Untenured
Faculty from Everywhere

NOVICE PROFESSORS AND EXPERIMENTAL TEACHING

Late in the summer of 1965, a group of eighteen Russian
agricultural experts toured Simon Fraser University.
They were impressed by the architecture and surprised
that the designers were Canadian: they had assumed
that Canada was too underdeveloped to produce architects of this calibre. And they were suitably amazed at
the speed with which the university had been built: they
had seen nothing like it in the Soviet Union. These were
their responses to the leading questions that people at
SFU asked. None of the Russians spoke English, so the
entire exchange was through translators. But the Russians had one unsolicited observation. The professors
that they met both at the University of B.C. and at SFU
seemed very young. They did not have the grey hair that
the Russians associated with academic standing and
achievement. In the 1960s, Westerners worried about the
apparent superiority of the Russian education system,
so this comment had an edge to it. The comeback,

offered by the translator, a Poultry Science professor from UBC, was that the professors on Vancouver's two campuses were youthful "because they're smart."[1]

With expansion, Canadian universities were already well into a youth movement. But SFU, as in so many aspects of its early development, was an extreme example. While the students, on average, were older than at other universities, the faculty were younger. Figures for the Physics Department illustrate the point. Seven years after SFU opened, a physicist from Toronto, Harry L. Welsh, looked at the ages of the faculty in Physics at SFU. He was writing a report on the department as part of the general program of departmental review that SFU instituted in the early 1970s; and he had high praise for the research reputation that Physics had already achieved. But he found the undergraduate program too idealistic and utopian: too intimidating for too many students. His explanation was the unrestrained youthful ambition of the faculty. In 1972 the oldest professor in Physics was forty-four and the youngest was thirty. Welsh calculated the average age at thirty-six. In 1965 they had been seven years younger—and that much more idealistic when they set up their program. Moreover, he observed, nearly everyone in the department had taught at SFU and nowhere else. Collectively they had little prior experience. Physics had hired a couple of its more mature faculty members from industry, but they were also new to teaching. Across the university, more than half of the faculty hired before 1970 had not taught before. Even in the first year, the faculty divided evenly between those who had taught at another university and those who had not.[2]

Those with teaching experience generally did not have a lot of it. The historian R. Craig Brown, also from Toronto, undertook a review of SFU's History Department in 1974. In History more than half of the faculty had taught only at SFU. Of the rest, only a few had taught previously for more than a couple of years. The variety of their teaching experience was extraordinary: in England and Wales, West Africa, the West Indies and Ceylon, as well as in the U.S. But what was striking for Brown was that the History faculty had mostly learned their trade at SFU. He had no comment on what that meant, except to observe that they had developed a laissez-faire attitude, allowing each other maximum latitude in what they taught and how they taught it and offering students a very flexible program to follow.[3] A youthful group of faculty in Physics had created a highly structured program. In History they had done the opposite.

Chris Taylor, after a long career in the federal civil service, retained an enthusiastic memory of his encounters with young professors in the 1960s. Taylor went to high school in Kitchener, Ontario, and entered SFU after working two summers at a fishing resort on the B.C. coast. In his second year, in the fall of 1967, he enrolled in a resource management course in geography with Hong Kong-born Shue Tuck Wong, newly appointed to SFU and still finishing his PhD at Chicago. As Taylor remembered, Wong came to the first class with breaking news: the City of Vancouver was proposing to build an elevated freeway through Chinatown—a project that ultimately did not go through. The merchants of Chinatown and others were fighting it and Wong was involved. He gave his students an option: either to follow the course as scheduled or to use the Chinatown freeway as a case study, taking their efforts off-campus, attending public hearings and assessing the proposals from both sides. He put it to a vote and the students chose to learn about public policy by getting involved. It was a wonderful educational experience according to Taylor.[4]

The geography course that achieved by far the most fame, applause and controversy was Michael Eliot Hurst's 101, The Geography of Technocratic Society. Eliot Hurst was a charter member of the department with a PhD in economic geography from the University of Durham, completed a year after he started at SFU. His lectures in 101 were awesome multimedia productions with several projectors running side by side to show film, video and slides—backed up by audiotape—all carefully selected and timed to illustrate the themes he was addressing. Without our contemporary advantage of PowerPoint software, he was putting on a show rarely seen then or now. He could maintain the drama of the presentation with sufficient force for a full two hours, not only to keep his own students spellbound but to draw in a crowd from other departments and even from off the hill. What he also did, with considerable criticism from a few colleagues and some students, was to allow students to determine the kind of assignment they completed for credit. He wanted serious work and commitment from them, but left the door open to their imaginations.

One of his teaching assistants has left behind a report on the challenge of handling tutorials for Eliot Hurst. This was Cam Murray, a New Zealander who had taught secondary school in his home country for five years before coming to SFU for graduate studies. He described himself as an innovative teacher, but from a straitlaced educational background. His conclusion after eight months with Eliot Hurst was that his courses had a place in a modern university: in fact, they were vital. But Murray had found the role of a tutorial leader and marker difficult. The first problem was that the tutorials seemed mundane after the extraordinary lectures. But the second and greater problem had to do with grading. When free to undertake any kind of assignment, many students still chose the conventional essay. From 165 students, Murray received sixty essays. The rest produced photo essays, films and videotapes, audiotapes, poetry projects, original music compositions, paintings, murals, batiks, "involvements" and "static displays." One "static display" was a totem pole carved with indigenous tools. One of the "involvements" was the effort of a student to organize and lead a church service. Assigning grades was never easy. But what Murray found most harrowing was the outraged reaction of his fellow graduate students—those not teaching in the course—when they saw these assignments coming in. Some of their comments were fair, he conceded, but most were "vitriolic and highly emotional." In these cases, Murray found it futile to argue that for many students this might be the first creative act since kindergarten.[5]

What Eliot Hurst was doing was conservative in comparison to what was advocated by some professors in the Education faculty. It was conservative in the sense that he and his teaching assistants were assigning grades. They ended up giving more As and Bs than they would have with traditional assignments; but they could explain that their students were putting in more effort. What they did accept was a responsibility as instructors to assess and grade. From a more radical pedagogical perspective, this was wrong. It inhibited individuality and free thinking.

Faculty had arrived with many understandings of what grades meant. In PSA, Tom Bottomore had given his colleagues a typically British scheme that mystified most North Americans—a scale that included grades like B++?+, expressing the fine difference between a high and a very high B. By the time classes started, he realized that it needed simplification. And when senate reconsidered a university-wide grading system, a majority voted for a stripped-down scale with As, Bs, Cs and Ds and no pluses or minuses. This decision reflected a debate that went beyond SFU: only a year later, Yale introduced a simplified grading scheme that was very similar. But in the fresh, unformed, charged and youthful environment of a new university, questions remained open for some time. In September 1967, senate was still debating grades. Science faculty wanted no change; in Arts most wanted pluses and minuses; and Education faculty argued for a pass–fail system. The Education idea was to take competition out of the learning process. In the end, the Arts position carried the day; and a grading system descending from A+ to F is what the university has had ever since.[6]

Two statements by student leader Martin Loney—given during SFU's most intense period of turmoil—sum up the radical critique of grades and their place in higher education. Loney put the radical case against the modern university with great economy in a column in *The Peak* in February 1967: "Maybe I'm wrong, but I always thought a university education was more than just a glorified supermarket which shoveled information down the throats." Loney wanted students to get active in the fight against the administration and "the business interests that lurk behind it." There were more important things to do, he said, than to engage in academic trivia. He had an explicit agenda. The minimum first step, he said, would be to get rid of grades and, of course, exams. He had been both student and, as a TA, a teacher. He had seen the battle over grades from both sides and he couldn't see their educational value. But his main point was that without grades, faculty had no power over students.[7]

Loney was giving a radical direction to the thought that runs through an instructor's mind when confronting a pile of essays or exams—teaching would be more fun without the marking. And to the extent that he was talking about student-centred education, he was promoting a 1960s notion that had shaped SFU's own Faculty of Education and infiltrated the thinking of faculty across the campus. Toronto's distinguished literary critic Northrop Frye spoke for traditionalists when he said that university education should be subject-centred, not student-centred.[8] Archie MacKinnon, SFU's thirty-eight-year-old founding dean of Education, had tried to balance the two by sending Education students to academic departments for credit work while enrolling them in open-ended, non-credit courses in Education.

MacKinnon had launched his Education Faculty with an eclectic group attracted by the broad vision he presented. He had not looked for school administrators or practising teachers, then the usual recruits for an Education Faculty. One of his senior appointments was Tom Mallinson, who at the age of forty-six was one of the oldest charter faculty members at SFU. Mallinson, like most of his colleagues in Education, had never taught school; and as an academic, he was closer to the beginning of his career than his age suggested. He had started university late, after working for much of his late teens and twenties in sales and accounting. As a teaching associate in the Department of Psychiatry at Toronto, he knew MacKinnon, and their conversations and shared ideas on education made him a candidate for a position at SFU. In retrospect, Mallinson recognized how utopian he and his colleagues had been. As he put it, it seemed like a great opportunity to be at a new university with no tradition: "no dead weight of past practice."[9]

Shortly after he retired in 1984, Mallinson wrote up recollections for a collection of essays about SFU by some of its early faculty. (The collection was never published but is available in the SFU archives.) Here he explained the broad concept around which the original Education Faculty designed itself.

Initially, Education students put a lot of energy and enthusiasm into non-credit work, creating their own programs and giving public presentations in music, theatre, dance and the visual arts. "It was a rare noon hour that did not have one or more offerings." But in the long run, non-credit could not compete with credit. When pressed for time, students put their effort into work that made a difference to their academic record. Perhaps it should not have been a surprise, but by the second and third years Mallinson and most of his colleagues were concluding that non-credit was not working. Education Faculty members began developing credit courses, although these courses really had no place within the original conception of the Education program. When a budget crunch came in the fourth year, they felt vulnerable and began a long discussion leading to the complete restructuring of the Faculty of Education. The brave experiment was clearly over by the time Dean MacKinnon resigned in January 1970.[10]

The Politics, Sociology & Anthropology (psa) Department was the locus of the most extraordinary adventure in pedagogy at sfu—a melting pot of Marxist and Dewey notions. By reputation it was both a bizarre and exciting place. Faculty from other departments passed around amazing stories, such as the one that Norman Swartz from Philosophy heard about a sociology professor in psa who supposedly gave grades inversely according to the income of a student's parents: the wealthier the parents, the lower the grade. Dale Sullivan, dean of Arts from 1968 to 1973, gave credit to accounts he heard of students in psa voting on their grades. Sharon Yandle, the student senator, *Peak* columnist and psa student, recalled the complaints she got from students and faculty in other departments about psa giving away free As. She herself had been in more than one psa class in which the professor asked students to grade themselves. She saw nothing irregular in it, because she assumed that the professor would not automatically accept a student's own self-assessment. But Yandle also said she did not consider herself a fool; and because she believed she had earned it, she would give herself an A. When other students tried to dismiss her student record, she had an effective answer. She had also taken a lot of History courses and she had done just as well in them.[11]

Yandle also remembered some of the young instructors in psa as very good teachers and very conscientious. They including Mordecai Briemberg and Louis Feldhammer, who were among the faculty who went on strike in 1969. Her memory of Feldhammer in his mid-twenties was that "he was kind of one of us" and that he conducted engaging classes with lots of invited speakers brought in by students as well as himself. (Feldhammer, who went on to teach sociology at Ryerson in Toronto, received an award for outstanding teaching at that institution in 1999.) Yandle also had classes with Kathleen Aberle, another of the striking faculty in 1969, and as an instance of Aberle's thoroughness and dedication remembered that her comments on an essay were as long as the essay itself.

What went on in psa was the talk of the campus, and there were enough strange stories to keep the talk going. Dean Sullivan understood that there was a professor in psa who encouraged his student to go into stores to shoplift and to bring the loot to class so they could discuss the experience. Yandle had a professor obsessed with Angola who regularly collected bags of clothes in class to ship to Africa. But what tore the department up from the inside was the charge that a core group had become so insistent on radical ideological conformity that their commitment to activism and collectivism was stifling free intellectual thought.[12]

These stories do not capture the passion and enthusiasm that faculty in PSA were able to generate among their students. The department had many defenders from outside as well as inside. One quote can serve as an example. In 1969, at the age of fifty-six, Harry Magdoff was the new editor of the *Monthly Review*, the independent American periodical of the Left. He had contacts with the PSA Department, mainly through Kathleen Aberle, who was to become a frequent contributor to the *Monthly Review* in the 1970s; and he had come up to SFU for several days in 1968 to lecture under the auspices of the PSA Department. When events at SFU concerning PSA were widely publicized in North America, he wrote a letter to *The Peak* to describe his time in the department as "uniquely rewarding and stimulating." He said that he had lectured at a number of American universities, including the most prestigious, without ever encountering a group of graduate and undergraduate students who were as vital and intellectually curious. He admitted to being perplexed and skeptical when he learned how far the department had gone to give students an equal share in its government: student participation was desirable, but in PSA he wondered if it had gone too far. So he spent as much time with students as he could. He was impressed by their maturity: by the way they weighed evidence, refused easy generalizations and proceeded tentatively towards conclusions. It seemed to him that their democratic experience in taking part in the running of the department was a major factor in the development of their maturity. What had been going on in PSA, he thought, was an intriguing experiment—unprecedented by anything he knew. "How sad," he ended his letter, "that it is being ruthlessly uprooted in its infancy."

DEMOCRACY AND THE COLLAPSE OF THE HEADSHIP SYSTEM

PSA was the extreme case, but in 1968–69, across the university, departments were opening up committees and department meetings to student representatives. They did so under combined pressure from student activists and faculty sympathizers, and typically only after hot debate. Generally, departments drew a line at student involvement in decisions about grades, graduate admissions, hiring and salary, tenure and promotion. But student representation—token or otherwise—was quickly carrying the day in Canadian universities from coast to coast. Indeed, some politicians were already ahead of faculty. In Ontario, in March 1969, when the provincial legislature debated new legislation for Carleton University, members of the Liberal and NDP opposition stood up to criticize the absence of guaranteed student representation on Carleton's senate.[13]

Geography at SFU took student involvement as far as any department other than PSA. This involvement was a big part of Chris Taylor's student experience in Geography. He had the chance to see the good and not-so-good sides of faculty, and thought he learned from both. What he appreciated was their openness, and he absorbed that as a lifetime lesson in management practice. But he also learned, at age eighteen or nineteen, that people with PhDs were not necessarily well organized or even competent in handling department business. That lesson can encourage confidence as well as skepticism in a young person. In his second year, Taylor became president of the Geography Students' Union and he was on several department committees, including Appointments, Renewal of Contracts, and Course Planning. "We were absolutely committee-ed to death." But the students had an impact. Their union would survey everyone taking geography each semester to find out what courses they wanted in the future and would insist that popular courses be offered even if the regular professors weren't planning to do them. While Taylor was still a student representative, Geography struck a committee of twelve, half students and half faculty, to search for a new department chair. On this occasion, parity meant that student opinion was decisive.[14]

One of the most dramatic and unexpected single outcomes of student participation occurred in History—which had a somewhat liberal, but scarcely radical group of faculty. The occasion was a department meeting and the issue a motion of support for the PSA Department and its striking faculty. Presiding was John Hutchinson, History's newly elected chair, who had been a central player in the faculty revolt that led to Patrick McTaggart-Cowan's resignation, but who was now a supporter of President Ken Strand and Dean Sullivan in their dealing with

PSA. The vote carried: eleven in favour, five opposed and six abstentions—with the students voting as a block of six in favour. Without the student votes it would have been an absolute deadlock, but Hutchinson, taking the principle of democracy to heart, resigned; and the students, to their surprise, found they had turned out a chair.[15]

As these events in History, Geography and PSA suggest, SFU's academic departments went through a revolution in government between 1965 and 1969. The board of governors, trying to catch up with what had happened, declared in July 1969 that department heads or chairs should not be authoritarian, but should work within a committee system and consult their faculty.[16] In fact, most departments were already operating that way and in a remarkably egalitarian—although frequently fractious—spirit. Seniority had largely disappeared as a criterion for leadership. It seems to have happened too fast for those involved to fully understand it as a historical or sociological phenomenon.

Norman Swartz has spoken of the extraordinary difference he found between McGill and SFU, all within the space of two years. In 1965, McGill had been his first teaching job, obtained on completing a PhD at Indiana. He had been hired as a part-time lecturer to teach the philosophy of science, and he found himself at the bottom of a McGill pecking order that allowed him no part in the running of the department. Senior professors made all the decisions, and junior people like himself discovered whether or not they were being rehired only by looking at a bulletin board to see if their names were on a list. When he came to SFU in 1967 he felt like he had been catapulted six hundred years forward, from the fourteenth century to the twentieth. To compound the contrast, two years after Swartz started at SFU he was chair of his department. But when he was at McGill, he said he wasn't sure what to think of his treatment. He found it a bit offensive, but didn't know what the practice was elsewhere—even at Harvard or at Indiana, the universities at which he had been a student. One suspects that, like Swartz, many of SFU's new faculty began to think seriously about the way universities were run only after starting to teach at one.[17]

In the early 1970s, when a number of outside scholars had a chance look at SFU, they seldom missed commenting on SFU's departmental democracies. These outside scholars were the external reviewers who would come in teams of three and spend three days talking to faculty, staff and students in a given department before writing reports. (It was the same review process that SFU follows today, although by 2005 it had acquired more procedures, and the management of it had moved further up the administrative hierarchy.) As a rule, what external reviewers could do, after just three days of investigation, was to throw up a mirror by reporting back to departments what their faculty and students said to them. If they thought there was a problem, it was likely because they had been told so by a good many people.

Their findings revealed early frustration at SFU with democracy at the department level. For example, Hungarian-born George Gratzer from Manitoba said the SFU Mathematics Department was too democratic to be efficient; Benoît Robitaille from University of Ottawa saw faculty unhappiness in Geography with the radical democratization that students like Chris Taylor were enjoying; Robert Binkley from Western Ontario believed that democracy in Philosophy wasn't working at all well because a significant subgroup lost every critical vote and felt left out; and Roy Daniells from UBC believed that SFU's English Department was overlegislated and overregulated. Daniells was repeating what he had been told by SFU faculty members like Stanley Cooperman, who had previously taught at Hofstra University on Long Island, New York. Cooperman claimed that in all the years he had taught, he had never been at a place like SFU, where measures were so maddeningly sidetracked into committees that reached no conclusion.[18]

SFU had taken a direction that other Canadian universities were following; and what the external reviewers were saying carried overtones of a nationwide discussion. One has a slice of this discussion in the words of Walter Gordon, the economic nationalist who had served as finance minister in the Liberal government of Lester Pearson and who was on the board of the University of Toronto. Gordon appeared before a University of Toronto commission in April 1969 to complain about "the jungle of committees" that Canadian universities had started to acquire. When it came to running departments by committee, he thought it a very poor idea—the end of good administration and a great inhibitor of new ideas. He was supporting a notion that the good old days were those of strong department heads who shouldered personal responsibility. Not surprisingly, Roy Daniells shared this notion. Daniells had been the long-time head of English at UBC. What was his advice to the Department of English at SFU? He thought the department should replace its formal regulations with common understandings and a reliance on precedents and common sense.

He was talking about the authority of people rather than of rules, and he was talking about the past, the way things had been at Canadian universities. Even at SFU that past was not far away. A system of strong, permanent department heads was what Shrum intended, and its collapse within three or four years he could not have predicted.

Several factors at SFU accelerated this collapse: all related to the youthfulness of the university and its faculty. The original heads were themselves relatively young, running in age from Rudi Haering, who was thirty-one when the university opened, to Tom Bottomore and Geoffrey Bursill-Hall, who were forty-five. A majority had been in their mid- to late teens when the Second World War started and six had seen wartime military service: Ron Baker, Archie MacPherson and Allan Cunningham in the Royal Air Force, Bottomore, as an infantry captain at General Headquarters in India, Bursill-Hall in the British Army Intelligence Corps and Parzival Copes, as a bilingual, Dutch-speaking teenage recruit into the Canadian army in the field in the Netherlands. There was a mostly silent gap in experience between these men and all but a few of the faculty that they hired. The latter were teenagers in the late 1940s or 1950s. Some of them had done national service in the immediate post-war era, when both Britain and the U.S. maintained the draft. The youngest of the group had been of draft age in the Vietnam War era.

As academic administrators, the original heads were mostly novices. They were men of experience and talent who had seen and done much, but who were tackling something they had not attempted before, and at an embryonic university. Baker had been an assistant to Roy Daniells at UBC and had taken on assignments in the president's office there. Nelson had been co-chair of his department at Queen's for a year. That was the sum total of the group's experience in academic administration. Moreover, they did not have a lot of common ground. In their most recently held positions, they been at various institutions: UBC, Queen's, Waterloo and Memorial in Canada; Oxford, the London School of Economics, Newcastle on Tyne and Edinburgh in the U.K.; and Washington (in St. Louis, Missouri) in the U.S., and, in Kendall's case, in a research position not associated with any university.

As they had arrived, one by one, McTaggart-Cowan added them to his advisory group, which became known as the Committee of Heads. There they sat with the bursar, registrar, librarian, dean of Education and dean of women as well as the president. In 1965, 1966 and 1967, this was the university's central administrative committee, the locus of power under the jurisdiction of the board. This was the way Shrum wanted it: no vice-presidents or permanent deans. All this held out the exciting promise of a weighty role in shaping the university. And the founding heads assumed other responsibilities by default. In the beginning they supplied the membership of the University Appointments Committee and the University Salary and Promotions Committee. A lot of power and responsibility was concentrated in very few hands.

After a few months of classes, the heads were looking for relief. As Brian Pate in Chemistry put it, the university was running on his stamina and that of the other heads, and on their ability to continue teaching, administering departments, fostering research and taking care of the administration of the university. But most of them, with Bottomore a leading voice, were fundamentally committed to Shrum's idea of no administrative layer between department heads and the president. The heads were hesitant even to give administrative assistants to the rotating deans, although they did in the end agree to that.[19] They also decided in December 1965 that they should have an administrative officer in each department to take over routine matters. That is how people like Ken Conibear, Rhodes scholar, author and former tugboat operator, and Ralph Kerr, retired Canadian army signal instructor, found places at SFU as departmental assistants in English and Physics.[20]

At the end of the first year, Pat Robertson, SFU's third registrar, took stock of the university's administrative structure. He was prompted by a couple of beefs he had with the micro-managing of the board and he suspected that others would soon be feeling the same way. The board had not learned to change its style now that it had a functioning university with faculty, staff and students. Robertson saw the university moving along from its beginnings when a small, tightly knit group of heads and board members could function with great informality. It was inevitably going to transform into a large, formal, sprawling organization with a bureaucracy and a fat book of policies and procedures.[21]

Robertson saw—before McTaggart-Cowan—that the style of the operation needed to change. The board had to stop looking at the

nitty-gritty and limit themselves to overall fiscal policy and external relations. And he had doubts about the continuing viability of the Committee of Heads. They had managed magnificently in the first year in
co-operatively hashing out budget allocations. But that would not be
the future, Robertson thought. They were likely to get more proprietary
as time went on. Without change in the way business was done, Robertson believed that the president was going to burn himself out, running
between the board and the faculty committees he was chairing.

The heads were feeling the physical and emotional demands of SFU's
turbulent beginnings; and by 1969 they had a health record that some
saw as evidence of collective stress.[22] Lorne Kendall was in his mid-
thirties in the summer of 1966 when he stepped down as head of Psychology with a heart condition. That same summer, Bruce Attridge had
relinquished the directorship of the Centre for Communication and the
Arts after a disabling illness that began with an infection. Don Nelson
discovered the seriousness of his leukemia in January–February 1968
and immediately resigned as head of Biological Sciences. Don Baird, the
librarian, had a stroke; and Allan Cunningham had to take leave in the
spring of 1968 to recover from tuberculosis.[23]

When he resigned as head of History in the middle of the summer of
1968, Cunningham wrote a long letter to Archie MacPherson, who had
become the temporary acting president. One reason for his resignation,
he said, was that he wanted to resume his scholarly career. He and his
fellow heads had put their research on hold from the time they took up
the SFU challenge. He said he found the headship too demanding to
keep without seriously shortchanging his teaching and scholarship.[24]

That was not Cunningham's only reason. He may have been getting
to the core of the matter when he spoke of the "total evisceration" of the
office of head. Heads, he said, had been reduced to routine administration while being stripped of real authority: "It is like having the hang-
over without having the party." He emphasized the evisceration that had
been executed from above: the president was not taking the advice of the
heads on administrative appointments or on enrolments; and open
budget planning was a charade because new programs were appearing
without their sanction.

What he did not mention were the problems coming from below. A
faction in his own department were organized to vote him out of office.
He had written his letter of resignation two days before the crucial

meeting and he caught his opponents by surprise. He had already lost his moral authority with a large number of his faculty, especially the younger ones. So carrying on would not have been easy. At sfu this was not a singular development, but followed a pattern repeated in most departments. The notable exceptions were the departments of Physics, Biological Sciences and Economics & Commerce, where there was positive consensus about the directions taken by the original heads, Rudi Haering, Don Nelson and Parzi Copes.

The heads probably did not expect the dissent that emerged by the second year. Several of them had invited their colleagues at the very start to share in the conceptualization of their departments; and that generally meant open discussion with everyone included—not the scenario that Norman Swartz encountered at McGill. The minutes of the first meeting of the psa faculty suggest the way things started off in many departments. This meeting was held a month before classes began and included two associate professors and three junior people who had yet to complete their PhDs, as well as Bottomore. The senior people did most of the talking, but on the table were fundamental questions about the future. How far would they take the integration of anthropology and sociology? What emphasis would they give to kinship studies or peasant studies or political parties and elections, and how could that be combined with African, South Asian or local studies? It was collective decision making involving everyone.[25]

The initial semester in most departments called for closer co-operation and more team teaching than happened later. History offered just one large introductory course with everyone sharing the lectures and taking tutorials. After doing the first round of hiring on their own, heads brought their colleagues into the hiring process, reading files, conducting interviews and ranking candidates. Some heads chose to distribute the work by making up a different committee for each position they were filling. Others took along a few of their colleagues for interviews at the cattle markets, the annual meetings of the various learned societies. All of this encouraged a sense of collective ownership of a department and its program. It also encouraged complaint when heads lapsed and made arbitrary decisions without consulting.

The second and third rounds of hiring had an overwhelming impact on the university and on nearly every department, and if the system of heads was fated to go, this drove the process. With two big intakes in 1966 and 1967, a faculty of 126 in the first year jumped to 274 by the third. After that, the university entered a long period of slow growth. But the effect of the second and third intakes was to make a young faculty still younger. Most of the senior appointments had been made in the first year. In 1967 more than three-quarters of the faculty were assistant professors and instructors. All this contributed to a dynamic that most heads could not control.

By 1967, Baker had forty-one faculty in English, up from the eighteen with which he had begun. His was one of the two largest departments, but in nearly every one, the nucleus of faculty from the first year had been swamped by the additions of the next two. Quick growth made it difficult to insist on a single vision. When debates about policies and priorities became bitter, new arrivals were conscripted into the fray. Disagreements found new life when fresh people gave them energy. Evan Alderson, who joined the English Department in 1966, found himself mistakenly under suspicion from the Left because he happened to have been interviewed by people from the Right (as the department then defined its divisions). That was the politicized nature of sfu by then. The Duff–Berdahl Report on university government, when it appeared in the spring of 1966, gave ammunition to everyone critical of the headship system; and throughout the university, departments began legislating steering committees, procedures, terms of reference and constitutions, all designed to rein in the heads. The ultimate goal of the majority was a system of rotating chairs, which by 1970 became the university-legislated system.[26]

The first instinct when heads resigned was to give the job to the next most senior person. When Kendall in Psychology stepped down in 1966, the president chaired the committee that named Bernard Lyman, who, at the age of forty-two, happened to be the oldest person in the department. Similarly, in psa David Bettison, who by 1967 was a full professor, was selected to follow Bottomore. By 1968 the selection process had become democratic: departments were voting on new heads or chairs. Still, when Cunningham resigned in History, the automatic choice was Peter Kup, the only other full professor. In Biological Sciences, Glen Geen replaced Don Nelson; and in Physics, John Cochran followed Rudi Haering. In each case the choice had been made from the senior rank.

This did not last. With a shortage of full professors and with an abundance of assistants and instructors, a system of rotating chairs quickly led to the election of junior people.

Within their departments and within the university, junior faculty had a voice. They were listened to, heard and able to influence the development of the university. They had helped create an egalitarian environment with little consciousness of rank; and that is what kept many of them at SFU. Some senior faculty had great difficulty with the new order. In 1971, Geoffrey Bursill-Hall expressed this in a letter to Brian Wilson, who was then only a few months into his influential tenure as vice-president. Senior faculty in Arts were becoming alienated, said Bursill-Hall, and the problem was the practice of making decisions by majority vote. "The opinions of senior faculty, who are inevitably in a minority, are either simply ignored or overruled." This was a disgruntled former head, seven years after he had begun planning his department.[27]

RECRUITING OUTSIDE CANADA AND THE CANADIAN ISSUE

With weeks to go before opening ceremonies in 1965, John Arnett, the *Vancouver Sun*'s education writer, wrote a story on the faculty that SFU had recruited. He featured three—David Bettison, Philip Stigger and A.H. Somjee—under a headline that said the world was beating a path to SFU.[28] Bettison, the South African, had been running an Australian National University research project in Papua New Guinea. Stigger, who came to SFU to teach African history, had been a magistrate in Tanzania through the transition from colonial rule to independence. A.H. Somjee was a political scientist from the University of Baroda in India, and a visitor at the London School of Economics during the previous year. Both Stigger and Somjee stayed at SFU for the duration of their careers. Bettison ended up in New Zealand.

For Shrum and McTaggart-Cowan, the international character of SFU's charter faculty was a matter of pride. When two of SFU's prospects—K.S. Viswanathan in Physics and T.W. Kim in Modern Languages—had visa problems, both Shrum and McTaggart-Cowan went straight to the top in the Canadian Department of Immigration to press their entry and that of other foreign scholars. They made the point that this was a national issue because Canada was producing only about one-third of the PhDs needed. But they also wanted specific recognition of

SFU's ambitions. Gordon Shrum had a chance to bend the ear of the deputy minister of immigration, Claude Isbister, during a visit to Vancouver; and Shrum got across the message that SFU needed help because it was recruiting staff "from all over the world."[29]

Some heads felt they had no choice but to look outside Canada. This was the case with Bursill-Hall in Modern Languages, who was creating a department unlike any other in the country with an emphasis on teaching the spoken language. This presented a much greater challenge than assembling a conventional literature department. Most of the faculty that he hired in the first round came out of American graduate schools. Their national origins, however, were diverse and the department ended up with a number of Europeans (British, French and German), Latin Americans and a few Asians, along with a contingent of Americans.

Shrum and McTaggart-Cowan had given a green light to searches that focussed outside Canada. Twenty years after the fact, Allan Cunningham claimed that nobody had ever suggested he make a special effort to select Canadians: "the colour of the passport was irrelevant." In his first round, Cunningham hired two Canadians (out of eight), and that happened because they were studying at the University of London and came to see him in London. In the second round he hired one out of ten, and that was someone completing a PhD at UBC who had been hired originally as a teaching assistant.

Cunningham did his initial interviewing in London and then, two weeks after unpacking in Vancouver, he went off to the annual meetings of the American Historical Association, which in December 1964 were held in Washington, D.C. The next year, with three of his new colleagues, he went to the AHA meetings in San Francisco; and between that and trips back to London he recruited most of his department. Should a later generation be shocked that he headed off to the U.S. without a cursory look in Canada? He did not think so. For one thing, he understood that some Canadians attended the AHA meetings, so there was a possibility of encountering them there. And what he had heard from McTaggart-Cowan and others made him pessimistic about attracting Canadians from the East.[30]

Bottomore also began selecting faculty while he was still in London. One of the first was an American, Roy Carlson, who was then an assistant professor at the University of Colorado. Carlson had a major research interest in the Pacific Northwest; he was married to a Canadian and his mother-in-law had been sending him reports of SFU. He came up to Vancouver to see McTaggart-Cowan; but the interview that counted was with Bottomore, and that was possible because Carlson passed through London on the way to Egypt, where he was involved in an archaeological survey in the Nile Valley (before the flooding caused by the building of the Aswan Dam). Over lunch at the London School of Economics, Carlson and Bottomore found a common subject in the archaeologist Vere Gordon Childe, the great prehistory synthesizer who, like Bottomore, was an intellectual Marxist and not an activist. That conversation persuaded Bottomore to add the archaeologist Carlson to the PSA mix.

Bottomore's British perspective and his years as editor of the international journal *Current Sociology* gave him a global view of the disciplines in PSA. His situation at the London School of Economics was also a factor because scholars from overseas were coming and going all the time. He had known and respected A.H. Somjee for several years before Somjee came from Baroda to spend a year at LSE. His decision to bring Somjee to SFU was a natural consequence. Bottomore's idea was to organize his department around two main fields, theoretical problems of the social sciences and changing institutions of developing countries. These he intended as primary teaching and research fields. Africa, Latin America, South Asia (India, Pakistan and Nepal) and Southeast Asia were all regions he targeted. Bob Wyllie, who was then a lecturer at University College of Cape Coast in Ghana, was one of the first people he interviewed in London. He also hired Bettison while in London, and thereby got a senior scholar who knew South Africa and Southeast Asia. And he was making decisions based on the files arriving in his mail; as a consequence he also hired Tom Brose, an American Fulbright fellow doing research on Mexico. In Brose's case, an interview was not possible and Bottomore dispensed with one. He made the same judgement in other cases as well. In this way he completed most of his first round of hiring before reaching Vancouver.

Ron Baker, on the other hand, knew the Canadian scene and was looking for people in the best populated discipline in the country. His first appointment, even so, was Ralph Maud, a British-born American who was teaching at the State University of New York in Buffalo. Maud was Baker's senior appointment. He had written in the spring of 1964 after seeing SFU advertised in *The Times* of London and had met Baker at the Modern Languages Association Meeting in San Francisco that June. A few months before classes started in 1965, Baker and Maud were corresponding about course outlines. This exchange makes interesting reading because it shows Baker both aware of Canadian sensibilities and unwilling to dictate course content. For a course on twentieth-century verse, Maud had chosen a lineup of American poets. Where were the British poets? Why was there no Canadian? Baker warned that these were objections that Maud would face from some Canadian colleagues and students. On the other hand, Baker said he would support Maud, whatever he chose to do.[31]

Baker was talking to high-school English teachers: all a matter of recruiting students out of grade twelve. As soon as he could, he distributed to teachers a description of the faculty in his department, with an emphasis on their teaching interests but mentioning something about their background. One question that teachers had been asking was about the national origins of his faculty. Baker disowned the question. "I am never quite sure why this is of interest," he said. However, he was armed with a reply. In 1965, one-third of his department were born in the United Kingdom, one-third in Canada and one-third in the United States. With one exception, he added, they had all done graduate work or gained university experience in North America. He might have added that seven out of seventeen had earned undergraduate or graduate degrees from UBC; but that was a more parochial picture than he wanted to promote.[32]

When it came to hiring in Canada or bringing Canadians back from elsewhere, the two departments that did it the most were in the Faculty of Science—Physics and Biological Sciences. Both departments had Canadians as their founding heads—Rudi Haering and Don Nelson; and Canadian PhD programs in the sciences had developed ahead of the arts. This meant more Canadian PhDs to be found, and heads who knew the networks that could find them. Beyond that, the research foci that Haering and Nelson conceived for their departments, and their approaches to recruiting, increased the chances that they would search in Canada or turn up Canadians.

Haering aimed to make an impact by creating a research department that concentrated on one branch of physics—condensed matter, or solid-state physics. As Haering explained, he wanted a "critical mass" of faculty doing related research. The result was the creation of a Canadian powerhouse in solid-state physics. His strategy was also practical in allowing the department to concentrate its expenditures for equipment and research facilities to maximum effect. And as John Cochran and Klaus Reickhoff have said, the faculty in Physics came together from the beginning as a cohesive and compatible group. They all bought Haering's vision.

Haering did not wait for applications but wrote to people like Cochran and Reickhoff after getting their names from former teachers or supervisors. Cochran was in Cambridge, Massachusetts, at MIT, where he was an associate professor. Reickhoff was working for IBM at their research laboratory in San Jose, California. Both had studied physics at UBC in the Shrum era: Cochran straight out of high school in Moose Jaw, and Reickhoff after resuming an education interrupted for eight years following his escape from the Russian-occupied zone of East Berlin in 1947. He had immigrated to Canada and struggled to get himself and his family established after landing in Vancouver with $7.00 in his pocket: his first job was on the docks chalking bags and weighing cargo.

The people that Haering recruited possessed considerable international experience. Reickhoff had a German education, three degrees from UBC and his time at IBM. Cochran had done a PhD at Illinois and post-doctoral work at Oxford and Leiden. Dave Huntley's PhD was from Oxford and Bob Frindt's was from Cambridge. K.S. Viswanathan, who had been an undergraduate at Madras, had an MSc and a PhD from California at Riverside. Others had done post-doctoral work abroad. But among the charter ten physicists at SFU, six had one or more degrees from UBC and three had one or more degrees from Alberta.

In Biological Sciences, Don Nelson took the exceptional step of recruiting a third of his faculty members from a federal government Agriculture Research Institute in the Ontario city of Belleville. Negotiating this deal took until September 1967, when these people started at SFU, but Nelson had anticipated success and held faculty spaces open for them. The Belleville people were experienced and senior researchers. And they were an international group, including an Irishman, Bryan Beirne, trained in Dublin; a German, Manfred Mackauer, trained in Frankfurt; an Indian, K.K. Nair, trained in Madras and Bombay; two

Englishmen, John Webster and Peter Belton, trained in London; as well as native Canadians J.S. Barlow, Thelma Finlayson and A.L. Turnbull. Turnbull was the one ex-Vancouverite among them. Their common field of research was biological methods of pest control. Nelson had already hired an American, John Borden (who had been an undergraduate at UBC), whose work on pheromones or sex attractants for bark beetles made him a good fit. Their research had both forestry and agricultural applications.[33]

Bryan Beirne had been the director of the Belleville Institute since 1955. It was a major research centre with thirty professional staff and one hundred support staff. Since 1962 he had been angling to move the institute to Vancouver. He wanted a university affiliation to allow his staff to take graduate students; and he considered the West Coast, with its great variety of micro-environments, the best place in Canada for the institute's basic research. In 1964 Shrum became aware that the institute might be movable and made inquiries.[34] As head of Biological Sciences, Nelson took over the file. A protracted negotiation with the Department of Agriculture lasted until 1967. In the end, Beirne and seven others joined SFU, but the institute stayed in Belleville.

Like Haering, Nelson hired former UBC students. Five of his first twelve appointments had been at one time or another UBC graduate or undergraduate students. But he had found people from much further afield. In 1965 his department had begun with six faculty: Nelson and R.C. Brooke, two Canadians, and Fulton Fisher, William Vidaver, Lalit Srivastava and A.P. van Overbeeke—a New Zealander, a Californian, an Indian and a Netherlander.

No easy generalization covers the recruiting of faculty for SFU. What happened in Biological Sciences and Physics on one hand, and in English, History, PSA and Modern Languages on the other, were different scenarios. And these departments didn't exhaust all the variations. Each discipline presented its special challenges; each head came to the task independently and with more or less familiarity with the Canadian networks in his discipline, or with the American, or the British.

In the 1960s, SFU, like other Canadian universities, offered better salaries than universities elsewhere in the world except the U.S. If an individual was willing to move from the United Kingdom or Australia or West Africa, then talking salary was the easy part of the discussion.

Within North America, however, Canadian money did not talk so loudly. One of the young American graduate students that sfu was trying to recruit in 1965–66 was Douglas Cole. He had met Allan Cunningham at the AHA meeting in San Francisco, and he sat on Cunningham's offer of a job at sfu while he waited to hear from the University of Kentucky. He did end up at sfu, where he taught for more than thirty years until his premature death in 1997. His choice in 1966 might have seemed obvious because he was from the Pacific Northwest and was completing a dissertation on Canadian constitutional history. But he hesitated. His early take on sfu, as he told his graduate school buddy, Bill Sampson, was that it had pretensions "somewhat out of line" with its salary and drawing appeal.[35]

A great many American colleges and state universities paid less than sfu. That could be seen in the salary tables that the American Association of University Professors published in its *Bulletin*. In 1965–66, salaries at sfu were better than at 80 per cent of American universities and colleges. But that still left about 180 American universities, beginning with Harvard, that had richer budgets and higher salaries.[36] sfu and other Canadian universities ranked themselves within the upper echelon of universities in North America. And to a graduate from an American university, Canada could look better than many of the choices at home. But Cole's comment is a reminder that sfu did not have a fat purse or necessarily a lot of prestige when recruiting in the U.S.

Two things helped. One was the size of the American system and the number of PhDs it produced. The second was the Vietnam War and its unsettling effect on many Americans. Tony Arnott's case conveys a sense of the times. In 1968 Arnott walked unannounced into the physics lab at sfu, having decided to leave the U.S. because his sons were nearing draft age. Rather than apply for a job in the conventional way, he went to Canadian universities, "interviewing" them. When Rudi Haering realized that Arnott was a senior research physicist from the Ford Motor Company Scientific Laboratory with previous teaching experience at the Carnegie Institute of Technology, he found a way to take him on, even though Physics then had no openings. The answer was to get him involved with the federally funded Tri-Universities Meson Facility (TRI-UMF), a joint sfu–ubc–Victoria project that had just been approved by Atomic Energy of Canada.[37]

What made Arnott's case singular was his seniority. Ann Messenger—who was to spend twenty-one years in the English department at SFU before retiring for health reasons—drove up from Berkeley through fog, slush, wind and rain in January 1966 with her husband Bill to check out Vancouver and its universities. The result, after a couple of days running from one campus to the other, was a job for him at UBC and, a year later, a job for her at SFU. After Richard Nixon's victory in the American presidential election of 1968, Messenger wrote to her parents in Pittsburgh: "We can become Canadians in another two and a half years."[38]

In December 1968, the Canadian edition of *Time* magazine ran a feature on foreign faculty on Canadian campuses, following the lead of the daily press. By then 50 per cent of the faculty at Canadian universities were foreign-born. Seven years earlier it had been 25 per cent. And in the preceding year (1967–68), according to Department of Manpower figures, Canadian universities had hired 1,013 American academics, 545 British and only 362 Canadian. The novelist and McGill University professor Hugh MacLennan called it "a program of national suicide." Two Carleton University professors, Robin Mathews and James Steele, gained national attention and notoriety with their campaign for corrective action. Their evidence and arguments can be found in the book they published in the summer of 1969, *The Struggle for Canadian Universities*. As this book shows, they generated a lot of heat, but ran into opposition from Canadian academics—foreign- and Canadian-born—when they suggested quotas based on citizenship.[39]

For Mathews and Steele and their allies, SFU was the ultimate demonstration of the problem. As the freelance writer Herschel Hardin put it in the spring of 1969, Canadians at SFU formed "just small enclaves in their own institution." About 30 per cent of the SFU faculty were Canadian by birth or naturalization. The other 70 per cent were not. In explaining the threat to Canadian identity, Hardin gave the example of History at SFU. In the first year, the history of Canada had been "lost in the shuffle" and only in the second round of hiring did Allan Cunningham look for someone to teach it; and he did so by going to the AHA meetings in San Francisco.[40]

Student radicals had their own take on the issue; and the person who expressed it best at SFU was John Conway. Today, Conway is chair of the

Sociology Department at the University of Regina. In the late 1960s and early 1970s he was a PhD student at SFU. Before that he had been a high-profile student activist at Regina and Saskatchewan; and when he arrived at SFU in 1968, he was instantly in the thick of things—elected that summer to the Student Society executive on the radical Martin Loney slate. When the foreign issue made headlines in the mainstream press, Conway wrote an article for *The Peak.*

The problem for Conway, as it was for other commentators from the Left, was not just the importation of American and other foreign faculty; it was the extensive Americanization of the whole country, economically, culturally and intellectually. This he believed was a much deeper concern than current hiring policies; and he charged Canadian universities and Canadian faculty with complicity. Too many Canadian professors had been schooled in the U.S. "Every discipline in Canada is American biased whether taught by Canadians or not," he wrote. In Conway's world, Americans who came to Canada in protest against the war or right-wing American politics were welcome. Those who were merely careerists were not.[41]

That was the critique from the Left. Gordon Shrum had earlier made headlines when he blamed the furor at SFU on malcontents from the United States and Great Britain. He really had in mind members of the PSA Department.[42] But in the heat of battle he was guilty of a more sweeping statement. So immigrant professors were absorbing shots from the Right as well as the Left. A deeply anti-American tone found its way into a letter from Ron Baker to Patrick McTaggart-Cowan a few months after McTaggart-Cowan had left SFU and after Baker had resigned as department head. Baker was expressing a discomfort felt by many Canadian academics. He told McTaggart-Cowan that he was seriously thinking of leaving SFU because it was no longer British or Canadian but American, with an American acting president, an American chair of joint faculty, an American dean of Arts and an American head of English. Five years earlier he had claimed not to be concerned where faculty came from. That indifference had gone.[43]

When he left, Baker thought the situation at SFU beyond repair: a university that he had been instrumental in starting had succumbed to an "academic-political style" that he found foreign and alienating. That is what he told McTaggart-Cowan. He added that other Canadian universities "could be saved" if the country would spend the money needed to produce homegrown talent. (People like Mathews and Steele were saying that the homegrown candidates were there, but being ignored.) Shortly after writing to McTaggart-Cowan, Baker accepted the presidency of the University of Prince Edward Island.

One of the national voices in the debate about foreign professors was Pauline Jewett, who happened to be a colleague of Mathews and Steele at Carleton. In an article in *Maclean's* in March 1969, she asked if Canadian universities were doing enough to attract Canadian talent. Five years later she was president of SFU; and during her term (1974–78), 80 per cent of new appointments were Canadians.[44] The hiring frenzy of the 1960s was over; and in the 1970s Canadian universities were overproducing graduate student, so it was a greatly changed environment. No one at SFU was disputing the desirability of hiring Canadians. But as president, Jewett raised hackles when she questioned and, on occasion, turned back appointments because she did not think an adequate Canadian search had been made.[45]

Jewett was leading a Canada-wide shift towards Canadian hiring; and by the late 1970s the argument had been settled by the Canadian government, which introduced immigration regulations giving clear preference to Canadian citizens and landed immigrants.[46] Since then we have had a quarter of a century of mostly Canadian hiring. Since 2000, departments have been itching to take advantage of a new willingness in the immigration department to allow international searches. It will take a while, however, to return SFU to the situation with which it started.

THE TENURE ISSUE

The tenure and promotions policy that SFU finally adopted in 1968 was one of things that left Ron Baker feeling out of place. This policy has been modified since, but its essential structure was set then, and in a way that Baker could not have anticipated when he first addressed the question on behalf of the board. A resolution of the tenure issue contributed to a fundamental change in the environment at SFU. But the university was so much in flux that the negotiation of tenure policy escaped notice by the great mass of faculty members. What they could eventually applaud was a new regime in which elected committees instead of heads made recommendations about tenure promotions and renewal. What many did not foresee was that this would bring a new insistence on research and publications.

Baker had written the skeletal academic freedom and tenure statement that the board adopted in May 1964. It was published in the handbook given to faculty when they arrived in 1965. This statement, slightly revised in 1966, was all that the university had until 1968, by which time half a dozen draft policies and two referenda had gone into the trash.

Faculty members, if they were paying attention, generally blamed McTaggart-Cowan for false starts and delays in developing a fully stated tenure policy, but it is hard to go through the surviving documentation and leave the main fault with him. On Baker's advice, McTaggart-Cowan and the board made a commitment to negotiate a policy with a Faculty Association as soon as one had been formed. Under the circumstances, this seemed a reasonable way to proceed. But with hindsight, an infant Faculty Association at a newly formed SFU seems to have been poorly equipped for the job.

First there was the matter of low membership. Halfway through the third academic year, only half of the faculty at SFU were Faculty Association members. This compared badly with an average 80 per cent at other Canadian universities. Many at SFU never belonged; and that was one reason why the bursar, Donald Ross, initially refused to institute automatic payroll deductions for Faculty Association dues. On the eve of the first censure of SFU by the Canadian Association of University Teachers, Howard McCurdy, the CAUT president, could not resist comparing SFU with Windsor, his own university, where membership was at 90 per cent. He was saying that the SFU association would be more effective if it had more members.[47]

Second was the crippling problem of an inactive membership. How many people would turn out for a Faculty Association meeting? Occasionally, quite a few. In 1968, following the student occupation of the administration building, the number was 123; but this was after a major campus confrontation. (The university then had a faculty of over 350, so 123 was good, but lots of people were not there.) Most faculty, then as now, paid attention to the association only when something went extraordinarily wrong. Then they would turn out at the next meeting to try to repair the damage. In the second year, the association reduced its quorum to ten—except for the annual general meeting. At times, meetings barely drew that number.[48]

Low attendance and a small quorum made Faculty Association meetings vulnerable to capture by any rump that waited until attendance thinned. This happened with critical effect at a Faculty Association meeting in October 1967.[49] Towards the end, with just thirty-six people still present, twenty-one votes were more than enough to carry a motion to scrap the Faculty Association's brief on academic freedom and tenure. The executive resigned immediately. This brief represented over twenty months of work; it had just been approved in a referendum of all members by a vote of ninety to twenty; and it was to go to the board for approval in two days.[50]

That meant another meeting four days later to try to put things back together. Even then, the turnout was only eighty-five, and the main debate was whether people really wanted a Faculty Association.[51] Dale Sullivan, the future dean of Arts (who was to win election as dean as a candidate of the Left), was among those busy distributing membership forms for a faculty union to replace the Association. This effort stalled at about sixty members, and the Faculty Association survived.[52] The next six months, however, proved to be critically important as the board and McTaggart-Cowan waited for the Faculty Association to bring back a new policy proposal. Within the Faculty Association all sides found a way to blame the president for an impasse; and he was the person who paid the greatest price in reputation and respect.[53]

These events created a stir across the campus. But this stir did not mean that the average faculty member was paying careful attention. The negative evidence is there in the faculty votes on three referendum ballots taken from 1966 to 1968. Under the right circumstances, the faculty would vote for almost anything.

The three ballots were on successive drafts of the university's tenure policy. The last draft bore little resemblance to the first. The most obvious changes were in length: step by step, in negotiations between the board and the Faculty Association, the policy statement grew and changed radically. Yet each time the faculty balloted, they voted yes. This can be explained somewhat by a process of constant re-education on the issues. But it also seems that most faculty at sfu wanted to trust the Faculty Association and the board to get it right.

This was understandable, given the many first-appointment professors at a new university with their own departments and courses, and theses or other research projects to worry about. Their inattention was one of the challenging conditions under which the Faculty Association laboured. A second was the sharp criticism of the evolving draft policy by a small number who were paying attention. And a third was the absence of guidelines. The Faculty Association and the board were negotiating policy in an area without Canadian models.

Baker had complained about that when he first addressed the tenure question in 1964. As far as he could tell, there was not much out there he could appropriate for an SFU policy.[54]

In the early summer of 1967, the secretary of SFU's Faculty Association, the McGill-educated serials librarian Charlie MacDonald, wrote to twelve Canadian universities asking for their tenure and sabbatical policies. What he found out was that older universities were still working on them. The largest English-speaking university in the country, Toronto, was only then adopting the principle of "tenure," and it did not have CAUT-approved procedures until 1975.[55] At some universities, nothing was happening. And MacDonald discovered that resistance to the idea of a tenure policy was strong among faculty members at some of them.

This was true at McMaster, where many faculty saw the existing system as "*de facto* tenure" without the drawbacks of a formal tenure system. They were referring to the traditional Canadian practice of making probationary appointments followed by regular continuing ones. Their fear was that an official tenure policy would make a continuing appointment harder to get. An ominous example of what might be coming was the Harvard Department of Economics, where nine out of ten people did not get tenure and had to move on.[56]

This helps explain Baker's attitude when he wrote SFU's first tenure statement. Baker did not see academic freedom as an issue in Canada—not the issue that it was in the U.S., where it had been under attack more frequently. In his experience, it was "almost unheard of" for anyone who held a faculty position for any length of time at a Canadian university ever to be released. Whatever you called it, Canadian academics enjoyed permanent or continuing employment—or tenure. Stamping it with a name and spelling it out as a policy, he believed, was more a "psychological sign of good faith" than a legal commitment.

What were the tenure expectations of SFU's charter faculty? They did not have anything on paper beyond the statement in the faculty handbook; and yet they had cheerfully come to SFU without much evident worry. The handbook said that appointments "without term" were awarded after three years to full professors, after four to associates and after seven to assistants; and that they would not be awarded automatically, but only after review by "the President and the Board of Governors." Beyond that, new faculty members received no statement of their terms of employment. After a candidate accepted a job from a department head, and after the board approved the appointment, the president sent him/her a form that stated rank, department, term and rate of pay: nothing more. Everyone except the founding heads got a fixed term of one to three years depending on rank. Everyone understood that their appointments were probationary but renewable.

Most people initially seemed unconcerned about their own security at SFU. For a glimpse into the thinking of those who did get involved in drafting tenure policy, we have a letter from John Mills to Clark Cook. The two of them were instructors—graduates of UBC with MAS from American universities—and charter members of the English Department. Within four months of starting at SFU, they joined a five-person Faculty Association committee charged with writing a tenure brief. The other three on the committee were two assistant professors and one associate. Only two of the five had PhDs and only one had taught at another university. No one within the Faculty Association seemed to think that seniority, rank and experience were needed to map out tenure policy.

In reality, tenure policy had a different look for those at the bottom of the ladder. Mills wrote to Cook in June 1967 after discovering that the Faculty Association executive—in negotiating with the board—had accepted major changes to their tenure brief. The revisions made the process more formal: specifying a hierarchy of tenure committees at the department, faculty and university levels; and recasting the adjudication committee in dismissal cases so that half of its members would be named by the president, rather than all by the Faculty Association. From a junior faculty member's perspective this was more threatening, especially because the tenure committees were to be composed of senior people. Mills, Cook and their drafting committee had assumed that tenure cases could be handled simply and expeditiously: heads would recommend to the president and the president would go to the board. No one else would be involved. Mills had quite a bit to say in his single-spaced, one-page letter to Cook, but one sentence stands out: "Tenure should be automatic."[57]

Automatic tenure was not going to be the outcome. A number of tolerant or "soft" features of SFU's largely informal initial policy disappeared in the negotiations between the Faculty Association and the board between 1966 and 1968. Faculty members themselves—with a collective commitment to high standards—were responsible for driving negotiations in this direction. This was true not just at SFU but at other Canadian universities. It could be seen in the leadership that the CAUT was giving. The policy that SFU adopted in 1968 followed the CAUT guidelines that had finally appeared in 1967. It bore no resemblance to the 1966 draft that Cook and Mills had worked on.[58]

What was different? In the beginning, Baker as academic planner and head of English told applicants that SFU did not plan to have an "up or out policy."[59] By that he meant that SFU would not imitate elite American universities like Harvard, but model itself on UBC as he knew it up to that point. Charter faculty at SFU understood that they could likely stay on with further appointments even if they did not get tenure at the first try. This offered a less pressured existence for everyone from the rank of assistant professor up.

The dividing line, then as now, between instructors and assistant professors was generally the PhD, but this was far from cut and dried. Founding heads like Baker and Bottomore would promote people without PhDs, and McTaggart-Cowan was willing to withhold promotion from people who had earned PhDs. He did not see promotion as a right. Instead he linked promotions to openings: an instructor could move up only when an assistant professor position became available. Only in January 1968, under pressure from below and with the sanction of the board (which had to deal with the budget implications) did he introduce the open-ended policy that SFU has kept ever since. Performance would be the only criterion for promotion. In theory, everyone could eventually make their way to full professor. That was not McTaggart-Cowan's first instinct. His original position would have created a university with a very different ethos, one in which seniority mattered far more and a professor waited for promotion until the department expanded or a more senior person moved on.[60]

In SFU's initial tenure statement, instructors could not get tenure; and so it has remained, despite an attempt in one Faculty Association brief to make instructors tenurable. But the way SFU started out, instructors could expect, if they did not get promoted, to continue on a succession of one-year contracts. For a moment in 1968, it seemed that this informal state of things would be codified in an explicit statement that instructors could be reappointed repeatedly "with no limit on years of service." The rule, however, became a maximum of seven years.[61]

During the summer of 1968, while the campus had its eyes on a parade of presidents—Ellis, MacPherson and Strand—SFU's ultimate tenure policy took shape. The Faculty Association kept negotiating as one president succeeded another. By the end, SFU had a system like those of the more prestigious American universities. Assistant professors had six or in some cases seven years to get tenure, or they were out and had to find jobs elsewhere. Instructors had seven years to be promoted to assistant professor or they were out.

With this policy, SFU instituted elected tenure and promotions committees. And unlike the earlier tenure briefs, this policy reserved spots on department tenure committees for assistant professors, although not for instructors. A number of the founding heads tried to resist this innovation because they thought one should be judged by one's peers: a full professor by full professors; an associate by full professors and associates, and so on.[62] But in 1968 at SFU, that was a losing argument. The movement was towards a more inclusive and egalitarian way of proceeding. That did not, however, mean open proceedings. From the beginning, these committees met *in camera* under strict rules of confidentiality.

Whether or not people anticipated it, the committees were generally tougher than the heads had been. Or one might say that they were less likely to make exceptions or to treat anyone as special. In the early 1970s, the outside scholars conducting departmental reviews were hearing complaints of a publish-or-perish culture—just what Shrum and Baker had promised that SFU would not have. The turning point was the commencement of the new tenure and promotions regime, and this was not just at SFU.[63]

In a letter to her parents late in 1969, Ann Messenger offered a glimpse of UBC, where her husband Bill was teaching. The new tenure and promotions regime had arrived there. A new broom was sweeping very clean at UBC, she said, "and stirring up much muck and wrath along the way." Bill Messenger had "worked like a slave" to get into print and his prospects for tenure in a year's time were good. But others had been slow to recognize the new urgency to publish; and four or five of his colleagues were under the axe. One of them had been hired without a PhD and was told at the time that it was not essential. Now he learned that it was.[64] Like many, he had been caught in a sea change in Canadian academic life.

What had happened across Canada was the adoption of tenure policies modelled on the CAUT statement of 1967. SFU had fallen in line in the summer of 1968 while it was under CAUT censure. The leadership of the CAUT were defenders of what they perceived to be traditional values at Canadian universities, which they believed were threatened by governments expecting a utilitarian—business and economy—orientation in exchange for increased funding. When Percy Smith, executive director of the CAUT, addressed members of the SFU Faculty Association in January 1968, he spoke of the invasion of university life by a business corporation approach. This, he said, had been the CAUT's main concern "over the past several years."[65]

The CAUT was promoting an American-style academic freedom and tenure regime to defend the liberal intellectual values of Canadian academia. To explain it, one has to recognize the long battle that the American Association of University Professors (AAUP) had fought to defend academic freedom in the U.S. When Canadians looked for a statement on academic freedom and when they looked for due process procedures, the AAUP was the body that offered them.

Everyone at SFU could have been spared confusion if the CAUT had defined and published its tenure policy guidelines earlier. When the guidelines did appear in November 1967, the Faculty Association and the board were already heavily invested in the draft policy they had been developing from scratch; and this they only abandoned when negotiations collapsed in the fall of 1967. In the summer of 1968, with the university under censure, the Faculty Association at SFU turned to the CAUT guidelines as their model. They then had to recast everything they had done; and that meant that fundamental questions, like the composition of tenure committees or the renewal of instructors, had to be revisited. Remarkably, in all the turmoil of that summer, the Faculty Association executive and the administration did reach a resolution that the faculty accepted; and SFU had a new policy.

This policy affected nearly everyone. The board of governors had formally given tenure to the founding heads in September 1967.[66] (The heads had originally been appointed permanently, so this was not a substantive change for them.) Everyone else had terms of one to three years. Altogether, several hundred faculty at SFU faced tenure, renewal or promotion decisions in a two-year period beginning in 1968. These were the guinea pigs for untested procedures, and as a consequence there was a new tension in the air. The arrival of a radically new tenure policy at the last hour—with its implications yet to be fully understood—changed the playing field for a collection of young faculty who also happened to have roots in several national academic traditions. But other Canadian universities were going through the same thing at the same time. Ann Messenger's report of turmoil among young professors at UBC reminds us of that.

7

Specialization and Interdisciplinary Studies

Arvid Grants was the founding chair of Philosophy at Simon Fraser University and a member of the Philosophy Department for nearly a decade. When he eventually left Vancouver, some time after he left SFU, it was to teach painting at the branch of Malaspina Community College located in the B.C. coastal town of Powell River. Since retirement he has continued as a flute instructor at the Powell River Academy of Music, an institution of an excellence that might not be expected in a pulp and paper town, but one that has grown up over the past thirty years around an internationally acclaimed boys' choir.

Grants was a Latvian who had sung as a young man with the choir of the Riga opera company. After the war he immigrated to Montreal, where he attended the Ecole des Beaux Arts on a scholarship. In 1952 he came to Vancouver after hearing that the Vancouver Symphony was losing a flute player. For a time he was the symphony's first flutist and he played for the CBC Concert Orchestra. While doing that he began taking courses at the University of B.C. and he completed a BA and an MA in fine arts. At that point he won a Canada Council doctoral fellowship to study Philosophy at Cambridge. His interest was in aesthetics. He had been at Cambridge for less than two years when McTaggart-Cowan and Ron Baker interviewed him in London. To his surprise, McTaggart-Cowan offered him an appointment in Philosophy as the first chair. He says that he protested that he was far from an expert, but he took the job.[1]

Grants's appointment was a mystery to many at SFU. This was not a conventional choice, especially for a leadership position. By the time he hired Grants, McTaggart-Cowan had given up on finding a senior philosopher as founding head. There did not seem to be one available. But he was impressed enough with Grants to see him as an interim solution. What impressed him? Ray Jennings, who joined the Philosophy Department in 1968, offers an insight. Prior to coming to SFU, Jennings knew McTaggart-Cowan as an old friend of his in-laws in Montreal. As Jennings puts it, McTaggart-Cowan thought of a philosopher as "a very cultured gentleman." In Arvid Grants that is what he had.[2]

At Cambridge, Arvid Grants himself had seen that analytic or linguistic philosophy had become the focus of the discipline in Britain; and when he selected people for SFU, he looked for analytic philosophers. They were not hard to find because that is what British and American schools were producing; and Grants was successful in giving his department an impetus in this direction. What Grants understood—and McTaggart-Cowan did not—was that leading British and American philosophers were now regarding their craft as technical and scientific. It was no longer an encompassing humanistic discipline taking in politics, science, psychology, metaphysics and history. Members of the Philosophy Department found themselves explaining this to students who wanted to take philosophy for the wrong reasons.

Larry Resnick, who did his graduate work at Cornell and came to SFU as chair in 1973, made no bones about his department's commitment to analytic philosophy in a 1977 statement of its goals. He warned that Philosophy was not the place for students who wanted to "sample the wares" of Oriental philosophy or mysticism: his department would not "pander" to popular demands for other-world views.[3]

As a new department of the 1960s, Philosophy at SFU caught an international trend in philosophy head-on. It became a department of analytic philosophers almost to the exclusion of any other kind. Arvid Grants, who had started the department in this direction, was a poor fit for it. McTaggart-Cowan's notion of a philosopher proved wildly off the mark. When Grants failed to finish his Cambridge thesis, his days at SFU were numbered. The decisions that tenure committees began making at SFU after 1968 made little room for exceptions. When Robert Binkley from the University of Western Ontario reviewed the department in 1977, he suggested that its "publish-or-perish mentality" had got out of hand. By then Grants had been denied tenure and had moved on.[4]

INTERDISCIPLINARY EXCHANGE

McTaggart-Cowan's choice of Grants suggests that he (McTaggart-Cowan) had a wonderfully anachronistic notion of philosophy. Perhaps he half understood that: his correspondence with Shrum suggests that was the case. For this there was a larger frame of reference that he shared with Shrum and Baker. At SFU they wanted to reverse what seemed to be a remorseless march towards specialization and disciplinary fragmentation. Intellectually, on these matters, McTaggart-Cowan was the junior partner. About the sciences, Shrum had opinions developed over a long career. Baker was the informed party when it came to the humanities and social sciences. McTaggart-Cowan could speak with some legitimacy about the sciences, but his knowledge of the arts did not go very deep. Still, he embraced the ideas of the other two. These included an interest in interdisciplinary approaches and a preference for large and inclusive departments. Erickson's architecture complemented these ideas.

Shrum also understood from the Macdonald Report that SFU's special mission was to offer the liberal arts and sciences as well as teacher education. These were the areas in which SFU needed to relieve UBC of an enrolment burden. The only professional program it was intended to have was teacher education. UBC would remain the only home for Engineering, Medicine, Forestry, Agriculture, Pharmacy, etc. Under pressure from board member Arnold Hean, Shrum did accept one departure from this rule—with the inclusion of Commerce. But this decision involved a compromise: Commerce was located in Arts, under the umbrella of the Economics Department.

This conception of SFU appealed to many of the faculty who took jobs there. They liked the promise of interdisciplinary exchange and the emphasis on the liberal arts and sciences. Len Berggren is an example. He received an offer of a position in Mathematics at SFU while residing on the island of Cyprus, where he was writing his thesis. (He was from Spokane and the degree he was working on was from the University of Washington, but his wife, a Fulbright scholar at Washington, was a Cypriot.) He had heard a lot about SFU. His friend David Eaves was already teaching there, and Berggren had been told by various people that it was an exciting, innovative place that had been physically designed to mix up the disciplines. Once he got there, he found that the architecture did not live up to his expectations; but Bergren was one of the early Science faculty members who sought opportunities to talk to philosophers, historians, sociologists and political scientists.[5]

Don DeVoretz in Economics is another who, nearly forty years later, speaks memorably about the excitement of his first few years at SFU. He had applied to SFU from the Philippines, where he had been employed on a Ford Foundation agricultural project as a statistician. He knew Mike Lebowitz, Peter Kennedy and Larry Boland, who were at SFU in Economics ahead of him, because all four had been at Wisconsin. He says that he was lured to SFU by the prospect of interdisciplinary teaching, although it never worked out for him: "It just was not going to happen." But there were compensations. What he remembered as most dramatic were not things like the student occupation of the administration building but tremendous discussions and debates on Marxism, feminism and free-market economics among some members of his department and a few of their colleagues from Philosophy, English and History.[6]

The newness of SFU could be a real plus for some faculty—just as it had been for some students. Jerry Zaslove, while completing a PhD at the University of Washington, turned down UBC and chose SFU for that reason. He had a background in comparative European literature; and he was looking for an interdisciplinary environment. The English program at SFU, coupled with possibilities in Modern Languages and perhaps in Education, promised him the latitude he wanted. Above all, he expected more freedom to cross disciplinary boundaries in a place that was just starting out.[7]

All this illustrates the impact of SFU's early self-promotion: its promise to be different and its intended emphasis on the liberal arts and sciences. Opposition to professional programs seems to have been strong among its early faculty. For many, an institutional commitment to education in the broadest sense was hugely important. Anything that smacked of professional training was suspect.[8]

Professors at SFU were carrying on old arguments about what a university should be, and with marked intensity because they were at a new university and in a period of expansion. Cardinal Newman's famous 1852 definition—written when he was seeking to establish a Catholic university in Dublin—was still alive at SFU with those who saw a broad or liberal undergraduate education as the main reason for having a university. A much smaller number at SFU believed deeply in research as the university's first mission, subscribing to a view articulated as early as 1918 by the American economist Thorstein Veblen. And those who might have accepted the classic professions (medicine, law, etc.), but who objected to other occupation-oriented programs, were also echoing Veblen or the educationalist Abraham Flexner and his critique of American universities of the 1920s. Finally, for the many who sought an intimate, integrated university community with shared goals, there was the threatening (but realistic) term coined in 1963 by Clark Kerr, the president of the University of California: "the multiversity." Many of SFU's faculty still held the nineteenth-century ideals of Cardinal Newman and regarded the 1960s example of the vast and fractured multiversity with dismay.[9]

Many American-born faculty at SFU had attended elite colleges in the U.S., where the liberal arts tradition was strong. Others had gone to huge American universities like Berkeley and not liked what they saw. Many had attended both kinds of institution: the liberal arts college as undergraduates and the megauniversity as graduate students. In Canada the expansion of the post-war era was pulling larger universities along Berkeley's path. By 1965, Claude Bissell, as president at the University of Toronto, was likening his university to Berkeley. It too had become a multiversity with all the challenges and problems that entailed. Among the problems that Bissell listed was "the slighting of the undergraduate."[10] The original vision of SFU offered by McTaggart-Cowan, Baker and Shrum was something different; and many faculty—wherever they came from—had been attracted by that.

The Politics, Sociology & Anthropology Department was a major battleground in the confrontation over the goals and objectives at SFU. For charter members of PSA like A.H. Somjee, it was immensely disappointing to see a "tentative interdisciplinary concept" overwhelmed and destroyed by radical ideology.[11] Why didn't interdisciplinary studies survive in a radical department? A part of Somjee's answer was that in PSA the democracy that came with radicalism meant that everyone did their own thing. Everyone taught what they wanted to teach. The inevitable result was that people reverted to their original disciplines. The political scientists went one way and the sociologists and anthropologists another, and consequently they left the notion of a shared and integrated program to twist in the wind.

The first discipline to leave PSA was Archaeology, and this was largely in reaction to PSA-style democracy. Archaeology's transition to department status took three years of negotiation; but when it was achieved in 1971, it emerged as a new kind of academic creature. Archaeology at SFU was just about the only North American Archaeology program—besides one at Calgary—that was completely independent of Anthropology. SFU had initiated a new area of undergraduate specialization and it was an enrolment success from the beginning, drawing a loyal following of majors and minors. The field school in Archaeology, starting with an excavation on Mayne Island in the summer of 1968, has provided undergraduates with a unique sense of common interest and experience. The annual digs in which these students have joined have been immensely important in unlocking the secrets of British Columbia's prehistory. Since the 1960s, legislative protection for archaeological sites has created a considerable field of employment for archaeology graduates. But the separation of Archaeology from PSA was a milestone in revising SFU's original academic plan.

Archaeology had begun with Roy Carlson's appointment in PSA, which he took up in 1966. Carlson says that Tom Bottomore, when he hired him, really wasn't expecting a digging archaeologist—which is how Carlson has described himself—but a synthesizer, one who sat in a library putting together the large pieces of the prehistory puzzle. Such an archaeologist might have been happier than Carlson was with Bottomore's interdisciplinary department—if that department had held together.

What Carlson saw, even before he came to SFU, was a huge opportunity in British Columbia, where little previous archaeological work had been done; and where prehistoric sites were awaiting attention up and down the coast and in the interior. He was keen to get on with it and immensely annoyed in early 1967 when his efforts to hire an experienced archaeologist out of the American government were thwarted by his PSA colleagues, who democratically voted to appoint his candidate, but not at the rank the man expected.[12] A year later, David Bettison, who was sympathetic to Carlson and thoroughly frustrated with their colleagues, warned him to get out "and get out fast." PSA had become unmanageable. This was a message from a department head on the verge of resigning. Carlson lost no time in looking for an exit. By then he had an ally in fellow archaeologist Phil Hobler, who had come to SFU from the University of Montana in the fall of 1967.

One argument that their PSA opponents threw at Carlson and Hobler was that an independent Archaeology program would be professional training, not liberal arts or humanist education. It did not belong at SFU. They cited courses that Carlson and Hobler projected, such as Technical Analysis of Material Cultures and Computer Programming of Archaeological Data. They did not see this as appropriate undergraduate education; and because it contributed to the multiplication of disciplines, they saw it as contrary to SFU values.[13]

Carlson and Hobler were taking a subdiscipline of Anthropology, one that students—till then—explored in depth only in graduate school, and they were making it a full discipline on its own. One of the complaints against them was that they were designing courses for undergraduates that really belonged at the graduate level. Specialization was coming too soon.

Was there anything wrong with bringing graduate training or education down to the undergraduate level? Carlson could not see it. As he put it, curricula were in constant flux, with new subjects appearing and old ones dropping away. Knowledge was "discovered, generated, discussed and debated" through research and teaching at the most advanced level; and if it survived this critical process it moved down the educational ladder, eventually to the high schools and the general public. So it should be with Archaeology.[14]

Some of this debate was window dressing for more fundamental political issues. Hobler and Carlson took their case to Ken Strand in the summer of 1968 after he became acting president. He was not worried about the disciplinary logic of PSA; and he wanted the two to stay in the department "as a steadying influence." And within PSA, opposition to the separation of archaeology was driven by a fear that it would lead to the dissolution of the department. Hobler and Carlson themselves were dismayed by the radical and democratic direction that PSA had taken.[15]

The archaeologists had keen student supporters who lined up beside them. These students had been easy to organize in the late spring of 1968 with the first Archaeology field school underway. Carlson was running it at Helen Point on Mayne Island—where he and his students were unearthing five-thousand-year-old weapon points, pebble choppers for woodworking and distinctive antler harpoons—and Hobler and three graduate students were conducting a survey of the mainland coast and finding thirty-five archaeological sites in the complex waterways between Ocean Falls and Bella Coola (communities that are only sixty kilometres distant). Hobler went down to Mayne Island, where everyone put down rakes, shovels and brushes to join the discussion. Carlson and Hobler went over the situation with the students, and collectively they made the decision to seek separation.[16] At this moment began the negotiations that took three years for final success.

SPLITTING UP PSA

For a brief period, the chair of PSA was sixty-five-year-old Maurice Halperin, a faculty member in Education before being parachuted into this department. He was one of the more remarkable individuals ever to teach at SFU, and the subject of an engaging biography by the SFU historian Don Kirschner.[17] Halperin had been chief of the Latin American branch of the U.S. Office of Strategic Services (the Second World War precursor to the CIA). In the McCarthy era, while teaching at Boston College, he had been accused of espionage by an FBI informant, Elizabeth Bentley. He was one of more than eighty people that she fingered whom the FBI never charged because they found no evidence. But Halperin was pessimistic about his chances of clearing his name and absconded to Mexico and then Russia. After three years in Moscow, he went to Cuba at the invitation of Che Guevara; and he lived there for six years before arriving at SFU in 1967. As an old-style American leftist with first-hand knowledge of the Russian Soviet regime, and of Communism under Castro, Halperin received an enthusiastic welcome from sfu's left-leaning faculty. But his role in psa was to preside over the final collapse of an interdisciplinary experiment that in the eyes of most of the university had gone badly wrong.

It was on Halperin's watch that psa decided to split into two departments, Political Science and Sociology/Anthropology. The vote was taken in October 1972, a year after Archaeology achieved department status. Dismissals after the strike in the fall of 1969, along with resignations and a series of negative tenure and renewal decisions, had cut a huge swath through psa. A purge, many called it. psa numbers had fallen from twenty-five to twenty-one, and there were only five people left who had been there before 1968. What the new people heard about the old psa was not good. Ted McWhinney was one of the senior people that sfu recruited despite a second Canadian Association of University Teachers (caut) censure. After listening to all the stories, he decided that a large part of the psa problem had been personalities: "quarrelsome, mutually incompatible people."[18]

A.H. Somjee was there from the beginning. In 1965, along with Tom Bottomore and four other colleagues, he had mapped out a course for disciplinary integration within psa. Before four years had passed, he had seen the attempt at integration largely abandoned. By 1973, Somjee was watching impatiently as psa proceeded through all the jumps and hurdles of formally splitting. He wanted it done as fast as possible. He thought that too many psa professors, given the opportunity to teach within a disciplinary melting pot, had abandoned the standards of any or all disciplines.[19]

With hindsight, Somjee believed the experiment he had joined had been utopian. Even if, as he described it, the "calibre, dedication and intensity" of the initial dialogue in the department about its interdisciplinary objectives had continued beyond the first couple of years, the concept was too ambitious. He now thought it should have been tried first as a graduate program and only around a few carefully selected themes. Once it had been explored and developed, it might be brought down to the undergraduate level. This was a notion similar to Carlson's of a natural downward migration of knowledge. But with his psa experience to guide him, Somjee had become leery of experimental programs for undergraduates.

THE MULTIPLICATION OF PROGRAMS

The twelve academic departments plus Education with which SFU began have increased over the past forty years to thirty-one departments and schools plus Education and Business Administration. In part this is explained by a manifold growth in the size of the university and in its enrolments, which together support a much greater diversity of aims and objectives. In part it is explained by a steady addition of professional or pre-professional programs as SFU has taken on functions that government and society expect of it. But it is also explained by an irresistible process of specialization and disciplinary subdivision that has a trajectory reaching back for more than a century.

Since the 1870s, American universities have led the way in subdividing, refining and inventing academic subjects, sometimes—from a traditionalist's perspective—taking the exercise to the point of the ridiculous. It was more than seventy years ago that the American commentator Abraham Flexner complained that university education was trivialized by courses on advertising, judo and food etiquette.[20] But in constantly adding courses and programs, Canadian universities have followed in the wake of American. Shrum, Baker and McTaggart-Cowan, with their desire to arrest the subdivision of disciplines and their emphasis on the liberal arts and sciences, seem like Canute ordering back the tide.

ECONOMICS & COMMERCE

PSA was the interdisciplinary experiment that people at SFU talked about. But it was not alone in SFU's original academic plan. The interdisciplinary department that best exemplified the long-term trend towards specialization and professional programming was Economics & Commerce. In this department, without much reflection, Shrum had accepted a marriage of academic and professional disciplines. He had switched sides in an argument between Ron Baker, who thought that Business or Commerce did not belong at SFU, and Arnold Hean, a Burnaby lawyer and a board member who was keen to see SFU offer something in this area. Placing Commerce in an Arts department was a compromise that had many precedents.[21]

The argument between Baker and Hean had been around for a long time—since the last decade of the nineteenth century, when business schools first appeared at a few American universities and when they mostly taught accounting. These schools justified themselves by drawing students and by attracting funding from business. But they were not warmly welcomed by traditional academics. With the introduction of subjects like Economics and Sociology into the Business curriculum, critics had an added concern: that there would be a conservative and employers' bias to courses taught in a business school.[22]

What happened in the U.S. was closely paralleled in Canada, beginning with a diploma program in Commerce at Toronto in 1901. The University of Western Ontario, borrowing the Harvard case-study method, introduced Business Administration in 1922; and in the 1960s it still had the leading program of its kind in Canada. Most Canadian universities still kept Commerce and Business Administration within Arts. This was despite some occasionally hot debate over the previous thirty years. UBC, with its separate Faculty of Commerce, was one of the few exceptions.[23]

In putting Commerce in with Economics, Shrum and the board were not doing anything radically new, even if they broke with the UBC example. But over the next decade at SFU, the two disciplines pulled in an uneasy harness. Under Copes, the department tried to create a uniquely integrated program. And he looked for people qualified in both subjects who could bring them together in their teaching and research. He made good appointments and managed one of the university's most stable departments. But it developed imbalances that became exaggerated with growth (from an original five faculty to fifty-two after fourteen years). In 1979 it split into two departments within a single school—still located in the Faculty of Arts. Two years later, Business Administration became a Faculty in its own right, and Economics stayed in Arts.

Larry Boland was one of the people in Economics & Commerce who deeply regretted the split. In his case, it was because he subscribed to the original concept, which he saw as beneficial for Economics students as well as for Commerce. From the start, Economics at SFU got a heavy dose of what Harry Johnson, the Canadian-born Keynesian economist at Chicago, called scientific economics. By that he meant a highly theoretical and largely mathematical approach. Boland was one person at SFU who thought Economics students needed to be exposed to the business perspective to get beyond a theoretical and isolated view of the world. And he thought that Business students needed the academic rigour one got from Economics.[24]

Economics & Commerce, as a combined department, had its first and only external review in 1975. It got high marks for its research record: the best in Canada, according to Stephen Peitchinis, the economist from Calgary. But he and his fellow reviewers judged the experiment in integration a failure. The two disciplines were sharpening their differences, beginning with their research and continuing with the way in which the graduate program in Economics had developed.[25]

One factor that the reviewers were quick to note was the unequal development of the two sections of the department. Commerce was decidedly the junior partner. Copes had tended to look for Commerce professors with interests in Economics, but not for Economics professors with interests in Commerce. As someone said, he hired "undiluted" economists. And the kind of Commerce professor he wanted was hard to find. Consequently, the Commerce side was understaffed.[26]

Economics & Commerce avoided the democratic revolution that swept through SFU's academic departments in the 1960s. It retained a strong top-down administrative structure with policies developed in committee and programs run by program coordinators. The department rarely met as a whole, and compared with what went on in other departments, this seemed to be an efficient and trouble-free way of management. But an outsider like Peitchinis also suspected that this style of management encouraged little interaction. And there were pockets of deep alienation: among Economics professors who did not want to be associated with Commerce, and among Commerce professors who did not want to be assessed for salary, tenure, renewal or promotion by their Economics colleagues.[27]

By 1975 an outsider could see that radical change was needed. One could look at other universities to see what was likely to happen. Commerce was a growth area driven by enrolments. When Commerce faculty did not get the resources they needed, they were in a strong position to demand more, and if they could not get it within a combined department, then separation was their way out. Under Copes, the department had already petitioned for faculty status with separate departments of Economics and Commerce—which would have given Commerce independence while retaining the relationship.[28] The creation of a school within the Faculty of Arts might have been a first step towards that. Instead, severance was complete and final in 1981, when Commerce became the nucleus of a Faculty of Business Administration, and Economics elected to stay in arts.

The flagship of the old Economics & Commerce Department was its Executive MBA, involving both Economics and Commerce faculty—an example of integration working. Forty years later, with more than twelve hundred alumni and its own building about to open in downtown Vancouver, generously donated by SFU's seventh chancellor, Joe Segal, the program is an institution. The concept was a first in Canada: a three-year MBA taken on weekends and evenings. Two of its graduates, Paul Cote and Barbara Rae, have subsequently served as SFU chancellors.

MODERN LANGUAGES

Geoffrey Bursill-Hall's Languages Department had a parallel, although more perplexed story. In 1978 the Department of Modern Languages changed its name to Languages, Literatures and Linguistics—DLLL. This was after several years of desultory discussion. The new name acknowledged divisions that had not been intended in the beginning, but that manifested themselves early on. As DLLL, the department lasted another eleven years, until 1989 when it dissolved and gave way to three new departments: Linguistics, French, and Spanish & Latin American Studies. No one considered Geoffrey Bursill-Hall's original Modern Languages curriculum to be interdisciplinary. What was new and revolutionary about it was his emphasis on teaching the spoken language. But the people he collected had quickly organized themselves into disciplinary divisions.

Bursill-Hall started with the conviction that language study—as distinct from literature study—was a discipline "in its own right." The problem he addressed was that the instructors who taught language courses at Canadian universities were generally literature specialists. He wanted instructors teaching the spoken language to be experts in what they were doing. As a consequence, his first requirement in designing a language program was to separate language study from literature.[29]

Even with the four European languages with which he started—French, German, Russian and Spanish—he faced a challenge in finding qualified faculty. He wanted structural linguists (linguists trained in the description of languages as spoken in the present or, as in the case of classical Greek and Latin, as spoken at a specific time in the past, rather than linguists concerned with the history of language or with changing language forms); and he wanted every language major to have a linguistics component. To his credit, he gathered at SFU the largest concentration of linguists west of Ontario. But he could not avoid hiring literature specialists. The market was too restricted to do otherwise. And he could not miss the latest wave in linguistics inspired by Noam Chomsky's theory of transformational grammar. One of Bursill-Hall's earliest appointments, Jim Foley, was a Chomsky student with a letter of recommendation from Chomsky. The interest of these linguists in the "deep structures" of language had little immediate relevance to a language-training program.

Bursill-Hall believed that he needed linguists to develop course materials, to lecture on the structures of specific languages and to train language instructors or "native speakers" to handle small-class drill sessions. He did not plan an independent undergraduate program in linguistics, but that is what followed as a number of the people he hired pursued their real interests; and their offerings drew in students from other departments who liked the interdisciplinary nature of linguistics courses that bordered on subjects like psychology and anthropology. Four years after the founding of the department, its members could still agree that literature had not been in the initial plan. But some literature had been added in the second year, again in response to student and faculty demand.

Bursill-Hall's Modern Languages Department was handicapped by SFU's decision to scrap foreign languages as an undergraduate requirement. The idea was Ron Baker's and, on the positive side, it opened up university education to students who otherwise would not have attempted it. But it also encouraged B.C. students to avoid foreign languages in high school, and a disproportionate number arrived at SFU with no inclination to try one. At the launching of the university, Bursill-Hall quickly built a large department—much faster, for example, than Parzi Copes in Economics & Commerce. Then low enrolments made the department look expensive—more expensive than at UBC, where language was compulsory—and that was an incentive for its faculty to broaden their appeal.[30]

By the late spring of 1969, members of the department felt confounded by a Catch 22, especially those who were in literature. They wanted a degree program in literature, and felt they were losing students because they did not have one. But Dean Sullivan and the higher administration, and the rest of the university—as reflected in the deliberations of senate—resisted. They did not want to add courses in a department that was already underenrolled. One way out was to develop interdisciplinary programs like Latin American studies with linkages to other departments. But the idea of breaking up the department was on the table: Literature might get better support from the university if it were on its own.

Under the circumstances, the survival of the department as Modern Languages and then DLLL until the late 1980s is remarkable. Neville Lincoln and Charles Bouton, who served as chairs in the 1970s, probably deserve major credit. SFU's revolution of 1968–69 left no one in the senior administration with any commitment to the idea that Bursill-Hall had had in the beginning—the one the university had been so quick to announce when they first hired him. Instead, in the early 1970s a new dean of Arts and a new vice-president academic, thinking of efficiency, were asking bluntly why the SFU department did not teach language the way everyone else did and accept classes of forty or fifty students.[31]

The department had long before expanded beyond the central commitment to language training that Bursill-Hall had intended. By 1975 the chair of the French division, Barrie Bartlett, for one, was describing something quite different; and because he was reporting for his colleagues, what he said presumably represented a consensus. He had prepared a statement for the department's upcoming external review. Although his statement still contained a passionate endorsement of Bursill-Hall's pedagogy, this was within a much more complex departmental framework. He and his colleagues were trying to make senior administrators at SFU understand that languages, literatures and linguistics were three domains requiring three kinds of academic competence. A French-speaking linguist was not automatically prepared to teach a French-language class and might even be a "positive menace" to the language program. Bartlett's subtext was that specializations created incompatibilities.[32]

On top of this, the department was divided by language: French, Spanish, Russian and German. The latter two struggled for enrolments and did not survive the university's cost cutting of the early 1980s. Up to that point, the department maintained the five organizational divisions on which it had settled after intense debate in 1968—the four languages plus linguistics. As Charles Bouton, the department chair, said in his statement for the 1975 external review, the Department of Modern Languages had the structure of a small faculty. It already contained the divisions that would eventually form the lines of complete fracture.

To add to the mixture, Burslll-Hall had hired linguists with wildly differing convictions: people who did not agree on fundamental notions about the nature of language. He had done so deliberately, in the interests of academic exchange and to expose students to a wide variety of linguistic teaching. But he had welcomed profound academic disagreements into his department.[33]

With all this going on, one must be impressed with the extraordinary diplomacy of key members of the department in holding it together for as long as they did. In the large picture, Modern Languages/DLLL was moving progressively with the times in making linguistics an undergraduate specialization, while also reverting to what had been traditional at Canadian universities: departmentalization by language and an emphasis on literature.[34]

THE ELECTIVE SYSTEM

When Heribert Adam described the SFU he discovered on arrival from Durban, South Africa, in 1968, he naturally compared it with European universities. His education and training had been at the University of Frankfurt and the Frankfurt Institute for Social Research. A seasoned professor in Germany, he said, would blush, "and not necessarily with envy," at the communication skills of a first-year sessional lecturer in North America. Adam attributed the difference to a North American system of rewards for teaching. At SFU he discovered that tenure, salary and promotion were affected by what students said of their teachers; and as he saw it, that was turning instructors into entertainers. He thought he saw a relationship between trendy courses, offered on the "pretext" of relevance, and teacher popularity.[35]

Adam was thinking of the options available to students at SFU in what he called the "smorgasbord" of topics "marketed as social science." At SFU he had been introduced to the phenomenon of electives and their corollaries, experimentation and specialization. The idea of giving students a lot of choice in their studies had come late to Canada. There were several reasons. One was a continuing belief in a core curriculum. One was the Canadian emphasis on honours programs that did promote specialization, but followed a largely prescribed set of courses. The third was cost. A small university (and that describes most in Canada up to the 1960s) could not afford a great array of electives.[36]

Ron Baker's academic plan had thrown out the prescriptive system. Science students had to take some arts, but social sciences and humanities students could (and did) avoid science. No one had to take English or a foreign language. The Baker plan catapulted SFU into an American-style elective system that left students with wonderful freedom to explore a great tangle of course offerings. One stabilizing feature was that they did have to declare a major and take the courses that their major specified. In Economics, that meant some mathematics. But in most departments, requirements for a major were exceedingly elastic—as they have generally remained.

Once again, one just had to look south of the border to see where all this was heading. Where choice was available, everyone—students and professors—tended to narrow their focus. In English at SFU, Baker stuck with Canadian practice by keeping composition and literature together. If Baker had imitated an American university like Michigan, he would have taught the two subjects separately. In fact, at Michigan, English Composition and English Literature first became separate subjects, then separate departments. Then the Composition Department at Michigan had spawned departments of Speech, Journalism and Radio and TV.[37] This was the elective system at work, encouraging the creative development of specialties in response to student demand.

Electives had been creeping into Canadian curricula, and with them the idea of majors. Gone was the old notion that either a student went deeply into a subject as an honours student, or became a generalist and took a "pass" BA. In the generation before SFU opened, a degree of specialization in a "major" subject became standard for all students at Canadian universities. SFU carried it further by permitting and expecting students to take more courses in their "major" than had been the case at older universities. UBC was quick to move in SFU's direction, but SFU was the leader.

In the large literature devoted to higher education in the U.S., one can find various critiques of the elective system. Looked at positively, it was a progressive response to the broadening of the social base of the university. Elite institutions could require Latin or mathematics and a foreign language of students whose futures were assured no matter what they studied. But when universities enrolled more students, and less privileged students, choice became an issue. What could a university offer that students would find practical and meaningful and that would help them get jobs? It followed that the best indicator was student demand. This was the kind of argument that justified electives.

From the radical Left in the 1960s came a counter-argument: the elective system was too market oriented. It served business by promoting specializations in fields that business was interested in. It reduced the university to producing the new proletariat needed in a technological age.[38]

For traditionalists, the elective system was profoundly regrettable because it led students down so many individual paths that they ended up with little common knowledge. This was compounded when the secondary-school system began imitating universities by offering more electives, as was happening in B.C. in the 1960s. The optional nature of an imaginative new high-school physics program, introduced in 1966, let most B.C. students skip a lot of physics. The Physics Department at SFU had to adjust to the difference. Electives in high school were adversely affecting other disciplines as well. History was a prime example.[39] So the complaint became this: as choice and specialized knowledge worked their way down through the education system, so too did yawning gaps in what students knew.

The American experience with electives included prolonged debate about their consequences and an early search for correctives. The "general education" movement in the U.S. dates from the 1920s; and the influential Harvard model, with its historical, interpretive and interdepartmental first-year courses, dates from the 1930s. The "University of Chicago Plan" emphasizing the great books of the Western world was another 1930s reaction to specialization. In the 1960s, Canadian universities found themselves on the same elective path with the same concerns about what it meant. York made a commitment to "general education" when it finally broke free of Toronto in 1964; other universities introduced first-year requirements with similar objectives.[40] SFU went unreservedly the other way, although the file has not closed on the subject. Nearly forty years later, at the instigation of Academic Vice-President

John Waterhouse, a university committee reinvestigated the issues. The result has been the legislation of breadth requirements effective at SFU in 2006.

In the 1960s at SFU, the elective principle faced pockets of resistance. Physics ran the most prescriptive program. On the other hand, Mathematics, like most departments, allowed its majors a lot of choice. The head of Physics, Rudi Haering, complained that Mathematics had no program at all, only courses: Mathematics let its students wind their "merry way" through a maze "with no guidance whatever."[41] Choice left Mathematics students free to specialize within one of its optional programs. In Mathematics at SFU, however, students seem to have appreciated the choice they had.

SFU's mathematicians described their department as "broadly based" with "clusters of faculty."[42] Ron Harrop and his colleagues had followed an organic strategy, letting the department shape itself step by step during the first few years of hiring. If they had an opportunity to hire one specialist in relativity and quantum mechanics, then they looked for two or three more. Physics did it the other way, by picking an area and focussing on that; but the objective in Mathematics was to be as comprehensive as possible (but not to make its students take everything). The idea of creating "clusters of faculty" with common interests led to concentration in four areas: pure mathematics, applied mathematics, statistics and computing science.

In three of these areas, SFU was doing something distinctive as well as job oriented. In 1969 the dean of Science, Lionel Funt, boasted that SFU's group of applied mathematicians was the strongest in the country.[43] Other Canadian universities were not doing much in statistics despite an increasing demand for statisticians from business and government. And in the late 1960s, Computing Science was just on the verge of tremendous growth and impact as a discipline; Harrop for one saw the future coming and became directly involved in creating computing science courses.

All of these areas potentially led to employment after graduation, with teaching only one of the options. But a strong contingent of pure mathematicians at SFU ensured a commitment to mathematics for its own sake. The department advertised itself this way to students. They could take math to find employment, but they could also choose it because it was aesthetically satisfying. In this spirit, the Mathematics Department built a large measure of choice into its undergraduate program.

In 1976 the Mathematics Department conducted a survey of its graduates, asking them about their careers since graduation and about the value of their math program. One question in the survey asked if Mathematics should be more employment oriented. Some graduates said no: a university was not a job-training centre. Some suggested a modest employment orientation but warned that the future directions of the job market were unpredictable (expressing some support for general education). Others called for a strong employment orientation. But running through these answers was a common belief that students should have freedom of choice. Graduates were not challenging the elective system they had known.[44]

COMPUTING SCIENCE

Mathematics and Computing Science were another SFU combination that did not survive the early 1970s. Computing Science had been a teaching subject in which the Mathematics Department anticipated growth, even after Ron Harrop stepped down as head. Briefly this seemed possible. In 1969, Lionel Funt, in his second year as the dean of Science, made Computing Science his number one priority.

Funt was a McGill-trained physical chemist who had risen through the academic ranks at Dalhousie and Manitoba. His first diagnosis of SFU, when interviewed for the dean of Science position, was that this was a university that needed a period of consolidation after the stress and strain of its first few years. But Computing Science was a special case. He understood that the discipline had an exciting future. And he believed that students recognized this and wanted to be part of it and that they knew that jobs would be waiting for them. The proof was at Toronto and Alberta, which had been running graduate programs since 1964.[45]

The technology for students and faculty to get involved in hands-on computing was already on the campus. In the spring of 1969, SFU upgraded its computer system with an IBM 360/50 in place of the 360/40 that had been purring twenty-four hours a day in the library basement—flashing little lights on its console and spinning reels of magnetic tape in cabinets lined along the wall. SFU had used some of its original capital budget to purchase a 360 when IBM first began to deliver models of that series in 1965. The 360 series, although it appeared five years before the commercial production of the computer chip, was a huge advance on what had been available.

What had become outdated was the kind of equipment the University of Toronto acquired when it purchased the first electronic computer in Canada in 1952: a research machine that operated with hundreds of vacuum tubes and that filled a large room in the Toronto Physics Building.[46] SFU's IBM 360 belonged to a new generation made more compact with transistors. But it was also far more versatile than anything built earlier, adaptable for commercial, administrative and scientific purposes. With its 360/40, SFU boasted the most automated library in North America; and after a disastrous attempt at manual registration in the fall of 1965, the Registrar's Office turned to the computer to cope with the triple burden of record keeping necessitated by the trimester system. In 1969, with the upgrade to the 360/50, the university added sixteen remote terminals, with twelve available to students and faculty. This was a first step in making computer technology generally accessible to the campus population.[47]

The 360/50 had a fraction of the capacity of the laptops that people nowadays lug through airports or tap at in coffee shops. But what it could do stimulated interest in applications for research in many disciplines. Tom Peuker in Geography at SFU knew about computer cartography from his time as a visiting fellow at the Laboratory for Computer Science and Spatial Analysis at Harvard. Another pioneer was Ray Koopman in Psychology, who had become interested in computing data in 1965, while still a graduate student at Illinois, before coming to SFU.

When SFU created a Computing Science Department in 1973, it was one of the first five in Canada and one of the first sixty-five in North America (out of more than fifteen hundred degree-granting universities and colleges). It began with undergraduate students and added graduate students after seven years. For a new discipline, this was a reverse order: the programs at Toronto and Alberta had begun at the graduate level. The term "Computing Science" instead of "Computer Science" also delivered a message: the subject was to be the use of the computer rather than the computer itself. The first director, Theodor Sterling, had been chosen because his thinking ran emphatically this way.

Sterling had been hired away from the Department of Applied Mathematics and Computer Science at Washington University in St. Louis. He was a pre-war Austrian immigrant to the U.S. who had served in the U.S. infantry in the Pacific and then completed four years of high school in one year after the war. After he had earned a PhD, he had been funded to do experimental work in developing computer applications, and he had begun developing computer applications for the rehabilitation of the blind, deaf and paralyzed.[48]

Sterling's orientation towards application made him a natural advocate of a computing program open to students from every part of the university. An interdisciplinary approach made abundant sense to him. Students could learn what they needed to know and apply it wherever their interest lay—in English, Languages, Psychology, Geography, Physics or Chemistry. Very few of the staff that he recruited had degrees in Computing Science—an indication of the infancy of the discipline but also a reflection of his philosophy.

Sterling chose not to adopt the pre-existing Mathematics courses for his program. Instead, he introduced similar courses under his own rubric and then persuaded Ron Harrop to teach them. His point—which Harrop accepted—was that Mathematics for interdisciplinary Computing Science students had to be taught differently.[49] These students wanted the application and not the formal mathematics. What Sterling sought to support was an understanding of the computer as a tool for everyone. This was an imaginative conception for the time, but one that has become more and more redundant as computer technology has become increasingly accessible. Too many of us can now use a computer without ever taking a course. SFU's present-day Computing Science Department, located in the Faculty of Applied Science, now advertises a greater focus on computer theory.

A FACULTY OF INTERDISCIPLINARY STUDIES

Sterling had been hired by Brian Wilson, SFU's vice-president academic from 1970 to 1978. The Belfast-born Wilson was an astrophysicist with fifteen years of Canadian experience, first with the National Research Council, and then with the University of Calgary, where he had been dean of Arts and Science. He had confidently moved to SFU even though the university was under the cloud of impending CAUT censure. On his second day on campus he gave a characteristically pragmatic, intuitive and brief reply to a reporter's question about censure. SFU did not have any reason to worry, said Wilson. There were no longer many academic jobs around: good people were going to be available despite censure.[50]

Wilson brought a fresh and forceful personality to SFU at a critical juncture. He was a central figure in the second phase of SFU's development, a phase that became a revision of the first and a set of new adventures. With Computing Science, Wilson put his considerable weight behind the idea that it should be in a new, catch-all Faculty of Interdisciplinary Studies (first called the Division of General Studies, and before that, the Faculty of University Programs). The presence in Arts of people like Tom Peuker and Ray Koopman suggested to Wilson that computing science was an interdisciplinary subject and not just a science.

In Interdisciplinary Studies, Computing Science found company in a mixed group of experimental departments: Kinesiology, Communications, Fine and Performing Arts, and Criminology. The faculty was also a collecting place for interdisciplinary programs that were not organized as departments: initially in Canadian Studies, Latin American Studies, and African and Middle Eastern Studies, and later in Women's Studies, Natural Resource Management, Management and Systems Science, and Gerontology.

Bob Brown was the first dean of the faculty, accepting the job only a few years after starting at SFU with a freshly earned PhD in Geography from Michigan State. Altogether he was to spend twenty years in senior administration, first as dean of Interdisciplinary Studies and then as dean of Arts. In his second year at SFU, during the turmoil of 1968, he had been drawn into university politics through the university's popularly chosen president, Ken Strand, with whom he struck an easy friendship. Together Brown and Wilson fostered a remarkably supportive environment for new programs.[51]

When he spoke about it in September 2000, Brown placed his Faculty of Interdisciplinary Studies within an SFU tradition that started with Gordon Shrum and with the architecture of Arthur Erickson. To make the point, Brown mentioned his first office in the Academic Quadrangle, where he had a professor of Philosophy on one side and a professor of English on the other. Conversations and friendships with people in other disciplines came naturally with proximity and daily encounters.

Brown is one of many who remembered with enthusiasm the intellectual cross-pollination of those early days. That, he explained, was what the Faculty of Interdisciplinary Studies continued to promote.

The Faculty of Interdisciplinary Studies also, and somewhat conversely, took SFU further along the path of specialization and professional education. It meant more departments within the university, not fewer, more divisions of the curriculum and more programs with an employment focus. In this sense it represented a redirection and an abandonment of the admittedly tentative and hasty conception with which SFU began. Bob Brown has explained it another way. He accepted the idea, which he attributed to Wilson, that traditional disciplines did not adequately address many areas of social concern. Interdisciplinary Studies was SFU's response: an innovative structure that focussed attention on such subjects as crime in society, the birth of the information age and women's issues.

There were also pragmatic reasons for a new faculty called Interdisciplinary Studies. It was part of what nearly everyone saw as a necessary revision of the university's original academic plan. General Studies or University Programs would have served as names for the new faculty, but Interdisciplinary Studies was better. It took in three programs from Education: Kinesiology, Communications, and Fine and Performing Arts. Discussion of a new interfaculty or interdisciplinary structure had begun with Kinesiology and then Communications and Fine and Performing Arts, all loose pieces in the SFU puzzle.[52] By putting them together, Wilson had the nucleus of a Faculty of Interdisciplinary Studies.

Of the three, Kinesiology had the most straightforward development. The term and concept—the science of human movement—have been widely adopted throughout North America, but the SFU program was the first of its kind anywhere. It brought together concerns with body mechanics, the physiology of exercise, neuromotor coordination, kinesthetic senses, motor learning and sports psychology. The exploratory authors of the kinesiology idea were two charter members of SFU's Physical Development Centre, Glenn Kirchner and Stephen Strattan. Kirchner was a former associate professor of Health and Physical Education at Washington State College. Stratton had ten years of teaching experience in B.C. elementary and secondary schools and at the college and university level in Washington and Oregon.[53]

Kirchner and Stratton had wanted to offer a degree in Physical Education, which they tried to locate in the Science Faculty. They had come up against Gordon Shrum's rule that Education students should take their majors in Arts or in Science. Could Physical Education be recast as a science with a large chunk of Biology? Stratton and Kirchner thought Biological Sciences might be interested. It was not, but by then they had the outlines of the Kinesiology idea with its science and research emphasis.[54]

Kinesiology gained an energetic and persuasive advocate in Eric Banister, who came to SFU in 1967 from UBC, where he had been a professor in Physical Education. Banister had studied chemistry at Manchester and applied physiology at Illinois, as well as physical education at UBC, and he was an ideal recruit for the kinesiology concept with his science training as well as his research record. When Kinesiology gained department status, he was the first chair.[55]

COMMUNICATION STUDIES

Kinesiology had developed out of a proposal for a Physical Education degree. By comparison, Communications and Fine & Performing Arts were reinventions—necessary once senate decided that Archie MacKinnon's ideas for Education were too amorphous to work. In the open and democratic culture of the Education Faculty at SFU in the 1960s, reinvention took a lot of talking. One wonders now that anything ever resulted—so much of the discussion was unfocussed: long discourses on first principles and on pet projects, everyone seemingly pulling a different way.

That explains the time it took for a group of professors in Education to coalesce as a Department of Communication Studies. First they came together as an administrative unit within Education, and then they searched for a concept, a definition and a name for a program. The group included three philosophers, one musician, one visual arts specialist and one specialist in special education. Then there was an anthropologist, a sociologist, a specialist in world games and a specialist in communications. Finally there were two or three educational psychologists, a student of the future, a person engaged in sensitivity training and a social policy expert.[56]

Communication Studies was the name that senate accepted for eight of these professors and the new department they formed. The alternative names they had tried out were Human Relations, or Human Relations & Communication Studies. The social psychologist who shaped the proposal, Tom Mallinson, made the definition as elastic as he could.

Mallinson had been the communications specialist in what had been called the Centre for Communications and the Arts. His link with the arts had been his interest in creativity and group processes. It was from this angle that he taught communications. Now he persuaded a number of his Education colleagues that communications was their common concern. He imagined he could bring in Murray Schafer, the musician and composer, with Schafer's conceptions of the soundscape and of noise pollution. It all fell within Mallinson's definition of the subject: human communications and their effects.[57]

At Mallinson's request, SFU had asked an anthropologist from the University of Oregon, Alfred G. Smith, to review Mallinson's Communication Studies proposal. Smith was a specialist in communication theory. He read the proposal and talked to the principals and then, without sounding a great alarm, put his finger on something that foreshadowed trouble. This proposal, he said, was "planning by laissez-faire"—a democratic search for ways to bring people together by leaving everything as open-ended as possible, skirting differences in academic objectives and personal style.[58]

Still, Smith was encouraging. Since the mid-1950s, many American universities had started departments, schools or colleges of communication—bringing together, in various combinations, programs in journalism, radio, TV and film, theatre, speech and behavioural science. The University of Michigan had been one of the first. Stanford and Texas had well-known programs. The Department of Communication at the University of Washington in Seattle had a mandate much like the one proposed at SFU. "All very legitimate," said Smith.[59]

He made a point of saying "legitimate" because he knew Communication Studies had critics at SFU. It potentially trod on many toes, especially in the Faculty of Arts. It overlapped Psychology, Philosophy, Linguistics and Sociology; and it threatened to steal students in an era of shrinking enrolments. (This was the contracting early 1970s.) And many in the Faculty of Arts doubted the competence of this collection of professors from Education to teach what they proposed to teach.[60]

The Communication Studies Department at SFU got off to a rocky start, mainly because its original staff was such an unlikely mix of personalities and pursuits. The low point came in 1977–78, when President Pauline Jewett suspended one professor and then reassigned him and a colleague to a kind of academic limbo as floating faculty without any academic department. (There was no longer anywhere to put them.[61]) This was to take some of the heat out of a Communication Studies Department riven with conflict. But by then one could see the discipline gaining ground elsewhere. Other Canadian universities were adopting similar programs. The first issue of the *Canadian Journal of Communications* had appeared in 1975; and members of the SFU department were prominent in the founding of the Canadian Communication Association in 1980.

FINE AND PERFORMING ARTS

Murray Schafer left SFU in mid-career in 1975 to purchase a farm near Indian River in eastern Ontario and to devote himself to composing. He had already achieved international recognition as one of Canada's most adventurous and talented composers, and more recognition was to come. He had given up on the promise of a department of Fine and Performing Arts. With a little bitterness, he observed that Computing Science and Criminology had been set up quickly, but the wheel turned slowly for Fine and Performing Arts. Utilitarian subjects, he thought, were getting the nod.[62]

Schafer had been at SFU from the beginning, a star catch for the Faculty of Education's biggest gamble, the Centre for Communication and the Arts. In the fall of 1965, so many students had wanted to participate in the Centre's activities that there was no time for planned development. What Schafer, Mallinson and their colleagues had in mind was a small experimental institute that integrated the arts. They were thinking of the Bauhaus School—the innovative German example of the 1920s and early 1930s with its integration of art and craft. Their objective was to do something not done anywhere else in North America by bringing together all of the fine and performing arts in one place.

After a couple of years, Schafer became one of the more disappointed members of the Centre when he concluded that the ideal was not being realized. He had expected that students in theatre or filmmaking would also take part in music and in visual arts, but in the second year he could see it was generally not happening. Perhaps this was inevitable given the non-credit nature of the centre's programs: its students followed their enthusiasms in what for them was extracurricular activity.[63]

The centre's successes—and the list was impressive—were mostly confined to work within artistic disciplines: filmmaking, visual arts and so on—rather than interdisciplinary collaborations. The centre quickly acquired a reputation in the arts community for creative energy; and it won over an enthusiastic student clientele. In music alone in the first year, 240 students had been involved in the concert band, or the choir, jazz group, symphony orchestra or chamber music group, or in music appreciation. At the peak of its activity the centre was using every square inch of the SFU Theatre—holding workshops, seminars and training sessions in offices in the basement, in passageways, closets, storage areas, dressing rooms and rehearsal areas. Theatre, film and video, still photography, drawing and painting, sculpture, pottery, dance and mime all jostled for space.[64]

The centre ran an intense schedule of films, lectures, dance recitals, plays and exhibits as daily events throughout the year. In its third year it attracted nearly fifty thousand people to performances and exhibitions. By the fall of 1968, the centre's scrapbook included seven hundred reviews in the public press. And its faculty were winning national attention. Schafer's opera *Loving* was performed for the first time on CBC in July 1966, and Michael Bawtree's play *The Last of the Tsars* premiered at the Stratford Festival that same summer.

But the centre had a rich budget that other units in the university envied. The centre was also vulnerable because it was unconventional and looked inessential. As Schafer acknowledged, the name "Communications and the Arts" sounded fishy to many on campus.[65] When the centre offered traditional theatre or music or art, it made friends, but experimental works easily made enemies: like a tongue-in-cheek noon-hour performance called Zen Rock Concert, which, when the curtains rose, proved to be nothing more than a small pyramid of rocks.

McTaggart-Cowan, although he had no great familiarity with the arts, was a strong supporter of the centre. Yet he had given it only three years to prove itself; and after he was gone, no one in the administration had any commitment to it. When people with disappointed expectations, like Schafer and the visual artist Iain Baxter, complained that the centre was loosely run and loosely structured, or that it lacked a clear statement of goals or had no definite identity, that was ammunition for outside critics.[66]

What followed eventually was its dissolution. Senate began debating what to do with the centre in 1969, and over the next two years senate separated the centre's service and academic functions. A senior non-academic administrator, Stan Roberts, vice-president, university services, assumed the overseeing of theatre facilities and public performances, workshops and non-credit courses. (The person actually running the operation was the centre's former publicist, liaison officer and program manager, Nini Baird, who has since been a prominent member of the B.C. arts scene as an administrator and promoter.) The Faculty of Interdisciplinary Studies got Fine and Performing Arts as a new academic department. But while Senate had decided on this division by 1971, it took several years to get an academic Department up and running. Schafer attributed the delay to administrative neglect; but things would have moved faster if there had been more agreement about the kind of department SFU should have.[67]

The first problem was sorting out what was academic about fine and performing arts. In the U.S. this question had long been resolved: degree programs in the visual and performing arts were commonplace. But this was not so in Canada. By the early 1970s, only a third of all Canadian universities offered any kind of academic degree in art. A number had introduced studio programs leading to degrees; but typically Canadian universities emphasized art history and appreciation. UBC had recently introduced studio programs, but 85 per cent of its fine arts enrolments were in art history.

It was very traditional to believe that non-credit activity was important (or even vital) in a student's education. McTaggart-Cowan had said so of his time at Oxford: on reflection he thought his coursework the least consequential part of his experience there. But non-credit work also had revolutionary potential. For students and instructors in a centre for the arts that sought to push boundaries and to break barriers, credit-free workshops gave a licence that would have been hard to find in examination-bound courses. A number of the artists associated with the centre embraced it as a radical alternative to degree-granting or diploma-granting programs elsewhere. That was the loss they regretted when the centre was phased out.[68]

However, the voices that prevailed were those that insisted that studio work was perfectly appropriate for academic credit. One belonged to James Felter, who had joined the centre in 1968 as a visual artist and curator and who became the director of the SFU gallery when it opened in 1971. Another belonged to Iris Garland, who had been teaching dance in Physical Studies/Kinesiology and in the Centre for Communication and the Arts from the time she started at SFU in 1965. A third was Murray Schafer's. Before he left SFU, he had been ready to settle for what he called a conventional but realistic solution. In 1975 the Department of Fine and Performing Arts at last began offering courses, some new and some that had been in Kinesiology (dance), or Communication Studies (music), or under the designation of General Studies.

Few in the visual arts, music, theatre or dance at SFU wanted a standard department with studio courses plus art history and appreciation. What a majority did want was less obvious. Vice President Academic Brian Wilson had decided to bring in an outsider—a consensus builder, not an artist—and the person he chose was Evan Alderson, who had proven himself as a mediator during a term as chair of English.

Alderson had his own radical credentials. As a graduate student he had been at the epicentre of the student disturbances at Berkeley in the fall, winter and spring of 1964–65. At the defining moment at Berkeley, when the student leader, Mario Savio, had mounted the roof of a police cruiser to give an impromptu address, Alderson and a friend had managed to broadcast his voice to a gathering crowd of hundreds by finding a mike, a speaker and enough extension cord to reach an outlet in the administration building.[69]

In Fine and Performing Arts, Alderson's job was creative management. On one side were artists—particularly in dance and music—who saw technique as indispensable (and insisted that their students have large blocks of studio time). On the other side were iconoclasts—more likely in the visual arts—who viewed technique as the enemy of creativity. (This was a modernist debate, and the struggle was to find a balance.) Alderson confesses to being rather naïve at the start about the rigour of the training required in various arts. But new faculty as well as the old initially embraced the interdisciplinary concept.

Alderson was the director until 1981. With hindsight, he places the founding of the department in a passing "modernist moment." Much of what then seemed critically important did not have staying power. And from the beginning the department's long-term plans contained the seeds of more conventional programming. Alderson and his colleagues anticipated incremental growth, beginning with minors in each of the arts and an interdisciplinary major, but leading eventually to the introduction of majors in music, dance, theatre, film and the visual arts. That is the way that the department (now the School for Contemporary Arts) has developed. Perhaps it should not be a surprise that each of the disciplines has become more self-contained and self-sufficient—more traditional in its sense of separate identity.

CRIMINOLOGY

The fifth department launched in Interdisciplinary Studies by the fall of 1975 was Criminology, which had no roots in earlier experiments or programs at SFU. At the time, the only other Canadian degree programs in Criminology were at Montreal, Toronto and Ottawa. SFU's founding chair, Ezzat Fattah, had come from Cairo to do graduate work in the Montreal program and had stayed there to teach. He had seen first-hand how Montreal had started with graduate studies and then introduced undergraduate studies six years later. At SFU, Fattah did it the other way around: he sold the idea to Bob Brown, Brian Wilson and the professionals advising them.[70]

With Criminology, SFU seized an opportunity that UBC had rejected. A group of professionals in law enforcement and corrections had petitioned for criminology-related courses from the UBC departments of Sociology, Psychology, Psychiatry and Law, and they had asked for a School of Criminology to offer graduate work. When they got a negative response they came to SFU. Discussions began in 1971, and by 1973 Fattah was working on an SFU proposal.

Thirty years later, Criminology, the School for Contemporary Arts, Communication Studies, Kinesiology and Computing Science were all established successes; and they survived and flourished in a way that SFU's earliest interdisciplinary experiments did not, perhaps because each had a career orientation, or because they were born in calmer days, or because they developed more deliberately with more planning. The Faculty of Interdisciplinary Studies did not last beyond the early 1980s. By then it was looking untidy: an arbitrary collection of academic units. In a period of financial exigency, its departments and programs were reassigned either to the Faculty of Arts or what was then a new Faculty of Applied Science. Yet it possesses a special place in SFU's history. SFU had two bold and creative phases in its first twelve years: the Shrum era from 1963 to 1968, and the post-Shrum era from 1969 to 1975. In the second, the Faculty of Interdisciplinary Studies was the incubator of experimental programs.

WOMEN'S STUDIES

The Faculty of Interdisciplinary Studies added a Women's Studies Program in 1975 (with the first courses available in 1976). By then, a smattering of Women's Studies courses had made their way into university curricula throughout North America. Toronto offered its first courses in 1970–71 and had a program by 1974. UBC introduced five courses in 1973–74. At SFU, Geography offered a seminar course on women in the fall of 1971; and the Canadian Studies program began to give a course on women in Canada in the fall of 1974.

Pauline Jewett was president of SFU when senate—after some stout challenges—approved the Women's Studies Program in the summer of 1975. One of the senators present was Klaus Reickhoff from Physics. In 1982 the university took the unusual step, while Reickhoff was still a senator, of naming the senate chambers after him. (The plaque remains in place, although the space has been renovated and is now a reception area.) The naming recognized Reickhoff's exceptional service as a perennial senator with broad concerns about the university, always thorough, always unwilling to take anything for granted and always ready to question. He still felt, when interviewed in 2003, that under Jewett's leadership Women's Studies had been pushed through; and he did not hesitate to raise concerns about it at the time.[71]

Andrea Lebowitz was the first coordinator of Women's Studies. She had been teaching English at SFU since 1965 when she arrived as a twenty-three-year-old MA graduate from Wisconsin at Madison. Ten years later she was defending a Women's Studies proposal on the floor of senate. In an address she gave in 1999, Lebowitz recalled that experience as a struggle. One senator, she remembered, had dismissively said of the women behind the proposal that they had commitment and enthusiasm "but no knowledge." He meant they did not have an academic subject. Another, she remembered, warned that to let "these women" teach

Women's Studies would be like allowing prisoners to teach prison education.[72] What many members of senate feared was a women's academic ghetto without disciplinary standards. They were insistent, when they accepted Women's Studies, that its professors should hold appointments in established departments such as History or English.[73]

In addressing senate, Lebowitz was facing a room full of men. Very few women had been on senate up to that point. When Lebowitz started at SFU in 1965, only sixteen women had regular appointments in a university with 126 regular faculty; and most of these women were instructors. Most departments had no women. (English, Modern Languages, Psychology, Chemistry and Education were the exceptions.) And the hiring that SFU did over the next few years favoured men by such a margin that the proportion of women actually dropped (from 13 per cent in 1965 to less than 10 per cent in 1972).[74]

By the time senate approved the Women's Studies Program, the university had a seasoned band of feminists. Their collective history went back seven years to the summer of 1968. In the vanguard were a group of student mothers who seized a section of the student lounge—then located on the second floor of the Academic Quadrangle. They took the space for a co-operative daycare centre, which they proceeded to run without a budget, licence or even formal leadership. Each of them contributed four and a half hours a week to supervising their children. They had acted pre-emptively rather than going through the nuisance and the uncertainty of applying to the administration for permission.[75]

In that same summer, a number of students, support staff and teachers at SFU became active in the broader concerns of the women's movement. As on so many other campuses, these were women who had been caught up in the politics of the New Left, as supporters of the Students for a Democratic University (SDU) or other activist organizations. Like women in these movements elsewhere, a time came when they revolted at being taken for granted by a mostly male national and local leadership. As they told a reporter for *The Peak,* they were tired of being asked to type or put up posters or canvass and never to organize, theorize or speak. They did the same thing that like-minded women did at other universities and began to meet separately as a women's caucus. Generally in North America, this was a development of the 1967–68 academic year. At SFU it began in July 1968, during SFU's summer of upheaval, with a group who first called themselves the Feminine Action League and then the Women's Caucus.

This is the subject of an invaluable MA thesis by Frances Wasserlein, who was a graduate student in History in the 1980s. Wasserlein herself was a feminist activist from the mid-1970s, when she was an undergraduate at UBC, before she came to SFU.[76] She interviewed nineteen women, some of the most engaged members of an organization that regularly drew thirty-five or forty to its meetings and that at the height of its activity had a mailing list of about three hundred. Her interviewees were from SFU and UBC and from off-campus, reflecting the diversity achieved after their meeting place moved downtown from Burnaby Mountain. In August 1969, the Women's Caucus had begun renting an office in the Labour Temple (at $30 a month.)[77]

At SFU, the Women's Caucus brought together faculty who were young and students some of whom were older, with little consciousness among them of difference. Wasserlein gathered that this was typical of early SFU—or of the Left at SFU—where students and faculty worked together without a strong sense of "us and them." But it seems to have been particularly characteristic of the women who banded together at the dawning of the women's liberation movement. No one assumed precedence: everyone was on a path of discovery. These women were not content just to read Simone de Beauvoir's *The Second Sex* or Betty Friedan's *The Feminine Mystique;* they were activists with a set of issues that they articulated during the summer and fall of 1968: birth control and abortion; equal pay for equal work; daycare, and the stereotyping of girls during childhood.[78]

A few names will suggest the diversity of SFU's feminist activists. One of the women that Wasserlein interviewed was Marcy Toms, a seventeen-year-old in 1967 when she chose SFU over UBC and enrolled in PSA, wanting to "get involved." Another was Marge Hollibaugh, a middle-aged woman with a grown daughter, who in 1968 had left California with her husband Ace in reaction to the Vietnam War. (Ace Hollibaugh was the mature PSA student who served several terms as student ombudsman.) A third was Jean Rands, who from the fall of 1968 was a typesetter for *The Peak.* She was not a student but an employee of the Student Society who the year before, at the age of twenty-three, had been the League for Socialist Action's fringe candidate in Vancouver's mayoralty election. A fourth was Liz Briemberg, mother of two small children and the British-born wife of Mordecai Briemberg, who had come to Vancouver in 1966 when he joined the PSA Department. In age, experience and background, each brought something different.[79]

PSA was, in fact, a common denominator for many of the SFU activists who formed the Women's Caucus. If they were not PSA students, they belonged to a social group that revolved around PSA. That explains how Maggie Benston got involved. She had started at SFU in 1966 as an assistant professor in Chemistry. She told Wasserlein she was not at all political when she landed at SFU. She said she was so uncritical of the world in which she had grown up that she would burst into tears at a party when someone suggested that what the United States needed was a revolution. That changed when she began making friends within a PSA crowd.[80]

Early in her involvement with the Women's Caucus, Benston wrote an article on women's liberation from a feminist–Marxist perspective. She prepared it for a major conference organized by the Women's Caucus and published it in the American socialist periodical *Monthly Review* in September 1969. Harry Magdoff was the editor of *Monthly Review* at the time and he remains an editor thirty-six years later. In a long interview published in *Monthly Review* on the thirtieth anniversary of his editorship, his interviewer asked specifically about the Benston article. Magdoff explained that he had been up in Canada, had met Benston, thought she had a marvellous point of view and asked her to write it up.[81]

Over a three-year period, a small group of women invested a tremendous amount of energy in the Women's Caucus. Benston was one of them. They directed this energy towards research, discussion, propaganda, workshops for working women and for high school students, protests and demonstrations and the publication of a monthly paper, *The Pedestal.* They began in the fall of 1968 with a clinic at SFU providing birth control and abortion information; and when they advertised in *The Peak* they got inquiries by phone from as far away as Saskatchewan—evidence of how extremely difficult it was for women to get this information. It was only in 1969 that the Canadian Parliament legalized therapeutic abortions and decriminalized contraception—although doctors had been prescribing the pill to married women since 1961. Between November 1969 and June 1970, the Vancouver Women's

Caucus mounted an ambitious nationwide campaign to legalize all abortions. It culminated in the Abortion Caravan, which left Vancouver at the end of April 1970 and ended with a demonstration on Parliament Hill in Ottawa two weeks later. Prime Minister Pierre Trudeau gave the demonstrators a cool reception.

The Vancouver Women's Caucus dissolved a year later. A minority wanted to focus on the abortion issue. A majority wanted a multi-issue approach, which they saw as the best way to draw in the largest number of women. Frances Wasserlein found the women she interviewed unwilling to say much about these differences; but the surviving files show a confrontation between a minority who belonged to a Trotskyite organization and were following a party line and a majority who wished to preserve the independence of their organization as a coalition of women. A similar struggle was being played out in the women's liberation movement in many cities.[82]

One of the projects of the Vancouver Women's Caucus had been a Working Women's Workshop, which was the genesis of a Working Women's Association, which in turn inspired the formation of an independent feminist union, the Association of University and College Employees (AUCE).[83] But out of the Women's Caucus also came the impetus for a Women's Studies program. The beginnings were a Geography course in the fall of 1971, then a non-credit SFU course at Burnaby's McGill library during the following summer and another non-credit course on campus in the fall of 1972. A group of students and faculty, including Lebowitz and Benston, began developing a proposal in December 1973. By the time they got it through senate, they had abundant evidence that they were offering something that many women badly wanted.[84]

Women's Studies at SFU also faced criticism from women who thought it served women poorly by letting them join cozy women's seminars instead of competing with men and getting into programs like engineering.[85] The proponents of Women's Studies at SFU, like Lebowitz, were conscious of another issue: across the campus women were in a minority—more of a minority than men are today. The proportion of women in the undergraduate population had slightly declined in SFU's first six years, from 38 to 37 per cent. Only in Education were women students a majority.

In the early 1970s, feminist scholars had begun critiquing the social sciences—beginning with Psychology, Sociology, and Anthropology—and finding them male centred.[86] Feminist questioning of the centrist assumptions and methodologies of academic disciplines began at that time. It was then that some feminists began advancing the idea that science was, or could be, bent to a male logic. When Andrea Lebowitz spoke about teaching in 1999—at the invitation of the president, in recognition of her own outstanding teaching—she touched on this. Women's studies, she said, had challenged the foundations of scholarly activity because it started with the premise that what was being taught was inadequate or blind when it came to "the various lives" of half the population.[87]

"The good news," said Lebowitz in 1999, was that SFU supported Women's Studies, first as a program and, after fifteen years, as a department. She believed the Faculty of Interdisciplinary Studies had the right structure to nurture new programs like Women's Studies; and she was one of those who regretted the faculty's eventual dismemberment.

8

A Succession of Crises

For faculty, staff and students, the 1960s at Simon Fraser University were like the emotional roller coaster of a summer field school. With a field school, one can generally predict the storyline for a group of fifteen or twenty young people thrown together for a month and a half in a foreign environment: the gathering of strangers; the expectations, excitement and discoveries, the new friendships and the bonding of the whole group; and then the difficulties, disagreements, fallings-out, ruptures and tears; and finally, when it is over, the surprising nostalgia. The difference at sfu was that this was a five-year drama rather than six weeks.

A professor from Oregon had a glimpse of what had happened at sfu when he spent a few days on Burnaby Mountain in March 1972. This was the anthropologist Alfred G. Smith, who had been invited to the university to review a Communication Studies proposal. He was immediately and singularly struck by the level of involvement that almost everyone felt in the history of "this young and tender institution." During his very first morning on campus he was told the SFU saga so many times by so many people that by noon he was sure that "solely from hearsay" he could recite the names of all the SFU presidents in chronological order. All this telling made him wonder if the history had yet been fully absorbed or resolved.[1]

Everyone seemed to have a version whether or not they had been there from the beginning. Ace Hollibaugh, the seven-semester ombudsman, the middle-aged Politics, Sociology & Anthropology student radical and refugee from California, published his in *The Peak* in January 1970. He had first enrolled at SFU in 1968, but he had its history all worked out (with PSA at the centre). It fell into three philosophical periods dominated by individuals: periods of promise, excitement and deflation. First came Gordon Shrum and Tom Bottomore, the promoter and Marxologist, and with them what Hollibaugh called "radical rhetoric"; then Mordecai Briemberg and the "heady atmosphere" of intellectual freedom and radical humanism; and finally the administration of Ken Strand, which Hollibaugh summed up as "reason without dialogue."[2]

In a letter to her parents in Pittsburgh, Ann Messenger tried to explain what was going on at SFU on the Friday in May 1968 when the board of governors fired President Patrick McTaggart-Cowan. She was still teaching part-time at the University of B.C., but was on the verge of accepting a position at SFU; and she was getting filled in by her future colleagues in English. There was no doubt in her mind that McTaggart-Cowan deserved his fate and that the Canadian Association of University Teachers (CAUT) had been right to censure his administration. But she also understood from her sources that McTaggart-Cowan was not the whole problem. The other part was the chancellor, who was also "head" of the board. For her parents, she characterized Shrum as "a very big businessman in B.C., electricity and dams and things, old and stuffy." Her sources had not mentioned Shrum's long career as a professor at UBC.[3]

Between the Faculty of Science and the rest of the university lay a sharp divide in the way things were told. John Cochran was a charter member of the Physics Department and its first chair after Rudi Haering moved up to become vice-president academic in the fall of 1968. Cochran was near the centre of the action in his faculty from the beginning; so it is interesting to examine what he did and did not remember during an interview in December 2002. His blank spots speak volumes about a perception gap between professors in Arts and in Science. What he remembered of assemblies of joint faculty was sitting for days on end at "bloody meetings" with people "ranting and raving." What he could not remember was what McTaggart-Cowan did to arouse the ire of faculty or why he was "turfed out."[4]

Back in October 1969, Cochran had told his own department that they had an image problem that they did not deserve. This was in a report he prepared as a department chair going into his third semester. His concern then was that although the department had an excellent reputation internationally among physicists, it had a poor reputation locally among high-school students and teachers—simply because it was at SFU. This was making it hard to recruit high-school graduates. "I am personally convinced," he said, "that the stream of nonsense which emanates from certain sections of our Arts Faculty has cost us a good many students."[5] His views about this period of SFU's history have not changed.

From the beginning, the telling of SFU's history shaped itself around a succession of crises. The early crises were the undoing of McTaggart-Cowan; and the later ones were the testing and confirmation of Ken Strand and of his leadership in remaking the university. These crises kept SFU in the news; and they came so frequently, accounts of SFU ran continuously in the media. SFU became the media's automatic example of student and faculty unrest, although nothing happened there like the $2-million fire set by student protestors in the computer centre at Sir George Williams in 1969, or even the $3,000 in damage done at UBC by Jerry Rubin's crowd in their occupation of the Faculty Club in 1968.[6]

THE SHELL SERVICE STATION

The first major crisis and the first demonstration of student power at SFU was a protest against the construction of a service station. Students and faculty were defending SFU's architectural integrity and its natural setting. The earliest hint that they could be mobilized in this way had been a "plant-in" at the end of the spring semester when about thirty professors and students spent a muddy afternoon planting grass and trees to stave off a designated parking lot.[7] A couple of months later, a Shell service station presented itself as a much bigger issue.

McTaggart-Cowan was generous in his memory of the anti-Shell protest, saying that he had never had any fear that SFU students would damage their own buildings: they were too proud of the architecture, and the Shell protest was proof. The result of the protest had been a compromise. The protestors did not stop the construction of the service station—which operated for nearly thirty-three years before Shell shut it down in 1999—but they did secure modifications in the design. In retrospect, McTaggart-Cowan conceded that the original design had been wrong, and the protestors had been right in objecting.[8]

At the time, McTaggart-Cowan had wryly watched a protest begin over a scenic view that had not existed before the service station lot was cleared; and then he had been unable to get ahead of the misinformation that pushed the protest along. The original idea had seemed unremarkable: to provide a basic service that would bring in revenue for the university. Chevron and Shell stations at UBC caused no comment, and a lot of cars would be coming to Burnaby Mountain. While the campus was still a construction site, workers had problems with vehicles breaking down and no repair or tow-truck facilities nearby.

With the plan for a service station came a creative addendum: the station would be sitting on university land, and if the company operating it prepaid twenty-five years' rent ($116,000), SFU would have a capital sum to put towards a men's residence. The prepayment of rent would show up in company books as an asset, so for a large company this would be quite manageable: a bookkeeping entry. This idea materialized within the board and it was a board member with connections at Shell, Charles Bloch-Bauer, who negotiated the details. In the summer of 1965, before the university opened, the board invited major oil companies to submit tenders. Shell's proposal—including a profit-sharing scheme and an extra $15,000 thrown in—was accepted during the second week of classes in the fall of 1965. By then the board had decided that the service station should be located centrally, on the concrete loop road near the transportation centre. And they had agreed that the architecture of the service station should be in keeping with the architecture of the university: no streaming pennants, tire displays, flashy contest signs, arc lights on tall poles or Shell's usual large yellow sign.[9]

For several months in the spring of 1966, SFU commuters enjoyed a magnificent view towards Burrard Inlet and the mountains of the North

Shore—a view created when a contractor for Shell toppled alder and hemlock trees on the far side of the loop road opposite the campus bus stop. The SFU community seems to have enjoyed this view without noticing that it was new or realizing that trees had been cut for a purpose. Then word spread that a service station was going in. It had not been a secret, but came as a surprise. A sod-turning ceremony and a story in *The Peak* in February (with an artist's conception of the design) had slipped nearly everyone's attention. The appearance of a construction shack and the laying of foundations at the beginning of June did not.[10]

One might gauge the strength of the campus-wide reaction by the generally conservative Physics Department, where eight of eleven professors registered objections to the service station (the other three were out of town).[11] In all faculties, students and professors were quick to express opposition. Aesthetics was one issue and catering to a big oil company another (everyone assumed that Shell had taken the initiative, not the board); and that was compounded by the board's decision to call the men's residence Shell House. Then there was the larger matter of taking campus opinion into account: the board had acted without consultation. At a new university in the post-Berkeley era, this complaint could be expected. But it carried added force because the Duff–Berdahl Report had just appeared and its whole point was that faculty and students ought to have a say in the running of universities. How could they be ignored in regard to something that so profoundly affected the appearance of the campus?[12]

The university and Shell went ahead with the service station, because the oil company would not withdraw without compensation and the university could not afford to pay the costs. As far as the company could tell, most students wanted a service station, although not on the spot that had been chosen. Moving it was not an option that Shell would consider once they had spent heavily on design, site development and construction. The concession that they agreed to—with student leaders, the Faculty Association and board members all involved in the negotiations—was to soften the appearance by moving the service bays to the rear and increasing the height of the shrubbery screen that they already planned to put along the road. The gas pumps stayed at the front.

The protest erupted in June and died down two weeks later, when Shell promised changes. Then when students enrolled for the fall semester—most of them having taken the summer off—the protest started up again. The service station site was still a mess because student demonstrators had briefly halted construction in June, and then Shell's contractor had waded into labour problems: a carpenters' lockout. In September a "Shift Shell" rally in the mall brought out a thousand students, and by the end of September student organizers had fifteen hundred signatures on a petition that they delivered by a cavalcade of cars to Shell officials in downtown Vancouver.

The Shell station controversy showed how fickle a university community could be under a trimester system. The Student Society president in the spring semester was Tony Buzan, who attended the sod-turning ceremony in February without a hint of concern. The summer president, Alex Turner, astutely put himself at the head of the protest and then contained it by negotiating and supporting Shell's changes. In September, yet another president, John Mynott, was leading a cavalcade of cars downtown to present Shell with fresh demands to relocate the station.[13]

SFU got the service station, but the protest had a legacy. First of all, activists had an appetizing taste of confrontation. At the beginning, in June, three hundred picketing students and faculty had managed to stop construction for two days. They had invaded the Shell site first thing in the morning and in the excitement the operator of a front-end loader had charged and scooped up a first-year science student, Don Cavers. The incident had shaken the construction crew more than the students: work had stopped and within an hour Shell's division manager had promised to negotiate. *The Peak* under Allen Garr's summer editorship led a cheering section: at last something was going on; the campus "has come alive."[14]

A second legacy was the beginning of the radicalization of student leaders, not just those who gravitated to the extreme left, but those who occupied the liberal centre. Stan Wong, then the student ombudsman, revealed the state of his thinking in a blast in *The Peak* at the end of June. He found the Shell fuss unseemly, but he put a large share of blame on the university's style and form of government: the administration had no way of listening to students; and the protest—he called it semi-riotous—was a consequence. He had decided that the most important action students could take would be to promote the Duff–Berdahl

Report and pressure the administration for student representation. His thinking, of course, put him in the mainstream of a national student movement.[15]

A third legacy was the aggravation felt by members of the board. Most had served from the fall of 1963 and taken on far more than they would have at any older university. They had helped make key decisions shaping SFU and had a proud and grateful sense of participation in the creation of an enterprising new university.[16] Collectively, the board saw the Shell protest as a setback, especially with the business community; and the feedback they got downtown told them that fundraising was going to be more difficult. Unhappily, board members were reading *The Peak* and even on occasion responding to invective directed at them on its pages by students and by a few faculty. All this served to shape their actions in the crises that followed.[17]

AFTER SHELL: THE TA AFFAIR

In late November 1966, the Shell station pumped 352 gallons (1,337 litres) of gas during its first day of business. The next morning, four students brought in cars for repair, and when Division Manager J.L. Hayes spent a couple of hours there, all four service bays were busy. That closed the file on the Shell controversy. From then on, the service station operated without disturbance, until 1999 when it shut its doors—finally and without warning, a victim of changing business strategy in the service-station industry. When that happened, with no sense of irony, students living on Burnaby Mountain protested its loss.[18]

About three and a half months after the Shell station opened, a fracas outside an east Vancouver high school precipitated the firing of five teaching assistants and a second SFU crisis. SFU students had been present at the high school; the police had been called to the scene and had made two arrests; and the story was in the papers and being chewed over on open-line radio programs. The board fired the five TAs who had been involved. In the aftermath, the vehemence of the campus reaction to these firings caught members of the board completely by surprise.[19]

For students and faculty (with some crusty exceptions) the issue was free speech: the board was disciplining students for off-campus activity and denying them basic rights as free citizens. Members of the board had quite another take. They had cracked down on behaviour that they thought harmed SFU, and they had done so without entertaining any doubts about their own authority. Then, in the face of a stormy campus, with students organized for a strike, they beat a retreat and reinstated the five TAs, who along with their supporters celebrated a victory with many speeches in a final meeting in the mall. All this happened within the space of a week, but the repercussions reverberated for a long time after.

The high school was Templeton Secondary, one of east Vancouver's ten secondary schools. SFU students turned up there after the principal at Templeton suspended a grade-twelve student for writing a parody of the school's literary magazine (and of his English teacher's literary taste) and then refusing to retrieve the twenty-five copies he had handed out.[20]

Among those who remember the incident, but who were not directly involved, the impression has lingered that the Templeton affair began as a PSA class project. The actual beginnings seem to have been as follows. On a Thursday an article appeared in the Vancouver newspapers about the suspended student. On Friday, without further investigation, a group of SFU TAs distributed an open letter to Templeton students. That evening they met a few Templeton students at the Burnaby apartment of an SFU undergraduate, Thomas Tyre, who had become a go-between; and together they made plans for a rally in the park adjacent to the school on Monday. They went back to the PSA Department late on Sunday to crank off a second open letter, and they hired a public address system for $10. During the weekend they contacted students at UBC and members of the Company of Young Canadians—the brief-lived Trudeau-government experiment in funding community action by youth—all with the objective of bringing out a supporting crowd.[21]

When the police showed up at Templeton during the noon hour on Monday, one of the PSA TAs, the soon-to-be-famous Martin Loney, was addressing a crowd of five to seven hundred people by loudspeaker from a station wagon. He ignored several police warnings to desist. The scene had become rough because the Templeton football team, wearing purple leather jackets, were out in force and trying to break up the rally; they were defending school territory rather than free speech. The police saw enough to make two arrests: Martin Loney and the undergraduate, Thomas Tyre, whom they charged with creating a disturbance. Ultimately the two students paid fines totalling $350, which the magistrate imposed along with a good stiff lecture.[22]

One can judge how seriously McTaggart-Cowan and the board regarded the negative publicity by their haste to respond. In the crowd at Templeton were about forty SFU students. Out of these, McTaggart-Cowan had six obvious names: Thomas Tyre, Martin Loney and four other graduate students who had signed the letters circulated at Templeton. On Wednesday, Tyre and four of the graduate students were summoned before SFU's disciplinary body, the Faculty Council, made up of administrators and professors with McTaggart-Cowan presiding. (A year later the Faculty Council ceased to function, a casualty of the student revolution.) Loney could not attend because he was back in custody: on Tuesday he and Tyre had defiantly proceeded from the magistrate's court to Templeton Secondary, where Loney had been arrested a second time on the same charge.

Of the five graduate students who signed the Templeton letters, four were in PSA and one in English. Geoff Mercer and Martin Loney were the main authors of the Templeton letters. Loney had been attending SFU for only seven months, mostly without attracting attention, except for a story and a picture in *The Peak* and an open-line radio interview a month earlier after he was detained at the border and searched for drugs.[23] Mercer was a regular contributor to *The Peak*. Mercer and Loney were British and fellow graduates of Durham University. The other two PSA students, Chris Huxley from York and Phil Stainsworth from Leicester, were also British. All four had been attracted to SFU by the presence of Tom Bottomore. The one Canadian was John Edmond, a graduate of UBC who was doing an MA in English.

What really upset board members, the administration and some faculty was the publicity. Was generating bad publicity for the university a punishable offence? McTaggart-Cowan and the Faculty Council agreed that they had no jurisdiction over students off-campus. But they did ask if these students had been guilty of dereliction of duty or abuse of privilege. Had the five TAs got involved on university time (skipping teaching duties)? Had they used university facilities? And had they intended to associate the university with their actions? The cases were so weak that they left the Faculty Council debating whether to do next to nothing or nothing at all. Tom Bottomore and a significant minority would have done nothing. The majority agreed to let two TAs off with reprimands. To be sterner with Loney, Mercer and Huxley, they asked

McTaggart-Cowan and Bottomore to review their academic standing before giving them further TA-ships.

The next day (Thursday), the board met and threw the fat in the fire by dismissing all five TAS instantly. In protest that evening, Bottomore resigned as dean of Arts. (The job of dean then was not a big one, but for Bottomore this was a turning point; and eight months later he left SFU for Sussex.) On Friday, with the campus in an uproar—stacks of a special issue of *The Peak* ready first thing in the morning, an early-morning meeting of the Student Council, a noon rally of two thousand students in the mall, a three-hour meeting of the Faculty Association and a threatened student boycott—the board agreed to hear an appeal on Monday. It was in the spirit of great emergency that a group of businessmen and lawyers who normally met once a month accepted a second meeting in five days.[24]

On Monday the board rescinded the dismissals after ten hours of hearings and debate that started in the middle of the afternoon and lasted past midnight. The board meeting began against the background noise and commotion of another mass student rally in the mall; and hundreds of students continued a vigil until twenty minutes after midnight, when they enthusiastically got the results.

Two contemporary comments summed it up. On the CBC Radio morning program *Viewpoint,* a UBC political scientist, Walter Young, pronounced the SFU board's flip-flop an "incredible performance." Young said it showed why professors and students could not afford to stick to their studies and leave university government to their lay boards.[25] Stan Wong, by then a nineteen-year-old president of the Student Society, was more generous. Wong had been at the centre of the action, organizing and chairing the student rallies and delivering student ultimatums to the board. He was the hero of the hour. At a victory rally held the morning after, he suggested that the board deserved applause for admitting they were wrong.[26]

OPEN MEETINGS OF SENATE

SFU was the first university in Canada to include students on senate; UBC and Victoria followed within a year, as did Alberta, Lethbridge, Guelph and Sir George Williams, but SFU set the precedent.[27] For representation on the board, students had to wait until W.A.C. Bennett finally lost a provincial election and a New Democratic Party government brought in a revised Universities Act in 1974. But the rules governing senate allowed it to introduce student representation on its own; and it did so just ten months after the publication of the Duff–Berdahl Report. The motion passed in February 1967, and the first student senators (Stan Wong, Sharon Yandle and Simon Foulds) took their places in June. By chance, the Templeton affair had blown up in the interval.

The debate in senate about student representation is interesting on three counts. First, board members spoke in favour, showing that they actually were moving with the times. (Up to 1974, three lay members of the board as well as the chancellor had seats on senate as well as six lay members chosen by convocation.) Second, senate set the number of student representatives at three, which was more than the students themselves had been expecting.

Finally, as an outcome of this debate, senate agreed to open its meetings to the public—despite worries that student journalists would be inaccurate and unfair in reporting senate proceedings. The real problem proved to be somewhat different: the belligerence of the student crowd that came in. The experiment lasted just over a year and a half before senate shut its doors and substituted cameras with feeds to video monitors in the adjoining cafeteria. A majority of senators had had enough of a riotous, paper dart-throwing public gallery that cheered some speakers—student leaders and their faculty allies—and heckled, hissed and jeered at the rest. The same senator who had recommended opening senate meetings made the motion to close them. He had originally argued for open meetings to promote communication. His experience told him he was wrong.[28]

In the period of open senate meetings, the SFU campus turned upside down. The climactic moment came when a faculty member cried out, "We did it. We did it. We took over the university."[29] But the call was premature. A majority of student and faculty wanted stability, not continued turmoil; and the motion to close senate meetings was evidence of that.

THE BURSTEIN AFFAIR AND THE TENURE CRISIS

SFU's greatest crisis was fuelled by the Burstein affair. Kenneth Burstein was an assistant professor in Psychology who started at SFU with a two-year appointment from September 1966. The head of his department recommended against renewing his contract; and what made this controversial was that there was no question of Burstein's competence, but only of his collegiality. He had vigorously opposed his department head, Bernard Lyman, who was a stop-gap replacement for a health-compromised Lorne Kendall. And the word from a couple of former colleagues at Texas Technical College, where Burstein had taught for two years, was that he was disruptive. Burstein appealed to the Faculty of Arts Committee on Salaries and Promotions and then to the University Committee. (Both committees were made up of department heads or their designates.) When each of these committees recommended a one-year renewal (with the implication that this would be terminal), he appealed to the president.[30]

McTaggart-Cowan had seen this case coming from the start and had expected Burstein to fight for his job—which he had done. When the case reached him, McTaggart-Cowan named a special subcommittee; and on its advice he wrote to Burstein to say that he would receive a normal two-year renewal. If McTaggart-Cowan had been lucky, that would have been the end of it. These proceedings had taken up the fall semester of 1967.[31]

Everyone relaxed over Christmas; and then the board, at its January meeting, overruled McTaggart-Cowan and renewed Burstein for just one year. One member of the board had argued against any renewal on the principle that the board should back up a department head. No one on the board seemed to think it necessary to back up the president.[32]

At the very moment that the board made this decision, a Canadian CAUT investigating team were roaming the hallways of SFU. The board later dismissed them as "three professors from the east." They included James B. Milner, professor of Law from Toronto; Percy Smith, secretary of the CAUT, based in Ottawa, and Alwyn Berland, dean of Arts and professor of English at Regina. They had been expected, but the board had chosen to ignore them. Percy Smith had seen this behaviour by a board before. He had been on the staff of United College a decade earlier when it was investigated by the CAUT (in the CAUT's only previous investigation); and he had resigned his position there in opposition to the United College board.

Smith and SFU also had a history. Percy Smith had not forgotten Shrum's provocative anti-tenure declaration of more than four years ago, and Shrum had not forgotten Smith. The investigative team were on campus at the invitation of the executive of the SFU Faculty Association, which had asked the CAUT to investigate a "breakdown in communications" with McTaggart-Cowan. By chance, the investigating team's week-long visit included the Thursday when the board delivered its Burstein decision.[33]

In their report, Milner, Smith and Berland gave McTaggart-Cowan full credit for accessibility: the people they talked to described a president who was "uncommonly easy" to get hold of—one who boasted that his door was always open and who worked hard to make it so. Milner, Smith and Berland gathered that the problem with him was not communications but his failure to get the right results from the board. Not surprisingly, given what they had witnessed, the CAUT team saw this as a grave problem. Their explanation was wordy but everyone got the point. They blamed "an absentee management and an undemocratic distribution of power along certain lines." They were pointing their fingers at the board and at the system of heads.[34]

By this point there may have been little that McTaggart-Cowan could do to save his presidency, even if he saw how precarious it was. Milner, Berland and Smith finished their report in early February and the CAUT released it immediately. McTaggart-Cowan and Shrum found it an extremely one-sided document. One example will serve. Milner, Berland and Smith thought that a new university like SFU should have adopted the principles of the Duff–Berdahl report from the start. Shrum's impatient but unpublicized answer was that he had begun planning in SFU in 1963 and the Duff–Berdahl report had been published in 1966. How could he have taken it into account? And how could he be expected to do what no other Canadian university had yet done?[35]

McTaggart-Cowan made appeasing noises in a public statement, saying the CAUT report contained "some excellent points" and would receive full consideration. Three months later, the CAUT president, Howard McCurdy from Windsor, spent two days at SFU. With him he had two members of the CAUT Academic Freedom Committee. One was a professor of history from UBC and the other an academic administrator in Continuing Studies from Calgary. Together they decided that matters at SFU were not improving, but if anything getting worse. Nine days later the governing body of the CAUT, the National Council, passed a motion of censure against McTaggart-Cowan and the SFU board of governors. Only one delegate voted against it.[36]

In 1968, faculty associations from forty-four Canadian universities and colleges sent delegates to CAUT Council. The council, with members attending from universities as distant as St. John's and Victoria, met in Ottawa just twice a year, in the fall and in the late spring. McCurdy had come out to SFU after final exams at his own university and in time to report to the late spring meeting of the CAUT Council. That brought the calendar to Wednesday, May 29, 1968, when Vancouver listeners heard on the evening radio that an organization called the CAUT had passed a motion of censure against SFU.

In a situation like this, a president has no manual that says what to do next. In the fall of 1971, when the CAUT censured SFU a second time (over the dismissal of striking members of the PSA Department), President Ken Strand saw no need to convene the entire faculty. He preferred to make statements in *The Peak* or the public press or to circulate memoranda. The political environment had changed, and the pressures he felt were very different. But his inclination not to call a faculty meeting helped him to keep a lid on things.

McTaggart-Cowan, on the other hand, could not have moved faster in calling a meeting about his CAUT censure. The ink was scarcely dry on the Thursday morning headlines when McTaggart-Cowan stood up in front of 190 faculty in room 9001, one of SFU's large, theatre-style lecture halls. The official term for such a gathering was a meeting of joint faculty. These occasional Athenian-style assemblies of the whole faculty were a feature of early SFU that did not last beyond that year. McTaggart-Cowan himself had reservations about them. He saw the democratic direction that some faculty wanted to take and he did not think it realistic.[37] But McTaggart-Cowan evidently hoped to dampen the impact of the censure with a prompt, open discussion.

Of course, it did not work that way. He immediately lost control of the meeting: first by agreeing that motions were in order; then in being presented with a motion demanding his resignation; and then in being voted out of the chair on the proposition that he could not preside over a debate on his own fate. One striking memory that many carried away from that afternoon was of McTaggart-Cowan's dignity in adversity. The meeting ended after a little more than two hours with a secret ballot vote of 125 to 61 in favour of his resignation.[38]

At that hour, McTaggart-Cowan had no intention of giving up his job, and he said so when his opponents, with the vote in their favour, told him he had to. He said the same on radio and TV that evening. He was clear in his own mind that because the board had hired him, only the board could fire him; and as long as he had its confidence, he was the president. But he was on weaker ground than he realized. Some board members had been saying in private that they needed "to do something about the president." In fact, they had gone to Shrum before the previous board meeting to get the subject on the agenda, and Shrum had put them off. Arnold Hean, a particularly strong-willed member of the board, was a ringleader. He might have re-examined his own role, but instead he focussed on the president.

In the Templeton case, Hean had advocated firing the five TAs and he had stuck to that while the rest of the board reversed themselves. Hean had opposed renewal for Burstein. Yet he was progressive on some issues: in favour of faculty representation on the board and student representation on senate. His thinking was that the board needed better information: if it knew more, it would make fewer mistakes; and in that thought he expressed a want of confidence in McTaggart-Cowan.[39]

On Friday morning, the day after the joint faculty meeting, the board fired McTaggart-Cowan, after deliberating for only thirty minutes. (McTaggart-Cowan remembered it as fifteen minutes: he had been sent outside and then brought back in what seemed to him exceeding haste.) They were in the boardroom on the twenty-first floor of the B.C. Hydro building in downtown Vancouver. Meanwhile, Martin Loney—now the newly elected Student Society president—was organizing a noontime rally and threatening sit-ins, marches and strikes, whatever it took to get both the president and the board to resign and give students and faculty control of a restructured university government.

Loney's rally began in the noon hour without anyone there knowing that the board had already dispensed with the president. They got the news after the rally had started. One moment reported in the *Vancouver Province* expressed the temper of the crowd of nine hundred. A mature student, a mother of five, stood up to ask if Loney and his followers wanted another Paris. (Students there had been battling riot-garbed police three weeks earlier.) The roar from the crowd in the SFU mall was "Yes!"[40]

George Suart was an incredulous witness to these events. At the age of thirty-seven, he had just been hired as SFU's vice-president administration. His appointment followed a board decision ten months earlier to beef up SFU's administrative structure. In the stripped-down administration that Shrum had specified, about fifteen people reported directly to the president—everyone from the director of information services to the librarian—plus twenty committees, including the Committee of Heads. Shrum himself could see that this could not continue; and as a large part of the answer, Suart arrived from Toronto, where he had a background in marketing and administration.

Suart had been on the job at SFU for six days when he sat in on the joint faculty meeting that voted for McTaggart-Cowan's dismissal. The next morning he was sitting outside the B.C. Hydro boardroom alongside McTaggart-Cowan while the board was deciding to fire the president; and by 12:30 he was back on campus watching the student rally. A few days later he dictated a long diary entry. At the meeting of joint faculty, particularly, he had felt perturbed that a president who, as far as he could see, had been putting in a full-time effort for more than four years, "perhaps twenty hours a day," should be treated the way he was.[41]

In the meeting of joint faculty, the mover of the motion for McTaggart-Cowan's resignation had been Kenji Okuda. Okuda was a Harvard-trained economist and a former advisor to the Economic Planning Ministry of the government of Nepal. He had started at SFU halfway through the first academic year and he had been elected president of the Faculty Association in November 1967. This was a month after a radical rump in the association had derailed tenure policy negotiations, precipitating the resignation of the previous executive. In the commonly understood divisions among SFU faculty at that moment, Okuda was a solid and sensible moderate.

The first thing that Okuda and his new executive did on taking office was to invite the CAUT to investigate what was happening at SFU. Okuda and his executive made this decision with breathtaking speed: they were elected on a Wednesday and by the weekend Percy Smith and the CAUT executive had named their investigating team—Smith, Berland and Milner. There were no rules for doing these things. The CAUT had little experience and the SFU Faculty Association had less. Okuda and his executive based their action on a motion passed by a vote of thirty-six to eighteen in an October meeting that had provoked the resignation of the previous executive. After the CAUT's investigating team got to SFU, they realized that this had been a "spur-of-the-moment" resolution, one drafted in mid-meeting and not very precisely. That did not stop them from going ahead with their task and expanding it into a wide-ranging criticism of the way SFU was run.

Ron Baker was in the small circle of McTaggart-Cowan supporters at SFU who found the whole procedure most unprofessional: the general membership of the Faculty Association had never had a chance to accept or reject the involvement of the CAUT or to debate the terms of reference for the investigation; and the terms of reference were vague. And what he was thinking was also going through the minds of presidents and board members at other Canadian universities. The evidence is in a carefully phrased letter from the president of the Association of Universities and Colleges of Canada (AUCC) to the president of the CAUT. The gist of it was that the CAUT's action at SFU had been highly flawed and had made the situation at SFU worse than it had been.[12]

One can understand why someone like John Cochran could be unclear about what caused the tempest that brewed all through the spring semester. Much of what happened was below the radar for most of the campus population. During their week at SFU in January, the investigating team had talked to just thirty faculty members, mostly from Arts and including nine department heads and deans. They had two sessions with McTaggart-Cowan and two sessions plus a lunch with Okuda and his Faculty Association executive. They also met the three leaders of an ultimately unsuccessful drive to unionize SFU's faculty; and they met a few students. They were talking to accusers and defenders, and scarcely anyone else. With their notes from these conversations, they proceeded to write up their report.

When Howard McCurdy and two members of the CAUT Academic Freedom Committee showed up without publicity in May, it was a little more of the same. The three of them talked mainly to Okuda and his executive, although they also saw the president; and McCurdy had lunch with Shrum and four other members of the board. Shrum, for one, gained no hint of the step that McCurdy and the SFU Faculty Association were contemplating: he thought it a pleasant lunch, a courtesy call. Okuda travelled to Ottawa the next week to urge the CAUT Council to censure SFU—assuming that this was what his membership wanted, but without meeting with them or taking any formal soundings. He was back in time to present his motion against

McTaggart-Cowan. The CAUT had delayed notifying the press long enough for Okuda to make the return trip.[43]

For Okuda and his executive, the proof that they were right was the vote that they secured against McTaggart-Cowan. After two hours of debate at that extraordinary meeting of joint faculty, 125 members of faculty had agreed with them. Okuda talked about it in an interview with an SFU student in 1982. He mentioned the Duff–Berdahl Report and the Burstein affair and a heightened level of protest among faculty after the board decision on Burstein. In general, he and his executive believed that the president was not supporting faculty the way he should and that SFU urgently needed procedures to ensure that faculty had a voice. That was why he and his supporters had acted.[44]

Okuda and his executive shared what seems to have been a widespread view at SFU then—especially in Arts—that "the primary responsibility" of the president should be to represent faculty to the board of governors. And in the spring of 1968, they felt that they had reached an impasse with McTaggart-Cowan because he would not accept anything stated so simply. They were claiming the authority of the Duff–Berdahl Report, which said that a president should be "the chief spokesman of the academics" to the lay people on the board. This statement actually gave McTaggart-Cowan no problem; but the version of it adopted by Okuda and others did. McTaggart-Cowan tried to explain that a president had other responsibilities besides representing faculty: that the university's chief executive officer had many interests to serve; but to their ears he simply sounded intransigent.[45]

Kenneth Burstein, whose case had figured so prominently in the CAUT investigation of SFU, eventually emerged a victor; but he had to wait for the fallout from McTaggart-Cowan's dismissal. In the spring, the board had gone through a process of reconsideration and ended up with the same decision—a one-year contract. But in the immediate aftermath of the CAUT censure, during the brief presidency of John Ellis, the board had agreed to look at the Burstein case again, and Burstein ultimately received a two-year renewal, which put him on track for a tenured position. He taught at SFU until his sudden and unexpected death in October 1987.

Burstein could be a compelling teacher, but he was never an easy colleague.[46] When the Psychology Department underwent its first external review in 1973, each of the reviewers got an earful about Burstein: his colleagues all described him as a troublemaker—an extraordinarily disruptive force whenever he disagreed with the decisions of his colleagues. Among his strongest advocates in his fight for a regular reappointment had been a group of twenty-five or thirty campus radicals, concentrated in English and PSA but including people in several other Arts departments and in Education, as well as Maggie Benston in Chemistry. In the months following the settlement of his case, Burstein emerged as a frequent hawk on campus issues. As Benston explained to a student interviewer in 1982, the point had not been Burstein's politics, but the principles that his case represented.[47]

In the board meeting that fired McTaggart-Cowan, Shrum's vote made it unanimous. He cast that vote after putting up a brief resistance. In the aftermath he wanted to tell Okuda that instead of running off to the CAUT he ought to have given McTaggart-Cowan more help, and that he had done more "irreparable" damage to SFU than "any one person can ever do." But Shrum reconsidered the politics of such a statement and struck it from a letter he sent Okuda on June 14. In August, McTaggart-Cowan left for rest and relaxation at his retreat in the Muskoka country near Bracebridge, Ontario, and for some job hunting, at which he was quickly successful. Within a month he was named the director of the Science Council of Canada, a federal government position in Ottawa.[48]

The following February, Shrum wrote to Ron Baker, who had just been appointed president of the University of Prince Edward Island. In his letter Shrum found himself reflecting on McTaggart-Cowan's dismissal: "I lost a life-time friend and without any compensating result." In 1983 he told the oral historian Peter Stursberg that the day of McTaggart-Cowan's dismissal had been one of the saddest of his life. This was from a man who had been through two divorces and who had survived the battle of Vimy Ridge.[49]

THE REVOLUTIONARY SUMMER OF 1968

In the two months following McTaggart-Cowan's dismissal, SFU went through the throes of a second birth. Allan Fotheringham, then a featured columnist for the *Vancouver Sun,* focussed on the image projected by a new president, Ken Strand, who assumed office at the end of that two-month period. For Fotheringham, Strand's close-cropped hair, horn-rimmed glasses, stylish ankle boots (a fashion of the late 1960s), knit tie, broadcloth shirt and tweed jacket spoke volumes. Gone, said Fotheringham, was the old "slightly fusty" semi-British civil service way of things and in its place "the very picture of a young, bright American career academic."[50]

Strand led a university with an augmented administrative super-structure: two vice-presidents (and three from 1971), plus more power-ful deans. The development of intermediate administrative layers between department heads and the president had been projected during the last year of McTaggart-Cowan's presidency, but became a reality under Strand. A vice-president administration, George Suart, had ar-rived in May; and the board was on the point of hiring an external can-didate as vice-president academic when they lost him in the confusion of firing McTaggart-Cowan. Six months later an internal choice, Rudi Haering, became the first vice-president academic. Lionel Funt from Manitoba had already been taken on as a permanent dean of Science; and the yearly rotation of Arts deans ended with the election of Dale Sullivan, a creative writer in the English department, in October 1968.

The collapse of the headship system during the summer and fall of 1968 made the new vice-presidential and deanship levels of administra-tion doubly significant. The democratic revolution that undid McTag-gart-Cowan followed a parallel course at the department level. The heads of PSA, History, Psychology and English—Bettison, Lyman, Cun-ningham and Baker—all resigned between May 29 and August 31. The heads of Geography, Modern Languages, Philosophy, Mathematics, Chemistry and Physics—MacPherson, Bursill-Hall, Bennett, Harrop, Pate and Haering (to become vice-president academic)—followed in the fall.

The succeeding system of elected rotating chairs took root at SFU at the insistence of faculty at the department level: under pressure, the once all-powerful heads resigned and chairs came in, now constrained by newly drafted departmental constitutions. By July 1969 this system had become university policy, endorsed by the board.[51] In the new structure, chairs were far less influential than the heads they replaced, not just in their relations with their department colleagues but in the broad shaping of university policy.

Strand took office on the first day of August 1968 as the third acting president in two months—after John Ellis, a board choice who took the position on a Friday and then resigned on a Monday (May 30 to June 3); and then Archie MacPherson, who, as a faculty choice, accepted the presidency with the proviso that he would do it for only six weeks. Classes continued; the library functioned; the staff in the registrar's and bursar's offices carried on their work (with difficulty); *The Peak* kept publishing (with much to report), but the two summer months of June and July 1968, between the firing of McTaggart-Cowan and the appointment of Ken Strand, were the two most extraordinary months of SFU's entire history.

Student activists found themselves frustratingly on the periphery, even though this was the summer of the radical Students for a Democratic University (SDU), with Loney and his supporters running the Student Society. The members of the SDU who were not actually on the Student Council were the keenest to provoke a situation, but still showed restraint, held back by the mood of the main student body. In a ballot of seventeen hundred students following McTaggart-Cowan's dismissal, a majority voted to hold a week-long strike for student and faculty control of the university; but those who assembled in a mall meeting, before the counting of the ballots, prudently designated this an extraordinary measure requiring a two-thirds majority. So there was no strike.[52]

On the eve of McTaggart-Cowan's dismissal, the SDU had been threatening a sit-in at the president's office; and in the next week an initial thirty SDU supporters started a sit-in the registrar's office, and then shifted to the boardroom after one of the young women on the registrar's staff told them that they were just getting in the way and that they ought to move closer to the place of power. Up to forty students stayed in the boardroom for five days—over a weekend and into the next week—before quietly leaving on their own. When they first brought in their sleeping bags and food on a Thursday evening, they made a mess of a staff coffee room, but otherwise did no damage; and Suart handled the matter by temporarily relocating staff (who were upset) and setting up new phone lines for them.[53]

The SDU commanded the active support of only a fraction of the 2,500 students enrolled in that summer semester. When Loney's SDU Council proposed to change the name of the university from Simon

Fraser, "a white colonizer," to Louis Riel, "a Metis liberator," 300 students persisted to the close of a three-hour rally to vote four to one to keep the name as it was.[54] In early August, with exams looming, Loney could not get a quorum in the mall for a rally against Strand's appointment. Only 150 students turned out for Loney's rally, well short of the needed 250.[55]

That summer visited great turmoil on the board. They had sent a president packing without calculating their next step; and they did not know what to expect of the faculty or students or the government. A number of board members had voted against McTaggart-Cowan as an indirect revolt against Shrum: after five years of Shrum's domination, they threw his man out. Arnold Hean seemed to feel that a new order had arisen when he took it upon himself to call on McTaggart-Cowan with the message that he had to give up the president's house and car without delay. When McTaggart-Cowan quoted Shrum about staying in the house and keeping the car until the university needed them (or until Christmas at the latest), Hean answered that Shrum no longer had much influence. Suart was witness to manoeuvring on the board to get Shrum out of the chair, which he eventually surrendered in October. His term as chancellor ended the next spring.[56]

This was a summer when the board sought the security of many off-campus meeting places: the B.C. Hydro building, the Bayshore Inn, the Grosvenor Hotel, the Villa Motel in Burnaby, the courthouse in Vancouver and the Jockey Club (the last thanks to board member Jack Diamond, the club's co-founder). Even at these locations they could not always escape student pickets.[57]

At the Villa Motel, for the first time, the board invited faculty members to one of its sessions. There were six of them, all department heads (all approaching the point of quitting), and they were there because board members wanted to pump them for ideas about what to do. By then, straightening out the SFU situation had a new urgency because the B.C. government was holding back funding for phase III of construction—the building of the science complex and the classroom block, to the north and to the south of the Academic Quadrangle.[58]

Neither the premier, W.A.C. Bennett, nor the new minister of education, Donald Brothers, was offering comment, but Shrum had some dire warnings. If the situation got out of control, he was quoted as saying, the university could be closed. Suart, fresh on the scene but wanting to reassure support staff, urged the board to announce that SFU was staying open, and they did that immediately.[59] In mid-June the board got reports that the B.C. government was going to cut SFU's operating budget as of the coming fall. And at the end of the month Shrum got word from the Ministry of Education to stop phase III construction, which was at the excavation stage. Within days the contractor had laid off everyone on the site.

No one on the board could mistake the evidence that W.A.C. Bennett was discouraged and upset with SFU. In the last week of July, as the board moved in disorderly fashion towards the appointment of Ken Strand, they heard rumours that the government was going to amalgamate SFU with UBC and do so immediately. That rumour found its way into the *Vancouver Sun*. Shrum had already reported a phone conversation with the senior bureaucrat in the Department of Education, Deputy Minister Neil Perry, who said that if Shrum and the SFU board did not put their ship in order, and if they appointed a president they did not really want just to appease faculty, "then it is all finished."[60]

Throughout this, the government continued to hold back phase III funding. In mid-September, Bennett called the new SFU president, Ken Strand, over to Victoria. Shrum and Strand went together. Strand was geared up to make a case for SFU, but the turn of the premier's conversation was folksy. Towards the end, Bennett pointed through his window to the sea ducks on the surface of Victoria's inner harbour. His point was that they rode the waves: now in the trough but now on the crest. Then he paused before asking Strand if he thought universities had a role in politics. Strand answered, "No, no more than politicians have a role in universities." About two weeks later Bennett announced the release of phase III funding.[61]

Strand had emerged as a presidential prospect through his chairing of meetings of joint faculty in June and July after McTaggart-Cowan's dismissal. These were marathon meetings attended by most of the faculty available during a summer semester, with the future of the university apparently at stake and the whole campus focussed on the outcome. And these meetings were a contest among faculty factions: radical, moderate and conservative. Very quickly, procedural motions became weapons, employed astutely by radicals and then, in self-defence, by moderates and conservatives. In the struggle it became vital for each side to have its experts in Robert's Rules of Order, who knew their points of order and points of privilege, the precedence of motions, what motions were debatable and on what basis the chair could be challenged. The people who entered this battle with the greatest relish seemed to be from Arts and particularly the PSA Department. In the sciences, faculty lurked in their offices or labs, trying to get on with their work but always with delegates posted in the meeting, ready to summon them when a crucial vote was coming up.

The press attended these meetings, witnessing the apparent collapse of a university. What did they make of it? Wilf Bennett, the education reporter for the *Vancouver Province,* described bitter sessions that repeatedly threatened to get out of hand, in which "some of the more articulate Englishmen and Americans on the faculty" hijacked proceedings with continuous amendments to amendments and point of order after point of order. Exhibitions like this impelled an editorial writer in the *Province* to say that the democratization of a university was "a mischievous process."[62]

A good many people attending one those meetings in late July applauded when Peter Kup from History briefly assumed the chair and refused to recognize the first person who rose on a point of order. He said he was not going to spend the afternoon with that kind of time-consuming tactic. He got away with it because after two months of procedural warfare, the majority had long passed their limits of patience.[63] But the scrupulous maintenance of the rules of debate had undoubtedly helped to keep tensions in bounds. This was a faculty under the spotlight and feeling the pressure. A reporter canvassing the campus in early June, developing a story for the *Vancouver Province,* found the atmosphere strange and unreal. Faculty members had all turned into politicians, unwilling to say what they really meant if their names were going to be used in print: afraid of the twist that one side or the other might put on their words.[64]

Strand had not been involved in the politics of SFU before May 30, 1968, and he had not been widely known outside his own department, Economics. He had started teaching at SFU in the middle of the second academic year after leaving Paris, where he had been employed by the Organization for Economic Development and Co-operation (OECD). The attraction of SFU was that it was in the Pacific Northwest and close to Seattle. He had grown up in Yakima, Washington. When Parzi Copes interviewed him in Paris and gave him a sales talk on Vancouver's climate, he answered that he knew all about it: "I know it rains there."

As president at SFU, Strand gained a reputation as a procedures man and a tough negotiator. He had a background in industrial relations, mostly as a researcher but also on the practical side. Before pursuing advanced graduate studies he had worked for a large construction company, building pipeline at the Hanford, Washington, nuclear energy facility, and as an executive assistant there he had dealt directly with jurisdictional disputes between trade unions: carpenters and machinists. What he saw and experienced there became the basis of a PhD thesis completed at the University of Wisconsin at Madison. As a consequence, he had thought more than most about negotiation and power: their relationship and their use, pertinent considerations for a university president in the 1960s.

As an undergraduate at Washington State College, Strand had taken a short course on parliamentary procedure. In an interview many years later, he recalled that he had not done well in the course, but had grasped the principles. In 1968 he still had a copy of *Robert's Rules of Order* on his shelf; and this copy went into action at the end of May. Strand's entry into the fray began during a lunch with Kenji Okuda and John Hutchinson, then a twenty-nine-year-old assistant professor of history and the vice-president of the Faculty Association. From lunch they went straight into the joint faculty meeting that unseated McTaggart-Cowan; and the procedural strategy that Okuda followed was one that Strand had advised. At that meeting Strand found himself giving direction from the sidelines to the person elected to replace McTaggart-Cowan in the chair—Archie MacPherson. On the following Monday, Strand was voted into the chair, and he remained there with little relief for the rest of a meeting that went on for twenty hours over three days. He was the cool, decisive and neutral arbitrator of a hot debate. That image propelled him to the top of a list of potential presidents, at least for most faculty members.

Strand could not have had a more awkward introduction to the board than when he met them for the first time as a candidate for president. The board wanted Strand to come in alone, without the Faculty Search Committee, as in a normal interview. After much haggling between the committee and the board, Strand finally walked in alone, made his way around the table shaking every board member's hand and then left without saying a word. The message from the search committee and from Strand was that faculty were choosing the president and their choice was not submitting to examination by the board. Suart, who was present, recorded in his diary that it was a scene he had never quite witnessed before.

That scene was the result of what had gone on with the appointment of two previous acting presidents. The board had twice in short order been administered a collective slap by faculty; and faculty members like Okuda and Hutchinson looked capable of handing out more. The first slap was the rejection of John Ellis, and the second was the election of Archie MacPherson. On the afternoon of the day that they fired McTaggart-Cowan, the board, largely on Shrum's advice, had appointed John Ellis as temporary acting president. He was one of the more senior people in the university and the director of one of its most original and successful programs, a Canadian from Vancouver, a person whom Shrum had sensed was independent and tough minded, and someone who by chance had written a sympathetic letter to Shrum in the midst of the troubles of the previous February.[65]

Ellis resigned after seventy-five hours. He had worked hard from the Friday afternoon through the weekend, first to define what might be required to get the CAUT censure lifted and then to get the board to agree. During his consultations with faculty, so many SFU people came and went from his North Vancouver house that the toilets in it were blocked by Saturday afternoon. On Sunday he met with the board at the Bayshore Inn in Vancouver and they accepted all seven of his demands. On Monday he presented these to the joint faculty.

He thought he was close to resolving the crisis: the board would accept the CAUT statement on academic freedom and tenure (if that was what faculty wanted); they agreed that the Universities Act should be reexamined; they would accept a new recommendation on Professor Burstein's renewal; they were open to modifying the positions of head and of dean, and they would consult faculty before appointing an acting president, as Kenji Okuda had demanded on the previous Friday. Ellis took the "temporary" in his title of temporary acting president to mean just that: he was there for only as long as it took the board and faculty, working together, to select an acting president. When he announced the board's concessions at the Monday meeting of joint faculty, there was applause. But then speaker after speaker—moderates and radicals—rose to take issue. What they seemed to agree on was that this was not enough and that the board should be listening, not proposing. *The Peak* reported an intervention by Okuda at one point. "We are the ones who take action in this university."[66]

Ellis resigned late in the afternoon. He announced his decision to joint faculty and immediately sent a telegram to Shrum. During the meeting he had heard enough to decide—right or wrong—that this was a situation in which he could accomplish little. The meeting adjourned to caucus over the dinner hour and reassembled to elect someone else. This proved to be Archie MacPherson, the head of Geography and also the recently elected dean of Arts, a generally popular figure, known to be sympathetic to student demands for a role in university government, and a head whose style within his own Department of Geography had been consultative and inclusive. MacPherson had also emerged over the previous year as a critic of McTaggart-Cowan. Shrum's immediate reaction, reported in the press, was that this election was illegal: the board appointed presidents; that was not the job of joint faculty.

Two days later the board reluctantly appointed MacPherson as their second temporary acting president, although Shrum, for one, never accepted him as legitimate. MacPherson had been elected by faculty and presented himself as a faculty man. It might seem a small thing for a president to doodle during a board meeting—drawing pictures of animals. But MacPherson did it while the board was discussing a letter from McTaggart-Cowan's lawyer about the minutes of the May 30 meeting. Board members thought the doodling was deliberate: a statement that MacPherson was not one of them.[67]

A letter that Kenji Okuda wrote to Gordon Shrum illustrates what was at stake, or what both sides thought was at stake. It was a private peremptory letter that Shrum answered tersely in the negative. In this letter, Okuda asked Shrum to step down immediately as chairman of the board and to stop attending board meetings, with the threat that if he did not do so, the matter would come to a vote in joint faculty with all the attendant publicity and headlines.[68] Okuda wrote out of a belief that Shrum had become a liability to SFU and with the knowledge that this was a widely held opinion. But his letter also assumed that faculty could dictate—that SFU was on the verge of faculty-run government. In fact, it was on the verge of administration-run government, which is a different thing; but Okuda shared with many the expectation that faculty rule was on its way. From the board side, this was a dangerous expectation, one that would not go down well with the premier; and board members did not want a president who looked at things only from the faculty side.

These were the circumstances of Ken Strand's first meeting with the board when he made no statement and accepted no questions, but simply appeared and left. From what they had heard about him, board members were actually favourably disposed towards him. He had the advantage, as he himself recognized, of not being identified with any faculty faction: he had been the neutral chair of the proceedings of joint faculty and had taken no stand on any issue. The board understood that he was his own man. But they wanted an opportunity to judge for themselves. From Thursday, July 26, when they first met him, until the following Wednesday, they wrestled with their decision. Up to the last moment, they were prepared to ignore the faculty Search Committee and appoint Lionel Funt, the dean of Science, and one of the most experienced academic administrators on faculty. However, after some negotiation, Strand had returned for a second meeting, having established that there would be no grilling. That had gone well. Strand was appointed on the last day of the month and took office the day after.[69]

The new order became evident at the next board meeting, which happened to be at B.C. Hydro. Shrum interrupted several times while Strand was speaking and Strand walked out, leaving the meeting in a shambles. The next morning he told Dick Lester, the secretary of the board, that it was himself or Shrum. Someone had to go. It did not come to that, and the two managed to tolerate each other until Shrum's term as chancellor ended in May 1969. But Strand had made his point.[70]

THE STUDENT OCCUPATION OF THE ADMINISTRATION OFFICES

In November 1968, which was Ken Strand's fourth month in office, nearly 180 students, led by campus members of the SDU, occupied four floors of the administration offices, still located in the library building. Thus began SFU's fourth crisis. The students maintained their occupation for fifty-four hours, until Strand brought in the RCMP, who cleared

Students voting at a general meeting held in the gym in the summer of 1968.

"Who's my Alma temporary acting Mater today?"

"... and why should we continue to put up with overcrowded classes and facilities?"

TOP LEFT: A cartoon by the *Vancouver Sun*'s Len Norris, poking fun at SFU turmoil in June 1968. SFU LIBRARY

BOTTOM LEFT: Cartoonist Norris, still having fun at SFU's expense in September 1968. SFU LIBRARY

ABOVE: Ken Strand in his presidential office. SFU INSTRUCTIONAL MEDIA CENTRE PHOTO, SFU ARCHIVES

ABOVE: Protestors with signs at convocation, 1968. SFU ARCHIVES

TOP RIGHT: Student Senator Simon Foulds speaking in the mall. SFU ARCHIVES

BOTTOM RIGHT: Ken Strand speaking in Freedom Square, September 9, 1968, early in his term as acting president. VANCOUVER SUN AND PROVINCE INFOLINE

ABOVE: Ken Strand's audience of 2,500 students, staff and faculty in Freedom Square, September 9, 1968. VANCOUVER SUN AND PROVINCE INFOLINE

TOP RIGHT: A cast member of *Coriolanus,* which was being rehearsed at the theatre during the occupation, in the mall with police officers at about 2:30 AM on November 23, 1968. PEAK PUBLICATION SOCIETY

BOTTOM RIGHT: Students occupying the administration section of the library building, November 1968. VANCOUVER SUN AND PROVINCE INFOLINE

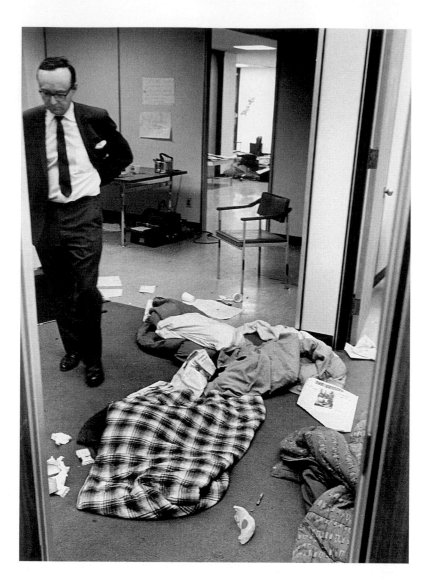

ABOVE: George Suart, vice-president for administration, checking for damage minutes after police cleared student occupiers out of the administration building, November 23, 1968. VANCOUVER SUN AND PROVINCE INFOLINE

TOP RIGHT: Police line behind the occupied administration/library building in the early hours of November 23, 1968. VANCOUVER SUN AND PROVINCE INFOLINE

BOTTOM RIGHT: Kathleen Aberle speaking in support of strike at a general meeting of PSA students and professors, September 1969. PEAK PUBLICATION SOCIETY

"NOW DON'T POUT KENNY, ALL I DID WAS TELL THEM THAT THEY COULD APPLY FOR POSITIONS AT S.F.U. I DIDN'T SAY THEY COULD HAVE THEM."

TOP LEFT: Sandy Wilson's graphic response to the trusteeship imposed on PSA, published in *The Peak* in July 1969. PEAK PUBLICATION SOCIETY

BOTTOM LEFT: A cartoon by Sandy Wilson in *The Peak,* November 1974, following news that President Pauline Jewett had written to the PSA seven, inviting them to apply for vacant positions. PEAK PUBLICATION SOCIETY

ABOVE: A protest during convocation in 1973, about the splitting up of the PSA Department. SFU ARCHIVES

CLOCKWISE FROM TOP LEFT: Gordon Shrum at B.C. Hydro, February 1971; President Pauline Jewett (SFU Instructional Media Centre photo); Brian Wilson, vice-present academic (Campbell Studios photo); Ron Baker, founding head of English and academic planner (Williams Brothers photo). SFU ARCHIVES

CLOCKWISE FROM TOP LEFT: Geoffrey Bursill-Hall, founding head of Modern Languages (John Helcermanas photo); Rudi Haering, founding head of Physics (Williams Brothers photo); C.D. Nelson, founding head of Biological Studies (John Helcermanas photo); Brian Pate, founding head of Chemistry (John Helcermanas photo). SFU ARCHIVES

CLOCKWISE FROM TOP LEFT: Ronald Harrop, founding head of Mathemetics; Parzival Copes, founding head of Economics & Commerce (John Helcermanas photo); Allan Cunningham, founding head of History (John Helcermanas photo); T.B. Bottomore, founding head of PSA. SFU ARCHIVES

CLOCKWISE FROM TOP LEFT: Archibald MacPherson, founding head of Geography (Williams Brothers photo); Lorne Kendall, founding head of Psychology (John Helcermanas photo); Lorne Davies, director of Athletics (John Helcermanas photo); Lolita ("Letty") Wilson, dean of women and acting registrar in the fall of 1965 (SFU Audio Visual Centre photo). SFU ARCHIVES

CLOCKWISE FROM TOP LEFT: Klaus Reickhoff, charter member of the Physics Department and long-term SFU senator (SFU Audio Visual Centre photo); John Ellis, founding director of the Education Development Program (SFU Audio Visual Centre photo); Dale Sullivan, first continuing dean of Arts (SFU Audio Visual Centre photo); Don Baird, first librarian (Williams Brothers photo). SFU ARCHIVES the building and arrested 114 students who had chosen not to leave voluntarily. This operation occurred in the early hours of a Saturday morning, beginning with a police warning at 2:30 AM and then police entry half an hour later.[71]

Altogether, over one hundred unarmed police officers were on the scene; and they achieved surprise by blocking off the road to the university while Vice-President Suart cut off both pay phones and regular phones in the occupied building. The students inside did not resist and were taken out the back door one at a time—with a police officer on either arm—and through a fifty-man police corridor to a succession of paddy wagons pulling up one behind the other. A fire truck stood in the shadows in case it was needed. There were spectators at that early morning hour. A crowd from a dance in the cafeteria had formed behind the library where the paddy wagons were lining up, and linking arms they began singing "We Shall Overcome." Mingled with them was a crowd that had emptied out of the theatre.

The only violent sounds came from an amplifier temporarily blasting into the night from the roof of the theatre. John Juliani, SFU's avant-garde resident theatre director and his troupe had been rehearsing a bizarre adaptation of Shakespeare's *Coriolanus* (a play about arrogance and arbitrary power); they had emerged onto the mall in makeup and strange costumes, a weird-looking group of bystanders; and they had the extremely mischievous idea of broadcasting a recording of ack-ack fire and bursting bombs at full volume for a continuous twenty minutes. They started this while the police were gathering in the mall and cutting a chain across the entrance to the occupied building and then going in. What the theatre group did was more stunt than calculated protest; and it was ignored by the RCMP commissioner on the scene; but it proclaimed in surreal fashion the unprecedented nature of what was taking place.[72]

Strand's decision to bring in the police defined his presidency: it accurately caught the mood of the majority on the campus and in the general public; it impressed the board and it gave him credibility with the government. The student occupiers had a just cause, but their tactics left them isolated. On the Monday, the SFU switchboard handled one thousand calls from members of the public who applauded Strand's action. One could hear the same thing on hot-line radio and read it in the editorial and letters-to-the-editor pages of the newspapers. And, as if to drive the point home, the tenor of the calls to the university reversed a couple of days later, when it seemed that Strand was going soft by asking the attorney general to drop the criminal charges against the arrested students.[73]

The public wanted a crackdown against campus agitators. And a majority of students and faculty were not so different. Nearly 2,500 students lined up—some for hours—to vote two to one against a strike in support of the 114 occupiers who had been charged. A Faculty Association ballot two months later backed Strand's decision to bring in the police by 84 to 24 (with a lot of faculty not stirred up enough to vote). In that atmosphere, the attorney general, Leslie Peterson (the former minister of education), felt no compunction about letting the charges stand. The charges were eventually reduced in magistrate's court but the students were not allowed to walk away from legal consequences altogether. Most received fines of $250 or two months in jail; a couple who expressed repentance were fined $25.[74]

The central issue for the students who occupied the administration offices was transfer credit. They had encountered a puzzling design feature in B.C.'s expanded system of higher education: college and university programs did not mesh. The first students to run into the problem were graduates of Vancouver City College, the earliest of the new two-year community colleges. Like SFU, Vancouver City College had been operating since 1965, and in 1967–68, its students began going on to university, seeking to enter their third year. They then discovered that they could not get university credit for all the courses they had taken at the college. The reason they got from the SFU registrar's office was that many of their college courses did not conform to what was offered at SFU.

Back in 1962, the president of UBC had recommended a system of community colleges independent of the universities: free to determine their own curricular programs without supervision by SFU, UBC or the University of Victoria. He knew that meant that there would not be perfect transferability from the colleges to the university; and from his perspective that was welcome: it let the colleges take creative initiatives while preserving university standards and expectations. And it would help cut down the flow of students from the colleges to the university.

But when Vancouver City College students realized that they could do two years of work at the college without getting two years of credit towards a university degree, they quite justly did not like it.

This issue reached explosive proportions early in the tenure of Harry Evans, SFU's fourth registrar. Evans had been hired by McTaggart-Cowan but started while MacPherson was acting president. He took over an office that had been without a registrar for six months; and that long gap accounts for some of the confusion in the way SFU was handling admissions. What he brought from the Department of Education in Victoria, where he had been registrar, was long experience in a fair-minded and compassionate approach to applying rules. He understood as well as anyone the complexity of the transfer credit issue. One of his first tasks at SFU was to sort out how it was being handled in his own office. In his naturally circumspect language, "there were problems."[75]

The solution was to establish in advance what SFU would say to a student about any given community college course: whether or not it had an SFU equivalent and, if it did not have an equivalent, whether it would still be counted towards a degree. This was the recommendation of John Ellis, who accepted a commission from senate to investigate transfer credit. He did so in the aftermath of the student occupation. Ellis visited Berkeley to see what was done in California, which had a much larger and more complex system of higher education than B.C., including separately governed community and state colleges as well as the multi-campus University of California. At Berkeley, Ellis saw booklets that detailed course equivalents within the California system, and the good sense of that idea was something he adopted for his report. He was thinking mainly of SFU, but his recommendations ultimately led to province-wide Articulation Committees representing the colleges and universities that met, discipline by discipline, to deal with transfer credit issues.[76]

So the students who occupied the administration offices had an issue that deserved prompt attention and one that actually was solved quite readily once it was addressed. They did not get much sympathy from the great mass of students or the faculty or the administration because they were associated with the SDU and because the SDU seemed bent on escalating protest. The agitation over transfer credit began in the fall semester following a resounding defeat of the SDU in student elections; and that made it look like an SDU attempt to reclaim the limelight. It appeared that they wanted an occupation whatever the issue. Moderate student leaders close to the action believed that was so. As Ken Strand explained in an interview in 2000, that had been his take on the situation.[77]

The lead-up was exceedingly brief; and the administration and senate had little time to look into what was happening with transfer credit before the protest got ugly. On October 16, the student ombudsman, Ace Hollibaugh, and student senator, Donn Korbin, an economics major and briefly an SDU activist, brought the matter to the Senate Admissions Committee. On November 4, SDU members from SFU met at Vancouver City College with students there. On November 11 they wrote to Harry Evans, the registrar, with three demands: free transfer of course credits throughout the province; the opening of the registrar's files for review by a student committee (they wanted to look at correspondence between SFU and the colleges); and the creation of an elected faculty–student appeal board to review admissions cases.

On November 14 the SDU called a noon-hour rally, which led to a sit-in involving two hundred students, first in the registrar's office and then on the fourth floor above. This lasted until 7:00 PM. By now they had a fourth demand: increased university funding. Both Strand and Evans talked to the students, saying that there were processes to follow but promising to start working on solutions: they recognized that something had to be done. On the 20th, Korbin made the four demands at a tumultuous meeting of senate, and then broke up the meeting and initiated the occupation. In one month and four days, the SDU had progressed from bringing an issue to a senate committee to taking illegal action.[78]

Nothing in Simon Fraser's brief past suggested that the administration would react to a student occupation by swiftly calling in the police. What would Strand's predecessors have done? That we cannot answer, but we know what they did in similar circumstances. McTaggart-Cowan anticipated a sit-in in his own office when the board took that problem away from him by firing him. He had put all confidential papers in the vault and arranged for an office in the Physics Department so he could run the university from there. He did not intend to call in the police except if it got rough—fighting among student factions—or if students did physical damage to the building. Otherwise he intended to wait it out. In McTaggart-Cowan's opinion, the police had been called in too early and too often on American campuses.[79]

In the first week of June it fell to Archie MacPherson and George Suart to deal with a sit-in by forty students in the registrar's office and then the boardroom. When the press asked MacPherson if he was going to let the students stay there, his answer was "Why not?" After five days and six nights they left of their own accord.[80]

In November, by contrast, Strand let the occupation continue for just two nights and two days before resorting to the police on the third night. He had in fact been prepared to bring them in on the second night. They had been loaded in their vans at the RCMP station on Gilpin Street in Burnaby, ready to move, with ropes and scaling ladders and riot gear and shields (none of which they needed); and they had been miffed when they learned they were not going to be used that night. George Suart had first contacted them early in the day, soon after arriving at the university and discovering that he could not get into his office. For him, the thought that police might be required had been instantaneous.[81]

This was an occupation, not a sit-in. And the numbers were much greater than at previous sit-ins. An occupation meant that the students inside were controlling access to the building. They had pushed filing cabinets against all entrances but the main one. There they had fastened a heavy steel chain that allowed the door to open only forty-five centimetres; and they were selectively challenging people who wanted to come through. The president could not get in, nor the vice-president, although a couple of administrative officers did enter and stay into the second night, and the occupiers allowed a security guard in to protect the filing room.[82]

The people inside were from Vancouver City College and UBC as well as SFU. Two reporters got in: one from the *Vancouver Sun,* who spent an hour inside on the last night; and one from the *Vancouver Province,* who was inside for five hours. They had minimally disguised themselves by doing things like taking off ties and jackets and messing up hair.[83] (A student, apparently, was someone with messy hair.) The people around Strand suspected that many outsiders were there. Probably less than half the occupiers were SFU students, although the vast majority were undoubtedly students who intended to come to SFU if they were not already enrolled.[84]

One of the older students arrested was a *Peak* reporter, twenty-six-year-old George Reamsbottom, who wrote about it in the next issue of the paper. He described an orderly occupation with rules: no dope, no destruction of property and no "do-it yourself" initiatives. This, more or less, is what the reporters for the *Province* and *Sun* saw while they were there. The former walked into Strand's darkened outer office to find many of the occupiers sitting there engrossed in Walt Disney's *Alice in Wonderland*, which was being projected against the office wall. Some pot smoking was going on, but it was being curbed by the objections of non-smokers. Two young men were trying to kick in the door of Strand's inner office, but they stopped after others protested. At the beginning students had opened up many offices; then they decided to lock them up to protect them against loss or damage. For the same reason they had admitted the security officer to watch the filing room. After receiving the police ultimatum to get out, some started a desultory cleanup (but the place was still a mess when Suart, in the wake of the police, brought in a cameraman to record it). An overwhelming majority voted down a motion to offer token resistance; and when most demonstrators elected to stay, they did so after giving everyone who wanted to a chance to leave.[85]

This was the occupation described from the inside. That picture does not capture the menace that Strand and his advisors perceived on the outside. The university had witnessed months of aggressive SDU behaviour at student rallies and at meetings of senate and joint faculty. The way in which the SDU had broken up the last senate meeting before the occupation was so belligerent, it is not surprising that those who witnessed it thought them capable of going much further. Two hundred SDU students had charged out when senate did not meet their demands and then returned to flick the lights off and on, switch off the mikes and back up their leader, Donn Korbin, who announced over a bullhorn that the meeting was over. "This body [the senate] is now irrelevant." Strand, as president, had been in the chair.

At that meeting Registrar Harry Evans could not help but recall the quiet and sanity of his years in the Department of Education in Victoria. He was responding not just to the bullying shouts and screams of the students who had crowded into the senate chamber, but the intimidating physical impact they had in a congested space, sitting all over the place. He was being pushed in the back and he had a large dog, brought in by someone, at his feet; and he was concerned for the two distinguished but older women present who were lay members of senate. At a later senate meeting, complaining of the impossibility of these conditions, one faculty senator put it simply: "We fear student power."[86]

We have a description of SDU tactics given by the education reporter for the *Vancouver Province*, Wilf Bennett. He told his readers that the SDU were at every student meeting, monopolizing the microphones, speaking to every motion, challenging the chair and keeping up a stream of procedural interruptions while their supporters packed the area near the platform, exerting the maximum psychological pressure and presenting a forest of hands in any open vote. They were effective, Bennett observed, because they managed to speak to the "vague liberalism" of a majority of students; and they had an influence beyond their numbers.[87]

The name of their movement—Students for a Democratic University—expressed the goal. They wanted a university run by students and faculty, not by businessmen and politicians. They spoke of restructuring society, with the university as a starting point. The question was: how far would they go? They were certainly lacking in decorum, but did they know when to pull back? Would they willingly let a situation become destructive or violent? Martin Loney was numbered as one of them, but to his credit he had urged the students to give up their occupation. The SDU was not as single-minded as it sometimes looked.

One glimpse of the apprehensions felt by the people around Strand can be found in a letter written by Bob Brown, the future dean of Interdisciplinary Studies. Brown was one of the people on whom Strand relied to negotiate with students. The letter in question was from Brown to the editor of the *Vancouver Sun* in reply to a feature article by John Conway, an SDU leader and PSA graduate student. The point that Conway tried to make was that the problems that he and other students wanted corrected were genuine: that it was wrong to attribute the troubles at SFU to hard-core militants intent on destroying the university. Brown's answer was to say that was just what was going on. The university, he said, was a pawn in an SDU game whose objective was social revolution.[88]

Another glimpse comes from George Suart's diary. He, quite understandably, saw the SDU as unreasonably impatient. As he put it, the SDU would have had a valid case if they had not expected Strand to rearrange the whole B.C. admissions system in three or four days. Suart had already been talking to an undercover RCMP officer. He first mentioned him in his diary about six weeks before the occupation; and as he began to talk to him regularly, he suspected that he was working with a partner. This officer was doing what police do, investigating groups considered a threat to society. In the 1960s, that included the SDU and SDS. As John Conway remembers, during the occupation students believed they had police *agents provocateurs* amongst them inside the building, urging all kinds of illegal activities. Suspicions ran so high that Southam News correspondent Duart Farquharson, on campus days after the occupation, found himself handicapped by persistent rumours that he was a plainclothes policeman.[89]

George Suart could have confirmed, if he had wished, that an undercover RCMP officer was at SFU. He did speak about it in an interview long after the events had become history and he remarked then on how uncannily accurate that officer's information was: he knew a day or two ahead exactly what student agitators were going to do. Suart's first conversation with this officer suggests how he was thinking weeks before the occupation. The conversation is another of his diary entries. What the RCMP officer said, after spelling out what he knew of the political situation at SFU, was that he thought the time had come for one university in Canada to take a strong stand: "A confrontation might ease the situation on other campuses." This assessment apparently spoke to Suart's own inclination.[90]

When the occupation took place, Suart was a key player. He later described his role as that of the chief cop on campus. The people that Strand turned to were senior administrators, academic and non-academic. On the first morning, they set up shop in the librarian's office. At the beginning the group included the president, the bursar, the registrar, the assistant to the president (Allan Smith, whom Strand had inherited from McTaggart-Cowan), the director of media and public relations, three deans (missing only the dean of students, Letty Wilson) and the two vice-presidents. The vice-president academic, Rudi Haering, was brand new on the job: his appointment was to go to the board that evening.[91]

Out of that tense initial strategy session, interrupted by the phone calls and the comings and goings of would-be student and faculty intermediaries, came an agreement to form a decision-making group made up of the three deans, the two vice-presidents and the president. The others then left. At that point, as Suart reported in his diary, the two hard-liners were himself and the dean of Arts, Dale Sullivan. The president was listening but keeping his counsel. Suart had already spoken to the RCMP commissioner in Burnaby.

Throughout that day they tried talking to the students in the building, while alerting the police that they could be called. Strand addressed a packed rally of two thousand in the mall and won cheers for his promise not to give in to a sit-in or occupation. At various times, each of the three deans and Strand attempted to convince the occupiers that they should leave the building. Strand made his second attempt in the middle of the night after deciding not to use the police then. During the first day, several faculty members recruited by the deans had also tried. The decision-making group was also communicating with the students through intermediaries like student ombudsman Ace Hollibaugh, student leader Stan Wong and PSA professors Tom Brose, Jerry Sperling and Mordecai Briemberg.

On the morning of the second day, after Strand had called off the police in the middle of the previous night, Suart observed what looked to him like a dispirited group gathered with Strand in the librarian's office. In his diary, Suart described the scene that followed. Ace Hollibaugh had phoned with yet another proposal and it was being discussed. Suart caught Strand's eye, and they went into an adjoining room. Suart says he spoke bluntly: this was not the time for procrastination: the president had to show he was decisive; that was priority number one. Strand gave no reply but walked back into the main office, told whoever was speaking to shut up, and said "Okay, we go tonight." Suart felt the energy change in the room instantly from depressed to electric. At that point, by common consent, all attempts to talk to the students stopped. The thinking was that if persuasion could not get them out of the building, perhaps the uncertainty of silence would. The students stayed, and the police arrived that night.

When the police did come, the great achievement all round was the avoidance of violence. For this the police deserved credit for the way they handled themselves; Strand deserved credit for bringing them out decisively in force in the middle of the night, and with surprise, and the students deserved credit for the self-discipline they exercised.

What did this episode mean in the long run? As Ken Strand was well aware, he had put to final rest the principle of *in loco parentis*. By turning to the police, the university completely disowned any parental responsibility for students, even on campus. A university was not like a family and did not try to sort out all its problems on its own. The implication was this: a student was under the university's guidance and discipline in academic matters only, and not in civil ones. Strand was clear on this distinction, although board members probably were not. For a majority of them, keeping students in line was the main thing, whether that meant bringing in the police or firing TAS for off-campus activity.[92]

The SDU continued to be a disruptive element at SFU for most of the following year; but they never attempted anything on the same scale again, and their weakness as a political force had been exposed. At SFU, as at universities throughout North America, the energy went out of the student movement around 1970. Part of the explanation, according to Murray Ross, the president at York, was that students had achieved a large part of their agenda. But most observers cited economic factors. The trend towards underemployment among university graduates, which first manifested itself around 1968, seemed to rob students of their idealism and to make them think more pragmatically about why they were at school. The change was one that many university teachers regretted.[93]

One important element in the handling of the occupation had nothing to do with students. It concerned the relationship between the president and the board. This is what Ken Strand emphasized when interviewed for this book. The board had no part in handling the occupation. Strand gave the board no accounting of what he was doing at the time; and to the annoyance of board members he stayed on campus and missed a board meeting at the Villa Motel that happened to fall on the second night of the occupation. After the fact, they accepted his assumption of full responsibility. Gordon Shrum actually complimented him on his timing in bringing in the police. As Strand saw it, the occupation was the moment that administrative power shifted decisively from the board of governors to the place it should have been all along, with the president.[94]

9

The PSA Affair

The PSA affair was a crucial part of Simon Fraser University's early history and probably the most notorious conflict on a Canadian campus then or since.[1] It was about radicalism, academic freedom and due process. From the beginning, one side characterized it as a political purge; but it was more complicated than that. At stake was the future of SFU: the direction the SFU adventure would take. The outcome, however, was predictable: the odds were all weighted against professors who went on strike.

Students and faculty in the Politics, Sociology & Anthropology Department took a strike vote at a general PSA assembly early in the fall semester of 1969. Over 750 had crowded into a lecture theatre designed to seat 504, with another one or two hundred massed outside. Sixteen PSA faculty members were on campus and most of them were present. Another six were on research leave; and whatever side they might have taken, they later counted themselves fortunate to have been away. There was little chance that they could have affected the outcome at a meeting that made every vote equal—student or faculty. A student activist presented the motion to strike, and student activists dominated much of the debate. They did have the unqualified support of five or six faculty members, including one of the most senior, Kathleen Gough Aberle, an associate professor with a long list of publications on kinship systems, peasant movements and politics in the Indian state of Kerala.

In the lead-up to the strike, half of the PSA faculty on campus were against it. In the meeting, however, most of these professors were silent. The one who did speak said that a strike was the wrong tactic, although he did not quarrel with its aims. Others would have argued about both aims and tactics but did not see this assembly as a welcome place to debate. Reports of the meeting gave these figures on the vote: more than seven hundred for a strike, thirty-six opposed and twelve abstentions. Hidden in those figures were the votes of faculty, for and against.[2]

The professors who accepted the authority of this vote and withheld their services knew that their action was not a legal strike under labour law. They were not unionized; they did not constitute a bargaining unit, and they had not conducted a legal strike vote. They had their own term for what they were conducting: an academic strike, which they conceded had no precedent but which they believed was demanded by the circumstances. When the strike began, forty-eight hours after the vote, six PSA professors met their classes and nine did not. Over the course of the strike, these numbers fluctuated slightly as one professor declared he was on strike, then not, and then on strike and then not.

About half of the approximately 1,250 students in PSA that fall sought to salvage their semester by transferring into other departments.[3] But half did not. Some of these stayed in the courses offered by non-striking PSA professors. But a large minority of several hundred PSA students stood solidly behind the strike; and their commitment was a significant—although generally unnoticed—element in the whole affair.

Maintaining this commitment took organization. A mimeographed strike bulletin appeared; and throughout the strike PSA students held daily meetings in the main cafeteria. When several departments hastily mounted additional courses for strike-displaced students, a student–faculty strike committee responded with pickets. On several occasions these pickets succeeded in disrupting classes by entering them or block-ing entrances with tables or milling about in the hall area outside or play-ing loud music, both recorded and live, or shouting over bullhorns.[4] President Ken Strand had already shown his willingness to turn to the police and the courts in the fall of 1968. In response to picketing in Octo-ber 1969, he obtained a court injunction naming three faculty members and nine students, who were ordered to stop disrupting classes.[5]

The picketing had begun in the second week when Strand suspended the nine striking faculty members and announced that he would be pro-ceeding with dismissals. Apologists later argued that it was a strike for only eight days and then a suspension, but it was a casuist's point: the strikers claimed to be on strike.[6]

The suspended faculty were still on the payroll and had access to their offices, but could not teach or supervise students or participate on committees. Most of the nine were braced for the serious consequences of the step they had taken. Some of them, however, were tentative. Harold Hickerson was one of the latter. Hickerson was an accomplished ethnographer, known for his work in British Guiana as well as on the Algonkian and Ojibwa people of the Great Lakes region. He had started at SFU in May 1969. Five months later he was in the midst of a highly partisan and emotional strike with the lines drawn not just between the administration and members of the PSA Department, but, more gut-wrenchingly, within the department between supporters and opponents of the strike.

Hickerson was the striking PSA professor who broke ranks after much uncertainty. But others also wavered. Keeping them onside were a group of militant students who rode herd on them, teaming up on the irresolute to stiffen their resolve.[7] As long as the strike lasted, there were professors caught up in it who were looking for a way out. More than one approached the Canadian Association of University Teachers in the hopes that the CAUT could negotiate a deal that would end the strike, save their jobs and still leave the issues over which they struck open for discussion. As long as the strike lasted, however, the CAUT kept out. Part of their calculation was political: the strikers had few friends at SFU other than the student activists concentrated in PSA.[8]

The strike collapsed after five weeks; and the striking professors an-nounced they were willing to return to teaching. Their courses had been cancelled, so they could not have gone back to classes that semester; none of them got their jobs back in the coming semester, and five of them never got them back. During the strike, Strand had served them with suspension and then dismissal notices; and the next phase of the affair became one of delayed, protracted, expensive and emotionally debilitating hearings.

Suspension hearings occupied the board in November 1969; next came the dismissal hearings. After Hickerson's reinstatement, there were eight cases to deal with. Within nine months, three cases ended in departures, although not through the hearing process. One of these was John Leggett (formerly an assistant professor at Berkeley), who had already been denied tenure and who was in his last contractual year. With one month left in that year, Strand reinstated him and let his contract run its course. The other two were Kathleen Aberle and David Potter. Potter was a Berkeley graduate with a London School of Economics PhD who, like Aberle, was an associate professor and who also published about India. Aberle and Potter had refused to go through a second round of hearings after Strand rejected the results of a first. Strand and the board used Aberle's and Potter's refusal as reason to terminate their contracts immediately.[9]

In the fall of 1970, one strike participant did win reinstatement—for the balance of his one-year renewal. This was Nathan Popkin, who had taught at SFU from 1967. He had chosen to separate his case from the others, and his dismissal committee found in his favour. Reinstatement allowed him stay on the SFU payroll until the following September, when his contract finally expired. His reinstatement left four cases unresolved: those of Mordecai Briemberg, Prudence Wheeldon, Louis Feldhammer and Saghir Ahmad.

This was a set of people drawn to SFU by many routes. Briemberg was a Rhodes scholar from Alberta. Wheeldon was a South African who had taught briefly at the University College of Rhodesia and Nyasaland. Feldhammer had enrolled for a year at Sir George Williams in Montreal before completing a BA at Berkeley and then beginning a PhD at Chicago. Ahmad had graduated from the University of Punjab in Pakistan before doing doctoral work at Michigan State and post-doctoral work at Alberta.

Feldhammer and Briemberg had been hired as instructors in September 1966. Wheeldon came a year later as an assistant professor.

Ahmad, the only one with a PhD, started in September 1969, just before the strike. At a PSA rally on his second day on campus he had stepped militantly to the mike to advocate a strike; and two weeks after joining SFU he was one of the nine who refused to meet classes.[10]

Eighteen months after the dismissal process began, Briemberg, Feldhammer and Ahmad were still under suspension; and their second set of dismissal hearings had not begun. They had agreed to a second set after Strand had rejected the findings of a first (which recommended reinstatement), but a fall and spring semester had passed without their new dismissal committees being set up. A committee had been formed in the Wheeldon case, but it made a ruling that Strand and his legal advisors found unacceptable.

This happened in June 1971. Strand's answer was to bring the dismissal hearing process to an end. He reinstated Wheeldon and immediately put the question of her one-year renewal before the University Tenure Committee. (Wheeldon still had not finished her PhD and therefore had not met the special condition required for her renewal. She was out.) Strand then asked the SFU board to scrap the university's dismissal procedures.

He had several reasons: board members were complaining of the cost; politicians were asking questions in the B.C. legislature about suspended professors still on full pay; he had found the procedures unworkable, and he was concerned that the situation was perpetuating a destructive atmosphere in the PSA Department and across the university. The problem was certainly absorbing a huge amount of his own time. Getting rid of the university's previously untested dismissal procedures freed his hands. He could now refer directly to the uncomplicated language of the Universities Act, which gave the president and the board the power to hire and fire. On Strand's advice the board immediately fired Briemberg, Feldhammer and Ahmad.[11]

Strand had been under pressure from three academic associations to reinstate all of the suspended PSA professors. His refusal had led the Canadian Sociological and Anthropological Association and the American Anthropology Association to censure SFU back in September 1970. The CAUT council entertained a censure motion in November 1970 without making a decision; but at its next semi-annual meeting in May 1971 the council voted for censure. This was several weeks before Strand and the board threw out SFU's dismissal procedures.

Strand and the board could ignore the CAUT and other academic associations because they had strong support from a majority of SFU students and faculty right to the bitter end. The strength of their position meant there was no quick patching up of differences with the CAUT: this censure of SFU lasted nearly six years. In contrast, the censure directed against Patrick McTaggart-Cowan had been imposed and lifted within the space of six months.

A PROBLEM DEPARTMENT

The PSA eight had gone on strike against what they called a purge. They were reacting to negative tenure, promotions and renewal decisions. At its most idealistic, their battle was not just about these decisions, but about how they were made. The PSA eight were demanding departmental autonomy, which they defended as the kind of grassroots democracy that one should encourage at an innovative and experimental university. And the democracy they were pushing for included student parity in all aspects of departmental government.

If the PSA eight had had their way, a student committee would have had a veto on tenure, promotion and renewal. Their opponents in the department, and outside it, saw an arrangement of this kind as a self-serving blend of principle and personal interest: a number of radical PSA professors would have fared better if judged by radical PSA students than by not-so-radical faculty. That was evident because when they were judged by faculty from outside the department, the results were negative. By September 1969, some members of the PSA eight saw little future for themselves at SFU and felt they had little to lose by striking.

During four full days of testimony at his own hearing, Nathan Popkin struggled to explain his motivation. Keeping his job was not an objective: if it had been, he said, going on strike was a disastrous way to do it. He had not thought the general public would understand what the strike was about; and he knew that the strikers were an isolated minority in the university. The best he could do to explain why he had joined the strike was to speak of its value in exposing what he thought was wrong at SFU: getting publicity that might bring light in. He also spoke of his commitment to group action.

As he put it, the idea of a strike emerged from mixed feelings of anger and demoralization. Doing something was better than "waiting around for our contracts to expire or moping around or begging people whom we really had no respect for to help us and take us back." The decision to strike had been an immediate boost to morale. "People's spirits began to lift," said Popkin of the embattled group in PSA, "and my own began to lift."[12]

The PSA eight were lost participants in a faculty revolution that had ended for most of SFU during the 1968–69 academic year: a revolution that had unseated a president, democratized departments (introducing elected chairs) and moved erratically and partially towards student participation in university and department government. Radical members of the PSA department had been in the forefront of the battles that produced these changes. Some of them, briefly, were major campus figures. But when the revolution stopped, their radical momentum did not. Instead it carried them far beyond the political and philosophical boundaries of the main body of students and faculty at SFU.

A note in the diary of Administrative Vice President George Suart suggests the power wielded by PSA radicals in the summer of 1968. Tom Brose, a charter member of PSA and associated with the radicals, was the chair of the Food Services Committee. Strand, then a week into his presidency, told the board that before finalizing a decision on the location of the cafeteria building, he had better get Brose's agreement. He was concerned that Brose might go to the mall and whip up student dissent.[13] A year later, Brose was one of the PSA professors denied a further contract. Twelve months had wrought a tremendous change.

The change affecting Brose could be summed up in two words: democratization and standardization. These were part and parcel of the CAUT-approved tenure policy that SFU adopted soon after Ken Strand became president. Gone was the discretion possessed by department heads. Now SFU had a policy that spelled out how a department should proceed to consider tenure, renewal and promotions cases. This became a problem for radical faculty and students in PSA when they wanted to set up their own procedures and then discovered that the dean, the president and the University Tenure Committee would not let them do so. They had to conform to the same procedural regime as everyone else. For a group of students and faculty in PSA, the story of the 1968–69 academic year was a rapid passage from heady triumph to defeat.

When did people at SFU begin to look at PSA as a problem department? It did depend on perspective. The scientists were quicker to bring accusations than their colleagues in Arts or Education. But the serious finger pointing against PSA did not begin until late in McTaggart-Cowan's presidency. Tom Bottomore, the founding head of PSA, believed he had left a functioning department when he departed from SFU in December 1967, although one that had already developed a disturbingly intense political culture. For his successor, David Bettison, matters seemed manageable when he assumed the headship at the beginning of 1968: it was later in the spring that he found the department impossible to run.[14]

Bettison's instincts had been democratic. Bottomore had not called votes at department meetings. He would listen to discussion and then sum up the consensus: he was the paternalistic leader who let everyone have their say while maintaining control. Popkin, as a junior member of faculty, initially liked Bettison, who called for motions and accepted the rule of the majority.[15]

The turning point for Bettison was in April 1968. It was then that he recognized a "saddening" and deep mistrust between PSA and much of the rest of the university. What made this mistrust unmistakable was the reaction in PSA to his decision to act as the director of his department, rather than its servant: to proceed as a head whose authority came from the president and the board rather than from his colleagues. Two linked developments had forced him to reveal himself this way: the University Appointments Committee had refused a visiting appointment that most of his colleagues wanted; and, under provocation, the dean of Science, Lionel Funt, had stood up in a special closed meeting of senate and made strong charges against PSA.

The rejected appointment was that of Andre Gunder Frank, an economist and specialist on Latin America who was then a visiting professor at Sir George Williams in Montreal. The PSA Department wanted him as a visiting replacement professor. Frank, an American-educated German citizen, was already internationally known for a book published in 1967 on economic underdevelopment in Latin America. He was an engaged and restless academic, having held appointments at universities in Canada, Mexico, Brazil and the U.S., all within the preceding dozen years. After 1966, however, he had been kept out of the U.S. When he applied to SFU, one did not have to dig very far to figure out why. He gave as a referee Paul Sweezy, one of America's leading Marxist economists, the founder of the leftist *Monthly Review* and, in

1957, one of the last American intellectuals targeted in the McCarthy era's anti-Communist witch hunt.

Bettison had recommended Frank's appointment and initially had no reservations about it. But when he defended it at a meeting of the University Appointments Committee he ran into heavy fire; and the committee ended up returning his recommendation and asking for more documentation. They questioned Frank's record, his referees and the faculty members who wanted to hire him. It all boiled down to a suspicion—or conviction—that a Marxist pressure group in PSA were pushing to hire Frank for ideological reasons without much academic justification. To add heat to the situation, the University Appointments Committee questioned two other PSA appointments around this time under similar circumstances.

In the ensuing argument, each side accused the other of ideological bias: one suspecting that a majority in PSA wanted only Marxists; and the other believing that people with influence in the university wanted no Marxists. Bettison found himself in the midst of bitter meetings in PSA; and he was unable to contain the rancour that many of his colleagues felt. This found expression in an intemperate public letter, signed by fourteen of them, accusing the University Appointments Committee and other committees of unprofessional conduct. The answering shot came from Lionel Funt, the dean of Science. At a stormy special closed meeting of senate, he read out nine accusations against PSA. Eighty PSA students stood outside the locked doors, rattling them, rapping on the walls and making so much noise that McTaggart-Cowan interrupted the meeting several times to send someone out to try to get them to be quiet.[16]

Bettison called the accusations against his department a smear, but he accepted a commission from McTaggart-Cowan to investigate. In the eyes of a majority of PSA faculty, and of a great many PSA students, his acceptance of this commission made him one of the enemy. The charges he had to investigate were of this nature: that there were professors and TAS in PSA who imposed a party line, who intimidated, mocked and ostracized students if they disagreed with them, who used their classes to collect money for leftist causes, and who subverted the whole academic enterprise through lenient grading and through frequent class cancellations to let students participate in protests and demonstrations. These accusations had an origin close to home. Student Senator Simon Foulds—a PSA student—was Dean Funt's source of information; and Foulds was reporting scuttlebutt from within PSA itself.[17]

The reaction in PSA to the prospect of an investigation was so negative that Bettison immediately resigned as head, only to have McTaggart-Cowan talk him out of it.[18] Bettison persuaded himself that PSA's best defence was an open inquiry, bringing out the facts, which he thought were mostly to the department's credit; but he could not convince a majority of his colleagues that this was the way to go. They feared a witch hunt; they closed ranks against him, and in a formal vote they refused to co-operate. For another six weeks Bettison struggled on, but he had had enough by the end of May, when he finally and decisively resigned. This was on the weekend that the board fired McTaggart-Cowan, and to many students and professors in PSA these developments looked like ultimate victory and vindication.[19]

Bettison had served in the South African Armoured Brigade in Egypt during the Second World War. When he finally left SFU for Lethbridge in 1969, he told Ken Strand that he had fought totalitarianism as a soldier and did not wish to stay in a totalitarian academic department. He had turned his back on South Africa rather than live under the apartheid system; and when he gave up an Australian National University research project in Papua New Guinea in 1965, he had intended to make Vancouver his permanent home.

The spring semester of 1968 changed that. He was the man in the middle: unhappy with a top-down administrative structure, but subject to unremitting attack from below. What he faced in his department he characterized as the power politics of mass rallies, propaganda by half-truths, private meetings and private caucusing, and rule by organized partisan power. This behaviour, he said, had crystallized in the spring of 1968; and he decided that he did not have the energy to combat it. He had been a defender of PSA, but within a short time he became a bitter critic.[20]

What were Bettison's opponents saying? In the summer of 1968 a junior member of PSA wrote to a new appointee who had not yet taken up his position. There had been a revolt of sorts, the letter writer said; and it had started in PSA. The head of the department was out and replaced by an elected chair. The university had been censured by the

CAUT, and the president was gone. And the students had voted in "the most radical student government imaginable." "All these elements have thrown the university into chaos which I find most encouraging and pleasant to be in."[21]

LEADING UP TO THE STRIKE

The excitement surrounding the first CAUT censure—with McTaggart-Cowan's dismissal and Strand's appointment—drove the PSA situation into the background. Bettison reported the meagre results of his investigation and resigned, and there the matter seemed to rest. More than that, the whole university was moving in concert with PSA towards a more egalitarian, democratic environment. Moreover, Strand had not been involved in earlier controversies and sought to make a fresh start.

In February 1969, nearly eight months into Strand's presidency, his focus came to rest on PSA. This happened after he read front-page headlines about PSA in the local papers. Some of the story was old business—what had happened the previous spring. Allan Cunningham, the ex-head of History, had exposed a can of worms during a debate at the University of B.C. with Louis Feldhammer by alluding to anonymous threats against the children of an SFU professor. He did not mention names, but a resourceful reporter from the *Vancouver Sun* dug out a story with quotes from David Bettison, Roy Carlson and two other departing PSA professors, all saying they had been harassed or threatened after differing with radicals in the department. According to the *Sun* story, Bettison's wife had received seven threatening phone calls during the last two months that he was head. And Carlson—in the midst of Archaeology's split from PSA—heard that a teaching assistant was suggesting to a class that they phone Carlson and ask if he knew where his children were.[22]

From this point on, mistrust and suspicion mushroomed between the dominant faction in PSA and the Strand administration. Initially the department mustered a strong showing of solidarity. Eighteen PSA professors demanded an apology and a retraction from the *Sun*. None of them, they declared, had had any part in making threatening phone calls to colleagues; none gave automatic As; none sought to hire revolutionaries regardless of academic qualifications; and all were proud of the department's procedures and its academic achievements. At this time

Strand resisted pressure to bring in the CAUT to investigate. What he did do was to write a letter to all faculty inviting anyone who had facts to bring them forward. He had given notice to PSA that it was again under scrutiny.[23]

In September 1969, on the eve of the strike, Vice-President George Suart gave an address on student unrest to a group of business people. He described PSA as a department in which fifteen out of twenty-two professors had a New Left viewpoint antagonistic to the capitalist system and identified the department as a breeding ground for the ideas of student extremists, who—he also wanted his audience to know—made up a small minority of the student body.[24]

Much of what Suart said was common knowledge at SFU: over two-thirds of PSA's professors readily identified themselves as Marxists, Marxist-Leninists, supporters of the New Left or radicals. However, they did not all march to the same drum. When Heribert Adam testified at the Popkin dismissal hearing, he said he had joined PSA in 1968 precisely because it had a progressive image. He started off, he said, as a member of the "so-called" ruling group and initially believed that the department was being attacked by the administration because it was radical. But he changed his mind and gradually withdrew from the group. He was one of several PSA professors who broke with the dominant faction after finding them too defensive, intransigent and unwilling to compromise.[25]

Seemingly minor issues could be threatening for his colleagues when they saw them as part of a general pattern of administrative harassment. Three examples will illustrate: one involving an advertisement, the second a fire bell and the third an airline ticket. All came up at the Popkin hearings because Popkin and his colleagues thought them evidence that the administration was out to get their department.

An advertisement for a new position in PSA had appeared in February 1969 in the *New York Review of Books* and in *Canadian Dimension.* What struck many at SFU unfavourably was the advertisement's identification of PSA as a department with a "radical orientation." President Strand questioned Mordecai Briemberg, the elected chair, about it. At the Popkin hearing Strand explained that all he wanted was recognition that the wording was a mistake. Instead he got such a defensive reaction that he felt quite disturbed. Months later, members of the PSA Department were still protesting that "radical" did not imply any particular ideology, and they were citing an armload of dictionaries and sociological articles to prove the point.[26]

The fire bell affair had to do with the testing of fire bells during the April break, when staff would be there but few faculty or students. Briemberg, as the PSA chair, objected to testing on a weekday when it would disturb the department's receptionist, secretaries and administrative assistant. How might he have handled it? The chair of English gave his staff time off while the bells were ringing, but Briemberg gave them the full day. The director of personnel told him he did not have the power to do so; and memos began flying between PSA and the administration. At the Popkin hearing, Briemberg said that the issue had been blown out of all proportion to its importance.[27]

The airline ticket belonged to Maggie Benston, whose home department was Chemistry. It had been paid for by the PSA Department, and that had led to a charge of misuse of funds. Benston had purchased her ticket to go to Montreal for the November 1968 CAUT meeting. She was representing a radical minority in the Faculty Association opposed to lifting the first CAUT censure. As Briemberg explained, the group behind Benston intended to pay for the ticket out of their own pockets before the charge actually went through the PSA account. Somehow they had failed to do so and the matter became an embarrassment. But Briemberg did not see why the administration made so much public fuss about it.[28]

In these things, Briemberg and his supporters saw a pattern of attack on their department. In the same things, the administration saw a department refusing to acknowledge the authority of the university's governing officers, committees and procedures: a department that acted as an institution unto itself. Neither side looked at these as isolated incidents.

The biggest issue of all was renewal, tenure and promotion. The problem from the administration's side was that PSA would not conform to the university's new Academic Freedom and Tenure Policy. First it was a case of delinquency: the department was slow to form an acceptable Tenure Committee. Then it became a problem of defiance: the department persisted in naming a committee and maintaining a procedure that the dean of Arts and the University Tenure Committee would not accept; and the department would not back down.

For the first time, SFU was following its CAUT-approved Academic Freedom and Tenure Policy in tenure, renewal and promotion cases. It was inevitably a ragged business. The deadline for completing the process was September 1, as in the past. However, the procedures were more complex and everyone was learning how they worked. To compound the challenge, the number of cases far exceeded previous years. There had been a bunching with professors on two- and three-year contracts coming up for consideration at the same time; and many of the previous year's cases had been deferred because the new policy introduced in 1968 was not in place until mid-September.

The PSA battle over academic freedom and tenure procedures began in September 1968 and continued through the fall and spring and into the following summer. The biggest disagreement was over PSA's involvement of students in assessing tenure, renewal and promotion cases, coupled with its policy of opening all files to general scrutiny.

From the beginning of the 1968–69 academic year, a majority of PSA faculty wanted to give students a decisive voice in the tenure, renewal and promotion process. It took some time to determine the formula, but by the end of April 1969 the parity idea had been worked out with its notion of parallel faculty and student committees, each with veto power. In its early experimentation with departmental democracy in the summer of 1968, PSA had discussed and approved tenure and renewal decisions in full department meetings with the professors under review present and speaking up for themselves: an open way of doing things but also a political pressure cooker. With the involvement of students, PSA extended the democratic principle further. In April and early May, PSA put its system to work—with members of a student tenure committee assessing professors' publications, teaching and service while members of the faculty were doing the same. The effort had no bearing on the decisions that the university ultimately made, because the University Tenure Committee would not accept PSA's committee or its procedures.[29]

The University Tenure Committee was a body created under the new tenure policy and itself an experiment in democracy. It had six elected members, two each from Arts, Science and Education, and the vice-president academic as chair. And among the responsibilities thrust upon it was approval of the makeup and procedures of department committees. Inevitably, the first time around was a scramble for everyone. In

February, four departments still had not set up acceptable committees and procedures. By April, however, PSA was the only one.

By then, time was running out. The tenure procedures were new but the time constraints were the same as before. The concern from the administration side was that the faculty handbook promised faculty members a year's notice if they were not going to get a renewal of contract. That made it imperative each year to resolve tenure and renewal cases before September 1. A department that procrastinated or created obstacles could make it impossible to meet the deadline, which would oblige the university to grant automatic renewals; and that could subvert the tenure policy before it had a reasonable trial.

In June the Faculty Association agreed that a dean should be able to name a tenure committee if a department failed to do so. The board adopted the change at its July meeting; and this option was available to Dean Sullivan with just over a month to go before the deadline. Sullivan attempted to use it right away because the PSA situation had reached a stalemate.

One hope for a better outcome had been a motion presented at a PSA Department meeting at the beginning of July. The author was one of the department's charter members, Robert Wyllie, who had been elected chair for the summer while Mordecai Briemberg took a semester's research leave. Like Adam and two or three others, Wyllie had previously supported the radical majority, but he was now hoping that his colleagues would compromise with the administration and the rest of the university. He had sounded out his motion with the University Tenure Committee and with Dean Sullivan, and it was acceptable to them. What he proposed was to amend PSA's procedures so that the student committee would be involved in tenure, renewal and promotion cases in a consultative way but would not have a veto. A majority of his colleagues objected and voted his motion down.

The failure of Wyllie's motion brought everything to a head. This probably did not come as a great surprise to anyone close to the action. Some of the key people who opposed Wyllie's motion had long before passed the point of compromise. We can see that in an assessment by Kathleen Aberle, who published an article on the PSA struggle in the May 1970 issue of *Monthly Review*.[30] One of the signal statements she made in that article was that she had felt that PSA's days were numbered from the moment it adopted student parity. It underscored her adherence to principle: she had supported student parity while believing it would lead to the "liquidation" (her word) of her department within one or two years.

The PSA Department rejected Wyllie's motion two months before the strike, although no one was yet talking seriously of a strike. Wyllie resigned as acting chair, and when PSA elected Briemberg by acclamation, Dean Sullivan refused to have him back, saying he no longer had confidence in him. Sullivan resolved the matter by putting PSA under trusteeship and naming four professors to a Trusteeship Committee that he would chair.

He had no trouble finding people who would serve, which was a measure of PSA's isolation. Three of these professors were from other departments—Economics, English and History. The fourth was Tom Bottomore, now well ensconced at Sussex but willing to take on this task from a distance. He thought he could be useful by providing background information and advice.[31]

These developments generated mountains of statements—justifications and counterjustifications—mimeographed or photocopied and circulated to everyone with a university mailbox, or else published in *The Peak*. Sullivan, Bottomore, Bettison, Wyllie and his supporters, and Briemberg, Aberle and their supporters, all had their say. When Sullivan met with the PSA Department before declaring a trusteeship, the department had the meeting taped and kept a transcript. When Sullivan met with Briemberg and told him that he was not acceptable as chair, the two agreed to tape that conversation in case one or the other should subsequently misrepresent what was said. In a discussion paper directed to their PSA colleagues, four PSA professors who dissented from the majority described a state of war between PSA and the administration "with semi-paranoid overtones on both sides."[32]

The clock on tenure, renewal and promotions was still ticking. Sullivan's first attempt to name a department Tenure Committee—using his new prerogative—was unsuccessful. The PSA professors he selected, radicals and moderates, would not serve without the endorsement of their department. That brought Sullivan to August 12 before he had a committee ready to work. And he had to recruit six of its seven members from outside PSA: from English, History, Modern Languages, Economics &

Commerce and Chemistry. The only PSA professor he could get to serve was A.H. Somjee—not a member of the radical faction. The tenure policy said little about how departmental committees should operate; and this committee wrote to no referees and consulted no students or colleagues. In any case, it had little time. In nine days it completed its review of the eighteen cases in front of it. Three days later these cases were before the University Tenure Committee; and two days after that, on August 27, all but two cases went to the board. It had been managed just under the wire, four days short of the end of the academic year.[33]

The whole process had been messy, rushed and improvised. This was perhaps inevitable under the circumstances; the haste and untidiness were both product and cause of the breakdown between PSA and the rest of the university. The elected PSA Tenure Committee—the one rejected by the University Tenure Committee—would have given positive recommendations to everyone up for consideration. As Kathleen Aberle testified at the Popkin hearings, it was a matter of solidarity: all standing together against the menace of the administration. By contrast, the PSA committee appointed by Dean Sullivan refused renewal in two cases, and in four cases made one-year renewal conditional on completing a PhD within eight months; and it denied promotion in three of four cases.

The appointed PSA committee did recommend tenure in six of seven cases and in the seventh—Aberle's—suggested that she be allowed to apply again before her current two-year contract expired. But the University Tenure Committee, after quick consideration, recommended that three people including Aberle not get tenure, and that she not get a second chance or another contract. What was the count by the time the University Tenure Committee was finished? Four PSA professors were threatened with termination as soon as their contracts ended in twelve months; and four others would likely be terminated at the same time for failure to finish their PhDs. In a department of twenty-two, that was a big housecleaning.

The two most questionable recommendations concerned Kathleen Gough Aberle and John Leggett, both denied tenure and renewal by the University Tenure Committee. The others affected junior faculty who had been teaching up to four years without yet completing a PhD. Some of them did protest that they had been hired without being told they had to get a PhD immediately; but that was not an argument that got much sympathy outside PSA, or even among a few of their PSA colleagues. Aberle and Leggett were different because they were established scholars and well known in their fields.

Aberle's vita had one immediately noticeable feature. Up to the time of her arrival at SFU, she had not held a permanent teaching position. Her seniority—she was an associate professor—had been earned though extensive research and publication. She was widely known through this research and also through her activism. And her frequent change of employment left her with contacts at many universities. She knew Herbert Marcuse from her time at Brandeis; she belonged to a circle that included Henry Magdoff of *Monthly Review,* and notoriously she had tangled with Margaret Mead at the 1966 meeting of the American Anthropological Association: Mead did not want Aberle's anti-war motion on the agenda of a scholarly gathering. In her own words, Aberle was an academic nomad. She had done six years of fieldwork in India and then had taught or held research fellowships at Harvard, Manchester, Berkeley, Michigan, Wayne State, Brandeis and Oregon.

There were two reasons why she had not settled anywhere before SFU. She was married to an anthropologist, David Aberle, and many institutions would not then hire a husband and wife in the same department. And she was a lifelong activist. She had spoiled her copy book at Brandeis by speaking publicly in defence of Fidel Castro during the Cuban missile crisis and at Oregon by refusing to assign grades because students with low grades were liable to be drafted. Already looking grandmotherly at the age of forty-four—if we accept a description by a young reporter from the *Vancouver Sun*—and speaking softly in a refined British accent, she did not fit the mould of a '60s radical; but she had the credentials.[34]

Leggett had started at SFU in 1966 after leaving Berkeley, where he had been an assistant professor. He was another SFU professor who had been present during the explosion of student unrest at Berkeley in September 1964. More than that, he had been a go-between in the tense negotiations between students and the Berkeley administration in the famous incident of the police patrol car: the vehicle with arrested student leader Jack Weinburg inside that was surrounded and trapped for hours in front of the Berkeley administration building by a crowd of hundreds of students.[35]

Leggett began his second year at SFU as an associate professor and he had produced his first book in 1968, a sociological study of Detroit's largely black working class. He was already stacking up research projects: studies of farm workers in California and also in New York. To push ahead with the New York study he took a year's unpaid leave of absence from SFU and accepted a contract to teach for that year at the University of Connecticut, closer to his sources.

This activity caused an uproar at SFU in the spring of 1969. Leggett's Connecticut contract had overlapped his resumption of teaching at SFU by two weeks. He committed no great crime from an SFU perspective and no one at Connecticut was taking action; and when President Strand got the full details he let the matter drop. But before he had the details, Strand had written a formal letter to Leggett to say that he could face dismissal. *The Peak* got hold of the letter and Leggett's reply and published them.[36]

Leggett's sojourn at Connecticut had come to Strand's notice in March 1969, after a lengthy *New York Times* article mentioned his involvement in a demonstration against Dow Chemical—a manufacturer of, among other things, napalm.[37] Rudi Haering, who was then vice-president academic, had phoned Connecticut and learned that the board at Connecticut had not been aware of Leggett's continuing connection with SFU (although the department chair had known). This led Strand to write Leggett formally to raise the spectre of dismissal. Strand's letter, when it became public, seemed proof to radicals that PSA professors were being targeted.[38]

Without the Aberle and Leggett cases, what kind of protest would PSA students and faculty have mounted? It might not have been much. These cases gave the strikers their best ammunition; and they were not alone in thinking this. Arthur Mitzman, who was very critical of the PSA eight, saw something wrong in the Leggett and Aberle decisions. Mitzman had joined the PSA Department in January 1970. When he started teaching he found himself mired in the deep mess that PSA had become. Still, he agreed to be acting chair in the summer of 1970. He was an activist, a veteran of civil-rights and peace demonstrations, including—sharing a page with John Leggett—an anti-Dow Chemical demonstration at Rochester. But his relationship with the strikers was never good. During his summer as acting chair his daily encounters with them were so hostile—shouting matches, pushing and shoving—that he took up residence in an office in History.[39]

Despite this, Mitzman called the Aberle and Leggett cases "gross and unambiguous injustice." For the PSA eight, these cases were what warranted collective action: they gave the most convincing evidence of a political purge. They were exhibits A and B, as Nathan Popkin put it. When Popkin testified at his hearing he emphasized Aberle's case and its value: she had a distinguished vita that could be published on the front page of *The Peak* to show how wrong the administration was. It was the Aberle case, Popkin said, that persuaded him to go along with the strike, rather than to petition on his own for his own unconditional renewal. Her case and Leggett's were the ones that ensured publicity and that made students and faculty in PSA believe they could achieve something—however nebulous—if they stood together.[40]

In all the excitement leading up to the strike, very few people noticed that Aberle's case did not go to the board. It was held back by Lalit Srivastava, the professor of biological sciences who was briefly acting president. One of Srivastava's last acts in that office was to hold back the University Tenure Committee's questionable recommendation for Aberle and one for another PSA faculty member. When Strand resumed office in September, he left these files as he found them; and the board never made a tenure decision for her, either to award or deny.

When Aberle went on strike along with her colleagues, her file sat with the president until it became irrelevant with the termination of her contract. She had been at the centre of the strike talk in PSA from the moment it first surfaced. She took an uncompromising stand from that point on and, after the dean's departmental committee recommended she not get tenure this time, she refused to appeal or to appear before the University Tenure Committee. She took a hard line at a mall meeting of PSA students on September 9, again on September 16 and finally on September 21 at the mass meeting of PSA students and faculty when the strike vote was taken.

What did she have to say? According to *The Peak*, at the mall meeting of September 9, Aberle began by defining her purpose in holding a university position. It was to work with colleagues and students in critical analysis of the problems of society: pollution, population, the bomb, the war and the oppression of the poor and of ethnic minorities. In 1969,

Aberle judged that all this was threatened and that if that was so, there was no point being a professor at SFU. That is how she connected the issues of departmental trusteeship and of tenure and renewal with larger social issues. "We cannot talk of oppression in the world and stand up for others if we cannot fight oppression where we stand." In encouraging PSA's radicals to go on strike, Aberle's firmness, along with her academic reputation, were critically important.[41]

THE STRIKE AND STUDENTS

Kathleen Aberle was a member of a group, and although she was the senior in age and academic standing, it would be a mistake to attribute the ideology and the actions of the PSA radicals mostly to her. The role that she played was to support the group.

This brings us to the question: what was the group? From testimony at the Popkin hearings and from the public press we get a consistent list of the most active radical professors in PSA: the opinion leaders. In addition to Aberle, they were Mordecai Briemberg, Tom Brose, Louis Feldhammer and Jerry Sperling, all junior faculty without PhDs.[42] But professors did not constitute the whole group. It included graduate students and undergraduates.

Mitzman made this analysis. There was not much difference in age, experience, credentials and social perspective between many of the young professors in PSA and the graduate-student TAS. They were drawn together, he thought, "like bees to honey." And in an energizing way, junior faculty were attracted to the radicalism of graduate students, rather than vice versa. This was a dynamic environment in which new ideas—like the rejection of "bourgeois," value-free social science—could gain currency in the group overnight. Within the group the most impatient, doctrinaire and confrontational were some of the students: they were the true guerrilla types, as one disenchanted PSA professor said.[43]

Sharon Yandle was in her fourth year at SFU at the time of the PSA strike. As a student senator, a regular contributor to *The Peak* and a PSA student she had been a close observer of all that went on. She wrote an account of the strike for the Winnipeg-published magazine of the left, *Canadian Dimension*.[44] One of her themes was the assertive role of a small band of PSA student radicals. They were the ones who demanded student parity and who received it as a gift from sympathetic faculty; and they were the ones who controlled the student committees and the student plenum. Many of the leaders of the PSA student union were also leaders of the Students for a Democratic University (SDU). They were prominent in the occupation of the administration building, as well as other sit-ins, mill-ins and teach-ins, and in repeated disruptions of senate and other meetings on campus.

One of the SDU leaders from PSA was John Conway, now a professor of sociology at Regina. As he saw it, PSA's militant students were a self-motivated group who did not need or take direction from their radical professors. His assessment of the tenure and renewal decisions of August 1969 and of the PSA strike and the dismissals that followed was that "they" (the faculty) were fired for what "we" (the students) were doing.

PRESIDENT STRAND AND THE DISMISSAL HEARINGS

In the summer of 1968, when Strand assumed the acting presidency, he promised students and faculty that he would do it for only one year. To understand why he would make such a promise, one has to remember the anti-establishment spirit of the moment, his sudden and unexpected emergence as a candidate and his status as the people's choice. Halfway through his term he was inclined to stick to the one-year limit, although many people were asking him to reconsider. By the next summer, however, he was willing to be president for another five years if the board could find a way to release him from his promise. There were other candidates, including Arnold Edinborough, the nationally known editor–publisher of *Saturday Night;* but Strand was the sole pick of a joint student–faculty search committee.

At the end of his acting presidency, with the board ready to appoint him president, Strand took a month off and Srivastava filled in. During that month the board ran student and faculty referenda on the question of releasing Strand from his promise. The student vote was 62 per cent for Strand to carry on as president and the faculty vote was 80 per cent.[45] These votes were expected. And they were a good indication of where faculty and students stood on the PSA issue. As we have seen, this made no difference to PSA faculty who went on strike. Strand returned to his office on September 8, and fifteen days later they were refusing to meet their classes.

Two months later they were preparing for dismissal hearings. The strike was over; they were still suspended from teaching and from participating on committees; the board had upheld their suspensions, and dismissal committees were being formed. Strand, drawing on his industrial experience, thought that the hearings would take three days. The PSA eight expected them to be over in a couple of months—by February 1970—and that their employment would end then.[46]

As the process dragged on, the PSA eight took encouragement: if the procedures were unworkable, perhaps they would keep their jobs after all. First there were hitches in setting up committees and then in getting them going, all of which caused delay. And the problems did not end there. The ultimate collapse of the process offers a useful lesson about the relationship of procedures to politics, power and goodwill.

SFU's Academic Freedom and Tenure Policy called for dismissal cases to be heard by three-member committees. The structure was like an arbitration committee, although the authors of the policy did not intend an arbitration process. Their objective was an equitable policy that gave a professor a hearing before being dismissed. But they made it complicated; and Strand, for one, eventually came to see it as one-sided: protecting the faculty member and not the university, and making sense only if one assumed that the university was "always wrong."[47]

Under the 1968 tenure policy the president named one member of a dismissal committee and the faculty member a second, and those two together named a chair. Six of the PSA eight agreed to go before a single committee, which promised to simplify matters. But the other two, Aberle and Popkin—as was their right—chose to go before separate committees. Initially that meant three committees: one for the six and one each for Aberle and Popkin. But by the time the process had been drawn out to its unsatisfactory conclusion, with incomplete committees and rejected findings, the number of projected committees totalled eight. Three committees actually met, two held hearings and Strand and the board accepted the findings of just one (in the Popkin case).

It had been difficult to put committees together. More often than not, the two sides disagreed on the choice of a chair. The tenure procedures anticipated this, and the next step was to ask the chief justice of the Supreme Court of B.C. to choose a chair. But he was not always able to do it right away; nor was he always successful. He reached a dead end several times: people were not willing to take on the job and the looming prospect of a CAUT censure was a factor.

At the start, Aberle's case showed how difficult it could be. When her committee had not been named after nine months, she asked to have her case rolled in with the other six. Up to that point, the committee for the six had only had a preliminary meeting. It had been delayed in finding a chair and then because Prudence Wheeldon, one of the six, had launched a legal challenge to the board's decision about her renewal. The committee decided to wait for court's decision because it had implications for the other PSA renewal and tenure decisions.

Wheeldon argued that SFU's decision to refuse her renewal was faulty because, in its haste, the university had not followed its own procedures. The university's answer was that the procedures were an internal matter and not enforceable in law. Three representatives of the Faculty Association, including Kenji Okuda, testified in court but did not help Wheeldon because they described the tenure policy as a "good faith" statement and not a legal document with legal consequences.[48] In June 1970, J.A. Hinkson, the judge who heard her case, ruled that SFU's Academic Freedom and Tenure Policy was not legally binding.

SFU's academic planner, Ron Baker, might have been called a prophet. Back in 1963 he had had doubts about the value of a university statement on academic freedom and tenure. He thought that SFU should have such a statement; but his reading and observation told him that it would not likely carry much weight in law. Now Strand and his legal advisors had Judge Hinkson's decision as proof; and from this moment they knew that they could probably discard the policy, or parts of it, without getting into legal difficulty. They did not take that step for another year, because Strand was not yet ready to strike sections from a policy that had been negotiated in "good faith" between the board and the Faculty Association. But he was in a strong position to insist that application of the policy was at the discretion of the board.[49]

Judge Hinkson's ruling was a major factor in the failure of the committee that finally assembled in July 1970 with seven cases on its docket: Aberle, Ahmad, Briemberg, Feldhammer, Leggett, Potter and Wheeldon. The chair of this committee was Earl Palmer of the University of Western Ontario, who had previously chaired a dismissal hearing at the University of New Brunswick and found for the university. At SFU, Palmer's committee met on two consecutive days before calling it quits and issuing a report without any hearings. It had plunged into a procedural quarrel with Strand, with the Leggett case a central issue. The quarrel might have emerged anyway, but Hinkson's ruling encouraged both sides to dig in their heels. As Palmer and his committee reasoned, if the seven professors had no appeal to the courts, then it was all the more important for their committee to be free of university control. And they quickly decided that they were not going to have the autonomy they needed.

They cited an instruction that Strand gave about Leggett. Leggett's contract ended on August 31, 1970, just five weeks away; and Strand told them that they could not consider his case after that. The Palmer Committee objected to Strand arbitrating the rules and this led into deeper waters. Strand warned the committee that he was not bound to accept their recommendations if they set their own rules; and they decided that the dismissal process at SFU was so flawed it could not lead to a just and equitable result. So they made their report brief and simple. There was no cause for dismissal, they said, because without a fair process, President Strand could not prove cause.[50]

Strand refused to accept the Palmer Committee's finding. As he put it, they had not done their work. They had only looked at the procedures, which they were not called to do; and they had taken no evidence or heard any argument on the charges, which was the task they had been assigned. He was on firm ground legally and politically. He had Judge Hinkson's decision; he had the support of the executive of the SFU Faculty Association, and he had the support of his faculty, who voted in a referendum on his action later that year.[51] The Student Society, now led by moderates, was also behind Strand.

The serious objections came from outside. For several academic associations the matter was black and white: the Palmer Committee had met and decided that there was no cause for dismissal. The CAUT, the Canadian Sociology and Anthropology Association, the Canadian Political Science Association and the American Anthropology Association all urged SFU to accept the Palmer Committee report and reinstate the seven. Strand's refusal led them to call for a CAUT censure, with the American association unhesitant about telling Canadians what they ought to do.[52]

The threat of a CAUT censure had little impact on Strand or on a majority of his SFU colleagues. As the next few years showed, SFU could ride out a censure without much consequence. If the accreditation of the university had been in danger, that would have been a different matter, but it was not. The accreditation body for Canadian universities was (and is) the Association of Universities and Colleges of Canada. In September 1970, the AUCC released a statement supporting Strand and taking issue with the Palmer Committee. The AUCC was the national voice for university presidents and administrators, and in it Strand and the SFU community had staunch allies.[53]

From the vast majority of the more than thirty academic societies in Canada came a great silence. This silence—as one would expect—never got any press; but it indicated how thin the concern was in the national academic community. The professional associations of the economists, geographers, historians, chemists, biologists and nearly all the others had nothing to say. Only in the three disciplines represented in the PSA department and in the national body for university teachers, the CAUT, were voices raised.

In the PSA affair, the CAUT did not rush to judgement, as it had with McTaggart-Cowan. Kathleen Aberle called it "excessive caution."[54] The CAUT file on PSA was already thick before September 24, 1969, when the PSA strike began. From the moment of the imposition of a trusteeship, PSA's radical professors had been asking the CAUT to get involved. They renewed their appeals in the dying days of August 1969, after the University Tenure Committee handed down its PSA decisions. And in response, Alwyn Berland, the CAUT executive secretary, accompanied by the chair of the CAUT Academic Freedom and Tenure Committee, spent two days at SFU in early September. They talked to key people in the administration and in the Faculty Association and to nine PSA professors, remarking on how polarized the situation had become.

Berland was critical of the University Tenure Committee and its "rather indecorous haste." But he was also disturbed by what he heard in PSA about the possibility of "direct action." He wanted the nine to disown the idea—whatever it meant. Nearly three weeks later, when he understood that direct action was going to be a strike, he sent a telegram from Ottawa to say that the CAUT would not support it. Lest there be any uncertainty, the president of the CAUT, Willard Allen at the University of Alberta, delivered the same message to PSA by telephone and telegram and in two news releases.[55]

As soon as the nine went on strike, Berland, Allen and the CAUT executive withdrew. If there had been no strike, they would have been willing to look into individual PSA tenure and renewal cases. Now they chose to wait and watch while the PSA suspension and dismissal story unfolded. When it was all over, they intended to reassess what they should do.

The waiting and watching ended when Strand rejected the Palmer Committee decision. But instituting a censure took another nine months, mainly because the SFU Faculty Association and the Student Society opposed it. Their representatives, Manfred Mackauer and Norman Wickstrom, were at the CAUT council's semi-annual meeting in Ottawa in November 1970, making that clear. Wickstrom was a history student who later wrote an extended honours essay about the PSA affair, mentioning his own role at this meeting. He observed a CAUT executive that was divided about censure: a majority for it but a minority against. And it seemed to him that most of the delegates from the fifty universities who now belonged to the CAUT had not given the SFU situation much thought before arriving in Ottawa. They assumed this was a straightforward conflict between an administration and a faculty, and they found it perplexing to have SFU's representatives telling them otherwise.

Two other universities were on the block, Mount Allison and Université du Québec à Montréal, and the votes to censure them were quickly taken. SFU provoked a long debate and a deferred decision. Six months later, at the May meeting, the censure vote did go through, but by a narrow margin. Wickstrom thought that his effort alongside Mackauer's had achieved something: the CAUT censure got less public notice when it eventually came.[56]

The committee that heard the Popkin case was the only one to reach a successful conclusion. And demonstrating that two paths can lead to the same place, this committee also recommended reinstatement. Strand's charges against Popkin, like his charges against the other seven, were that by going on strike, he failed in his contractual obligation to teach and in this way abused the trust of students. Proving that Popkin had gone on strike was not hard. For the committee the question was whether or not the act of going on strike justified dismissal. That led them into a lengthy review of what had gone on before.[57]

The chair of this committee was Gideon Rosenbluth, an economist from UBC and a past president of the CAUT. Under his leadership the committee made a full meal of their task: meeting for a total of 68 1/2 days between March and October 1970. About half of the meetings were given to hearings and half to deliberations. The committee took testimony from Strand and Dean Sullivan, as well as from Popkin and a number of his PSA colleagues—Aberle, Briemberg, Wheeldon, Adam and Wyllie.

Strand and Popkin, the two principals, were present for every day of hearings. Two university lawyers attended; and Michael Lebowitz, an economic historian and Marxist from the SFU Department of Economics & Commerce, acted as Popkin's counsel—giving up, as Popkin gratefully acknowledged, the equivalent of seven weeks of his own personal and professional life. He did so gratis because Popkin could not afford a lawyer.

The Rosenbluth Committee found Popkin guilty of misconduct, but not the gross misconduct that warranted dismissal. They were critical of the hasty process that had produced the tenure, promotion and renewal decisions of August 1969; they thought the PSA professors were justified in claiming "flagrant" violations of academic freedom; they believed that Strand was too quick to cut off negotiations with PSA and the strikers. What they would not endorse was the strike itself or the conditions for negotiation that the strikers set. The Rosenbluth Committee saw provocation by the administration; and they believed that the consequences of the strike were not all that serious. They also doubted that the same people would attempt another strike. They called for Popkin's reinstatement. Strand accepted their finding and reinstated Popkin for the balance of his contract.[58]

The reinstatement of Popkin in November 1970 left four of the eight PSA cases still pending: cases that had gone before the Palmer Committee and that Strand insisted had to go before new committees. Three of these stalled in failed efforts to find committee chairs. One went ahead: a committee for Prudence Wheeldon, which held twenty-five days of hearings in the first six months of 1971—until it made a ruling that precipitated the final breakdown of SFU's dismissal process. The Wheeldon committee was chaired by David L. Johnston, a young law professor from Toronto, who was soon to become dean of Law at Western

Ontario.[59] The Johnston Committee brought the whole dismissal exercise to an abrupt end with a ruling that the university—not the president alone—was a party to the proceedings. The ruling came after a dispute over the production of documents. Wheeldon, represented by two lawyers, claimed that the strike was justified because the administration's conduct towards the PSA Department had been so oppressive. She wanted hundreds of documents from the University Tenure Committee, from the dean of Arts and from other SFU officers and committees. The University Tenure Committee would not provide even a list; and Strand insisted he did not have the power to collect documents other than those in his own files. That led Wheeldon to ask for a ruling that the parties were Wheeldon and the university and not just Wheeldon and Strand.

The Johnston Committee gave Wheeldon the ruling she wanted. In his confrontation with the Palmer Committee, Strand had drawn a line in the sand, and now the Johnston Committee was stepping over it. Strand was defending the authority of the president and board: insisting that the board could not be a party to the hearings because it was the final arbitrator; it could not be both judge and prosecutor. That was how he and the university's lawyers read the Academic Freedom and Tenure Policy and the Universities Act.

To the board, the dismissal procedures were a charade: unlikely to reach any conclusion before the contracts in question expired. And the bills were mounting. The Wheeldon case was going to cost another $35,000. It seemed to Richard Lester, now chair of the board, that no committee of academics would ever recommend dismissal. So board members were asking themselves whether they should continue or seek a resolution either by reinstating Wheeldon, Briemberg, Ahmad and Feldhammer, or by paying them off to the ends of their contracts, or by suspending the procedures—after getting the sanction of the Faculty Association—and moving directly to dismissals. The Johnston Committee's ruling brought this discussion to a halt.[60]

Strand was ready to write *finis*. The CAUT council had passed its censure motion; so that damage had been done. Judge Hinkson's decision the year before had underscored the legal power of the board. Now, Strand decided that the time had come to use that power. He asked for an adjournment of the hearings and went straight to the board to get

Wheeldon reinstated, which he believed would render the Johnston Committee redundant. Then he recommended throwing out the dismissal provisions of the tenure policy and after that the immediate dismissal of Briemberg, Ahmad and Feldhammer. The board happily obliged.

This action had a couple of untidy consequences, but still closed the book on the PSA affair for Strand, if not for SFU. On the untidy side, in his resolve to stop the Johnston Committee in its tracks, Strand had not found time to consult the executive of the Faculty Association. The members of this executive had backed him fully up to this point. Now they were outraged and passed a motion of non-confidence.[61]

A second untidiness lay in the reaction of the Johnston Committee. Strand told them that they had no more work to do and no reason to exist. They disagreed and carried on to produce a report published in the *CAUT Bulletin*. They did this for the benefit of the many Canadian universities that had adopted similar procedures. Were these procedures workable? The Johnston Committee thought they were.[62]

The affair was over for Strand because he had the critical political backing he needed. From a public perspective and from a government perspective, what he had done was long overdue. And he had an effective majority of SFU faculty applauding him: not as many as earlier on, but more than enough. In a referendum after the non-confidence motion of the Faculty Association executive, Strand got an endorsement from 58 per cent of 227 voting faculty members, with 37 per cent against him and 5 per cent abstaining.[63] The numbers do not convey the strength of feeling on either side, which was considerable, but it was obvious that a majority were gratified to have president who was taking care of things.

McTaggart-Cowan's presidency had come to grief over an Academic Freedom and Tenure Policy statement. How remarkable it was, three years later, to see faculty agreeing with Strand and the board that the dismissal sections of their new policy had to go. What is a tenure policy without protection against arbitrary dismissal? The political climate at SFU had changed, priorities had changed, and everyone had seen how convoluted things could become. But the about-face was also a measure of the impatience that many felt towards the PSA Department and its radical professors.

After getting a vote of confidence from his colleagues, Strand was keen to turn to other things: long-term academic goals for the university and general operational and policy matters. PSA had been an overwhelming distraction.[64] Settling with the CAUT was not on his agenda; and when his term ended three years later, in August 1974, SFU was moving forward, adding programs, gaining students, hiring faculty and feeling little effect from censure. That summer, when he stepped down as president, Strand took out his Canadian citizenship, a step that only some American-born professors were imitating because—unlike today—it involved re-nouncing U.S. citizenship.[65] Becoming a Canadian, however, went with Strand's desire to stay in B.C. and at SFU, where he taught for the balance of his career.

Strand's successor, Pauline Jewett, insisted that SFU do something about the CAUT censure. While a candidate for the presidency, Jewett declared her sympathies with the CAUT and the dismissed PSA professors; she thought an injustice had been done, so there was no doubting her agenda. She came by her views honestly. She had been active in the CAUT and one of her referees, John Porter (the author of *The Vertical Mosaic*), had been on the American Anthropology Association commit-tee that investigated SFU. In 1991, during an interview with the SFU historian Robin Fisher (given when Jewett was terminally ill and under-going intensive chemotherapy), she admitted that she appreciated the SFU side of things better after she arrived, but she had felt "quite strongly" that SFU was in the wrong. Doing something about the CAUT censure was a condition of her candidacy. When she was hired, she said she could not stay at SFU if the censure continued.[66]

Even so, Jewett's willingness to take the job showed the great weak-ness of the CAUT: it could not stop ambitious people from taking jobs at SFU, even someone as sympathetic to CAUT aims and objectives as she was. Hers was one more case in which other considerations came into the picture. Jewett had not been recruited but had pursued the SFU pres-idency aggressively, knowing that it would be a milestone for women. With the exception of Mount St. Vincent, a Catholic women's college, no university or college in Canada had ever had a woman as president, nor had any coeducational university or college in the U.S. She had begun applying a few years earlier, when York, Prince Edward Island and Trent were all searching for presidents. When the SFU position was posted, she lined up her referees and campaigned energetically, getting all kinds of people to write and generating support among students at SFU.[67]

What were Pauline Jewett's credentials? She had something that Ken Strand lacked and that the SFU community now seemed to want: national visibility. One of her referees was Walter Gordon, the high-profile economic nationalist of the Liberal cabinets of Lester Pearson. Jewett was a vice-chair of an organization created by Gordon, the Committee for an Independent Canada (now the Council of Canadians). She had been a vice-president of the federal Liberal Party and had run three times in the federal Ontario riding of Northumberland, losing twice and winning once and serving in Parliament—as one of only four women MPS—for two years between the elections of 1963 and 1965. She had a national profile as a contributor to *Canadian Forum, Canadian Dimension, Saturday Night* and *Maclean's*. And she was a presence at Carleton, where she had taught since 1955 (when the entire professoriate could be seated around a single table) and where she had been a department chair and then director of Carleton's Institute of Canadian Studies.

Her entry into academic life had not been easy. She felt that doors had been closed because she was a woman; and she had reason. She was on the job market for five years—living with her mother in Ottawa—from the completion of her Harvard PhD until she landed her position at Carleton. She had applied to eighteen Canadian universities without being shortlisted once. When she was hired, her salary was 80 per cent of a male colleague's, although he was starting at the same time with the same qualifications. She was grateful for the job, she said; but it was gratitude tempered by awareness of salary discrimination. And she had a broader frame of reference, which she had developed while completing a study for the Canadian Nurses Association, her first job after earning her PhD. She had seen too many women who felt they had no option but to go into nursing when their real desire was to be doctors.[68]

During her 1991 interview with Robin Fisher, Jewett listed her main interests at SFU: women, hiring Canadians and ending the censure. In all three she showed leadership and left a legacy; and she could not have done it without co-operation and help from administrators, senators and the board. But she did not have an easy time. She pushed hard on her items—too hard for most of her vice-presidents, deans, chairs and faculty; and as she conceded in retrospect, she probably did not do enough on the items that were important to them.

One does not get a good report card on Jewett from many of the key people who were then at SFU. And her difficulties were public, advertised nationally in an article by the Vancouver writer Clive Cocking in the November 1975 issue of *Saturday Night* and locally in Allan Fotheringham's column in the *Vancouver Sun*. Cocking invented the term "the barons of SFU" to describe the two dozen top administrators—the all-male power elite—who were not happy with Jewett's presidency; and he quoted Jewett as saying that her first year had been rough. Robin Fisher interviewed Jewett and George Suart about twelve months apart in 1990 and 1991. Suart had been vice-president administration when Jewett arrived and continued long after she left. He said bluntly that Jewett had been a "zero" as an administrator. She said that she had been undermined by her vice-presidents.[69]

Jewett worked hard to lift the CAUT censure. The complexion of the SFU board had changed with four New Democratic Party appointments after an NDP victory in the 1972 provincial election. In her first semester at SFU, she got the board to institute dismissal procedures, ending a three-year hiatus without them. She had been thinking about the formulation of these procedures for several months before taking up her appointment; and the result provided for an independent arbitrator whose verdict would be binding on the board. Strand had been dead set against binding arbitration; so Jewett persuaded the board to make a remarkable reversal early in her presidency. And this measure was one that the CAUT had been insisting on.[70]

The CAUT had also been demanding reinstatement of the surviving seven dismissed PSA faculty. (One of the summer tragedies of 1971 had been the drowning death of the eighth, Saghir Ahmad.[71]) If Jewett had had her way, she would have reinstated all seven; but she encountered resolute opposition from her deans and chairs. In the fall of 1974, she began by writing to the seven, inviting them to apply whenever an appropriate position came up; several of them answered that this was not good enough. She persisted on this tack, asking the deans and chairs of Sociology & Anthropology, Political Science and Communications to identify suitable positions and advise the seven about them. And she put the dean of arts, W.A.S. (Sam) Smith, in charge of the effort.

Smith had been the first president at Lethbridge—appointed when he was thirty-seven—and he had been there at the time of the PSA strike. He carried no baggage at SFU and made an honest effort to do what Jewett asked: persuading the seven to submit their vitas; bringing some of them onto campus to hear what they had to say; circulating their vitas to various departments: History, Education, Economics & Commerce, Communication Studies, Geography, Continuing Studies, Sociology & Anthropology and Political Science, and prodding these departments to evaluate and respond.

The most obvious departments for the seven were Sociology & Anthropology and Political Science, which had arisen from the ashes of PSA with fresh outlooks bolstered by new appointments. Neither of these departments—nor any other—wanted Briemberg, Feldhammer or Wheeldon, ostensibly because they did not have PhDs or comparable scholarly publications. Political Science might have taken Popkin, who had co-authored a book published by Oxford University Press, but they wanted him only if it did not cost them another appointment.

Aberle had not left Vancouver. With her husband teaching at UBC, Vancouver had become her settled home and a career as a private scholar was her ultimate option. No one disputed the strength of her scholarly record; but Sociology & Anthropology flip-flopped about her, first saying no—that they did not need anyone in her area—and then voting yes. Leggett, now tenured at Rutgers, came to SFU for a public lecture and spent an hour and a half with three representatives of Sociology & Anthropology. They found him impressive; but when he stated that he required an offer that he could sit on for up to five years, they were turned off: they did not see it as a serious proposition. Political Science was interested in Potter, who had come to SFU as an associate professor with publications and who had been tenured in 1969. (He was the only one of the seven who had sacrificed a secure job.) Potter was now a senior lecturer at the Open University, the United Kingdom's "university of the air," which had admitted its first students in 1970. He was evidently happy there, and the way things worked out, he stayed with the Open University in Milton Keynes, Buckinghamshire, until he retired.

Jewett was trying to reconcile the three sides of an awkward triangle: the CAUT, the PSA seven and SFU's senior administrators. In theory, the president and the board had the power to reinstate the seven without consulting anyone. But if Jewett had tried to do that, the damage would have been great; and she knew it. She would have faced a revolt of her vice-presidents and deans. In the press some of them were quoted as saying the reinstatement would be made over their dead bodies. In May 1975, Brian Wilson reiterated the limits of the deal that they were willing to make. By then, Wilson had been vice-president academic at SFU for nearly five years. He had arrived a year after the strike, and he had won immense respect from the upper echelon at SFU—those who dealt with him most continuously and directly, he had been their preferred candidate for president at the time Jewett was chosen. He was presidential material: twice a candidate for the SFU presidency (1974 and 1978) and from 1979 to 1995 vice-chancellor (president) of the University of Queensland—Australia's longest serving vice-chancellor at the moment he retired.

In May 1975, Wilson—with the deans behind him—insisted that SFU do no more than consider the seven "on their merits" for existing openings. No position should be specially tailored for any of them; no department should think they could get someone extra by taking one of them in; no department should compromise its academic standards. Departments had been getting mixed messages, because Jewett was undoubtedly keen to reinstate the seven. Communications and Political Science both had the impression that they could gain a body by accepting one of the seven. To put this notion to rest, Wilson addressed Jewett in a stiffly worded "private and confidential" memo: a vice-president laying down the law to a president. He ended on this note: "I would like your assurance that the office of the President will not in future be used to pressure individuals, including Chairmen, into actions which they are unwilling to make for sound academic reasons."[72]

Jewett had already attended the spring 1975 CAUT council meeting and made a valiant but unsuccessful effort to have the censure lifted. All this set the stage for negotiations between SFU and the CAUT through the summer of 1975. Negotiations ended in agreement in October. The CAUT accepted SFU's determination not to reinstate all seven. Potter was to be offered an appointment in Political Science and Aberle in Sociology & Anthropology—with a qualification: her offer would be good only if it led to a final settlement with the CAUT. Leggett was to get "fair and impartial" consideration for a faculty position if he applied. No offers were to go to the other four. The CAUT had accepted SFU's argument that in the current "highly competitive" academic market, they did not have the necessary qualifications. But the CAUT had insisted that something be done for them; and the answer was to offer them research grants for up to two years to complete their PhDs, the funding to come from SFU but to be paid through a CAUT research grant program.[73]

The seven did not buy it. Briemberg, Popkin, Aberle and Leggett lost not a moment in going public with vigorous objections. They would not "collaborate"; none of them would apply for the research funding; Potter would not accept an offer, nor would Aberle. The suggestion that four of her colleagues were not qualified, Aberle said, added new injury to old. The only settlement that they would accept would be reinstatement of all seven.[74]

Jewett had hoped to get the CAUT censure lifted at the November 1974 CAUT council meeting, soon after she became president. What she could tell the council then was that SFU had reinstituted dismissal procedures and that she had sent letters to the seven, inviting them to apply for vacant positions. The council had decided to wait to see what happened. Jewett then aimed at the following May meeting and after that— with the CAUT–SFU agreement in hand—at the November 1975 meeting. The rejection of this agreement by the seven was a setback and the CAUT backed out of the agreement.

Jewett had little to add that would not stir up trouble for herself at SFU. So she set about persuading the CAUT that SFU had done all it could and that the PSA seven were "uncooperative." That took another year. A gesture in the fall of 1976—rescinding the original charges and renewing the offer the seven had rejected—served the purpose; and the CAUT council finally lifted its censure in May 1977. The seven made no public comment, but it was over; the story had limped to its close. Everyone was tired of it. The CAUT made its peace with SFU without any ringing principles to proclaim. The seven were left on the outside. A year later, Jewett announced that she would step down as president that fall. Her sojourn at SFU was over; she was preparing a return to politics, and in the federal election of 1979 she won election as an NDP candidate in the riding of New Westminster–Coquitlam.[75]

AN EPISODE OF THE TIMES

The collective cost of the PSA affair is incalculable. It made heavy demands on two SFU presidents; absorbed countless hours in meetings, negotiations and correspondence for the CAUT executive and council;

required large sacrifices in time and equanimity by nine members of three hearing committees; imposed an immensely stressful and prolonged ordeal on members of the PSA Department, whatever side they were on, and extended its disturbing influence at SFU well beyond the PSA Department.

The PSA affair was more than an artifact of the troubled beginnings of a new university. The issues were not just local, although a new university provided a very public battleground. More appeared to be at stake at SFU because the opportunity to be radically different seemed greater. But the PSA affair was just one of many confrontations at Canadian universities in those years, even if it was one of the most publicized. The elements that nourished the affair could be found across the country: university expansion and the hiring of many junior university teachers; the issue of democratization and university government; the student movement and, in the late 1960s, its final confrontational phase, and the professionalization of academia, with tenure and tenure procedures and standards vital instruments of the process. The mix was full of contradictions; idealism faced off with reality; students and professors at SFU and elsewhere were discovering where the boundaries were.

Epilogue
Shrum's University after Forty Years

In 1983, Gordon Shrum told oral historian Peter Sturs-berg that he had few regrets about Simon Fraser University: neither about his decisions nor about the way things worked out. Stursberg asked about the business community's frequent dismissal of SFU as a radical place; and Shrum repeated what he probably told his business friends—that SFU was more socialist than radical, and if it had more socialist professors than conservative, it was not the only university like that. His feelings about SFU were good. He said that nothing unpleasant had happened to him there, other than his final meeting with McTaggart-Cowan, "which was most distressing." Everything else he had taken in stride.[1]

Everything else included a bizarre moment at the 1970 spring convocation when Jim Harding, a student radical, kissed Shrum's foot. It was one of the last memorable public gestures of the radical camp. Harding was another activist from Regina who had chosen the Politics, Sociology & Anthropology Department at SFU for graduate studies. He had been a founding member of the Students for a Democratic University and one of the "firebrands" named in the court injunction that President Ken Strand obtained during the PSA strike. A few months later, when Harding had handed in his PhD thesis on the sociology of scientism, the turnout for his defence was so huge it had to be relocated to a large lecture hall. Paranoia had brought out a crowd of campus radicals: word had spread that he might be failed and they were there as observers to make sure the examiners were fair. For convocation Harding put on sandals and donned a multicoloured Somali robe—instead of an academic gown—and when he came grinning across the platform, scrip dangling from his neck, staff in one hand and degree in the other, he knelt and kissed Shrum's shoe. It meant, he said afterwards, that one learns to kiss the boots of the authorities. Shrum swung his foot, perhaps instinctively, but *The Peak* and the *Georgia Straight* reported it as a kick.[2]

Shrum was on the convocation stage because he continued to make time for SFU when he was no longer chancellor. Later presidents found him willing to help if they had occasion to use him. In the early 1980s, when he expressed pride in what SFU had become, he spoke of its progressiveness, its willingness to look at new ideas, "its excellent staff" and "very good students" and the smooth functioning of its governing bodies, which, he pointed out, included students at every level.[3]

In 1969, when Shrum stepped down as chancellor, he gave an interview to Ed Wong (Stan Wong's older brother), who by then was a graduate and the editor of the SFU alumni publication *The Bridge*. At that point, despite the ongoing turmoil and frustration, Shrum said that he had faith in SFU: all the elements were there and would come together eventually. One had to take the long view. Within ten years, he predicted, SFU would be well within the second echelon of Canadian universities. For Wong's benefit, he drew a distinction between Canada and the U.S.—a distinction that remains largely true today. Canada had great and small universities but the academic standards at all were much the same; and one could happily send an excellent student to a smaller Canadian university for graduate work if there was a professor there in his or her field. It was not like the U.S. with its elite universities, its middling universities and its very poor ones. Shrum did accord a special place in Canada to such universities as B.C. and Toronto, and he thought it unrealistic to expect SFU to overtake them, but he was sure SFU would take its place among the rest. A decade later he judged it had happened.[4]

Shrum died at the age of ninety in 1985, six years before *Maclean's* magazine began its annual ranking of Canadian universities. *Maclean's* was imitating *U.S. News and World Report,* which by then had produced four annual—and commercially successful—issues devoted to ranking U.S. universities and colleges. Before *U.S. News and World Report* got into the act, Americans had had a variety of special publications to refer to. The idea was a new one in Canada but one that proved effective in selling magazines.

Shrum might well have been among the many academics in both countries who decried magazine rankings and the methodologies behind them; one would expect that from him, given his belief in the essentially even quality of Canadian universities.[5] However, it would have been natural for him to trumpet SFU's placings in *Maclean's* from 1992 to 2002: first five times, second four times and third twice in the comprehensive university category (universities with a wide range of programs but no medical school). Reputation has been just one criterion for *Maclean's*. However, Shrum surely would have taken satisfaction from the 1994 ranking of all Canadian universities that put SFU fourth in reputation and the 1995 ranking that put it third—ahead of UBC and Toronto. He could have acknowledged the eccentricities of the *Maclean's* methodology and still have concluded that SFU had arrived.

In the thirty-six years since Shrum stepped down as chancellor, the student population has nearly quadrupled and the number of people employed by SFU has doubled—with the faculty–staff ratio a continuing 40–60 split. SFU has never confirmed a target population, although Shrum originally suggested eighteen thousand—a figure the university has passed if one goes by head count or is fast approaching if one speaks of full-time equivalents. SFU has reached these numbers in two bursts, one in the late 1970s and one beginning in the late 1990s and continuing to the present. And it has been gaining ground on UBC, which in 1970 had four times the enrolment and now has a little over twice.

SFU administrations—like those at the University of Victoria—have seen growth as a means to move ahead. They have accepted rising enrolments even when the provincial government was holding the line on budgets. One consequence has been an increasingly unfavourable ratio between students and full-time faculty. By 2002, Statistics Canada was reporting 18.4 students per full-time professor at UBC and 22.3 at SFU, although both draw from the same public purse. Those figures make UBC look better than most universities in Canada; SFU is average. To serve its students, SFU has followed a trend, evident in Canada from 1970 and increasingly so in the 1980s and '90s, towards employment of a floating supply of university teachers hired by the semester or the year. SFU has not adopted the other conceivable choices: raising regular faculty teaching hours or cutting off enrolment.[6]

Growth has given SFU some of the manoeuvre room needed to introduce new programs and initiatives when budgets were tight, as they have been perennially since the 1960s. Some robbing of Peter to pay Paul has helped: the systematic reassignment of vacated faculty positions from old programs to new or from static programs to growing—a matter of deliberate policy from the Strand presidency onward. And SFU has done remarkably well in recent decades in fundraising in the private sector and amongst its alumni. The university was launched with a great fundraising campaign in the 1960s and then suffered in the 1970s because it was a hard sell in downtown Vancouver; it was also handicapped as a new university with a youthful and still small population of graduates. George Pedersen, who was president from 1978 to 1983, found that he had a major task in re-educating the public and the business community about SFU, assuring them that there was more to it than the stories they had heard of its radicalism.[7]

Pedersen's successor, Bill Saywell, arrived in the fall of 1983 in the midst of a major recession, with deep government cutbacks and the most severe financial crisis SFU has faced (and the most severe that the university system in B.C. has experienced since the 1930s). But as the B.C. economy came back in the late 1980s, Saywell pressed on with an ambitious $30-million "Bridge to the Future" fundraising campaign that eventually raised $65 million—double its goal. This effort, plus large bequests and other campaigns that went on simultaneously or that have carried on since then, have contributed to the expansion and improvement of SFU's physical plant and facilities and to its endowment funds. By 2003, with an endowment fund of $123 million, SFU had climbed to sixteenth in endowment funding among Canadian universities. None of the universities ahead of it have had as short an institutional history.[8]

When SFU marked its twenty-fifth anniversary in 1990, Saywell made a couple of claims that had the ring of conviction and enough evidence to make an argument. SFU, he said, was "likely the most innovative" university in Canada" and "exceptionally responsive" to changing needs and demands.[9] If he had been referring to the past, he could have mentioned the first student senators in the country, the first woman president, the first computerized library and the first computerized registration system; and his list would have included a new approach to teacher training, an executive MBA program that was the first of its kind in Canada, and leadership in B.C. in launching a full continuing education university program in 1970, and in taking degree programs to the interior of the province in 1974 with a branch campus at Kelowna. And for the 1970s he would have added the development of kinesiology, criminology, computing science and women's studies programs within the Faculty of Interdisciplinary Studies.

Saywell was also thinking of the new programs of the 1980s: cooperative education, following Waterloo's example, which SFU had begun to push vigorously; natural resource management; gerontology, and engineering science. And he was thinking of SFU's downtown campus at Harbour Centre.

SFU has been transforming itself with a growing presence in the business–commercial–residential hub of Vancouver, taking initiatives that UBC has been slow to follow. The opportunity was there because Vancouver, unlike many other major Canadian cities—Toronto, Montreal, Ottawa, Edmonton, Winnipeg and Halifax—had no university campus within ten miles of the downtown core. SFU's administration had explored the idea of a downtown satellite in the late 1970s and tested it in 1980–81 with a skeleton program in rented space on Howe Street. The early and ultimately realized concept was of a self-funded facility for mid-career or continuing education that complemented the main campus and diverted no funding or resources from it. SFU was quite well established downtown by 1989, when it finally moved into its Harbour Centre campus in the landmark Spencer retail building—renovated at a cost of $23.5 million, all raised through private and corporate donations. Saywell has described Harbour Centre as a strategic move to raise SFU's profile in the city. And while people on Burnaby Mountain have occasionally muttered about the dispersal of energy—if not funding—that Harbour Centre represented, the downtown campus has been a winner with the general public and SFU's private and corporate friends.

Across the street from Harbour Centre, SFU now has the Morris J. Wosk Centre for Dialogue, a state-of-the-art international conference centre that opened in 2000 in a heritage bank building dating from 1919—a building that had fallen from grace before SFU took it over, but that has been restored with the exterior facade and decorative ceilings returned to their original detail. One block south and one block west of the Wosk Centre is the Segal Graduate School of Business, another SFU downtown institution, which is opening on SFU's fortieth anniversary in another restored heritage bank building. Both buildings have been redeveloped with large gifts from the donors for whom they are named. The development of the Woodward's site on Hastings and Abbott streets will bring another major SFU program downtown—the School for the Contemporary Arts.

No one has had a larger role in SFU's downtown adventure than Jack Blaney, who arrived from UBC in 1974 to be SFU's first dean of continuing studies. In his career at SFU he has been vice-president development, vice-president Harbour Centre and, from 1997 to 2000, president. Blaney was the architect of SFU's Continuing Studies Program, the "Bridge to the Future" campaign, the Harbour Centre concept and the idea and effort to create the Wosk Centre for Dialogue.[10] The Wosk Centre was born as Blaney looked from Harbour Centre across Hastings Street at an empty and decaying Dominion Bank building and wondered if SFU could find a use for it. Blaney's favourite word for SFU is "gutsy," and it has come out of his own approach and experience: he would have incorporated it in the university's mission statement when he was president if he had received any encouragement from the editorialists around him.

With its new satellite campus in Surrey, B.C., SFU has expanded once again, this time to rescue a New Democratic Party initiative that came to grief under the provincial Liberals. The Surrey campus began as a B.C. government plan to create a technical university offering courses in information technology and interactive arts. On-line education was one of TechBC's missions and close liaison with industry another. The legislation establishing TechBC had provoked controversy in 1997 because—shades of the past—the government proposed an all-powerful board, no senate and no tenure. The Canadian Association of University Teachers (CAUT), the B.C. Council of Faculty Associations and the College Institute Educators Association all objected, and the CAUT briefly blacklisted the new university. The blacklisting, however, was just a hiccup for TechBC. The main problem was the financial structure that had been imposed on it by an NDP government.[11]

One year after TechBC opened in a converted Zellers department store in a Surrey shopping mall, it folded under the weight of a multi-million-dollar rental agreement with the Insurance Corporation of B.C. The rental was for future space in an office tower that ICBC—a Crown corporation—was building in Surrey. TechBC could not afford it; and eight months after their 2001 landslide victory over the NDP, the Liberal government of Gordon Campbell turned TechBC over to SFU. This challenge was accepted under President Michael Stevenson in the same spirit as earlier administrations had taken initiatives like the downtown campus. Most of the four hundred TechBC students became SFU students, carrying on with equivalent programs; and nearly all of the TechBC teaching faculty were absorbed by SFU.[12]

SFU has assumed the Surrey operation to build it up, not wind it down—to double enrolments within three years and then keep growing, to expand programming and to establish a permanent satellite campus in the space intended for TechBC. The last was accomplished in the fall of 2004 with a move into the tower of ICBC's Central City complex, designed by architect Bing Thom and incorporating the university, a shopping mall and office space—a hybrid structure that Thom calls "a new suburbia." It is yet another architectural statement associated with SFU.[13]

Surrey has added more complexity to the operation of SFU, which by 2005 employed four vice-presidents, four associate vice-presidents, eight deans, seven associate deans and twenty-nine directors, including the director of the Surrey campus. Gordon Shrum's idea of a spare, bottom-weighted structure has long gone. Along with recent growth, SFU has arrived at the end of a natural cycle with the retirements that began in the mid-1990s and that have continued to the present. What has happened at SFU has been happening at universities across the country, but it stands out more sharply at an institution that was absolutely new forty years ago. SFU exemplified the stability of the Canadian university professoriate through the 1970s and 1980s—with few new positions created and little attrition through resignation, retirement or death. There was some turnover of junior faculty in the first few years of the tenure and renewal process introduced in 1968 (with Politics, Sociology & Anthropology an extreme example), but after that, new appointments came infrequently.

SFU entered the 1990s with 189 professors who had been there from 1970 or earlier. They were concentrated in the senior academic and administrative ranks; and they made up 40 per cent of the faculty. In 2005 only a handful of them remained as regular faculty, although many carry on in post-retirement teaching, research and administration. If one were to choose a symbolic moment for the transfer from old to new, it might be the retirement of Jock Munro in 2002 after thirty-six years in the Department of Economics. He had started as an assistant professor in July 1966 and served as chair of the Department of Economics and dean of Arts during the 1970s. In 2000, when he stepped down as vice-president academic after eleven years in that position—in three separate stints—he was one of the last administrators at SFU who could remember what the university had been like in the beginning.

In 2005, SFU was still mainly the Burnaby Mountain campus; and that showed no sign of changing soon. It had 85 per cent of the student enrolment, 99 per cent of the full-time faculty and nearly 75 per cent of the built university space. From 2003, tall construction cranes at either end of the campus were visible from the Production Way SkyTrain station south of the mountain. (The station opened in August 2002.) At the west end of the campus, three student residential towers have risen and, at the east end, the first phase of the UniverCity housing development, after years of on-again, off-again discussion.

Both projects have drawn fire from Arthur Erickson as departures from his original conception.[14] He would have maintained a low profile for all buildings and he would not have put the UniverCity development on a higher elevation than the Academic Quadrangle. Erickson's original plans provided for more student residences than were built at the time and he did map out a housing development, although he would have put it on the lower elevations to the west of the campus. These projects are intended over time to transform Burnaby Mountain into a thriving twenty-four-hour community with shops and services, including an elementary school—everything needed to keep its inhabitants out of their cars and on the mountain.

In 2005, excluding the UniverCity development and projects in progress, about half of the built space on Burnaby Mountain dated from the 1960s. The science centre complex has grown in every decade.

Otherwise, the main additions have been the administration building (Strand Hall), the classroom complex (Robert C. Brown Hall), the top two floors of the library, the west gym extension, the east concourse cafeteria and the student centre, all from the 1970s; the Applied Sciences Building, Education Building, Diamond University Centre, McTaggart-Cowan Hall and Halpern Centre from the 1980s; and the Maggie Benston Centre, West Mall Complex, Hamilton Hall and East Theatre Annex from the 1990s. What has been preserved over thirty-five years of building is the visual impact of the heart of the campus. Shrum wanted a campus that looked finished from the start, and he got what he wanted in Erickson's design. One proves it with every walk from the bus dismount by the transportation centre through the mall and to the Academic Quadrangle. It has not changed much.

During orientation week in 2004, Erickson's concept of the mall as the university's marketplace was alive and well. Frosh assembled three hundred at a time for what was billed as a drum café. They sat nine rows deep in a semicircle, looking east towards the Academic Quadrangle with the Maggie Benston Centre on their right and the W.A.C. Bennett Library on their left. They could be forgiven if the names meant nothing: just buildings with names.

They were sitting where students had held great rallies in the 1960s and they were looking towards the very spot where Jim Harding kissed Shrum's foot. But they were there for what lay ahead, not for silent reminders of the past. Every one of them had a seventy-centimetre-tall African drum between the knees and they were following Munkie Ncapayi, a drummer originally from Johannesburg, and the several professional drummers backing him up. Ncapayi and his associates have been successfully selling their franchised product—the drum café—to companies in Canada, the U.S., the U.K., Australia and South Africa for corporate "team-building" events. They had been "outsourced" to entertain SFU's newest students. From the SFU mall, the booming bass and the edge tones of the three hundred djembe drums that Ncapayi supplied easily reached the farthest windows of the Academic Quadrangle and reverberated along the walkways past the East Mall complex towards the student residences. A student from the 1970s was standing by, on assignment for the *Vancouver Sun*. His observation: "The campus may be quieter, but it is not silent."[15]

Notes

Works and sources cited frequently are abbreviated as follows: Simon Fraser University: SFU; Simon Fraser University Archives: SFUA; University of British Columbia: UBC; Canadian Association of University Teachers: CAUT

PREFACE | FREEDOM SQUARE AND SFU'S HISTORY

1 L. Robert Wilkins, "Freedom of Speech Exists Only in the Minds of People," *The Peak*, July 25, 1994.
2 Lester to Martin Loney, August 1, 1968, SFUA, F 74/3/3/20.
3 Amanda Camley, "A Space for Students," *The Peak*, July 12, 1999.
4 SFUA, Camley/Harter interview, July 31, 2001.

1 | THE INSTANT UNIVERSITY

1 The original audiotapes of the interviews and the transcript are in the SFU Archives. The autobiography published from this material is Clive Cocking, ed., with Peter Stursberg, *Gordon Shrum: An Autobiography* (Vancouver: UBC Press, 1986).
2 Transcript of Shrum/Stursberg interview, February 16, 1983, 338, SFUA.
3 *Vancouver Sun* and *Vancouver Province*, March 23, 1963.
4 P.B. Waite, *Lord of Point Grey: Larry MacKenzie of U.B.C.* (Vancouver: UBC Press, 1987), 123–4; Harry T. Logan, *Tuum Est: A History of the University of British Columbia* (Vancouver: UBC, 1958), 153; Transcript of Shrum/Stursberg interview, 194–97.
5 David J. Mitchell, *W.A.C. Bennett and the Rise of British Columbia* (Vancouver: Douglas & McIntyre, 1983), 281–82; Hugh Keenleyside, *Memoirs of Hugh L. Keenleyside: Vol. 2, On the Bridge of Time* (Toronto: McClelland and Stewart, 1982), 484; Transcript of Shrum/Stursberg interview, 226–35.
6 Transcript of Shrum/Stursberg interview, 342.
7 McCarthy/Stursberg interview, June 20, 1985, SFUA; Ellis/Johnston interview, October 10, 2002, SFUA.
8 Shrum Jr./Stursberg interview, July 4, 1984, SFUA.
9 David Daiches, ed., *The Idea of a New University: An Experiment in Sussex* (Cambridge MA: MIT Press, 1964), particularly contributions by Sir John Fulton, W.G. Stone and Granville Hawkins; Asa Briggs, "Developments in Higher Education," W.R. Niblett, ed., *Higher Education: Demand and Response* (San Francisco: Jossey-Bass, 1970), 102–3; Henry D.R. Miller, *The Management of Change in Universities: Universities, State and Economy in Australia, Canada and the United Kingdom* (Buckingham: Society for Research into Higher Education and Buckingham University Press, 1995), 14–15.
10 Henry Johnson, *A History of Public Education in British Columbia* (Vancouver: Publications Centre, UBC, 1964), 203–5.

11 For a contemporary reference see Claude Bissell, "Institutions of Higher Education in Canada," Niblett, *Higher Education,* 144–45.

12 March 1964.

13 Shrum to Stainsby, December 18, 1963, SFUA, F 33/2/0/3.

14 Erickson/Sandwell interview, July 8, 2001, SFUA.

15 Robin S. Harris, *A History of Higher Education in Canada* (Toronto: University of Toronto Press, 1976), 552–61; F.E.L. Priestley, *The Humanities in Canada: A Report Prepared for the Humanities Research Council of Canada* (Toronto: University of Toronto Press, 1964), 45; A.S.P. Woodhouse, "The Humanities," and B.S. Keirstead, "The Social Sciences," in C.T. Bissell, ed., *Canada's Crisis in Higher Education: Proceedings of the Conference held by the National Conference of Canadian Universities, at Ottawa, November 12–24, 1956* (Toronto: University of Toronto Press, 1957), 128–29 and 157; Nathan Keyfitz, "Sociology and Canadian Society," T.N. Guinsberg and G.L. Reuber, eds., *Perspectives on the Social Sciences in Canada* (Toronto: University of Toronto Press, 1974), 21–24.

16 Briggs, "Developments in Higher Education," 102–3.

17 V.W. Bladen and Association of Universities and Colleges of Canada (AUCC), *Financing Higher Education in Canada* (Toronto: University of Toronto Press, 1965), 4, 7, 13, 24; F. Cyril James, "Comparisons and Contrasts in University Financing: Canada, the United Kingdom, and the United States," Bissell, *Canada's Crisis,* 213–26; N.A.M. MacKenzie, President, UBC, "Government Support of Canadian Universities," Bissell, *Canada's Crisis,* 193; John B. Macdonald, "The West," Robin S. Harris, *Changing Patterns in Higher Education in Canada* (Toronto: University of Toronto Press, 1966), 51; Johnson, *Public Education in B.C.,* 198; Watson Kirkconnell, *A Slice of Canada: Memoirs* (Toronto: University of Toronto Press, 1967), 154–60.

18 Bladen, *Financing Higher Education,* 13. For general background see Doug Owram, *Born at the Right Time: A History of the Baby Boom Generation* (Toronto: University of Toronto Press, 1996), 159–82.

19 The Millennium Scholarship Foundation cites these figures for 2002–3: a 13.3 per cent university participation rate among eighteen- to twenty-one-year-olds in B.C. and a 9.1 per cent college participation rate. The all-Canada figures are higher: 19.7 and 14.3 per cent.

20 Paul Axelrod, *Scholars and Dollars: Politics, Economics and the Universities of Ontario, 1945–1980* (Toronto: University of Toronto Press, 1982), 23.

21 David N. Smith, *Who Rules the Universities? An Essay in Class Analysis* (New York and London: Monthly Review Press, 1974), 24; Axelrod, *Scholars and Dollars,* 23.

22 Axelrod, *Scholars and Dollars,* 23.

23 Waite, *Lord of Point Grey,* 174–79.

24 Ibid., 174–79; William Bruneau, *A Matter of Identities: The UBC Faculty Association* (Vancouver: UBC Faculty Association, 1990), 62.

25 Macdonald, "The West," 50; Johnson, *Public Education in B.C.,* 203; John Barfoot Macdonald, *Higher Education in British Columbia, and a Plan for the Future* (Vancouver: UBC, 1962), 44; UBC Archives, Macdonald Report on Higher Education in British Columbia Collection, William Tetlow (collector) 1962–1963, Box 2, files 1-16.

26 Reference to *Vancouver Sun* article in H.G. Hardwick, "Is This the Answer?" *B.C. Teacher,* December 1957, 125–26.

27 Baker's unpublished postscript written for Macdonald Report, SFUA, Ron Baker files.

28 Macdonald, *Higher Education in B.C.,* 19–24.

29 Johnson, *Public Education in B.C.,* 20; Waite, *Lord of Point Grey,* 185–86.

30 Macdonald, "The West," 43; President Macdonald's July 31, 1962 statement to the UBC Board on the Decentralization of Higher Education, UBC Archives, Macdonald Report Collection, Box 1.

31 Minutes of a special meeting of the UBC senate, August 8, 1962, UBC Archives, Macdonald Report Collection.

32 Macdonald, *Higher Education in B.C.,* 14–15.

33 Ibid., 47–56

34 John D. Dennison, Alex Turner, Gordon Jones and Glen C. Forrester, *The Impact of Community Colleges: A Study of the College Concept in British Columbia* (Vancouver: B.C. Research, 1975), 1–2; John D. Dennison and Paul Gallagher, *Canada's Community Colleges: A Critical Analysis* (Vancouver: UBC Press, 1986), 13–14; Christopher Jencks and David Riesman, *The Academic Revolution* (New York: Doubleday, 1969), 480–92.

35 *B.C. Teacher,* December 1957.

36 Macdonald, *Higher Education in B.C.,* 55, 118; F.E.L. Priestley, *The Humanities in Canada: A Report Prepared for the Humanities Research Council of Canada* (Toronto: University of Toronto Press, 1964), 5; R.W.B. Jackson and W.G. Fleming, "Who Goes to University? English Canada," Bissell, *Canada's Crisis,* 24.

37 Dennison and Gallagher, *Canada's Community Colleges,* 34–35.

38 Minutes of special meeting of the Higher Education Committee, September 8–9, 1962, UBC Archives, Macdonald Report Collection, Box 1.

39 Hardwick to Baker, October 19, 1961, SFUA, Ron Baker files.

40 Walter Hardwick, Report to UBC senate on the location of colleges in British Columbia, June 1962; Macdonald, *Higher Education,* 64–66.

41 The figure of eight thousand cars comes from Baker's unpublished postscript written for the Macdonald Report (SFUA, Ron Baker files); for staff, faculty and student numbers see Waite, *Lord of Point Grey,* 182, and President's report, UBC, 1960–61.

42 Macdonald, *Higher Education in B.C.,* 88–89.

43 Macdonald, "The West," 44.

44 MacMillan to Shrum, September 20, 1963, SFUA, F 3/1/0/20.

45 Quoted in *The Ubyssey,* January 28, 1963.

46 Board minutes, October 10, 1963, 7, SFUA, F 33/1/0/0/1.

47 Macdonald, "The West," 51.

48 Ibid., 50.

49 Macdonald, *Higher Education in B.C.,* 88–89.

50 Curtis/Harter interview, February 9, 2001, SFUA; conversation with Leslie Peterson, April 5, 2002.

51 J.H. Stewart Reid, "Origins and Portents," George Whalley, ed., *A Place of Liberty: Essays on the Government of Canadian Universities* (Toronto: Clarke Irwin, 1964), 17–19; Martin L. Friedland, *The University of Toronto: A History* (Toronto: University of Toronto Press, 2002), 200–9.

52 Reid, "Origins and Portents," 9.

53 "Preface," Whalley, *A Place of Liberty,* viii.

54 Bora Laskin, "Some Cases at Law," Whalley, *A Place of Liberty*, 188–94; Michiel Horn, *Academic Freedom in Canada: A History* (Toronto: University of Toronto Press, 1999), 220–45.

55 V.C. Fowke, "Professional Association: A History of the CAUT," Whalley, *A Place of Liberty*, 225–29; "The Reform of University Government," CAUT *Bulletin*, November 1960, 10–35; Donald C. Rowat, "The Duff–Berdahl Report," CAUT *Bulletin*, April 1966, 23–30.

56 Sir James Duff and Robert O. Berdahl, *University Government in Canada: Report of a Commission sponsored by the Canadian Association of University Teachers and the Association of Universities and Colleges of Canada* (Toronto: University of Toronto Press, 1966), preface, v and 93, appendix II; Minutes of staff meeting, February 23, 1965, SFUA, F 193/28/72/2/14.

57 Bissell, "Institutions of Higher Education," 142–43; C.W. Gonick, "Self-government in the Multiversity," Howard Adelman and Dennis Lee, *The University Game* (Toronto: Anansi, 1968), 43–44.

58 Hutchinson/Nielson interview, 1982, SFUA.

59 Bissell, "Institutions of Higher Education," 144–45.

2 | CHOOSING A SITE, A DESIGN, A PRESIDENT AND A TRIMESTER SYSTEM

1 Transcript of Shrum/Stursberg interview, February 16, 1983, 361, SFUA.

2 Telephone conversation with John Chapman, October 11, 2003.

3 Warnett Kennedy to Robin Fisher, December 22, 1987, SFUA, Fisher files.

4 Transcript of Shrum/Stursberg interview, 348.

5 Minutes of first meeting of SFU board, October 10, 1963, SFUA, F 33/1/0/0/1.

6 *Vancouver Sun*, May 4, 1963.

7 G.M. Shrum, "The Selection of a Site for Simon Fraser University," May 6, 1963, SFUA, Fisher files, Chancellor's papers.

8 SFUA, F 32/1/0/6.

9 Mackenzie to Shrum, April 4, 1963, and Shrum to Mackenzie, April 9, 1963, SFUA, Fisher files; Tucker to Shrum, April 28, 1963, and Shrum to Tucker, May 8, 1963, SFUA, F 3/1/0/19.

10 Warnett Kennedy to Robin Fisher, December 22, 1987.

11 Shrum to MacKinnon, January 15, 1969, with attachment: Shrum's notes to the architects, dated May 22, 1963, SFUA, Fisher files, Chronology.

12 The name of the firm in 1912 was Sharp and Thompson.

13 SFUA, F 32/1/0/6.

14 Ken Burroughs and Ron Bain; Gene Waddell, "The Design for Simon Fraser University and the Problem of Accompanying Excellence," Manuscript, February 5, 1998, 69.

15 Edith Iglauer, "Seven Stones," *The New Yorker*, June 1979, 42.

16 Ibid., 63; Erickson/Sandwell interview, July 8, 2001, SFUA.

17 Waddell, "The Design for Simon Fraser University," 39.

18 *Vancouver Sun*, July 24, 1963; Donald Stainsby, "Instant University," *Saturday Night*, March 1964, 18; *Globe and Mail*, March 21, 1964; Gordon Shrum, "Education," *Saturday Night*, November 1965.

19 Arthur Erickson, "The Architectural Concept," *Canadian Architect*, February 1966, 40.

20 Arthur Erickson, *The Architecture of Arthur Erickson* (Vancouver: Douglas & McIntyre, 1988), 32–37.

21 Abraham Rogatnick, *Architectural Review,* April 1968, 263–65.

22 "Simon Fraser University in Vancouver," *Interbuild,* February 1966, 12–17; "Simon Fraser University—Miracle on a Mountain, *School Planning Laboratory Reports,* January 1967, 1–8.

23 Donlyn Lyndon, "In Canada, The Continent's First Single-Structure Campus," *Architectural Forum,* 1965, 13–21.

24 Iglauer, "Seven Stones," 42.

25 *New York Times,* June 29, 1970.

26 Ibid., 50.

27 R.J. Thom, "Academe on a Mountain Top," *Canadian Forum,* January 1966, 225.

28 Erickson/Sandwell interview, July 8, 2001, SFUA.

29 Ibid.; Waddell, "Design for Simon Fraser University," 69 (citing interview of June 13, 1997).

30 Erickson, "The Architectural Concept," 40; Iglauer, in *The New Yorker,* June 1979, 65, quotes Erickson's description of concrete as "the marble of our times."

31 Warnett Kennedy to Robin Fisher, December 22, 1987.

32 Transcript of Shrum/Stursberg interview, 365.

33 *Vancouver Sun,* February 20, 1964; allocations in the spring of 1964 for the first years of construction as given by Waddell, "Design for Simon Fraser University," 185–87.

34 Waddell, "Design for Simon Fraser University," 127–28.

35 *The Peak,* May 21, 1969.

36 Waddell, "Design for Simon Fraser University," 250–70; Erickson/Sandwell interview, July 8, 2001, SFUA.

37 Shrum's list of potential presidents; Gordon Robertson to Shrum, May 29, 1963, and Shrum to Robert T. McKenzie, May 29, 1963, SFUA, F 32/1/0/13.

38 Petch to Shrum, August 14, 1963, SFUA, F 32/1/0/13.

39 McTaggart-Cowan/Fisher interview, September 6, 1986, SFUA.

40 Patrick McTaggart-Cowan, "Autobiographical Notes, dictated 1983–85," 209, SFUA, F 65/1/0/1.

41 R.J. Baker, "Notes for the History of Simon Fraser University, dictated 15 September–28 October 1970," 35–36, SFUA, F 34/2/0/14.

42 Ibid., 28.

43 McTaggart-Cowan to Shrum, September 5, 1963, SFUA, F 65/2/3/34; McTaggart-Cowan, "Autobiographical Notes," 194, F 65/1/0/1; Shrum to McTaggart-Cowan, September 13, 1963, F 65/2/3/34.

44 Richard Lester, "A View from the Board," 3, SFUA, F 70/2/0/15.

45 Ibid., 5.

46 Donald Stainsby, "Instant University," 18; transcript of Shrum/Stursberg interview, 390.

47 Confidential record of discussion with A.F.C. Hean, dictated by McTaggart-Cowan, July 16, 1968; McTaggart-Cowan, "Autobiographical Notes," 196–97, SFUA, F 65/2/2/10.

48 McTaggart-Cowan/Fisher interview, September 6, 1986, SFUA.

49 Richard Lester, "A View from the Board," 7.

50 McTaggart-Cowan to Shrum, 3 September, 1963, SFUA, F 65/2/3/34.

51 Shrum to Stainsby, December 18, 1963, SFUA, F 3/1/0/21.

52 Sidney E. Smith, "Educational Structure: the English Canadian Universities," C.T. Bissell, ed., *Canada's Crisis in Higher Education: Proceedings of a Conference*

held by the National Conference of Canadian Universities at Ottawa, November 12–14, 1956 (Toronto: University of Toronto Press, 1957), 14–15.

53 See Shrum quoted in Stephen Franklin, "The New Universities Break with the Past: Their Pioneer Approach Has Enabled Them to Find New Ways of Doing Things," *Weekend Magazine,* November 23, 1963, 24.

54 Notebook, Autumn 1963, SFUA, F 65/3/0/2.

55 Baker to Shrum, November 28, 1963, and Shrum to Baker, November 29, 1963, SFUA, F 3/1/0/21.

56 Baker/Harter interview, April 24, 2001, SFUA.

57 Dean of Educational Relations, University of California, to Baker, January 31, 1964, SFUA, F 48/01/2/21.

58 Registrar, University of Manitoba, to Baker, February 14, 1964, with attachment, SFUA, F 49/01/2/43.

59 David C. Webb was research director of the Canadian Foundation for Education Development, founded by lawyer Frank B. Common and retired industrialist Vernon E. Johnson. His report on year-round operations appeared in *University Affairs,* February 1964.

60 Ron Baker, Draft report on trimester system, January 17, 1964, SFUA, F 49/02/11/3,

61 Shrum to H. Greville Smith, November 25, 1964, SFUA, F 49/1/0/6.

62 Transcript of Shrum/Stursberg interview, 395.

63 *Globe & Mail,* February 25, 1964.

64 See Ontario Premier John Robarts, Canadian Universities Foundation Executive Director Geoffrey Andrew and University of Calgary Principal Malcolm Taylor quoted in *Weekend Magazine,* November 30, 1963, 27.

65 Committee on Year Round Operation of Universities, "Final Report," CAUT *Bulletin,* September 13, 1964, 2–32.

66 Woods, Gordon & Co., "Simon Fraser University Trimester Cost Study," January 1972, SFUA, F 27/3/1/184.

67 Suart to Strand, August 28, 1971, attachment (estimate of 20 per cent for 1970–71 and 13 per cent for 1972–73); President's papers (1971), Strand to T. Craig, November 25, 1971, SFUA, Fisher files.

3 | ACADEMIC PLANNING

1 John Arnett, *Vancouver Sun* education reporter, *Vancouver Sun,* April 9, 1965; McTaggart-Cowan to Peterson, January 5, 1964, SFUA, F 193/30/1/2/1.

2 McTaggart-Cowan/Fisher interview, September 6, 1986, SFUA.

3 Minutes of the general meeting of the UBC Faculty Association, November 7, 1963, SFUA, Fisher files, Shrum papers; Transcript of Shrum/Stursberg interview, February 1963, 401–2, SFUA; Ron Baker, "The Beginnings," 22, SFUA, F 70/2/0/5.

4 McTaggart-Cowan/Fisher interview, September 6, 1986, SFUA; Transcript of Shrum/Stursberg interview, February 1983, 401–2, SFUA, F 49/1/3/36; Southwell, assistant secretary, CAUT, to Baker, April 7, 1964, SFUA.

5 J.H. Stewart Reid to Gordon Shrum, November 30, 1963, and Shrum to Reid, December 6, 1963, SFUA, F 33/2/0/3.

6 Baker, "The Beginnings," 6; also see Shrum's comments to UBC professor William Gibson in a letter, July 26, 1963, SFUA, F 3/1/0/20.

7 Bora Laskin, "The CAUT and Tenure," CAUT/ACPU *Bulletin,* March 1965, 2.

8 Daniel A. Soberman, "Tenure in Canadian Universities," CAUT/ACPU *Bulletin,* March 1965, 5–36.

9   Draft terms of appointment for academic staff, attached to agenda for March 3,
    1964, meeting of Staff and Organization Committee with board of governors,
    SFUA, F 33/2/0/5.

10 Ibid.

11 Transcript of Shrum/Stursberg interview, 402–3.

12 Bora Laskin, "Some Cases at Law," George Whalley, ed., *A Place of Liberty: Es-
    says on the Government of Canadian Universities* (Toronto: Clarke Irwin, 1964),
    177–94.

13 See Michiel Horn, *Academic Freedom in Canada: A History* (Toronto: University
    of Toronto Press, 1999), 244–45; and V.C. Fowke, "Professional Association,"
    Whalley, ed., *A Place of Liberty,* 209ff.

14 Richard Hofstadter and Walter P. Metzer, *The Development of Academic Freedom
    in the United States* (New York: Columbia University Press, 1955), 487–91.

15 Soberman, "Tenure in Canadian Universities," 12–13.

16 Horn, *Academic Freedom in Canada,* 218–19.

17 Minutes of the board of governors, March 12, 1964, and April 9, 1964, SFUA,
    F 32/1/0/13; Minutes of the staff and organization committee, March 3 and
    April 3, 1964; Smith to Baker, June 30, 1965, and Baker to Smith, July 6, 1965,
    SFUA, F 49/1/0/9.

18 Soberman, "Tenure in Canadian Universities," 31–36.

19 *Vancouver Sun,* June 17, 1965; Baker made no headway in a conversation with
    Laskin at this time: R.J. Baker, "Notes for the History of Simon Fraser University,
    dictated 15 September–28 October 1970," 37, SFUA, F 34/2/0/14; Laskin to
    McTaggart-Cowan, September 9, 1965, F 49/1/0/10.

20 Baker, "The Beginnings," 4–5.

21 Sidney E. Smith, "Educational Structure: the English Canadian Universities,"
    C.T. Bissell, ed., *Canada's Crisis in Higher Education: Proceedings of the Confer-
    ence held by the National Conference of Canadian Universities, at Ottawa, No-
    vember 12–24, 1956* (Toronto: University of Toronto Press, 1957), 12; Martin L.
    Riedland, *The University of Toronto: A History* (Toronto: University of Toronto
    Press, 2002), 553–56.

22 See Roald F. Campbell, Thomas Fleming, L. Jackson Newell and John W.
    Bennion, *A History of Thought and Practice in Educational Administration* (New
    York: Teachers College Press, 1987), 150–55.

23 For 1960 figures see Robin S. Harris, *A History of Higher Education in Canada*
    (Toronto: University of Toronto Press, 1976), 515; for figures given for 1956 see
    A.S.P. Woodhouse, "The Humanities," Bissell, *Canada's Crisis,* 128–29.

24 Shrum to Erickson and Massey, August 13, 1963, with attached listing of pro-
    posed teaching departments, SFUA, F 32/1/0/9.

25 Text of advertisement for Canadian Universities Foundation, dated February 11,
    1964, SFUA, F 49/1/2/38; Press release, March 10, 1964, F 49/1/3/11.

26 Baker/Harter interview, April 24, 2001; Baker/Fisher interview, July 8, 1988, SFUA.

27 Board minutes, February 17, 1964, 8, SFUA, F 33/1/0/0/2. The board member
    was Arnold Hean: Baker, "The Beginnings," 15.

28 Baker, "The Beginnings," 6.

29 Baird to McTaggart-Cowan, January 11, 1964, SFUA, F (President: old list)
    F 27/4/3/1; Board minutes, February 17, 1964; McTaggart-Cowan to Shrum,
    December 31, 1963, (old list) F 27/3/1/57; McTaggart-Cowan to Shrum, January 7,
    1958, (old list)F 27/3/1/58.

30 Shrum to Litherland and Shrum to Brockhouse, December 23, 1963, SFUA, F 3/0/1/21.

31 W.H. Cook, National Research Council, to Shrum, January 24, 1964, SFUA, F 3/1/0/22.

32 John B. Macdonald, *Role of Federal Government in Support of Research in Canadian Universities* (Ottawa: Queen's Printer, 1969), 101–5.

33 Volkoff to Shrum, March 17, 1964, SFUA, F 3/1/0/24.

34 Shrum to McTaggart-Cowan, January 9, 1964, SFUA, F 3/1/0/22; McTaggart-Cowan to Shrum, April 8, 1964, F 3/1/0/25.

35 W.H. Cook to Shrum, January 24, 1964, SFUA F 3/1/0/22; McTaggart-Cowan to Shrum, Frederickson and Lester, June 16, 1964, F 3/1/0/26.

36 McTaggart-Cowan, personal notebook for November–December 1964, outlining points for a speech, SFUA, F 65/30/2.

37 *Vancouver Province,* February 26, 1964; *Vancouver Sun,* February 27, 1964; Paul Edward Dutton, "Geoffrey Bursill-Hall," *Historica Linguistica,* 1998, 247–49; Board minutes, February 17, 1964, 7, SFUA, F 33/1/0/0/2.

38 Geoffrey Bursill-Hall, press release, March 26, 1964, SFUA, F 49/1/5/31.

39 Shrum to McTaggart-Cowan, October 16, 1963, SFUA, F (old list) 27/3/1/57; Daniells to Shrum, October 21, 1963; Daniells to Shrum, November 26, 1963; Shrum to McTaggart-Cowan, December 2, 1963; Daniells to Shrum, December 23, 1963; Shrum to Daniells, December 27, 1963, F 3/1/0/21.

40 McTaggart-Cowan's personal notepad for October–December 1963, SFUA, F 65/30/0/2.

41 Sandra Djwa, *Professing English: A Life of Roy Daniells* (Toronto: University of Toronto Press, 2002), 342; SFU board minutes, November 14, 1963, 4, SFUA, F 33/1/0/0/2.

42 Whalley to McTaggart-Cowan, June 3, 1964, SFUA, F 3/1/0/26; McTaggart-Cowan to Shrum, July 18, 1964, with attached letters from Whalley to McTaggart-Cowan, July 17 and 20, 1964, F 32/1/0/13.

43 Shrum to McTaggart-Cowan, July 29, 1964, SFUA, F 3/1/0/27; Minutes of the board, August 10, 1964, 2, F 33/1/0/0/2; Conversation with R.J. Baker, March 12, 2004.

44 C.B. MacPherson, "After Strange Gods: Canadian Political Science 1973," T.N. Guinsberg and G.L. Reuber, eds., *Perspectives on the Social Sciences in Canada* (Toronto: University of Toronto Press, 1974), 52–75.

45 Pate to McTaggart-Cowan, March 14, 1964, SFUA, F 3/1/0/24; McTaggart-Cowan to Shrum, April 8 and May 12, 1964, Leo Yaffe to Shrum, April 27, 1964, and H.V. Alke to Shrum, May 4, 1964, F 3/1/0/25; Minutes of the Staff and Organization Committee, June 11, 1964, F 3/1/0/26.

46 Board minutes, September 10, 1964, and attached documents, SFUA, F 33/2/0/11.

47 Board of governors, agenda support papers, May 12, 1964; Recommendation for appointment of T.B. Bottomore, July 29, 1964; Recommendation for the appointment of A.B. Cunningham, July 28, 1964, SFUA, F 3/1/0/25.

48 McTaggart-Cowan/Fisher interview, September 6, 1986, SFUA.

49 Ibid. McTaggart-Cowan had forgotten Robinson's name. During a telephone conversation on October 11, 2003, Robinson said he had suggested MacPherson.

50 McTaggart-Cowan to Staff and Organization Committee, August 19, 1964, SFUA, F 3/1/0/27.

51 Baker, "The Beginnings," 20.

52 Baker to Bottomore, September 4, 1964, SFUA, F 49/1/5/2.
53 Watson Kirkconnell and A.S.P. Woodhouse, *The Humanities in Canada* (Ottawa: Humanities Research Council, 1947), 169.
54 Reickhoff/Johnston interview, October 10, 2002, SFUA.
55 William Bruneau, *A Matter of Identities: The UBC Faculty Association* (Vancouver, UBC Faculty Association, 1990), 40–42.
56 Richard Hofstadter and C. De Witt Hardy, *The Development and Scope of Higher Education in the United States* (New York: Columbia University Press, 1952), 123–32. See comments on the heads in the 1982 interviews conducted by Ken Nielsen with Margaret Benston, Robert Koepke and Michael Lebowitz, SFUA
57 See comment by Harris on the PhD in Canada up to 1940: Harris, *A History*, 1976, 601; see also H.G. Johnson, "The Current and Prospective State of Economics in Canada," T.N. Guinsburg and G.L. Reuber, *Perspectives on the Social Sciences in Canada* (Toronto: University of Toronto Press, 1974), 103; and C.F. Poole, "The PhD as a Qualification for University Teachers," *CAUT/ACPU Bulletin*, December 1965, 61–64.
58 T.R. McConnell, "Introductory Essay," T.R. McConnell, Robert O. Berdahl and Margaret Fay, *From Elite to Mass to Universal Higher Education: The British and American Transformations* (Berkeley CA: Centre for Research and Development in Higher Education, University of California, Berkeley, 1973), 23.
59 Shrum to E. Bruce Tregunna, Botany, Queen's University, November 28, 1963, SFUA, F 3/1/0/21.
60 Shrum to Hugh Grayson-Smith, Physics, University of Alberta, March 19, 1964, SFUA, F 3/1/0/24. The same ideas reappear in an article Shrum wrote for *Saturday Night*, November 1965.
61 Harris, *A History*, 20–22.
62 Henry Johnson, *A History of Public Education in British Columbia* (Vancouver: Publications Centre, UBC, 1964), 217–23.
63 S.N.F. Chant, *Report of the Royal Commission on Education* (Province of B.C., 1960), 214–37.
64 Ellis/Johnston interview, October 10, 2002.
65 Handwritten list on Château Laurier letterhead, headed "Potential Presidents," SFUA, F 32/1/0/13. This list includes names of possible deans of Education.
66 John Barfoot Macdonald, *Higher Education in British Columbia, and a Plan for the Future* (Vancouver: UBC, 1962), 36–37.
67 MacKinnon to McTaggart-Cowan, July 2, 1964, SFUA, F 3/1/14/10; Baker to MacKinnon, July 20, 1964; MacKinnon to Baker, August 3, 1964; Board of governors minutes and attachments, July 9, 1964, F 33/2/0/11.
68 Ellis/Johnston interview, October 10, 2002; Strand/Johnston interview, November 22, 2000; Baker, "Notes for the History," 19.
69 Baker to MacKinnon, July 20, 1964, and MacKinnon to Baker, August 3, 1964, SFUA, F 3/1/14/10. See also A.R. MacKinnon, "Simon Fraser Intends to Train Teachers Differently," *B.C. Teacher*, May–June 1965, 349–51.
70 *Vancouver Sun*, April 27, 1965.
71 Gordon Shrum, "Education," *Saturday Night*, November 1965; Gordon Shrum, "The Shape of Education in 1985," *Vancouver Sun*, February 10, 1965.
72 Duguid/Rossi interview, January 30, 2002, SFUA.
73 McTaggart-Cowan, autobiographical notes dictated between 1983 and 1985, 19–20, SFUA, F 65/1/0/1.

74 "Report of the Committee on Academic Standards, Faculty Association, UBC," prepared by Peter Harnety, SFUA, F 49/2/5/4.

75 Baker, "The Beginnings," 6.

76 Friedland, *University of Toronto*, 531–33.

77 *Vancouver Province*, May 6, 1964; Shrum to Peterson, March 13, 1964, and G.T. Cunningham to Shrum, March 17, 1964, SFUA, F 3/1/0/24; Peterson to Shrum, March 19, 1964, F 33/2/0/5.

78 Board of governors papers, J. Carnie to McTaggart-Cowan, March 26, 1964, SFUA, Fisher files; McTaggart-Cowan, "Working Paper No. 1 for the Fourth Meeting between UBC, University of Victoria and Simon Fraser University," June 9, 1964, F 33/2/0/8; "The Three Universities Capital Campaign Fund," July 17, 1964, F 33/2/0/10.

79 *Vancouver Province*, September 9, 1965; *Vancouver Sun*, September 9, 1965.

80 *Vancouver Sun*, September 10, 1965.

4 | BERKELEY NORTH

1 *Vancouver Sun*, September 17, 1965; Minutes of meetings of Committee of Heads, August 17, 24, 31 and September 1, 1965, SFUA, F (old list) 27/12/10/2.

2 *Vancouver Sun*, September 10, 1965.

3 Notes from interview with Stan Wong, November 19, 2003.

4 Martin and Marier/Harter interview, April 3, 2001, SFUA.

5 V.W. Bladen and Association of Universities and Colleges of Canada (AUCC), *Financing Higher Education in Canada* (Toronto: University of Toronto Press, 1965), 13.

6 Dean of Student Services to president of Student Society, October 27, 1969, with attached summary of September 1968, Housing and Transportation Survey, SFUA, F 54/3/1/89.

7 News Release no. 149, July 8, 1966, SFUA, Bursar's files; McTaggart-Cowan to Lolita Wilson, April 3, 1967, F 193/18/1/0/1; *The Peak*, October 8, 1969, 12.

8 Dean of women to General Services, February 21, 1966, housing accommodation, April 4, 1966, SFUA, F 54/3/1/50.

9 Dean of Student Affairs to chairman of Student Affairs Committee, January 24, 1968, with attached statistics, SFUA, F 52/3/0/70; "The University of British Columbia: Students entering for the first time at the first year level by school districts, 1968–69," F 52/3/0/77.

10 Lolita Wilson to archives, August 16, 1979, with attached student statistics from fall 1966 and spring and summer semester 1966, SFUA, F 54/3/1/73.

11 Dean of Student Affairs to president, March 14, 1968, SFUA, F 193/18/1/0/1.

12 Transcript of Shrum/Sturberg interview, February 16, 1983, 387–88, SFUA.

13 *The Peak*, November 22, 1967, R-6, for a transcript of Yandle's address.

14 *The Peak*, June 7, 1967, 1, and November 1, 1967, 5; Foulds to Peak board of directors, November 15, 1966, SFUA, F 17/2/0/31.

15 For example, see Yandle on Foulds in *The Peak*, October 25, 1967, R-11, and Foulds's column "Senate inside and out" in *The Peak*, fall semester, 1967.

16 SFUA, F 17/2/0/28.

17 *The Peak*, January 13, 1971; Frances Wasserlein, "'An Aimed at the Heart': The Vancouver Women's Caucus and the Abortion Campaign," 1969–1971, MA thesis, SFU, 1990, 42.

18 Birge/Harter interview, August 9, 2001, SFUA.

19 *The Peak,* November 15, 1967, 5.

20 SFUA, F 74/3/2/20.

21 Murray G. Ross, *The Way Must Be Tried: Memoirs of a University Man* (Toronto: Stoddart, 1992), 96.

22 *Saturday Review,* April 1, 1972, 35.

23 *The Peak,* July 26, 1967, 2; Douglas Marshall, "The Hippie and the Cop," *Maclean's,* July 1978, 20.

24 McTaggart-Cowan to Lolita Wilson, April 3, 1967, SFUA, F 193/18/1/0/1.

25 Diane Laloge, "Why did we want to liberate the Rotunda?" *The Peak Student Handbook,* fall 1985, 37–39.

26 Arthur H. Elliott to McTaggart-Cowan, February 26, 1968, and McTaggart-Cowan to Elliott, March 4, 1968, SFUA, F 193/18/1/0/1.

27 Robertson to Wong, March 28, 1967, with attachment, SFUA, F 74/3/2/12.

28 *The Peak,* April 5, 1967, 14.

29 Martin Meyerson, "The Ethos of the American College Students: Beyond the Protests," *Daedalus,* fall 1966, 713–25, see 726; John B. Macdonald, "The West," Robin S. Harris, *Changing Patterns in Higher Education in Canada* (Toronto: University of Toronto Press, 1966), 55.

30 Macdonald, "The West," 55.

31 Claude Bissell, *The Strength of the University* (Toronto: University of Toronto Press, 1968), 21–27, 28–34, 35–44, 45–53, 54–65.

32 Macdonald, "The West," 56, and Bissell, *The Strength of the University,* 105, cite Taylor's "The Academic Industry: A Discussion of Clark Kerr's 'The Uses of the University,'" *Commentary,* December 1964; and his "Portrait of a New Generation," *Saturday Review,* December 8, 1962. For Bissell's reference to Kerr and permissiveness, see *The Strength of the University,* 104. See also Doug Owram, *Born at the Right Time: A History of the Baby Boom Generation* (Toronto: University of Toronto Press, 1996), 159–82.

33 Philip G. Altman, "Student Politics and Higher Education in India," Seymour Martin Lipset and Philip G. Altbach, eds., *Students in Revolt* (Boston: Houghton Mifflin, 1969), 235–56.

34 Calvin B.T. Lee, *The Campus Scene, 1900–1970* (New York: David McKay, 1970); Michael M. Miller and Susan Gilmore, *Revolution at Berkeley: the Crisis in American Education* (New York: Dell, 1965); David Lance Goines, *The Free Speech Movement: Coming of Age in the 1960s* (Berkeley: Ten Speed Press, 1993); Michael Miles, *The Radical Probe* (New York: Atheneum, 1971); Bissell, *The Strength of the University,* 57; Macdonald, "The West," 55.

35 Jack Weinberg, "The Free Speech Movement and Civil Rights," reprinted from *Campus CORElator,* January 1965, and posted at fsm-aorg/stacksweinberg.html; Goines, *The Free Speech Movement,* 1993.

36 John R. Seeley, "Quo Warrento: The Berkeley Issue," Miller and Gilmore, *Revolution at Berkeley.*

37 *Burnaby Examiner,* October 15–31, 1965.

38 *Vancouver Province,* article by Wilf Bennett, September 18, 1967, 3.

39 Richard E. Petersen, "The Student Left in American Education," Lipset et al., *Students in Revolt,* 223; David N. Smith, *Who Rules the Universities? An Essay in Class Analysis* (New York and London: Monthly Review Press, 1974), 241; Ross, *The Way Must Be Tried,* 129–30.

40   *The Peak,* August 9, 1967, 1, and December 6, 1967, 1.

41   *The Peak,* October 25, 1967, 21.

42   *The Peak,* October 26, 1966.

43   Ibid., 1, and *The Peak,* November 2, 1966, 4.

44   Duguid/Rossi interview, January 30, 2002, SFUA.

45   Seymour Martin Lipset, "Introduction: Students and Politics in Comparative Studies," Lipset and Altbach eds., *Students in Revolt,* xvii.

46   Jim Harding, "What's Happening at Simon Fraser University?" *Our Generation,* January 1969, 52–67.

47   *The Peak,* January 31, 1968, 1.

48   *The Peak,* January 25, 1967, 10.

49   Stanley Aronowitz, "Rethinking C. Wright Mills," *Logosonline,* summer 2003.

50   *Vancouver Province,* March 27, 1969.

51   Cyril Levitt, *Children of Privilege: Student Revolt in the Sixties: A Study of Student Movements in Canada, the United States and West Germany* (Toronto: University of Toronto Press, 1984), 51, 131–32.

52   Lee, *The Campus Scene,* 122–43.

53   A. Belden Fields, "The Revolution Betrayed: The French Student Revolt of May–June 1968," Lipset and Altbach, *Students in Revolt.*

54   *The Peak,* May 15, 1968, 2, 8, 9.

55   Walsh to W.R. Sallis, December 18, 1968, SFUA, F 74/3/2/21.

56   Wilson/Johnston interview, September 26, 2002, SFUA.

57   SF *View,* October 4, 1965, SFUA; Committee of Heads, July 13, 1965, SFUA, F 193/28/72/2/19; Committee of Heads, August 31–September 1, 1965, F 27/12/10/20; House Committee to president, Student Society, January 19, 1966, F 74/3/2/2, President; McTaggart-Cowan to Wilson, October 6, 1966, F 193/28/72/2/19.

58   *The Peak,* July 13, 1966; Minutes of the special meeting of Faculty Council, July 9, 1966, SFUA.

59   Martin L. Friedland, *The University of Toronto: A History* (Toronto: University of Toronto Press, 2002), 171; Dale T. Alexander to McTaggart-Cowan, July 28, 1965, SFUA, F 193/18/1/0/2; Joan H. to President, October 29, 1969; Minutes of Committee of Heads, August 31–September 1, 1965, F 193/28/72/2/20.

60   *The Peak,* November 3, 1965, January 19, 1966, March 16, 1966, February 16, 1966, February 23, 1966, November 3, 1966, February 15, 1967, March 15, 1967; Report to senate from Faculty Council, March 28, 1966, and John T. Humphries to McTaggart-Cowan, March 14, 1966, SFUA, F 112/1/0/0/2; D.P. Robertson, paper for council, February 1, 1967, and Jim Shields to D.P. Robertson, January 24, 1967, F 112/1/0/0/4; Walsh to SFSS Council, February 1, 1969, F 74/3/2/22.

61   *The View,* October 4, 1965; *The Peak,* November 1, 1965; McTaggart-Cowan to Mynott, December 5, 1966, SFUA, F 74/3/2/9; McTaggart-Cowan to Weeks, December 2, 1967, F 74/3/2/18.

62   SFU *Yearbook: Charter Edition,* 67; *The Peak,* April 5, 1967, November 29, 1967, February 4, 1970; Co-chair, Winter Carnival Queen Committee, Waterloo, to president, Student Council, SFU, October 12, 1967, SFUA, F 75/3/2/16.

63   *The Peak,* April 6, 1966, September 13, 1967, February 7, 1968; Yearbook sales manager to president of Student Society, April 11, 1967, SFUA, F 74/3/2/13.

64   Achtemichuk/Harter interview, September 22, 2001, SFUA.

65   G.W. Hobson to McTaggart-Cowan, April 6, 1966, SFUA, F 74/3/2/3; Kay Sanson

to the registrar, October 23, 1966, F 74/3/2/8; McTaggart-Cowan to Tony Buzan, December 13, 1965, F 74/3/2/1.

66 *The Peak,* March 16, 1966, 4; October 18, 1967, 1; November 8, 1967, 5; November 15, 1967, 5; January 7, 1970, 1; January 14, 1970, 1, 3; McTaggart-Cowan to Tony Buzan, March 16, 1966, SFUA, F 74/3/2/3; McTaggart-Cowan to Weeks, November 9, 1967, F 74/3/2/17; McTaggart-Cowan to all faculty, October 11, 1967, F 112/1/0/011; Anne Yandle, "Breaking the Lounge Barrier," *SFU Compass,* February 1966, F 17/6/0/21.

67 *The Peak,* October 30, 1968, 1.

68 *The Peak,* June 1, 1966, 1.

69 D.J. Daly, External review report, April 1975, SFUA, F 29/4/0/23.

70 *SFU Fact Book,* 9th edition, March 1989, 149; Grades, fall 1966, SFUA, F 54/31/33; Report of the Grading Committee of the Faculty of Arts, 1972, Fisher files, Dean of Arts Advisory Committee, RG 8/3/023.

71 Faculty Council minutes, January 26, 1966, SFUA, F 112/1/0/0; Strand to Faculty Council, March 28, 1969, with attachment, F 112/1/0/0/8; Minutes of Faculty Council, July 18 and August 2, 1972, F 112/1/0/0/5.

5 | STUDENT JOURNALISTS, POLITICIANS, ATHLETES AND TEACHERS

1 Robert M. McIvor, *Academic Freedom in Our Time: A Study Prepared For the American Academic Freedom Project at Columbia University* (New York: Columbia University Press, 1955), 217–19.

2 *The Peak,* January 5, 1966; N. Alan Bell to board of directors, Peak Publications, July 22, 1966, SFUA, F 17/2/0/31; Michael James Campbell to registrar, July 13, 1966, F 112/1/0/1/3.

3 *The Peak,* January 5, 1966; November 23, 1966, 8; November 30, 1966, 2.

4 Wong to Foulds, April 3, 1967, SFUA, F 74/3/2/13.

5 Mynott to Steenhuus, September 28, 1966, SFUA, F 74/3/2/6.

6 Wong to Student Society executive council, January 18, 1967, SFUA, F 74/3/2/10.

7 *The Peak,* October 5, 1966, 3.

8 Ibid., 2.

9 *The Peak,* July 29, 1969, 4.

10 *The Peak,* March 25, 1970, 6.

11 *The Peak,* November 26, 1969, 4; *SFU Comment,* November 1970, 11–14.

12 Cyril Levitt, *Children of Privilege: Student Revolt in the Sixties: A Study of Student Movements in Canada, the United States and West Germany* (Toronto: University of Toronto Press, 1984) 52–53.

13 *The Peak,* May 13, 1970.

14 See Patrick Beirne to chair of Peak Publications Society, July 13, 1969, 3, SFUA, F 17/2/0/32.

15 *The Peak,* October 27, 2002, story by Stephen Thomson; and October 18, 2004, story by Nicole Vanderwyst.

16 *The Peak,* October 12, 1966, 1.

17 On card playing see G.G. Brett, assistant manager, general services, to Tony Buzan, president, Student Society, January 13 and February 16, 1966, and Martin and Marier/Harter interview, April 3, 2001, SFUA, F 74/3/2/2/2. On Welch see *SFU Comment,* August 1974, 2–3.

18 *The Peak,* October 1, 1969, 12.

19 *Bulletin* (SFU) September 8, 1965, 3.

20 *The Tartan,* September 17, 1965.

21 *The Peak,* October 13, 20, 27 and November 3, 1965.

22 Donald C. Rowat, ed., *The Ombudsman: Citizen Defender* (Toronto: University of Toronto Press, 1965); Ron Yamauchi, "This Ombudsman's for You," *Peak Student Handbook,* fall 1989, 8–12.

23 Rowat to Wong, March 7, 1967, SFUA, F 74/3/2/12; Wong to Rowat, April 11, 1967, F 74/3/2/13; Rob Walsh to R.A Summers, December 4, 1968, F 74/3/2/21.

24 *The Peak,* February 21, 1968.

25 Referendum document, March 13/14, 1969, SFUA, F 74/1/0/2.

26 Toronto *Star,* June 9, 1966; Notes for an address by Allan J. MacEachern for release March 13, 1966, SFUA, F 74/3/2/3.

27 Appendix II of CUS student means survey, February 1966, SFUA, F 74/3/2/11.

28 *The Peak,* November 23, 1966, 5; November 6, 1967, 6; President of Alma Mater Society, Victoria, to minister of education, February 9, 1966, SFUA, F 74/3/2/2; Joint brief by members of BCAS, January 27, 1967, F 74/3/2/10.

29 SFU student president and ombudsman to minister, March 30, 1966, SFUA, F 74/3/2/2; McTaggart-Cowan to Arthur Weeks, December 12, 1967, F 74/3/2/18.

30 *The Peak,* February 1, 1967, 7; February 15, 1967, 6; Bigsby to Wong, January 16, 1967, SFUA, F 74/3/3/10.

31 This is Cy Gonick's reading of the Duff–Berdahl Report: "Self-Government in the Multiversity," Howard Adelman and Dennis Lee, eds., *The University Game* (Toronto: Anansi, 1968), 43–44.

32 *The Peak,* October 19, 1965.

33 *The Peak,* August 2, 1967; Yorke to Mynott, July 30, 1966, SFUA, F 74/3/2/5.

34 Trevor Lautens in the *Vancouver Sun,* September 26, 1995, A-15; Dennis Bell in *Victoria Daily Times,* August 20, 1968, 5; Diana Geddes in *The Times* (London), June 8, 1974; Terence Corcoran (on Loney's book *The Pursuit of Division*), *Globe and Mail,* July 31, 1998; Christine Cosby interview with Martin Loney, *The Peak,* November 23, 1989, 9.

35 *The Peak,* May 29, 1968, 1; *Vancouver Province,* June 1, 1968, 1; Chronology of SFU, printout of March 12, 1986: reference to clipping from *Columbian,* October 16–31, 1965, SFUA.

36 *The Peak,* September 25, 1968, 1.

37 *The Peak,* September 24, 1969, 2; October 1, 1968, 12; November 5, 1968, 1.

38 Suart to Sullivan, November 18, 1970, as reproduced in *The Peak,* January 13, 1971.

39 *Vancouver Province,* January 10, 1966.

40 Report of interview with Dr. Shrum by Athletic Review Committee, July 23, 1971, SFUA, F 80/3/0/9.

41 Recommendation to appoint Lorne Davies, dated March 1, 1965, and effective May 1, 1965, SFUA, F 193/9/2/0/2.

42 Athletic Awards at SFU, paper 49, Committee of Heads, 1965, SFUA, F 193/28/72/2/26.

43 J.H. Wyman, "Report on a Study of the Simon Fraser University Department of Athletics and Recreational Services," December 14, 1970, 17, SFUA, F 80/3/0/4.

44 M.L. Van Vleit to Suart, February 25, 1971, and Suart to Van Vleit, March 1, 1971, SFUA, F 80/4/0/4.

45 Transcript of Shrum/Stursberg interview, February 16, 1983, 387, SFUA;
    Vancouver Province, January 10, 1966.
46 Wyman, "Report on Athletics," 16.
47 Dennis Roberts, "SFU Athletics Programme Tops for Canada," *SFU Week,*
    January 1977.
48 Jerry Kirshenbaum, "But is it Simon-pure?" *Sports Illustrated,* February 28, 1977.
49 Transcript of Shrum/Stursberg interview, 393.
50 *Vancouver Sun,* September 13, 1978.
51 Robert Pinkney, head football coach, Downsview Secondary, North York,
    Ontario, to Lorne Davies, February 6, 1968, SFUA, F 80/5/3/3; Lorne Davies
    memo on CFL draft picks, March 31, 1971, F 80/5/3/6; "Simon Fraser Football
    1971," F 80/5/3/7; Wyman, "Report on Athletics."
52 SFU Athletic Department resume on Cutler, circa January 1969, SFUA, F 80/5/3/5.
53 Wyman, "Report on Athletics," 15.
54 *1966 Clansmen Pressbook,* 27, SFUA, F 80/3/0/2; "Department of Athletics and
    Recreation Report for 1969–70."
55 Telephone interview with John Buchanan, January 25, 2004.
56 Ron R. Mills, "Resource Distribution in Athletics at SFU: Sexual Discrimina-
    tion," circa 1976, SFUA, F 80/3/0/12.
57 Wyman, "Report on Athletics," 10–11.
58 Ibid., 16.
59 *The Peak,* October 18, 1976; Karl Yu, "Shrum Bowl," *The Peak,* October 6, 2003;
    Arthur Weeks to *The Peak,* October 18, 1967, and Weeks to principal, Sehome
    High School, Bellingham, October 18, 1967, SFUA, F 74/3/2/16; Weeks to Denny
    Boyd, sports editor, *Vancouver Sun,* October 17, 1967.
60 Suart to Strand, May 22, 1973, SFUA, F 80/3/0/9; Suart to Matthews, November
    22, 1973, F 80/3/0/6.
61 Mills, "Sexual Discrimination."
62 Wyman, "Report on Athletics," 15.
63 *The Peak,* June 14, July 19 and 26, 1967.
64 Wyman, "Report on Athletics," 12.
65 Claude Bissell, "Ontario," Robin S. Harris, *Changing Patterns in Higher
    Education in Canada* (Toronto: University of Toronto Press, 1966), 92;
    Bottomore to president and Committee of Heads, October 26, 1965 (suggesting
    SFU offer graduate scholarships), SFUA, F 193/28/72/2/28.
66 Baker to Turner, June 21, 1966, SFUA, F 61/3/0/3.
67 Memo by Charles Hamilton, January 1966, SFUA, F 61/30/0/3; McTaggart-Cowan
    to deans, department heads, bursar, December 19, 1966, F 19/7/1/14; Bottomore to
    president and Committee of Heads, October 16, 1965, F 193/28/72/2/28.
68 Martin Meyerson, "The Ethos of American College Students: Beyond the Pro-
    tests," *Daedalus,* fall 1966, 730; John Perry Miller, "Under the Tower," *Ventures*
    (magazine of Yale Graduate School), 1966, 1–9.
69 Spencer to McTaggart-Cowan, September 13, 1967, and Spencer to Yandle,
    September 18, 1967, SFUA, F 74/3/2/16; SFU Graduate Student Union newsletter,
    September 5, 1973, F 38/1/0/5.
70 *The Peak,* March 27, 1968.
71 *The Peak,* September 28, 1967, 1; Robertson to Shaw, September 21, 1967, SFUA,
    F 75/3/2/16.

72 Brief of sFU Graduate Student Union to Eileen Dailly, minister of education, February 15, 1973, SFUA, F 38/1/0/5.

73 *SFU Comment,* December 1973, 10–11.

74 Freisen to Strand, February 25, 1972; Williams to Diamond, April 20, 1972; Strand to Daem, October 21 and 26, 1972, SFUA, F 38/1/0/2.

75 SFU Graduate Student Union newsletters, February 15, 23 and September 5, 1973, and January 2, 1974, SFUA, F 38/1/0/5.

76 Conversation with Percilla Groves, February 18, 2004.

77 Minutes of steering committee, September 8 and 16, 1976, SFUA, F 38/2/0/2.

78 Minutes of steering committee, September 25, 1976, SFUA, F 38/2/0/2.

79 Telephone interview with Tom McGauley, February 20, 2004.

80 Honoree Newcombe, "Coming up from Down Under: A Hopeful History of AUCE," Jill Stainsby et al., *AUCE and TSSU: Memoirs of a Feminist Union, 1972–1993,* 3–14.

81 Wilson/Johnston interview, September 25, 2002, SFUA. On the general subject of student wastage a decade earlier see T.H. Matthews, registrar, McGill University, "Academic Failures," Bissell, *Crisis in Higher Education,* 115.

82 Barbara M. McIntosh, Lolita N. Wilson and Beatrice Lipinski, "The Extent and Nature of Student Attrition in the First Five Years at Simon Fraser University," *Canadian Counsellor,* June 1975, 163–74.

83 Andrew/Harter interview, March 27, 2001, SFUA.

6 | YOUNG, UNTENURED FACULTY FROM EVERYWHERE

1 *Vancouver Province,* August 12, 1965.

2 Bonsall to Chase, January 28, 1970, SFUA, F 52/3/0/55; H.L. Welsh, External Review Report, 1972, F 19/3/0/1.

3 Craig Brown, External Review Report, March 1974, SFUA, F 29/4/0/42.

4 Taylor/Rossi interview, January 21, 2002, SFUA.

5 Cam Murray, "Reflections on Eight Months as a Teaching Assistant in Geography 101, 001, at SFU, 1971," SFUA, F 12/6/0/1.

6 *The Peak,* September 13, 1967, 5; October 4, 1967, 5; November 22, 1967, 14; Proposed marking scheme for PSA, September 14, 1965, and attachment, SFUA, F 20/4/6/1.

7 *The Peak,* February 1, 1967, 11; September 4, 1968, 5.

8 Northrop Frye, "The Ethics of Change: The Role of the University," Arthur Kestler et al., *A Symposium: The Ethics of Change* (Toronto: CBC Publications, 1969), 54.

9 *The Peak,* May 10, 1999.

10 Thomas J. Mallinson, "SFU—Then and There," 1986, SFUA, F 124/1/0/6.

11 Yandle/Rossi interview, April 2, 2002, SFUA.

12 Ibid.; Sullivan/Kohler interview, March 29, 1983; Somjee to Mugridge, September 26, 1973, SFUA, F 20/5/0/4; Heribert Adam, "The Teaching of Political Literacy at SFU," 6, F 70/2/0/13.

13 W.G. Fleming, *Postsecondary and Adult Education* (Toronto: University of Toronto Press, 1971), 241.

14 Taylor/Rossi interview, January 21, 2002, SFUA.

15 *The Peak,* September 25, 1969, 1.

16 *Vancouver Sun,* July 24, 1969.

17 Swartz/Rossi interview, December 19, 2001, SFUA.

18 Gratzer's review of Mathematics, 1972, SFUA, F 14/6/4/2; Robitaille's review of Geography, 1974, F 12/1/0/3; Philosophy, unaccessioned files, Binkley's Review of Philosophy, 1976; Daniells's review of English, 1974, F 25/5/0/1.

19 Minutes of meeting of Committee of Heads, November 2, 1965, SFUA, F 193/28/72/2/23.

20 SFU Comment, October 1972, 4–5; Hugh Atrill, "The Student's Best Friend," Physics Students Association Newsletter, November 1977, SFUA, F 19/14/0/2.

21 Registrar to president, June 3, 1966, SFUA, F 3/1/28/11.

22 R.J. Baker, "Notes for the History of Simon Fraser University, dictated 15 September–28 October 1970," 21, SFUA, F 34/2/0/14

23 Fisher/McTaggart-Cowan interview, September 6, 1986; McTaggart-Cowan to Baker, March 15, 1967, SFUA, F 27/4/1/12; Baker, "Notes for the History," 5.

24 Cunningham to MacPherson, July 16, 1968, SFUA, F 3/1/17/10.

25 Minutes of PSA Department meeting, August 9, 1965, SFUA, F 20/4/6/1.

26 For a glimpse of how that worked see Cole to Sampson, October 20, 1967, SFUA F 35/1/1/4.

27 Bursill-Hall to Wilson, December 1, 1971, SFUA, F 29/4/0/43.

28 Vancouver Sun, August 15, 1965.

29 McTaggart-Cowan to Isbister, July 12, 1965; G.C. Andrew to McTaggart-Cowan, July 6, 1965, SFUA, F 193/30/2/2/1.

30 Allan Cunningham, "For Richer, For Poorer," 5, 15, SFUA, F 70/2/0/0/6.

31 Baker to Maud, April 5, 1965, SFUA, F 25/2/1/2.

32 Baker circular sent to English teachers, 1965, SFUA, F 34/3/0/6.

33 Vancouver Province, July 5, 1967; B.P. Beirne, "The Belleville-Simon Fraser Affair, 1962–67," May 1, 1967, SFUA, F 5/7/1/1.

34 J.A. Anderson, director-general Department of Agriculture, to Shrum, March 26, 1964, SFUA, F 3/1/0/24.

35 Cole to Sampson, January 30, 1966, SFUA, F 35/1/1/4.

36 AAUP Bulletin, June 1965, 259–61; SFU Faculty Association, "A Brief on Salaries and Tenure . . .," February 9, 1966, SFUA, F 79/3/1/1.

37 Johnson/Cochran interview, December 11, 2002, SFUA; Hugh Atrill, "Dr. Tony Arnott," Physics Student Association Newsletter, January 1978, F 19/14/0/2.

38 Messenger's correspondence with her parents, January 1966–November 1968, SFUA, F 176/05/1966.

39 Robin Mathews and James Steele, The Struggle for Canadian Universities: a Dossier (Toronto: New Press, 1969). Mathews and Steele addressed 250 students at SFU in February 1970: The Peak, February 4, 1970, 1. See Wilf Bennett, "Americans Invading Canadian Colleges," Vancouver Province, December 14, 1968.

40 "Uncle Sam's Our Teacher Now," Vancouver Sun, April 12, 1969, 6.

41 John Conway, "Educational Imperialism," The Peak, March 12, 1969, 7; Patricia Jasen, "The Student Critique of the Arts Curriculum," Paul Axelrod and John G. Reid, Youth University and Canadian Society (Kingston/Montreal: McGill-Queen's University Press, 1989), 258.

42 The Peak, November 1, 1967, 5; Transcript of Shrum/Stursberg interview, February 1983, 410–15, SFUA, F 49/1/3/36.

43 Baker to McTaggart-Cowan, October 22, 1968, SFUA, F 65/2/2/7.

44 Judith McKenzie, Pauline Jewett: A Passion for Canada (Kingston/Montreal: McGill-Queen's University Press, 1999), 102; Pauline Jewett to acting director

general, Department of Manpower and Immigration, July 29, 1977, SFUA, Fisher files, Jewett papers, RG 3/3/1/3.

45 *Vancouver Sun,* "Unstacking the Deck," June 21, 1975; Clive Cocking, "The Knives Are Out for Pauline Jewett," *Saturday Night,* November 1975, 17; Pauline Jewett to board of governors, June 3, 1975; Evan Alderson to Pauline Jewett, June 12, 1975, SFUA, Fisher files, Jewett papers, RG 3/3/2/5/10.

46 J.L. Granatstein, *Yankee Go Home: Canadians and Anti-Americanism* (Toronto: HarperCollins, 1996), 214.

47 *Canadian University,* June 1969, 3; Rossi/Boland interview, May 1, 2002, SFUA; Minutes of Faculty Association meeting, May 16, 1968, F 79/0/4/1.

48 Minutes of Faculty Association meetings, December 3, 1968, and February 2, 1967, SFUA, F 79/0/4/1; Matthews to McTaggart-Cowan, July 24, 1967, Fisher files, McTaggart-Cowan papers.

49 Minutes of Faculty Association meeting, October 18, 1967, SFUA, F 79/3/1/1.

50 *Vancouver Sun,* October 21, 1967; *The Peak,* October 25, 1967, R12; Macdonald to Vidaver, October 16, 1967, SFUA, F 79/3/1/1/1.

51 Minutes of Faculty Association meeting, October 31, 1967, SFUA, F 79/3/1/1.

52 *Vancouver Sun,* October 23, 1967; *Vancouver Province,* November 24, 1968; *Canadian University,* June 1968, 3.

53 Minutes of Faculty Association meeting, January 18, 1968, Faculty Association executive to McTaggart-Cowan, October 19, 1967, and McTaggart-Cowan to Faculty Association executive, October 25, 1967, SFUA, F 79/3/1/1; Minutes of Faculty Association meeting, April 18, 1967, F 79/0/4/1; Cole to Sampson, November 9, 1967, 2, F 35/1/1/4.

54 Baker to Smith, July 1, 1965, SFUA, F 25/2/1/3.

55 Martin L. Friedland, *The University of Toronto: A History* (Toronto: University of Toronto Press, 2002), 565; CAUT, report on behalf of the Academic Freedom and Tenure Committee, May 13, 1975, SFUA, F 27/12/4/10.

56 Kirkaldy to Macdonald, May 25, 1967, SFUA, F 79/3/1/1; Lawrence S. Lifschultz, "Could Karl Marx Teach Economics in the United States," John Trumpbour, ed., *How Harvard Rules* (Boston: South End Press, 1989), 281.

57 Mills to Cook, June 24, 1967, SFUA, F 79/6/1/1; C. Cook, D. Berg, et al., "Side by Side Comparison of Two Briefs on Academic Freedom and Tenure," June 21, 1967. See Mills on the same subject in *The Peak,* September 10, 1969, 11, and January 14, 1970, 10.

58 Alderson, Steig, Mills et al. to Malloch, July 13, 1970, SFUA, Fisher files, Strand papers, RG 3/2 2/1-B-1.

59 Baker to D.R. Skeels, January 26, 1965, SFUA, F 25/2/1/1.

60 Tietz to McTaggart-Cowan, June 23, 1967, SFUA, F 193/10/7/6/1; McTaggart-Cowan to academic deans, January 3, 1968, F 193/28/88/0/9.

61 Hamilton to McTaggart-Cowan, July 11, 1966, SFUA, F 193/8/0/0/5; McTaggart-Cowan to Vidaver, February 24, 1967, F 193/8/0/0/3; Baker to Alan Smith, July 8, 1968, F 193/8/0/0/5; Statement on Academic Freedom and Tenure, September 19, 1968, F 193/28/88/0/38; Minutes of University Promotions and Salaries Committee, April 15, 1966, F 193/28/88/0/4.

62 Baker to Alan P.D. Smith, July 8, 1968, Copes to Smith, July 17, 1968, and Harrop to MacPherson, July 17, 1968, SFUA, F 193/8/0/0/5.

63 For a sense of this kind of politicking see Douglas Cole's correspondence, particularly Cole to Sampson, October 20, 1967, SFUA, F 35/1/1/4.

64 Messenger to her parents, December 13, 1969, SFUA, Messenger fonds F 176/05/1966.

65 Minutes of Faculty Association meeting, January 19, 1968, SFUA, Faculty Association fonds F 79/4/0/1.

66 McTaggart-Cowan to Vidaver, September 25, 1967 SFUA, F 193/8/0/0/3.

7 | SPECIALIZATION AND INTERDISCIPLINARY STUDIES

1 Telephone interview, May 18, 2004.

2 Jennings/Rossi interview, SFUA.

3 David Braybrooke, "The Philosophical Scene in Canada," *Canadian Forum,* January 1974, 29–34; Philosophy, unaccessioned files, external review, April 15–18, 1977, "Statement of Goal," SFUA.

4 Philosophy, unaccessioned files, external review, April 15–18, 1977, reviewer no. 1 (Binkley), SFUA.

5 Bergren/Johnston interview, December 18, 2002, SFUA.

6 Devoretz/Rossi interview, August 8, 2002, SFUA.

7 Zaslove/Rossi interview, February 21, 2002, SFUA.

8 J.H. Milsum, Review of Kinesiology Department, July 1973, SFUA, F 23/3/7/11.

9 John Henry Newman, *The Idea of the University* (Garden City NY: Image Books, 1957); Thorstein Veblen, *The Higher Learning in America* (New York: B.W. Huebsch, 1918); Abraham Flexner, *Universities: American, English, German* (New York: Teachers College Press, 1967); Clark Kerr, *The Uses of the University* (Cambridge MA: Harvard University Press, 2001); Roald F. Campbell, Thomas Fleming, L. Jackson Newell, John W. Bennion, *A History of Thought and Practice in Educational Administration* (New York: Teachers College Press, 1987), 155–56.

10 Claude Bissell, *The Strength of the University* (Toronto: University of Toronto Press, 1968), 21–27.

11 Somjee to Mugridge, September 26, 1973, SFUA, F 20/5/0/4.

12 PSA file, "Appointments declined 1966–70," SFUA, F 20/3/1/3.

13 Feldhammer to PSA Faculty, October 11, 1969; David Potter to Curriculum Committee, PSA, October 23, 1968; Briemberg to PSA Department, October 23, 1968, SFUA, F 4/1/0/1.

14 Carlson to Potter, October 24, 1968, SFUA, F 4/1/0/1.

15 Kristine Anderson, "The History of Archaeology at Simon Fraser University," April 1986, SFUA, F 4/1/0/4.

16 "Archaeological Breakthrough on Mayne Island," *SFU Comment,* April 1969, 4; Anderson, "Archaeology at Simon Fraser University," April 1986, SFUA, F 4/1/0/4.

17 Don S. Kirschner, *Cold War Exile: The Unclosed Case of Maurice Halperin* (Columbus MO: University of Missouri Press, 1995).

18 McWhinney to Mugridge, August 10, 1973, SFUA, F 20/5/0/4; McWhinney to Strand, August 29, 1972, Fisher files, Strand papers, RG 3/2 24/10-b-7.

19 Somjee to Mugridge, September 26, 1973, SFUA, F 20/5/0/4.

20 Abraham Flexner, *Universities: American and German* (New York: Oxford University Press, 1930); McWhinney to Strand, August 29, 1972, SFUA, RG 3/2 24/10-b-7.

21 Board minutes, February 17, 1964, 8. The board member was Arnold Hean; Ron Baker, "The Beginnings," 15, SFUA, F 70/2/0/5.

22 Richard Hofstadter and C. De Witt Hardy, *The Development and Scope of Higher Education in the United States* (New York: Columbia University Press, 1952), 80–94.

23 Robin S. Harris, *A History of Higher Education in Canada* (Toronto: University of Toronto Press, 1976), 242–45.

24 H.G. Johnson, "The Current and Prospective State of Economics in Canada," T.N. Guinsburg and G.L. Reuber, *Perspectives on the Social Sciences in Canada* (Toronto: University of Toronto Press, 1974), 84–122.

25 Boland/Rossi interview, May 1, 2002, SFUA; Stephen G. Peitchinis, External review of Economics & Commerce, April 1975, F 29/4/0/23.

26 D.J. Daly, External review of Economics & Commerce, April 1975, SFUA, F 29/4/0/23.

27 Boland/Rossi interview, May 1, 2002; Peitchinis, External review of Economics & Commerce.

28 Boland/Rossi interview; MBA Alumni to Mugridge, July 1974, SFUA, F 29/4/0/23.

29 "The Department of Modern Languages at SFU," October 17, 1974; Bursill-Hall, "Language study at SFU," SFUA, F 13/1/1.

30 DML Annual report, 1966–67, SFUA, F 13/1/0/1; DML enrolment figures, 1966–72, F 13/2/1/14.

31 Minutes of the DML Committee of Chairmen Meeting, March 26, 1974, and April 3, 1974, SFUA, F 2/1/1/19.

32 Report of French Division for 1975 external review, SFUA, F 13/2/8/1.

33 DML Annual Report, 1966–67.

34 A.S.P. Woodhouse, "The Humanities," C.T. Bissell, ed., *Canada's Crisis in Higher Education: Proceedings of the Conference held by the National Conference of Canadian Universities, at Ottawa, November 12–24, 1956* (Toronto: University of Toronto Press, 1957), 128–29.

35 Heribert Adam, "The Teaching of Political Literacy at SFU," Cunningham manuscript, SFUA, F 70/2/0/13.

36 Watson Kirkconnell and A.S.P. Woodhouse, *The Humanities in Canada* (Ottawa: Humanities Research Council, 1947), 11–12; Harris, *A History,* 594; Hofstadter and Hardy, *The Development and Scope of Higher Education.*

37 Harris, *A History,* 139, 250, 515.

38 David N. Smith, *Who Rules the Universities? An Essay in Class Analysis* (New York/London: Monthly Review Press, 1974), 74–76.

39 John Cochran, Report on Physics Department, October 1, 1969, SFUA, F 19/3/0/3.

40 Campbell et al., *A History of Thought,* 152–53; Murray G. Ross, *The Way Must Be Tried: Memoirs of a University Man* (Toronto: Stoddart, 1992), 31–32; Paul Axelrod, *Scholars and Dollars: Politics, Economics and the Universities of Ontario, 1945–1980* (Toronto: University of Toronto Press, 1982) 103–4.

41 Haering to dean of Science, October 22, 1968, SFUA, F 19/2/0/2.

42 Mathematics Department report, 1972, SFUA, F 14/6/4/2.

43 Report on Faculty of Science, December 1969, SFUA, F 14/6/4/1.

44 Alan Byrd and Elaine Iodice, "Report of the Results of a Questionnaire Concerning the Mathematics Degree at SFU, 1977," SFUA, F 14/6/4/3.

45 Report on Faculty of Science, December 1969, SFUA, F 14/6/4/1; Minutes of Mathematics Appointments Committee, February 2, 1968, F 14/2/2/3.

46 Martin L. Friedland, *The University of Toronto: A History* (Toronto: University of Toronto Press, 2002), 379–80.

47 *The Peak,* May 15, 1968, 2; and March 12, 1969, 5.

48 sfu *Comment,* October 1974, 2–3; Sterling/Roberts interview, 1974, SFUA, F 160 item 105.

49 Sterling to Ladner, August 14, 1972, SFUA, F 23/3/4/1; Sterling to Lachlan, May 29, 1975, F 23/3/4/2.

50 *The Peak,* September 16, 1970, 4; *Vancouver Province,* September 3, 1970, 16.

51 Carol Thorbes, "An Interdisciplinary Flavour," *SFU News,* September 7, 2000.

52 Proposal for procedure for senate to follow in Interdisciplinary Studies, SFUA, F 60/1/0/4.

53 Draft report to the president from the ad hoc committee in the interdisciplinary study of human movement, 1967, SFUA, F 60/1/0/4.

54 Proposal for interdisciplinary program for the study of human movement, 1967, SFUA, F 60/1/0/4.

55 Bernard C. Abbott, External review of Kinesiology, July 1973, SFUA, F 23/3/7/11.

56 Wheatley to John Chase, July 5, 1971, SFUA, F 23/3/3/2.

57 Communication Studies proposal, October 16, 1972, SFUA, F 23/3/3/2.

58 Alfred G. Smith, "Communication Studies at sfu," March 15, 1972, SFUA, F 23/3/3/2.

59 Alfred G. Smith to Mallinson, February 14, 1972, SFUA, F 22/8/5/4.

60 Lincoln to Sullivan, March 28, 1972; Elliot Hurst to Brown, March 18, 1972; Mugridge to Harper, March 17, 1972; Swartz and Tietz to Harper, March 23, 1972; Diamond to Brown, March 22, 1972, SFUA, F 22/8/5/4.

61 Report of President's Committee of Inquiry into the Department of Communication Studies, SFUA, F 193/12/2/6/7; Hudson to Jewett, December 19, 1977, F 193/12/2/0/6.

62 Schafer to Jewett, November 18, 1974, SFUA, F 193/12/2/0/3.

63 R. Murray Schafer, "The Third Year: A Recipe for Reformation," July 17, 1967, SFUA, F 109/1/0/0/2.

64 Centre for the Arts, a review of teaching research, operations, 1956–68, SFUA, F 109/1/0/0/5.

65 Schafer, "The Third Year."

66 Proposal by Brian Carpendale, Iain Baxter and Murray Schafer, December 1966, SFUA, F 109/1/0/0/3.

67 Daniel Birch, acting president, sfu, to W.M. Armstrong, chair, University Council, September 1976, SFUA, F 23/3/2/2; Schafer to Jewett, November 18, 1974, F 193/9/3/0/9.

68 Brian Freeman, "An Open Letter to the Centre for Communication and the Arts," March 27, 1969, SFUA, F 109/1/0/0/3.

69 Alderson /Johnston interview, February 11, 2003, SFUA.

70 Ezzat Fattah, A Proposal for a Criminology Program at sfu, 1973, SFUA, F 193/12/6/0/1.

71 Reickhoff/Johnston interview, October 10, 2003, SFUA.

72 Andrea Lebowitz, President's lecture on teaching, November 24, 1999, SFUA, F 164/0/10; the speaker was likely Reickhoff: see Reickhoff to Wilson, July 10, 1975, Fisher files, RG 4/2/2/3 1/3.

73 Wilson to Reickhoff, July 23, 1975, SFUA, Fisher files, RG 4/2/1/3.

74 Lolita Wilson to Carole Anne Soong, May 24, 1972, and attachment, SFUA, F 62/1/0/7.

75 Ros Pickett, "Family Co-op Active," *The Peak,* September 17, 1970, 16; Diane La-loge, "Why did We Want to Liberate the Rotunda," *The Peak Student Handbook,* fall 1985, 810; the SDU also made a pretence of liberating the boardroom and turning it into a nursery: *Vancouver Province,* June 7, 1968; Harding, "What's Happening at Simon Fraser University," *Our Generation,* January 1969, 59–60.

76 Frances Wasserlein, "'An Arrow Aimed at the Heart': The Vancouver Women's Caucus and the Abortion Campaign, 1969–1971," MA thesis, SFU, 1980.

77 "Women's Caucus: A History and Analysis," mimeographed document circa November 1970, SFUA, F 166/0/0/0/6.

78 Ibid.

79 Wasserlein, "An Arrow Aimed," 33, 39, 42, 47.

80 Ibid., 34–36.

81 Christopher Phelps, "An Interview with Harry Magdoff," *Monthly Review,* May 1999.

82 "First draft of paper by Liz Law, Esther Philips, Pat Hoffer, et al," SFUA, F 166/0/0/0/6.

83 Honoree Newcombe, "Coming Up from Down Under: A Hopeful History of AUCE," Jill Stainsby et al., *AUCE and TSSU: Memoirs of a Feminist Union, 1972–1993,* 3–14.

84 M. Beston et al., Proposal for a Women's Studies Program at SFU, July 1974, SFUA, F 164/0/4.

85 Eileen Morris in *Vancouver Province,* October 11, 1975; M. Benston et al., proposal.

86 Elvi Whittaker, "Towards a Feminist Ethic and Methodology," J.S. Grewal and Hugh Johnston, eds., *The India–Canada Relationship: Exploring the Political, Economic and Cultural Dimensions* (New Delhi: Sage Publication, 1994), 243–65.

87 Andrea Lebowitz, president's lecture on teaching, November 24, 1999.

8 | A SUCCESSION OF CRISES

1 Smith, Communication Studies at SFU, March 15, 1972, SFUA, F 23/3/3/2.

2 *The Peak,* January 7, 1970, 5.

3 Messenger to parents, June 1, 1968, SFUA, F 176.

4 Cochran/Johnston interview, December 11, 2002, SFUA.

5 John Cochran, Report on Physics Department, October 1, 1969, SFUA, F 19/2/0/3.

6 Strand/Johnston interview, November 22, 2000, SFUA; Mike Graham, "Strand Says SFU has Unfair Picture," *Vancouver Sun,* April 14, 1969.

7 *Vancouver Sun,* April 18, 1966, 16; *Vancouver Province,* April 19, 1966; *The Peak,* May 4, 1966.

8 McTaggart-Cowan/Fisher interview, September 6, 1986, SFUA.

9 Minutes of meeting of Committee of Heads, July 20, 1965, SFUA, F 193/28/72/2/19; Report to faculty on meeting of board of governors, September 16, 1965, F 193/28/72/2/21; Draft suggested statement [on Shell station] by the president, June 24, 1966, F 193/20/1/0/11.

10 McTaggart-Cowan to H.N. Matheson, October 5, 1966; McTaggart-Cowan to Reickhoff and Huntley, July 6, 1966; Draft suggested statement, SFUA, F 193/20/1/0/11.

11 Reickhoff, Cochran et al. to McTaggart-Cowan, June 21, 1966, SFUA, Fisher files, McTaggart-Cowan papers, RG 3/1 38/13-A-13.
12 *The Peak:* Stan Wong to editor, June 29, 1966; David Berg to editor, September 7, 1966; Clark Cook to editor, September 14, 1966.
13 Dennis Roberts to president, [September 29, 1966], SFUA, Fisher files, McTaggart-Cowan papers, RG 3/1 38/13-A-13.
14 *The Peak,* May 4, 1966, and June 22, 1966.
15 *The Peak,* Wong to editor, June 29, 1966.
16 Richard Lester, "A View from the Board," 4–5, SFUA, F 70/1/0/14.
17 *The Peak,* June 29, 1966, 6; Mr. Justice Branca to editor, October 12, 1966, 4; Shrum to Mrs. Sherwood Lett, March 31, 1967, SFUA, Fisher files.
18 Erin Fitzpatrick, "Shell Station Closes," *The Peak,* July 19, 1999; Hayes to McTaggart-Cowan, November 23, 1966, SFUA, F 193/18/1/0/2.
19 Lester, "A View from the Board," 17.
20 *The Peak,* March 15, 1967, 3.
21 *The Peak,* March 17, 1967; Meeting of Faculty Council, March 15, 1967, SFUA, F 112/1/0/0/4.
22 *Vancouver Province,* April 19, 1967.
23 Interview with Loney, *Vancouver Sun,* September 14, 1985.
24 Meeting of board, March 20, 1967, SFUA, Fisher files, Board of Governors papers.
25 Walter Young, CBC Viewpoint, March 24, 1967, SFUA, Fisher files, McTaggart-Cowan papers, RG 3/11 22/10-E-2.
26 *The Peak,* March 21, 1967, 1.
27 "Students Secure Senate Seats, Start Drive for Open Session," *University Affairs,* April 4, 1968, 7–13.
28 *Vancouver Province,* March 27 and 31, 1969; Allan Fotheringham, column, *Vancouver Sun,* April 9, 1969.
29 Evenden/Rossi interview, August 1, 2002, cited in Dionysios Rossi, "Mountaintop Mayhem: Simon Fraser University, 1965–71 (MA thesis, SFU, 2003), 133, SFUA.
30 See *Vancouver Province,* January 27, 1968, for a faculty member's statement to the effect that a one-year renewal meant Burstein was being fired.
31 The president to the board, October 29, 1967, SFUA, Fisher files, Board of Governors papers, RG 5/4 11/2, App. 7; Report on SFU by the Special Investigating Committee of the CAUT, February 9, 1968, F 32/0/1/28.
32 Hean to board of governors, July 2, 1968, SFUA, Fisher files.
33 For Percy Smith's version of events leading to the CAUT censure see his "Faculty Power and Simon Fraser," *Canadian Forum,* September 1968, 122–24.
34 "Report on Simon Fraser University," CAUT *Bulletin,* April 1968, 4–28.
35 Shrum to Milner, April 11, 1968, and Shrum to McCurdy, April 11, 1968, SFUA, Fisher files, Chancellor's papers.
36 *Vancouver Province,* June 6, 1968; McCurdy to Shrum, SFUA, F 32/1/0/28; Resolution of censure against the board of governors and president of Simon Fraser University, May 26, 1968, F 32/1/0/28.
37 President to board of governors, October 29, 1967, SFUA, Fisher files, Board of Governors papers, RG 5/4 11/2, App. T.
38 *Vancouver Province,* May 30 and 31, 1968; *Vancouver Sun,* May 30, 1968; *Globe and Mail,* June 1, 1968.

39 Hean to Shrum, July 2, 1968, Shrum to Baker, February 11, 1969, SFUA, Fisher files, Shrum papers; R.J. Baker, "Notes for the History of Simon Fraser University, dictated 15 September–28 October 1970," 29–31, F 34/2/0/14.

40 *Vancouver Province*, May 31, 1968.

41 Suart diary, about June 9, 1968, SFUA, Fisher files, Individuals; Suart/Fisher interview, April 18, 1990.

42 Baker, "Notes for the History," 39–41; Baker to G.C. Andrews, September 17, 1968, SFUA, Fisher files; Funt to Strand, with attachments, Strand papers, RG 3/2 1/1-b-1 (1968); Roger Guidon to C.B. MacPherson, July 17, 1968, and MacPherson to Guidon, October 21, 1968, Strand papers, RG 3/2 1/1-B-1 (1968).

43 *The Peak,* June 4, 1968, 2; Okuda/Nielsen interview, circa March 1982, SFUA; McCurdy to McTaggart-Cowan, May 27, 1968, F 32/1/0/28.

44 Minutes of Faculty Association meeting of March 5 and April 19, 1968, SFUA, F 79/4/0/1; Matthews to Arts heads, March 8, 1968, Fisher files, RG 8/3/0 1/2; Faculty Association memo, CAUT censure motion—a reply to critics, June 10, 1968, Fisher files, RG 3/1 22/10-E-2.

45 Faculty Association executive to president, March 13, 1968, SFUA, F 142/8/0/0/3; John Matthews, memo "Unsatisfactory Communications," March 6, 1968, Fisher files, McTaggart-Cowan papers, RG 3/1 19/10-13-9.

46 *Vancouver Province,* June 6, 1968; *Vancouver Sun,* June 7, 1968.

47 Benston/Nielsen interview, circa March 1982, SFUA; Ernest R. Hilgard, Review of Department of Psychology, October 15, 1973, F 2/3/6/2; Petition re: Burstein, October 13, 1967,F 79/4/0/1.

48 Shrum to Okuda, June 14, 1968 (draft and final), Fisher files, Chancellor's papers; Shrum to McTaggart-Cowan, July 2, 1968, SFUA.

49 Shrum to Baker, February 11, 1969; transcript of Shrum/Stursberg interview, February 21, 1983, 433, SFUA, Fisher files, Chancellor's papers.

50 *Vancouver Sun,* September 7, 1968.

51 SFU News Release, July 23, 1969, SFUA, F 150/0/1.

52 *The Peak,* June 4, 1968, 1.

53 Strand to Spinks, January 29, 1969, SFUA, Fisher files, Chronology; Suart diary, about June 9, 1968, 9.

54 *The Peak,* July 10, 1968, 3, and July 18, 1968, 1; *Vancouver Sun,* July 11, 1968, 37.

55 *Vancouver Sun,* August 10, 1968.

56 Suart diary, June 19, July 1, 23 and 26, October 17, 1968; McTaggart-Cowan, record of a phone call from Shrum, July 19, 1968, and record of a discussion with Arnold Hean, July 13, 1968,SFUA, F 65/2/2/10.

57 *Vancouver Province,* June 1, 1968.

58 *Vancouver Province,* June 3 and 6, 1968; Suart diary, June 6 and 19, 1968.

59 *Vancouver Province*; June 4, 1968; *The Peak,* June 4, 1968; Suart diary, dictated on about June 9.

60 Allan Fotheringham, column in *Vancouver Sun,* July 27, 1968; Suart diary, July 26, 1968.

61 *Vancouver Province,* September 30, 1968; Strand/Johnston interview, February 6, 2001, SFUA.

62 *Vancouver Province,* June 8 and August 12, 1968.

63 *The Peak,* August 2, 1968, 1.

64 Bob McConnell in *Vancouver Province,* June 8, 1968, 1.

65 Ellis to Shrum, January 31, 1968, and Shrum to Ellis, February 2, 1968, SFUA, Fisher files, Chancellor's papers.

66 *The Peak,* June 4, 1968.

67 Suart diary, July 16, 1968, 3, and September 16–21, 1968, 2, SFUA, Fisher files.

68 Okuda to Shrum, June 12, 1968, SFUA, Fisher files, Chancellor's papers.

69 Suart diary, July 26, 29, 30, 31, 1968.

70 Suart diary, August 12–17, 19–23; Strand/Johnston interview, November 22, 2000.

71 *Vancouver Sun,* November 22 and 23, 1968; *Vancouver Province,* November 21, 1968; *The Peak,* November 25, 1968. The papers reported that the occupation had lasted seventy-seven hours, but it had begun at 10:30 PM Wednesday and ended between 3:00 and 3:30 AM Saturday.

72 Suart diary, November 19–22, 1968.

73 *Vancouver Province,* November 29, 1968; Duart Farquharson, "Confrontation on Campus," Southam News Service reprints of November and December 1968 articles, 18; Suart diary, November 27, 1968.

74 *The Peak,* November 26, 1968, and March 20, 1969; *Vancouver Province,* January 18, 1969; *Trail Daily Times,* February 6, 1969; *Vancouver Sun,* February 7, 1969.

75 Evans/Johnston interview, October 29, 2002, SFUA.

76 Ellis/Johnston interview, October 10, 2002, SFUA.

77 Terry Devlin, "SFU: The Anatomy of Disorder," *Vancouver Sun,* November 30, 1968.

78 *Vancouver Province,* November 15, 1968, 16.

79 Account of May 31, 1968, board meeting, dictated by McTaggart-Cowan, July 19, 1968, SFUA, F 65/2/2/10.

80 *Vancouver Province,* June 7, 1968.

81 Suart diary, November 19, 1969.

82 *The Peak,* November 21, 1968, 4, and November 25, 1968, 1.

83 *Vancouver Province,* November 25, 1968, 7.

84 *Vancouver Sun,* November 23, 1968, 1.

85 *The Peak,* November 21, 1968.

86 Duart Farquharson, "Agitators Stir the Pot Well," *Vancouver Province,* December 7, 1968; Evans/Johnston interview, October 29, 2002; Simon Fraser University dismissal hearing, Nathan S. Popkin, Proceedings in camera, vol. 29, August 22, 1970, 20, UBC Archives.

87 *Vancouver Province,* November 30, 1968; Evans/Johnston interview, October 29, 2002.

88 Brown to editor of *Vancouver Sun,* December 20, 1968, SFUA, Fisher files, Strand papers, RG 3/2 13/8-B-1.

89 Telephone conversation with John Conway, May 10, 2004; Farquharson, "Confrontation on Campus," 8; Suart diary, October 9, 1968; Suart/Fisher interview, April 18, 1990.

90 Suart diary, November 19–23, 1968.

91 Lionel Funt, Chronology of some of the events of this evening, November 21, 1968, SFUA, Fisher files, RG 3/2 47/11-A-4a (1968) X; Suart diary, November 19–22, 1968.

92 Strand/Johnston interview, November 22, 2000.

93 Ross, *The University: The Anatomy of Academe* (New York: McGraw-Hill, 1976), 130–31; Cyril Levitt, *Children of Privilege: Student Revolt in the Sixties: A Study of*

of Student Movements in Canada, the United States and West Germany (Toronto: University of Toronto Press, 1984), 51. Levitt cites E.B. Harvey, *Educational Systems and the Labour Market* (Don Mills ON: Longman Canada, 1974).

94 Strand/Johnston interview, November 22, 2002.

9 | THE PSA AFFAIR

1 See Michiel Horn, *Academic Freedom in Canada: A History* (Toronto: University of Toronto Press, 1999), 313.

2 *Vancouver Province,* September 23, 1969, 9; *Vancouver Sun,* September 23, 1969, 1; *The Peak,* September 24, 1969; Aberle, Open letter to CAUT, April 28, 1970, 8, SFUA, F 131/4/6/05.

3 *The Peak,* October 15, 1969. The figure of 1,250 is based on Aberle's sensible estimate of the number students that a given number of enrolments would represent. Students might well take more than one course at a time in PSA. There were 1,500 enrolments but about 1,250 students. See Aberle's open letter to CAUT, April 28, 1970, 8.

4 Suart to all faculty, October 15 and 17, 1969; Buchanan to all faculty, October 21, 1969, SFUA, F 131/0/0/0/3; Council newsletter, October 14, 1969, F 85/1/0/0/1-3.

5 *The Peak,* October 29, 1969; John Cleveland and Brian Slocock, "The Strike in Retrospect," *The Peak,* November 19, 1969, 6–7.

6 "Arbitration at SFU: the Popkin Case," *CAUT Bulletin,* winter 1971, 13.

7 *Vancouver Province,* October 6, 1969. The reference to the student role in keeping pressure on sometimes hesitant striking faculty comes from a conversation in 1985 with William Hoffer, one of the student activists involved.

8 Alywun Berland, "Report on the Simon Fraser University Dispute," December 10, 1969, 49, SFUA, Fisher files, Strand papers, RG 3/2 1/1-B-1 (1969).

9 *Vancouver Sun,* August 17, 1970, 13, August 26, 1970, 8; *Vancouver Province,* August 1, 1970, 19, August 27, 1970, 30.

10 *The Peak,* September 10, 1969.

11 Strand to colleagues, June 18, 1971, SFUA, F 85/1/0/0/1-3.

12 Popkin dismissal hearings, May 28, 1970, 66–67, UBC Archives.

13 Suart diary, August 8 and 12–17, 1968, SFUA, Fisher files.

14 Bettison to Strand, July 15, 1969, SFUA, Fisher files, President's PSA Materials.

15 Letter to the editor from Roy Carlson, *Vancouver Sun,* August 22, 1969.

16 *The Peak,* Special Newsletter No. 3, April 10, 1968; Funt's Statement to senate, identified on document as March 29, 1968, but actually April 8, 1968, SFUA, F 32/1/0/19. For another view from the sciences see Huntley to Strand, September 27, 1968, Fisher files, Chancellor's papers, RG 2/3 25/10-B-7 August–September.

17 *The Peak,* Special Newsletter No. 3.

18 Bettison to McTaggart-Cowan, April 10, 1968, SFUA, Fisher files, Strand papers, RG 3/1 18/10-B-7; McTaggart-Cowan to Bettison and Matthews, April 9, 1969.

19 PSA Department minutes, April 9, 1968, SFUA, Fisher files, RG 8/15 3/34; Matthews to Bottomore, May 16, 1968, RG 57/1/4/1/2; Bettison to McTaggart-Cowan, May 28 and 29, 1968, Chancellor's papers RG 3/1 18/10-B-7.

20 Bettison to McTaggart-Cowan, May 29, 1968, SFUA, F 193/10/6/0.

21 Katz to Sharma, July 8, 1968, Private papers of Hari Sharma.

22 *Vancouver Sun,* February 14, 1969, 1, and February 15, 1969, 1.

23 Suart diary, February 24, 1969, 2; Press release signed by K. Aberle and seventeen others, February 18, 1969, Chancellor's papers RG 2/3 23/10-B-7 (1969) 1.

24 Suart text, September 1969, 4, SFUA, Fisher files.

25 Popkin dismissal hearings, vol. 30, September 19, 1970, 5–7, UBC Archives.

26 Ibid., vol. 14, June 20, 1970, 77; vol. 29, August 22, 1970, 17–18; Aberle, "A Reply to Dean Sullivan's Chronology," October 10, 1969, SFUA, F 131/0/0/0/3.

27 Popkin dismissal hearings, vol. 24, August 13, 1970, 24, UBC Archives.

28 Strand to university community, October 2, 1969, and attached chronology by Sullivan, SFUA, F 131/0/0/0/2; Briemberg to all faculty, October 8, 1969, F 85/1/0/0/1-3.

29 Minutes of special department meeting, August 1, 1968, SFUA, Fisher files, RG 8/16/1 1/6; Douglas, Hollibaugh, Lees et al., "Who has Broken Contract with Whom," September 20, 1969, 15, F 85/1/0/0/1.

30 Kathleen Gough (Aberle), "The Struggle at Simon Fraser University," *Monthly Review,* May 1970, 31–45.

31 Bottomore to Sullivan (for circulation), August 26, 1969, SFUA, F 131/1/0/01; Sullivan to Bottomore, August 11, 1969, Fisher files, RG 8/3/7.

32 Adam, Barnett, Collinge and Wyllie, "PSA Policy and Practice: A Working Paper for Internal Discussion," June 18, 1969, SFUA, F 131/1/0/0/2.

33 Summary of Aberle case, SFUA, Fisher files, Strand papers, RG 3/7 2/1 D 1 (1970).

34 *Vancouver Sun,* September 23, 1969, 1–2; Karen McKellin, "By Tempest Tossed: Kathleen Aberle and the Crisis in the Political Science, Sociology and Anthropology Department at Simon Fraser University in the late 1960s," unpublished essay for Professor Bill Bruneau, UBC.

35 David Lance Goines, *The Free Speech Movement: Coming of Age in the 1960s* (Berkeley: Ten Speed Press, 1993), 142–59.

36 *The Peak,* April 2, 1969, 3, May 28, 1969, 1, June 4, 1969, 5; Hickerson to colleagues, August 3, 1970, and attached letter of May 21, 1969, from Leggett to Wyllie, SFUA, F 131/1/0/0/4.

37 Suart diary, August 8 and March 12–13, 1969, 3, SFUA, Fisher files, Individuals.

38 *The Peak,* January 27, 1971, 8a–8d; Wilson to Eastwood, December 24, 1970, SFUA, F 22/8/4/1.

39 Mitzman, "For General Circulation to Colleagues in the Social Sciences," July 7, 1970, SFUA, F 131/1/0/0/5.

40 Popkin dismissal hearings, vol. 9, May 28, 1970, 68–70, UBC Archives.

41 *The Peak,* September 10, 1969, 1.

42 Duart Farquharson, "Confrontation on Campus," Southam News Service reprints of November and December 1968 articles, of November and December, 1968 articles, 8; Popkin dismissal hearings, vol. 30, September 19, 1970, 27: Heribert Adam's testimony.

43 Collinge to Strand, March 31, 1969, with attached "Supplementary on the PSA situation," SFUA, Fisher files, Strand papers, RG 3/2/3 4/4.

44 Sharon Yandle, "The End of PSA at Simon Fraser University," *Canadian Dimension,* February–March 1970, 16–19.

45 *Vancouver Province,* August 2, 1969, 7; *The Peak,* September 3, 1969, 3.

46 Strand/Johnston interview, November 22, 2000, SFUA.

47 Ken Strand, "Thoughts on University Dismissal Procedures," October 30, 1970; Ken Strand, "Thoughts on University Dismissal Procedures," September 7, 1971, SFUA, F 193/28/88/0/45.

48 Wheeldon v. Simon Fraser University, 15 DLR (3rd) 641, British Columbia Supreme Court, J. Hinkson judge, June 18, 1970.

49 See Strand to President, CAUT, November 16, 1970, SFUA, F 193/29/2/2/5; Lester, Chair of SFU board, to Brothers, B.C. minister of education, March 11, 1971, Fisher files, Strand papers, RG 3/2 5/2-A-2 (1970–71).

50 E.E. Palmer, J.S. Dupre and W. Livant, "In the Matter of a Hearing Relating to Dismissal Charges . . .," July 24, 1970, SFUA, F 131/0/0/0/3; Comment on hearing committee decision, July 26, 1970, F 131/0/0/0/5; Ken Strand, Statement by the president on the Palmer decision, July 26, 1970, F 85/1/0/0/1-3.

51 Faculty Association, Open letter to all SFU faculty, November 20, 1970, SFUA, Fisher files, Strand papers, RG 3/2 32/10-E-2; Executive committee, Faculty Association, to all faculty, July 30, 1970, F 85/1/0/0/3.

52 A.E. Maloch, L.F. Kristjanson and I.D. Pal, "Simon Fraser University," CAUT Bulletin, autumn 1970, 59–84; Aberle memo, May 26, 1970, with attached "Interim Report of American Anthropological Association," SFUA, F 131/0/0/0/5.

53 "Full Text of AUCC Statement," Takkali (Information Office, SFU), October 1970, 3; Vancouver Province, September 30, 1970, 10.

54 Kathleen Aberle, "The Simon Fraser University Dispute: An Open Reply to CAUT," SFUA, F 131/0/0/0/5.

55 CAUT Bulletin, winter 1970, 42–50. The chair of the Academic Freedom and Tenure Committee was Archie Malloch, and the president of the CAUT in 1970–71 was Willard Allen, a professor of chemistry at Alberta.

56 Norman Wickstrom, "The PSA Dispute at Simon Fraser University," circa 1974, 86–90, SFUA, F 150/0/1.

57 "No Cause for Dismissal: The Rosenbuth Committee Report," November 18, 1970, SFUA, F 131/0/0/4; "Simon Fraser University Dismissal Hearing, Nathan S. Popkin, Proceedings in Camera," transcript, March–October 1970, UBC Archives.

58 "No Cause for Dismissal." This report also appears in CAUT Bulletin, winter 1971, 3–29, under the title "Arbitration at SFU: the Popkin Case."

59 "The Wheeldon Dismissal Hearing Report," CAUT Bulletin, autumn 1971, 57–96.

60 Lester to members of the board, June 1, 1971, SFUA, Fisher files, Strand papers, RG 3/2 14/9-A-2 (1971).

61 "Report on Simon Fraser University, III," CAUT Bulletin, winter 1972, 3–5.

62 "Wheeldon Dismissal Hearing Report," CAUT Bulletin, autumn 1971, 62–64.

63 "Report on Simon Fraser University, III," 5; Bridwell to all faculty, "Referendum Results," July 2, 1971, and Strand to colleagues, July 5, 1971, SFUA, F 85/1/0/0/0/3.

64 Strand to colleagues, July 5, 1971, SFUA, F 85/1/0/0/3.

65 Editorial, Vancouver Sun, August 15, 1974; Jack Wasserman, column, Vancouver Sun, August 21, 1974.

66 Jewett/Fisher interview, June 1, 1991, SFUA; Press release, October 16, 1974, Fisher files, Jewett papers.

67 Judith McKenzie, Pauline Jewett: A Passion for Canada (Kingston/Montreal: McGill-Queen's University Press, 1999), 97.

68 Ibid., 37–48.

69 Clive Cocking, "The Knives Are Out for Pauline Jewett," Saturday Night, November 1975, 17–27; Allan Fotheringham, columns, Vancouver Sun, March 29 and April 2, 1975; Jewett/Fisher interview, June 1, 1991, and Suart/Fisher interview, April 18, 1990, SFUA.

70 SFU News Release, October 16, 1994, SFUA, F 193/33/2/0/3; Vancouver Sun, October 17, 1974.

71 *Vancouver Sun,* July 28, 1973.

72 Wilson to Jewett, April 26, 1977, SFUA, Fisher files, Jewett papers, RG 6/3/1/1 1/4.

73 Agreement with CAUT signed by Paul Cote and Pauline Jewett for SFU, October 9, 1975, SFUA, Fisher files, Jewett papers, RG 3/32/2 7/4.

74 *The Peak,* December 3, 1975, 9–10.

75 *The Peak,* February 19, 1977 (interview with Jewett) and May 26, 1977; McKenzie, *Pauline Jewett,* 106–10; J.R. Stevens, chair, CAUT Academic Freedom & Tenure Committee, to Jewett, October 8, 1976; David Williams, associate executive secretary, CAUT, to Jewett, May 17, 1977, SFUA, F 27/3/2/44.

EPILOGUE | SHRUM'S UNIVERSITY AFTER FORTY YEARS

1 Transcript of Shrum/Stursberg interview, February 21, 1983, 443, SFUA.

2 *Georgia Straight,* May 27–June 3, 1970, 3; *The Peak,* June 3, 1970; telephone interview with John Conway, May 10, 2004.

3 Transcript of Shrum/Stursberg interview, February 21, 1983, 443, SFUA.

4 *The Bridge,* April 1969, 1–3.

5 See Sarah Schmidt, "Universities Planning to Rank Programs," *Vancouver Sun,* October 19, 2004, A5.

6 Karen Neeham, review of Indu Rajagopal, "Hidden Academics," CAUT *Bulletin,* May 2003, 6–10; CAUT *Almanac of Post-Secondary Education,* 2003, 6, table 3.6.

7 Pederson/Harter interview, spring 2001, SFUA; *SFU Alumni Journal,* vol. 8, no. 2, 9.

8 "The Saywell Years" (interview with Bill Saywell), *Simon Fraser Week,* February 25, 1993, 2–3; CAUT *Almanac of Post-Secondary Education,* 2003, 6, table 3.5.

9 *Simon Fraser Alumni Journal,* vol. 8, no. 2 (Special Silver Anniversary Issue), 10.

10 Ken Mennell, "Blaney: The Man and his Leadership," *Simon Fraser University News,* November 30, 2000.

11 Robert Clift, "No Senate, No Tenure, No Academic Freedom," CAUT *Bulletin,* September 1997, 1–2.

12 SFU Surrey news releases, September 16 and December 3, 2004.

13 *Architecture Week,* June 14, 2004, N-1.2.

14 Kim Pemberton, "New Towers at SFU Are a 'Tragedy,' Architect Says," *Vancouver Sun,* September 13, 2004, B1; Erickson/Sandwell interview, July 8, 2002, SFUA.

15 See Glenn Bohn on orientation week at SFU in *Vancouver Sun,* September 24, 2004, B3.

Index

hockey, 161, 168
Hofstadter, Richard, 98
Hogarth, Madge, 136
Hollibaugh, Ace Leroy, 121–22, 251, 256, 286, 291
Hollibaugh, Marge, 251
honours program, 110–11, 234
Hope, Fred, 126
Horn, Michiel, 80
Huntley, David J., 204
Hutchinson, John F., 38, 192–93, 279–80
Huxley, Christopher V. (Chris), 263
Huxtable, Ada Louise, 52

IBM cards, 127
IBM 360, 238–39
Imperial College London, 55
in loco parentis, 136, 144, 292
Insurance Corporation of B.C., 336
interdisciplinary approaches, 83, 220–33, 239–54
Interdisciplinary Studies, Faculty of, 84, 239–42, 248–49, 254, 334
intramural sports, 168, 170
Iredale, W. Randle, 48, 57
Isbister, Claude, 201
Ivory, Paul E., 131

James, Ralph, 90
Java, terraced hills, 54
Jawaharlal Nehru University, Delhi, 55
Jefferson Airplane, 125
Jennings, Raymond E. (Ray), 219
Jewett, Pauline, 180, 209, 244, 249, 323–28
Johnson, Byron I., 17
Johnson, Harry G., 228
Johnson, Lyndon Baines, 130
Johnson, Philip Courtelyou, 46, 52
Johnston, David L., and committee, 320–22
Johnston, Patricia H., 4
joint faculty, meetings of, 208, 268–270, 277–79, 281
Jolley, Janiel, 139
Juliani, John, 104, 283

Kamloops, 19
Kelowna campus, 334
Kendall, Lorne M., 94, 97, 197, 199, 266
Kennedy, Peter E., 221
Kennedy, Warnett, 43–44, 55
Kerr, Clark, 52, 128, 222
Kerr, Ralph, 196
Kesey, Ken, 124–25
Keter, George, 150
Killam, Ruth, 45
Kim, T.W., 200
Kinesiology, Department of, 240–42, 248, 334
King Edward School, 25, 182
Kinoshita, Matsu, 140
Kirchner, Glenn, 165, 241
Kirschner, Don, 225
Kiss, Zoltan, 50, 57–58
Koerner Graduate Centre, UBC, 44
Kohler, Erika, 3
Koopman, Raymond F. (Ray), 238, 240
Kootnekoff, John, 164–65
Korbin, Donn, 286, 288
Kup, A. Peter, 199, 278

Labour Relations Act, 175
Lakehead University, 162, 181
Laloge, Diane, 126
Langley, B.C., 19, 28, 40–42
language requirement, 105, 231, 235
Languages, Literatures and Linguistics, Department of, 230–33
Laskin, Bora, 34, 35, 79, 82, 92
Latin American Studies, 230, 240
Lautens, Trevor, 157–58
Lawford, Peter, 113
League for Socialist Action, 251
Leary, Timothy, 124–25
Lebowitz, Andrea, 249–50, 253–54
Lebowitz, Michael A., 221, 320
Le Corbusier, 46, 58
lectures, 106–8, 198
Leggett, John C., 296, 309–12, 316–17, 326–27
Leme, Jose, 180

Madge Hogarth House, 118, 136–37
Magdoff, Harry, 191, 252, 310
Maggie Benston Centre, 51, 338
Magnussen, Karen, 169
majors, 234
Malaspina Community College, 23, 218
mall, 50–52, 57, 59, 135, 152, 264, 276, 283, 291, 299, 338
Mallin, Lorne, 146, 152
Mallinson, Thomas J. (Tom), 189, 243–44
Management and Systems Science, 240
Maple Ridge, B.C., 118
Marcuse, Herbert, 133, 310
Marier, Norma, 116–17, 119
Martin, Carol, 169
Martin, Jane, 116–17, 119
Massey, Charles Vincent, 45
Massey, Geoffrey, 45–47, 52, 54
Massey, Raymond Hart, 45
Mathematics, Department of, 84, 86, 90, 95, 194, 236–37, 239
mathematics requirement, 234–35
Mathews, Robin, 207, 209
mature students, 109–10, 120–22, 185
Maud, Ralph, 202–3
Mayne Island, B.C., 223, 225
Mead, Margaret, 310
Medical Research Council, 88
Memorial University, 109
Mercer, Geoff, 263–64
Messenger, Ann C., 207, 215–17, 256
Messenger, William E. (Bill), 207, 215–16
Meteorological Service of Canada, 60–62, 66
Mies van der Rohe, Ludwig, 46
Mills, C. Wright, 133
Mills, John, 213–14
Milner, James, B., 266–67, 270
Miss Canadian University pageant, 139
Miss SFU contest, 139
Mitchell, David J., 4
Mitzman, Arthur, 311–13
modernist architecture, 46
Modern Languages, Department of, 84–86, 90, 172, 201, 205, 230–33, 250, 274

Monte Alban, Mexico, 54
Monthly Review, 191, 252, 300, 307, 310
Montreal Olympics, 163
Mount Allison University, 319
Mount St. Vincent College, 323
multiplication of programs, 227
Munro, John M. (Jock), 4, 337
Murray, Cam, 187
Museum of Anthropology, UBC, 46
Mynott, John, 260

Naegle, Kaspar, 95
Nair, K.K., 204
Nanaimo, 23
Nanterre, France, 134–35
National Association of Intercollegiate Athletics (NAIA), 162–64, 166, 168
National College Athletic Association (NCAA), 161, 166, 168
National Conference on Canadian Universities and Colleges, 36–37
National Defense Education Act (US), 16–17
National Research Council, (NRC), 6, 88, 171
National Sciences and Engineering Research Council (NSERC), 88
national sports championships, 161
Natural Resource Management, 240, 334
Ncapayi, Munkie, 338
Nelson, B.C., 18
Nelson, C. Donald (Don), 89, 97, 102, 116, 197–99, 203–5
New Caledonia College, 23
New Democratic Party provincial government, 177, 265, 325, 335–36
New Left, 121, 132–33, 250, 304
New Westminster, B.C., 26–27, 118, 167
Newman, John Henry (Cardinal), 222
Nielsen, Ken, 3
Nixon, Richard M., 207
Non-Faculty Teacher's Union, 175
normal schools, 100, 102
North Burnaby Secondary, 116
North Shore, 7, 26–27

and athletic scholarships, 159–60, 163; and Premier Bennett, 7–10, 39; and board of governors, 65; and CAUT, 77–78, 266–67, 270–71; and choosing a president, 59–60, 62; and Committee of Heads, 196; and construction, 58–59, 76; and dentists' wives, 172; and Duff-Berdahl Report, 36–37; and Education, 100–101; and John Ellis, 280–81; and English requirement, 106; on faculty from U.S. and Great Britain, 208; and first registrar, 114; and founding of SFU, 5–10, 12–14, 20, 31, 39–40, 249; and graduate students, 30, 170, 172; and Jim Harding, 330–31; on lectures and tutorials, 47, 105–7; and librarian, 87; life and career, 6–9; and McTaggart-Cowan, 59–60, 62–66, 74, 273, 276; and recruiting, 88–96, 99, 200–201; and Rose Bowl, 161; and selection of departments, 86, 220, 227; and selection of a site, 40–44; and Sputnik, 16; and Ken Strand, 282, 292; and student signs, 135; at UBC, 6–8, 11; on SFU and its future, 331–32; on teaching and publication, 99, 215, 222; and tenure, 76–78; and trimester system, 67, 71, 74; unpopularity at SFU, 5, 256

Shrum Bowl, 163, 167

Sinclair, Rosalind, 139

Sir George Williams University, 71, 134, 139, 257, 264

sit-ins, 275

Slick, Grace, 125

Smith, Alfred G., 243, 255–56

Smith, Allan, 290

Smith, Gordon, 45

Smith, J. Percy, 35, 77, 78, 92, 216, 266–67, 270

Smith, Sidney, 83

Smith, W.A.S. (Sam), 325–26

Snedenko, Abe, 126

Soberman, Daniel, 78, 80, 81

soccer, 161, 163, 165–66, 168, 170, 182

Social and Philosophical Studies, Centre for, 103

Social Credit provincial government, 8, 18, 41, 111, 179

Sociology & Anthropology, Department of, 179, 226, 325–27

softball, 170

Somjee, A.H, 200, 202, 223, 226, 309

Spagnolo, Penny and John, 4

Spanish and Latin American Studies, Department of, 230

specialization, 220, 241

Spencer, Ian, 174–75

Sperling, Jerry, 291, 313

split summer system, 68

Spock, Dr. Benjamin, 128

Sputnik, 16

Srivastava, Lalit, 205, 312, 314

Staff and Organization Committee, 89, 94

Stainsby, Donald, 12

Stainsworth, Phil, 263

Stanford University, 68, 243

Steele, James, 207, 209

Steen, Donald, 165

Steenhuus, Sam M., 121, 146

Sterling, Theodor D., 238–39

Stevenson, H. Michael, 4, 336

Stigger, Philip, 200

Strand, Kenneth T. (Ken): and Kathleen Aberle, 312; acting president, 215, 275, 303, 314; and administrative structure, 274; and Archaeology, 225–26; and Premier Bennett, 277; and David Bettison, 302; and board of governors, 279–80, 282, 292; and Bob Brown, 240; and Canadian citizenship, 323; career before SFU, 278–79; and CAUT censure, 268, 317–18, 321, 323; characterized by Allan Fotheringham, 273–74; and dismissal hearings, 320–22; and Education program 102–3; and graduate student demands, 176; leadership of, 256–57; and John Leggett, 311–12, 317; president, 312, 314; and PSA Department, 295–97, 303–4, 314–23; and student occupation, 282–83, 286–88, 289–92; and tenure policy, 299